# Client/Server
# Architecture

## Titles in the J. Ranade Series on Computer Communications
### (J. Ranade, Series Advisor)

# Client/Server Architecture

**Alex Berson**

## McGraw-Hill, Inc.

New York   St. Louis   San Francisco   Auckland   Bogotá
Caracas   Lisbon   London   Madrid   Mexico   Milan
Montreal   New Delhi   Paris   San Juan   São Paulo
Singapore   Sydney   Tokyo   Toronto

**Library of Congress Cataloging-in-Publication Data**

Berson, Alex.
   Client/server architecture / Alex Berson.
     p.   cm.—(J. Ranade series on computer communications)

   Includes index.
   ISBN 0-07-005076-7
   1. Electronic data processing—Distributed processing.  2. Computer
architecture.  3. Computer networks.  I. Title.  II. Series.
QA76.9.D5B47   1992
004'.36—dc20                                      92-6831
                                                    CIP

       7 8 9 0   DOC/DOC  9 8 7 6 5 4

**ISBN   0-07-005076-7**

*The sponsoring editor for this book was Jerry Papke, and the
production supervisor was Suzanne Babeuf. It was set in Century
Schoolbook by North Market Street Graphics.*

*Printed and bound by R.R. Donnelley & Sons Company.*

# Trademarks

The following trademarks are listed in alphabetical order, not in the order in which they appear in the book:

AIX, AS/400, APPC/LU6.2, APPN, CICS, DB2, DISOSS, DRDA, ESA, IMS/VS, IMS/DC, LAN Server, Micro Channel Architecture, MCA, MVS, NCP, NetView, OS/400, PS/2, RS/6000, SAA, SNA, SQL/DS, VM, VSAM, VTAM are trademarks of International Business Machine Corporation.

AppleTalk, Macintosh are trademarks of Apple Computers, Inc.

Apollo is a trademark of Apollo Computer, Inc.

Unix is a registered trademark of Unix System Laboratories.

Banyan Vines is a trademark of Banyan Systems, Inc.

Berkeley Software Distribution and BSD is a trademark of University of California at Berkeley.

DEC, DECnet, DECWindows, DNA, ULTRIX, VAX, VMS are trademarks of the Digital Equipment Corporation.

CDC is a registered trademark of Control Data Corporation.

dBase III is a trademark of Ashton-Tate Corporation.

Display PostScript is a trademark of Adobe Systems, Inc.

Gupta, SQLBase, SQLWindows are trademarks of Gupta Technologies, Inc.

HP, HP-UX, NewWave, PRISM are trademarks of Hewlett-Packard Corporation.

IBM, PS/2, AS/400, OS/2 are registered trademarks of International Business Machine Corporation.

IDMS is a trademark of Computer Associates International, Inc.

Ingres, Ingres 4GL, Ingres-Star are trademarks of Ingres Corporation.

Informix, Informix OnLine, Informix-Star are trademarks of Informix, Inc.

Intel is a trademark of Intel Corporation.

InterBase is a trademark of Borland International, Inc.

*To Irina, Vlad and Michelle*

# Contents

# List of Figures

# CHAPTER 4

# CHAPTER 5

# CHAPTER 6

# CHAPTER 7

# CHAPTER 8

# CHAPTER 9

# CHAPTER 10

# CHAPTER 11

# CHAPTER 12

# CHAPTER 13

# CHAPTER 14

# CHAPTER 15

# CHAPTER 16

# Preface

The last few years have seen the transformation of personal computers into programmable workstations organized into local area networks and integrated with mainframe computers. This transformation has been combined with advances in microcomputer technology, graphical user interfaces, networking, and communications. As technology continues to evolve, users are capable of interconnecting various platforms efficiently and transparently to distribute data and applications across heterogeneous systems and networks. Users' desire to reduce hardware and software development and operational costs can now be realized by moving application development and operational systems from expensive mainframes to more efficient, less expensive, but just as powerful, workstations. These are the main reasons that new types of computing have developed. The revolutionary computing paradigms have resulted in a new, often confusing, vocabulary. The picture has become even more complex with the advances and acceptance of open systems.

Prominent among these new computing models is the client/server computing model and the underlying architectures of the cooperative and distributing processing. Almost every major business organization is considering the move toward distributed environment, cooperative processing, open systems, and/or client/server architecture.

These rearchitecturing, major system integration projects require significant investment in time, money, and resources. However, often the lack of proper expertise and confusion surrounding the issues of open systems, distributed cooperative processing, and client/server architecture lead to actual or perceived project failures that affect business and computer vendors alike.

Thus, the need to clarify the concept and architecture of the client/server computing model becomes very pressing indeed. Understanding the client/server architecture and relevant issues is central to the success of open distributed systems and cooperative processing.

The purpose of this book is to introduce readers to the power, advantages and complex issues of the client/server architecture. To do it properly, the evolution of the computing environment, discussion of standards and open systems, client and server platform specialization, client/server communications in local and wide area networks and major communication protocols (including Advanced Program-to-Program Communications) are used as a foundation on which the client/server architecture is explained. Client and server specialization is illustrated on examples of software and hardware implementations that may help readers make an informed decision when purchasing client/server platforms.

Based on this foundation, all major issues of client/server architecture, including distribution of presentation, applications, data and databases, transaction and workflow management, software distribution concepts, as well as several specific client/server environment implementations, are described.

## WHY THIS BOOK IS NEEDED

Even though the term *client/server* is relatively new and little understood by many, the amount of information related to the subject (though not necessarily directly) is tremendous. Some of the material, covered in this book, especially references to a particular vendor product implementation, can be found in various vendor publications, trade literature, and international standards materials.

However, to sort through this amount of information is extremely difficult. That is especially true because significant portions of the available information are being changed on a regular basis. Various emerging standards and continuous product updates are examples of this dynamic nature. In addition, various client/server implementations and related issues require detailed knowledge of different hardware and software platforms. Specifically, hardware platforms described in this book include mainframes, midrange systems, workstations, servers, and personal computers. Operating systems include MVS, VM, Unix/AIX, OS/2 and DOS. Description of open distributed environments include Open Software Foundation's Distributed Computing and Distributed Management Environments. Database management system discussions cover DB2, Oracle, Sybase, Ingres and Informix. Other client/server-related issues deal with programming languages, transaction monitors (e.g., IBM's CICS, AT&T's Tuxedo, NCR's Top End, Transarc's Transarc), presentation management (e.g., X Window System, MS Windows, etc.), communication protocols and techniques (e.g., IBM's APPC/LU6.2, Remote Procedure Calls, etc.), and various industry standards.

Unfortunately, even if one decides to read all available literature, it would be very difficult to obtain a clear picture of what client/server computing is and how it works. That is why the author's personal experience in developing client/server based open distributed environments proved to be invaluable in writing this book.

## WHO THIS BOOK IS FOR

This book has been written as a result of the author's participation in several large-scale system integration projects implementing distributed client/server architecture in open systems environments.

In discussing architecture, advantages, and benefits of the client/server computing model, the author met with many DP managers, system integrators and system administrators, database and communication specialists, network and CICS system programmers—all of which are potential readers of this book.

This book can be used as a guide for system integrators, designers of distributed systems, database administrators considering the issues of distributed databases and DBMSs for open systems, and systems administrators and network specialists looking for theoretical or practical knowledge of the distributed cooperative processing and client/server architecture. Specific client/server implementations described in the book can help DP managers, DBAs, network and communications specialists, and application developers make informed decisions when selecting platforms and products to implement client/server environments.

In fact, this book is a must for any system professional who deals with open systems and standards, distributed cooperative transaction processing, and client/server architecture. Anybody who is looking at communications issues in an open distributed environment and is involved with the Advanced Program-to-Program Communications (APPC/LU6.2), Remote Procedure Calls, LAN-to-WAN communications, and IBM's Distributed Relational Database Architecture (DRDA) should read this book.

Finally, those readers who are involved with the intersystem connectivity, open system architectures, and future standards in computer networking will find this book and its subject extremely useful.

## PREREQUISITE

Readers with any data processing experience can understand this book. Those who deal with only COBOL batch programs will find this book useful. Those with CICS, SQL, DB2 or any other database experience will benefit. Unix, OS/2 and MS DOS application and system

programmers, network designers and operators, AIX and SAA follow-
ers, and OSF and UI proponents should not have any problems reading
this book.

The author assumes readers have little or no previous knowledge
about client/server architecture. The book has been structured as a
self-teaching guide, where the client/server architecture and multiple
related issues are spread across five parts and gradually introduced to
the reader. Part 1 begins with the evolution of computing environments and introduction to the open systems phenomenon. Parts 2
through 5 methodically analyze various aspects of the client/server
architecture, concentrating on critical issues and demonstrating features and advantages of some client/server-related products over
others. Those readers already familiar with data communications,
LANs and WANs, may skip Part 3, and go directly from Part 2 to Part
4, even though Part 3 contains some useful references on various LAN
protocols and APPC/LU6.2.

## STYLE USED

The book includes a fair amount of diagrams, figures, examples, and
illustrations in an attempt to present a large amount of rather complicated material in as simple a form as possible. Client/server architecture is a complex, involved, and often misunderstood subject;
whenever possible, theoretical issues are explained with practical
examples. However, for those interested in theory, the book provides a
sufficient theoretical, architectural base.

In fact, this is the first comprehensive guide to the client/server
architecture that analyzes the subject from several angles, including
theoretical, architectural and practical viewpoints. Several major
client/server implementations, as well as hardware and software components, are discussed alongside the relevant client/server architecture topics. This book is about a very dynamic subject. All material
included in the book is current as of this writing. But the author real-
izes that as the client/server computing model continues to evolve,
changes may be necessary. He intends to revise the book if significant
developments in the client/server arena necessitate adding, deleting
or changing parts of the text.

## WHAT IS INCLUDED

Part 1 begins with analysis of the evolution of computing environments,
and introduces the definition and advantages of open systems. Open
Software Foundation's Distributed Computing Environment is introduced and used as the reference model for the client/server architecture.

Part 2 describes the specialization of clients and servers in distributed environments. Advanced hardware features beneficial to the server components are explained on examples of several available products. Client's specialization is illustrated on the example of presentation management—specifically, X Windows System.

Part 3 deals with the critical issues of networking and data communications in the client/server computing environment. Local and wide area networks and various networking protocols are described here. The Advanced Program-to-Program Communications (APPC/LU6.2) is also introduced in this part.

Part 4 provides a detailed look into the features of cooperative distributed processing as the foundation of the client/server architecture. Some of the features of client/server architectures, discussed in Parts 1 and 2 as characteristics of the client/server specialization, are revisited here. Specifically, presentation, application, and database components are discussed from an architectural point of view in Part 4. The issues of distributed databases and data management in client/server architecture, as well as the examples of client/server database implementations are also described in great detail in this part.

Part 5 of the book deals with the issues of transaction and workflow management in the client/server environment. X/Open's Distributed Transaction Model and such transaction monitors as CICS, Tuxedo, Top End and Transarc, as well as AT&T's Rhapsody and OSF's Distributed Management Environment, are described in this part.

*Alex Berson*

# Acknowledgments

First and foremost, I must thank Jay Ranade for encouraging me to write this book. Special thanks to John Pezzullo for giving me an opportunity to work on the leading edge of computer technology. My special thanks to Larry Johnson for his optimism, support, never-ending enthusiasm, and the guidance only he can provide. Very special thanks to Cynthia Wilson and Bill Stewart for giving me an opportunity to learn and to be creative in a very stimulating and challenging environment.

Thanks also to my numerous friends at IBM, New York Life, and Merrill Lynch for providing useful assistance, as well as a creative and challenging atmosphere, especially poeple like Mo Howes, Ilse Curto, and Kevin Riley.

Thanks to all those who have helped me with clarifications, criticism, and information during the writing of this book, especially to Carol Lehn, who patiently read the entire manuscript and made many useful suggestions.

I am grateful to Gerald Papke, senior editor, for his constant encouragement.

My very special thanks to Christine H. Furry and her colleagues at North Market Street Graphics for their expertise, patience, advice, and attention to details.

Finally, very special thanks to Irina, Vlad, Michelle, and the rest of my family for giving me time to complete the book and understanding its importance, and for their never-ending optimism, support and love.

## ABOUT THE AUTHOR

**Alex Berson** (East Brunswick, New Jersey) has more than 20 years of data processing experience as a systems architect, consultant, instructor, and writer. He specializes in database design, relational technology, distributed processing, and data communications. He is currently working as a systems architect on a large-scale insurance application project to create a distributed client/server environment. Mr. Berson is the author of *APPC: An Introduction to LU6.2* (McGraw-Hill, 1990).

# Foundation

*The evolution of intelligent workstations (IWS), the tremendous growth in their sheer computing power, and the availability of extremely impressive graphics are changing the way today's computing systems are utilized to meet ever more demanding business needs. One of the more pronounced trends is the enabling of rapid development of workstation-based applications. Another important trend is to increase cost-benefits in application development by forming user/developer workgroups. These workgroups can share distributed resources such as information, devices, services, and applications. Sharing of resources, when performed cooperatively through the interactions between clients (requesters of resources) and servers (providers of resources), can be achieved by employing a client/server computing model.*

*The term* client/server *originally applied to a software architecture that described processing between two programs—an application and a supporting service. At that time, the client program and the server program did not have to be physically separated—they could be a calling and a called program running on the same machine. Thus, usually the client/server discussions were limited to interactions between one client and one server. As computer science and the theory of programming evolved, however, the concepts of programs capable of providing services or managing resources on behalf of a number of other programs became widely accepted.*

*The client/server computing model represents a specific instance of distributed cooperative processing, where the relationship between clients and servers is the relationship of both hardware and software components. The client/server architecture, its software and hardware components, and their interrelationships are the subject of this book.*

Foundation

# Introduction to Open Distributed Systems and Client/Server Model

The client/server computing model covers a wide range of functions, services, and other aspects of the distributed environment. Relevant issues include local and wide area networking, distributed data, distributed processing (applications and presentation), distributed transaction processing and management, and standards and open systems. Our discussion of the client/server architecture begins with a look at the evolution of distributed application environments and an introduction to open systems and standards.

## 1.1 EVOLUTION

How familiar is the phrase, "Client/server computing is the way of the '90s"? Claims have been made that client/server technology will eliminate application backlogs, reduce software maintenance costs, increase application portability, improve systems and networks performance, and even eliminate the need for minicomputers and mainframes. Instead of getting into a debate about which of these promises (if any) is realistic, let's first look at the evolution of computing environments and find a place for the client/server model.

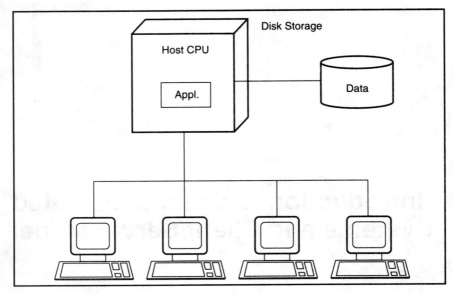

**Figure 1.1**   Host-based processing environment

### 1.1.1   Host-based processing

The client/server computing model implies a cooperative processing of requests submitted by a client, or requester, to the server which processes the requests and returns the results to the client.

Client/server cooperative processing is really a special form of distributed processing, where resources (and tasks affecting the resources) are spread across two or more discrete computing systems. While distributed systems are a relatively new phenomenon, operating system level distribution is well known and widely used. One example may be the distribution of arithmetical and input-output (I/O) functions between a central processing unit (CPU) and an I/O channel controller. Other examples include the distribution of network control functions between an IBM host running Virtual Telecommunications Access Method (VTAM) and a communication controller running Network Control Program (NCP), or distribution of operating system functions among multiple CPUs in a multiprocessor such as the IBM 3090/600 (six processors). However, for the purpose of this book, let's consider processing environments as they are viewed by a particular application.

Distributed systems evolved from the most primitive environment to support application processing. It is the host-based processing environment that does not have any distributed application processing capabilities. Host-based application processing is performed on one computer system with attached unintelligent, "dumb," terminals. A single stand-alone PC or an IBM mainframe with attached character-based display terminals are examples of the host-based processing environment. From an application processing point of view, host-based processing is totally nondistributed.

### 1.1.2  Master-slave processing

The next, higher level of distributed application processing is a master-slave processing. As the name implies, in a master-slave system slave computers are attached to the master computer and perform application-processing-related functions only as directed by their master.

Application processing in a master-slave environment is somewhat distributed, even though distribution of the processing tends to be unidirectional—from the master computer to its slaves. Typically, slave computers are capable of limited local application processing, such as on-screen field validation, editing, or function-key processing. An example of a master-slave processing environment is a mainframe (host) computer, such as IBM 30XX, used with cluster controllers and intelligent terminals.

### 1.1.3  Client/server processing

The client/server processing model has emerged as a higher level of shared device processing typically found in local area networks (LAN). In a shared-device LAN processing environment, personal computers (PC) are attached to a system device that allows these PCs to share a common resource—a file on a hard disk and a printer are typical examples. In the LAN terminology, such shared devices are called *servers* (a file server and a printer server in our example). The name *server* is appropriate, since these shared devices are used to receiving requests for service from the PCs for generic, low-level functions. In a typical LAN-based shared-device processing, these PC requests are usually limited to services related to shared file or print processing (a common file can be read by several PCs, and some report pages can be sent by multiple PCs to the same printer). The obvious drawback of such an approach is that all application processing is performed on individual PCs, and only certain functions (print, file I/O) are distributed. Therefore, an entire file has to be sent to a PC that issued a READ request against this file. If a file has to be updated, the entire file is locked by the PC that issued the update request.

Examples of shared device processing that allow a local area network to have a system dedicated exclusively to the file and/or print services are Novell's NetWare and Microsoft's LAN Manager.

The client/server processing model is a natural extension of shared-device processing. As local area networks grew in size and number of

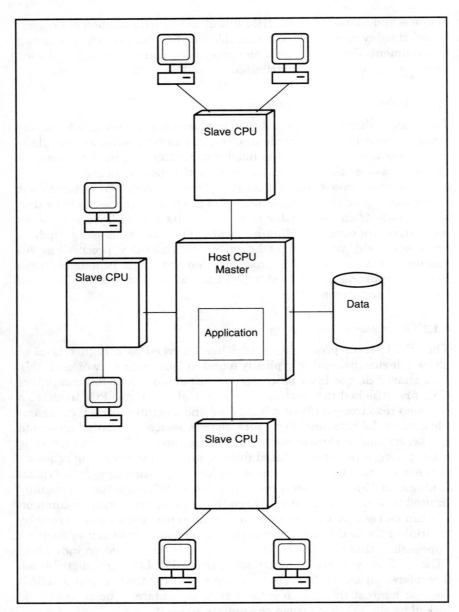

**Figure 1.2**  Master-slave processing environment

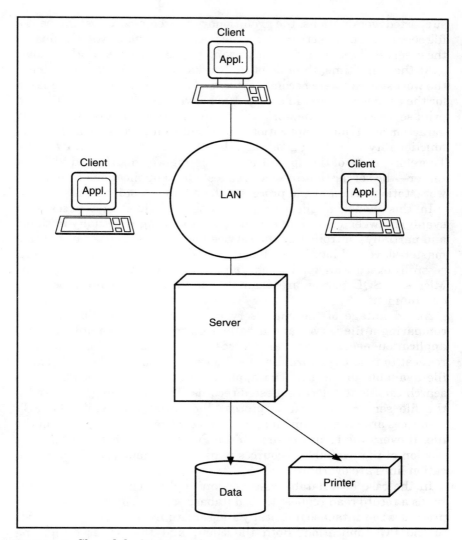

**Figure 1.3**  Shared-device processing environment

supported workstations, the evolutionary shared-device system, be it a file server or a print server, also grew in capacity and power. Gradually, these servers became capable of serving large numbers of workstations.

At the same time, the role of the workstations was also changing—the workstations were becoming *clients* of the servers. The main reason for the change was that in a large LAN environment sharing of file and print services among the workstations in a LAN group represented only a fraction of a typical application. The significant part of the application functionality was also a good candidate for sharing among LAN users. Therefore, some of the application processing was distributed to a new server—the server that receives requests from applications running on workstations (clients) and processes them for each of its clients.

In this model, application processing is divided (not necessarily evenly) between client and server. The processing is actually initiated and partially controlled by the service requester—client—but not in a master-slave fashion. Instead, both client and server cooperate to successfully execute an application. Database server such as Sybase or the Microsoft SQL Server are examples of the client/server processing environment.

An advantage of the client/server approach can be illustrated by comparing a file server and a database server. For example, if a PC application needs particular records from a shared file, it sends a request to read the *entire* file to a file server, which makes this entire file available to the PC. The application running on this PC has to search the file to select requested records. The computing resources of the file server are used to process the entire file, while the PC's resources are used to run an application that reads every record of the file. If every file record is sent to the PC for processing, a significant portion of the available resources is used inefficiently, and communication lines are overburdened.

In the case of a database server, an application running on a PC sends a record read request to its database server. The database server processes the database file locally and sends only the requested records to the PC application. Both the client and the server computing resources cooperate to perform the requested query.

To summarize, architecturally, client/server processing requires:

- Reliable, robust communications between clients and servers
- Client/server cooperative interactions that are initiated by a client
- Application processing distribution between a client and its server
- Server-enforced control over what services or data clients can request
- Server-based arbitration of conflicting clients requests

### 1.1.4   Peer-to-peer processing

A client/server model distinguishes between clients that request services and servers that service these requests. All participant systems in peer-to-peer processing, however, are equals and can request and provide services to and from each other.

This architecture is much more than Peer-to-Peer DOS LAN, for example. It is the ultimate in the distribution of application process-

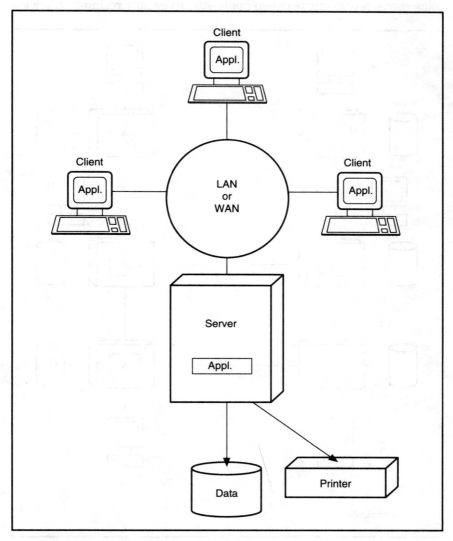

**Figure 1.4**   Client/server processing environment

ing. The processing is performed wherever computing resources are available, including shared devices, CPU, and memory. A single system in peer-to-peer processing can act as a client for other servers and as a server for other clients (including itself). In addition, in intelligent peer-to-peer processing, one server can distribute a workload among available servers, and can even optimize such a distribution based on servers and network characteristics.

Ideally, such a peer-to-peer environment provides for transparent cooperative processing between applications possibly residing on a wide

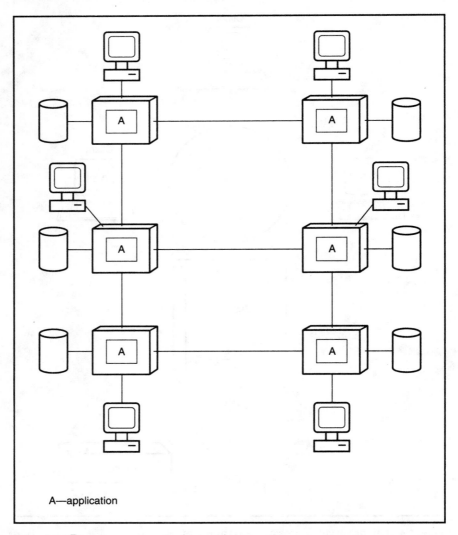

A—application

**Figure 1.5**   Peer-to-peer processing environment

variety of hardware and software platforms. One goal of the peer-to-peer processing environment is the support of networked databases, where Data Base Management System (DBMS) users will be able to move seamlessly between multiple heterogeneous (i.e., different) databases. Thus, practical implementation of the peer-to-peer computing environment is the goal of architects and designers of truly distributed systems.

### 1.1.5   Advantages of client/server computing

Very few products today even claim to support peer-to-peer processing. There is a spectrum of outstanding technical issues that make the implementation of peer-to-peer processing a rather difficult task. However, the client/server model, while not yet the peer-to-peer ideal, is a reasonable approach to the development of distributed systems. This model provides significant benefits and can be used in today's business solutions.

Aside from strictly marketing considerations—most of the development of application-enabling technology (including Computer Assisted Software Engineering, or CASE, tools) is being focused on client/server tools—there are real benefits in adopting a client/server architecture. Specifically:

- It allows corporations to leverage emerging desktop computing technology better. Today's workstations deliver considerable computing power, previously available only from mainframes, at a fraction (sometimes more than an order of magnitude) of mainframe costs.

- It allows the processing to reside close to the source of data being processed. (Client/server architecture is a special form of distributed processing—cooperative processing.) Therefore, network traffic (and response time) can be greatly reduced, and effective throughput and carrying capacity on a heavily loaded network is increased. Conversely, the network bandwidth requirements, and therefore cost, can be reduced.

- It facilitates the use of graphical user interfaces (GUI) available on powerful workstations. These new interfaces can be delivered to customers in a variety of visual presentation techniques together with easy navigation and standards-compliant consistency. Indeed, a picture is worth a thousand words. As a result, investment in training and education can be leveraged better, new products that exceed customer expectations, can be developed faster, and end-user resistance to accepting new products can be minimized.

- It allows for and encourages the acceptance of open systems. Indeed, the fact that clients and servers can, in fact, be running on different hardware and software platforms allows end users to free themselves from particular proprietary architectures, thus taking economical, marketing, and competitive advantage of the open market of available products.

To be sure, the client/server model is not perfect. There are some disadvantages to using a client/server model:

- If a significant portion of application logic is moved to a server, the server may become a bottleneck in the same fashion as a mainframe in a master-slave architecture. Server's limited resources will be in ever-higher demand by the increasing number of resource consumers (end users).

- Distributed applications, especially those designed for cooperative processing, are more complex than nondistributed. This is true for the application development, run-time environment, and tools used to manage this distributed environment. However, some of this complexity can be offset by reducing a large problem into a set of smaller, possibly interdependent problems, similar to modular system design.

There are certain claims made by various software vendors and industry experts relative to a client/server computing model. Some of them are probably true, while others look like a marketing/sales push. For example, the claim that client/server will turn nontechnical users into professional software developers is highly questionable. The same can be said about a claim that client/server will force minicomputers and mainframes to disappear.

However, it is highly probable that a *properly implemented* client/server model will reduce software maintenance cost, increase software portability, boost the performance of existing networks, and even eliminate application backlog by increasing the developer's productivity and shortening the development lifecycle.

Current trade publications emphasize only one side of the client/server model—the side related to the distributed data. However, the true client/server architecture encompasses much more than just data. It includes networks and data communications, distributed presentation and distributed transaction processing, standards, and open systems. This book attempts to look at all these issues in order to give a reader as complete a picture as possible of the client/server architecture.

## 1.2   STANDARDS AND OPEN SYSTEMS

Before discussing all aspects of the client/server architecture, it will be useful to look at the difference between an architecture and a product.

An *architecture* is a set of definitions, rules and terms that are used as guidelines for building a product. A *product* is a specific implementation of an architecture. The architecture alone, without a product implementing it, is not very usable. A product that implements the architecture is what makes that architecture usable.

Well-designed architecture should be implemented in one or more products, and should have a lifetime well beyond a specific product. To achieve these goals, such an architecture should be based on industry standards, and, conversely, may initiate the introduction of new standards. Products that implement such an architecture will promote and support standardization. The client/server computing model is an architecture, albeit not yet a mature architecture. Thus, the products that implement the client/server architecture, although offering some very useful features, differ significantly in functionality, interfaces, and even level of compliance to the standards that should regulate the architecture. What's more, not all standards relevant to the client/server architecture are finalized to date or even fully developed. Therefore, discussion of the client/server will start with a look at relevant industry standards, especially those related to open systems.

### 1.2.1 Open systems

From an information technology point of view, a typical business enterprise is a collection of different systems residing on a wide variety of different, quite often multivendor, mutually incompatible hardware and software platforms, running a myriad of business, scientific and engineering applications. Today, customers want to link their entire enterprise into a coherent whole, tying together all their systems, irrespective of the vendor platform on which these systems are running. Moreover, customers want to extend their businesses by linking enterprise-wide systems with the business's suppliers, distributors, and customers. To be able to interconnect all these systems and to move applications from one system to another, these existing proprietary systems should open their architectures by adopting standards-based interfaces. Even such giants of proprietary systems as IBM recognize the customer's desire for interoperability across multivendor platforms.

Interoperability means that existing multivendor systems should be able to talk to each other. Open interoperability means that new applications should be built in such a way that neither the design nor the implementation of the system would lock the application into a particular vendor hardware or software platform. In other words, open systems applications should be portable across all customer-specified platforms to avoid "lock-in" onto a particular system. In addition, as business applications grow in scope, customers should be able to move these applications to a larger, more powerful system without the need to modify applications—an open system should facilitate application scalability for performance and throughput.

Of course, in order for open systems to fulfill interoperability and application portability requirements, such systems must be built according to industry-accepted standards. Only when a system conforms to industry standards can it seamlessly interoperate with another standards-compliant system, and only then can applications be ported from one such system to another.

It is very important to notice that an open system does not automatically mean UNIX operating system. Openness is not a function of the operating system. Open systems should have the following features:

- compliance with industry standards for programming, communications, networking, system management, presentation, system services and interfaces between applications and system services
- portability of applications across systems
- scalability of application's performance and throughput
- interoperability across systems

In fact, the Institute of Electrical and Electronic Engineers (IEEE) Technical Committee on Open Systems (TCOS) offers the following definition of *open systems: . . . A comprehensive and consistent set of international information technology standards and functional standards profiles that specify interfaces, services, and supporting formats to accomplish interoperability and portability of applications, data and people.*

### 1.2.2   Openness and proprietary standards

Of course, some customers might be interested only in application portability, systems scalability, and interoperability. Such a position is usually justified by saying that these features bring the highest return-on-investment benefits. However, without standards compliance, the full potential of open systems cannot be achieved. For example, the stated goal of IBM's Systems Applications Architecture (SAA) is to provide application portability, consistency, and connectivity across all SAA-supported platforms—MVS, VM, AS/400 and OS/2. However, while the benefits are clear, SAA does not provide interoperability and portability between IBM and non-IBM platforms, thus limiting the openness of SAA-compliant systems.

If, however, all SAA systems were designed to comply with relevant industry standards, then SAA systems would have been truly open to all vendors and users that adhere to these standards. The standards in question are those for programming, communications, networking, system management, presentation, system services, and interfaces between applications and system services (the latter two are described by a POSIX standard). It is true, however, that IBM announced that its version of UNIX operating system (AIX) will be converging with the SAA and will be compliant with POSIX.

There are many important ramifications of the wide proliferation of proprietary standards:

- Customers that are locked in to one vendor's systems and are looking to change the vendor/system/architecture face very high costs of switching from one vendor to another.

- As a rule, users of proprietary systems had already written a large amount of business-related software and supporting documentation, and had trained their employees in system-specific skills. Not all these investments can be saved when migrating to another environment.

- Independent software vendors tend to develop software for vendors with large, installed customer bases, thus giving the largest system vendors additional competitive advantage.

Thus, many users are forced to be locked in to proprietary systems. The real problem arises when, for various reasons, a proprietary system's vendor no longer meets the customer's needs. The twenty-first century customer needs will be changing and growing dramatically.

In the last few years, broad-scale worldwide networks that attempt to connect hundreds of host processors, workstations, servers, and PCs are being developed. Since these networks typically consist of a wide variety of vendor systems, the structure of such large, heterogeneous networks proves to be extremely complex, and network management extraordinarily difficult. These facts result in a worldwide need for and acceptance of standards-based open systems. Client/server architecture and its implementations are no exception: standards will allow different vendor's clients and servers to communicate, to port applications from one platform to another without abandoning the client/server architecture, and to move applications to systems of different sizes to achieve scalable performance and throughput.

Among standards organizations that play key roles in the open systems arena are:

- POSIX—Portable Operating System Interface for computer environment—has been defined by IEEE TCOS to provide greater consistency across unlike operating environments.

- X/Open is a nonprofit organization founded in 1984 to solve problems caused by software and systems incompatibility. X/Open plays an important role in defining a Common Application Environment (CAE), specifications for which are contained in the X/Open Portability Guide (XPG3 in the third release of this guide).
- International Organization for Standardization (ISO) has as its goal developing, accelerating, and promoting various standards and the products that implement them. Among them is the Open Systems Interconnection (OSI) reference model.
- Corporation for Open Systems (COS) concentrates its efforts in the area of OSI, ISDN, standards conformance testing, and certification.
- Object Management Group (OMG) is an international organization involved in system and software development in the framework of the object-oriented technology.
- Open Software Foundation (OSF) and Unix International (UI) are two major technology providers for the open system environments. They are described below.

### 1.2.3    Role of UNIX

The UNIX system was created in 1969 in AT&T's Bell Laboratories. Since the beginning and by design, it has been easily portable to a wide variety of hardware platforms.

From that point of view, it was quite open, even though UNIX was primarily intended to be used for scientific, engineering, and technical applications.

Because the UNIX system is written in a high-level language, "C," and its source code is inexpensively licensed, UNIX became very popular in colleges and universities, where, over the years, it had undergone extensive modifications. Over 200 versions of UNIX exist today, the majority of which derive from the work done at University of California at Berkeley, whose version of UNIX is known as Berkeley Software Distribution (BSD).

Since UNIX is the registered trademark of AT&T, proprietary operating systems that are based on it have been called by different names. Examples of proprietary UNIX-based systems include XENIX from the Microsoft Corporation, ULTRIX from the Digital Equipment Corporation (DEC), and AIX from the International Business Machine Corporation (IBM).

The greatest growth in UNIX systems today is occurring on small-scale systems. In particular, the UNIX influence affects workstations, network servers, and hardware architectures based on the Reduced

Instructions Set Computing (RISC) technology. There are several reasons for such impressive acceptance of the UNIX system:

- UNIX-based systems are inherently more open and easily standardized than non-UNIX proprietary systems.
- Because of its openness, easy interoperability, relatively low price, and multitasking and multiuser support, the UNIX system is the preferred and recommended system for all U.S. government computer system development.
- UNIX-based systems can take advantage of the power of the RISC technology, and can thus deliver excellent price/performance characteristics.
- UNIX penetration into the workstations and servers market and the resulting improvements in price/performance make it the operating system of choice for the fast-growing client/server cooperative processing applications.
- UNIX is well accepted by European and Japanese vendors and customers.

According to the market research statistics, the various flavors of UNIX systems now control over 9 percent of the worldwide hardware market. Many vendors and system users believe that UNIX-based systems have the best potential to provide better systems interoperability, application portability, better network support, and better overall price/performance. One obvious disadvantage of the UNIX system has always been the existence of multiple, generally incompatible UNIX versions.

To support UNIX claims on open systems, new standards have to be developed and UNIX-based systems have to be standardized. Over the years, various user groups and standards bodies had been formed, and new, open systems standards are being developed.

However, standards groups do not develop systems. That is why special organizations have been formed to develop core software technology and supply them to the entire industry. Two major organizations of this kind are the Open Software Foundation (OSF) and the UNIX International (UI). Each organization attracted a number of hardware and software vendors. Each organization has similar goals and develops similar technology. Unfortunately, the competition among various UNIX system vendors has resulted in competition between OSF and UI.

Unless standards and technologies from OSF and UI converge into a common open systems continuum, there will always be questions and arguments among vendors and users as to which system is open and

which standards are to be followed. Hopefully, OSF and UI will converge their technologies so that both systems vendors and systems
users can benefit from standards-based open systems.

### 1.2.4  Beneficiaries of open systems

The ultimate goal of an ideal open computing environment is to make
possible truly distributed networks where:

- computing can occur transparently across the network
- applications, resources, functionality and power can be shared seamlessly throughout the environment
- users will be provided with the greatest possible portability, interoperability, and scalability of applications

Creation of such an open computing environment does not mean the
elimination of proprietary operating systems. Nor (and this is very
important) does it imply that open systems must be purely UNIX-
based. Open systems are more than UNIX. Open systems environments accomplish interoperability and portability of applications and
data by supporting a comprehensive and complete set of internationally accepted technology and functionality standards. And truly open
systems will coexist with proprietary operating systems, including various flavors of UNIX. This coexistence will be accomplished by providing interfaces and connection points, so that vendor lock-in is avoided
and the user's investments in existing technology, applications and
training are better leveraged. A truly open computing environment
will benefit system vendors, independent software vendors, and end
users in the following ways:

- Hardware and software system vendors will benefit from open systems by lowering the costs of operating systems development, thus
  shortening time-to-market for new products. Instead of spending
  time and efforts on creation of proprietary systems, vendors will be
  able to improve the architecture, features, and functionality of new
  products.
     Open systems do not eliminate competition. Conversely, vendors
  will compete and add value to their products to achieve specialization of products and hardware platforms, quality, service, and proprietary optimization solutions.
- Independent software vendors will benefit from an open computing
  environment by developing products based on international standards. Compliance with standard interfaces will practically guarantee new, wider markets for their products.

■ End users will be the biggest beneficiaries of the open computing environment. Their hardware purchasing strategies will allow end users to purchase systems without fear of buying the "wrong box." In open systems, end users will be assured of having the same operating environment with any system they purchase—mainframe, minicomputer, workstation, or supercomputer. Mixed vendor interoperability and networking connectivity will be simplified. Software development and training and maintenance costs will be lowered, and more off-the-shelf products will be available at more competitive prices. Entire corporations and individual business units will have more flexibility in choosing products and systems that best suit their business requirements.

While a truly open computing environment is still the future goal of many vendors, standards bodies, and end users, there are many encouraging developments today that bring us closer to the open systems environment. The already mentioned Open Software Foundation and UNIX International are two organizations which have stated that development of Open Systems is their main objective.

In fact, today, both organizations offer almost similar versions of the open computing environment. OSF offers the Distributed Computing Environment (DCE), while UI's solution is Open Network Computing (ONC). Granted, no one organization, no matter how big and influential, can manage to create such a complete and complicated environment and force the industry to accept it. That is why both the OSF and the UI find their strength in their membership. Practically all systems and independent software vendors belong to either one or both OSF and UI.

The discussion of OSF and UI, their strategies and differences, are beyond the scope of this book. This book is about the client/server architecture and its implementations. However, distributed cooperative processing is the foundation and key of the client/server architecture. And since distributed processing is one of the main goals and beneficiaries of truly open systems, it will be useful to look at one of the best known candidates to become a de facto standard for the open and distributed computing environments: OSF's Distributed Computing Environment.

## 1.3 DISTRIBUTED COMPUTING ENVIRONMENT

Even though both the DCE and ONC appear similar, the DCE might have wider acceptance. Indeed, even the European Commission (the coordinating body for Unified Europe) has picked OSF's DCE over UI's ONC for the development of the new generation of distributed applications for the multivendor computing strategy. The European Commission (EC) claims that the OSF's DCE is more complete than the ONC, and that support for the DCE is expected from both OSF and UI camps.

For all practical purposes, DCE and ONC seem to be incompatible on only one point: Remote Procedure Calls (RPC). This incompatibility is not critical; there are several vendors that are implementing the DCE on the UI standard operating system: UNIX System V release 4, often abbreviated as SVR4.

### 1.3.1   Background

OSF's Distributed Computing Environment empowers both end users and software developers to take advantage of truly distributed open systems. The DCE provides the foundation that is needed to use and develop distributed applications in heterogeneous hardware and software environments.

To develop the Distributed Computing Environment, OSF issued Requests For Technology (RFT). Through its open RFT process, OSF has selected and integrated the best technologies available to date. Over 50 vendors responded to the RFT (only 29 of those were actual OSF members). The selected technologies were mostly derived from the DECorum proposal jointly submitted by Hewlett-Packard (HP)/ Apollo, IBM, Digital Equipment Corporation (DEC), Microsoft Corporation, Locus, and Transarc.

By selecting DECorum technologies, OSF has positioned its DCE as an alternative to Sun Microsystems' Network Computing Architecture (NCA). The NCA has already been adopted by Sun's large installed customer base (Sun Microsystems is a member of the UI). This decision could have made the acceptance of the DCE a rather slow process. However, IBM's recent (Fall of 1991) announcements of the forthcoming interoperability between its Systems Applications Architecture (SAA) and its version of UNIX—Advanced Interactive eXecutive (AIX) operating system—plus OSF's decision to adopt a significant part of the AIX as a portion of its operating system kernel—OSF/1—make the development of bridges between SAA, AIX, and DCE a very real possibility.

As open distributed environments penetrate the commercial system markets, traditionally dominated by IBM and IBM-compatible products, SAA and AIX interoperability with the DCE will be an important requirement, as well as one of the deciding factors, for the DCE acceptance.

### 1.3.2   DCE architecture

In general terms, the Distributed Computing Environment is an integrated environment consisting of the following components:

- Distributed File System
- Directory Service
- Remote Procedure Calls
- Threads Services
- Time Services

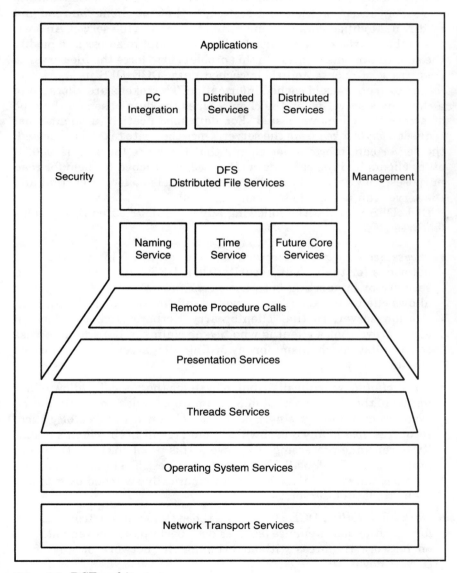

**Figure 1.6** DCE architecture

## Distributed file system (DFS)

Distributed file systems operate by allowing a user on one system that is connected to a network to access and modify data stored on files in another system. From a client/server architecture point of view, the system on which the user is working is the *client,* while the system in which the data is stored is the *file server.*

When data is accessed from the file server, a copy of that data is stored, or *cached,* on the client system, so that the client can read and modify it. Modified data is then written back to the file server. An obvious problem arises when multiple clients attempt to access and modify the same data. One solution to this problem is to force the file server to keep track of clients and their cached data. DCE DFS uses a set of *tokens* to keep track of cached information. The tokens are allocated to a client by a server when the client caches the data based on the type of access the client requested. For data modification, a client must request a *write token* from the server. Once the write token is allocated, the server can inform other clients that the write token is issued. If other clients had the same data allocated and cached to them for read purposes, they will be notified that their data is no longer current and the server can revoke their tokens.

DCE DFS provides the following advanced distributed file systems features:

- *Access Security and Protection.* While original UNIX systems were notorious for their weak security, DCE DFS implements enforced security by supporting both user *authentication* (*Kerberos* system allows clients to exchange encrypted information with the authentication server, so that clients carry Kerberos tickets which in effect prove that a client is who he/she claims to be) and an access control list mechanism for awarding file access to authorized clients.

- *Data reliability.* While distributed systems theoretically allow elimination of the single point of failure, improperly designed distributed systems may force a single client to rely on a number of critical resources, loss of any one of which would result in the client's inability to continue processing. To prevent this problem, DCE DFS supports *replication* for all its network services: if one of the servers becomes unavailable, a client is automatically switched over to one of the replicated servers.

- *Data Availability.* DCE DFS allows the system administrator to perform routine maintenance (such as data backup, file movement, etc.) on network resources without bringing the network or any of its servers down.

- *Performance.* DCE DFS is an efficient, extensible system. By caching file status information and data on a client system, DFS is reducing the number of data requests from clients, thus reducing a server and network's workload.

- *Manageability.* DCE DFS uses distributed databases to keep track of file location, authentication, and the access control lists used by both clients and servers. These databases are broken into separately administered and maintained domains that can be accessed by any client. In addition, these databases are self-configuring and easy to operate.

- *Standards Conformance.* DCE DFS conforms with the IEEE POSIX 1003.1 file system semantics standard.

- *Interoperability with Network File System (NFS).* DCE DFS provides gateways that allow clients using NFS to interoperate with DCE DFS servers, thus providing a migration path from NFS to DCE DFS.

DCE DFS is based on the Andrew File System from Transarc Corporation. It differs from the Sun's Network File System (NFS)—a current de facto standard—in these two main categories:

- DFS uses global file space (all network users see the same paths to accessible files). Global file names ensure uniform file access from any network node via a *uniform name space*. In NFS, each network node has a different view of the file space.

- DFS provides integrated support for both local and wide area networks; NFS was designed primarily to operate in a Local Area Network environment.

**Directory service**
Computer networks, like people, require names and directories to describe, record, and find the characteristics of the various services and information they provide. Like a real mail system, an electronic mail system must be able to locate a user's mailbox in order to deliver the mail.

In a distributed computing environment, the mail delivery application will contact a directory or name services application to look up the user's name and location (address). In the DCE, anything that can be named and accessed individually (e.g., network services, electronic mailboxes, computers, etc.) is called an *object*. Each object has a corresponding listing (an *entry*) in the directory service. Each entry contains *attributes* that describe the object. Name entries are collected into lists called *directories*. In the DCE, directories can be organized into hierarchies in which a directory can contain other directories. An example of such a hierarchy can be an international telephone listing that contains directories of individual countries.

The name and directory services are central to the DCE. That is because all DCE objects are defined by their names, and applications and services gain access to objects by accessing an appropriate directory entry and retrieving its attributes. Thus, object characteristics are separated (decoupled) from the object itself, and, most importantly, the *location independence* of objects is assured. Such an organization allows applications and services to access objects even if the object moves or changes several of its attributes.

The DCE Directory Service is integrated with the other DCE components, including DCE DFS, and possesses the same advanced characteristics (security, reliability, availability, manageability, performance) as the DCE DFS.

The DCE Directory Service is designed to participate in the CCITT's and ISO's (International Standards Organization) Open Systems Interconnection (OSI) X.500 worldwide directory service. Local DCE users can be tied into X.500 directory service and, conversely, users in other parts of the world are allowed to access local names via X.500. To implement this feature, DCE supplies naming gateways called *Global Directory Agents,* or *GDA.*

In a client/server DCE environment, a local client in one part of the DCE network (in one domain) that needs to look up the name of a remote client sends its request to a local GDA residing on a name server. The GDA on that server forwards the request to the worldwide X.500 service, which looks up a name and returns the result to the GDA, which in turn passes it back to its client.

To ensure portability and interoperability, and to isolate application programmers from the details of the underlying services, the OSF DCE uses a service-independent application programming interface (*API*). This API is based on the X/Open Directory Services (XDS) API specifications. Applications that use XDS can work with the DCE Directory Service and with X.500 without modifications.

### Remote procedure calls

Remote Procedure Calls (RPC) syntax, semantics, and presentation services represent the extension of high-level language subroutine calls. RPCs allow the actual code of the called procedure to reside and be executed on a physically remote processor in a manner transparent to the application. The RPC mechanism is the most critical aspect of the entire DCE architecture—it acts as the glue that holds all DCE components together. The basis of the OSF DCE RPC is the HP/Apollo's Network Computing System (NCS) version 2.0 Remote Procedure Call, submitted as part of the DECorum proposal. DCE's

RPCs are easy to use, and are designed to be transparent to various network architectures and to support threads (described below). According to the research done by the European Commission, RPC syntax, semantics, and presentation services represent the major differences between OSF's DCE and UI's ONC. One point worth mentioning is that OSF disagrees with the way ONC encourages fundamental RPC protocol modifications by users.

### Threads services

A typical network computing environment achieves its goals by linking all participating processors. Therefore, opportunities exist to implement a certain degree of parallel processing. Among many strategies in existence to implement the parallel processing code, OSF selected the threads strategy for its Distributed Computing Environment. The threads strategy uses subprocesses (threads) that exist and operate within a single instance of the executing program and its address space. The program itself can use special synchronization tools, such as semaphores, to control access to a common, modifiable resource shared by several users (memory variable, for example).

Of course, there are many other methods of implementing parallel processing (i.e., shared memory among multiple programs or use of explicit synchronization verbs to exchange messages among several programs). However, these methods usually involve resources external to the program. DEC's Concert Multithread Architecture (CMA) is the foundation of the DCE's Threads Services. It offers portability and supports the POSIX 1003 application and system services interface specification.

### Time services

The function of the time services component is to synchronize the clocks of all network nodes with the clock that controls the network as a whole. Due to its completeness and simplicity, OSF selected DEC's distributed Time Synchronization Service.

### The result—DCE client/server model

OSF DCE is designed to fit into the client/server paradigm. Therefore, DCE components must be present on the service requestor, DCE client, and the service provider, DCE server (see Fig. 1.7).

DCE is not simply a software package that can be installed on a server. In fact, DCE components are placed "between" applications and networking services on both the client and the server. Even though DCE is a multilayered architecture containing a number of basic services, the DCE client/server model hides actual details of these services from end users. Essentially, DCE components represent an

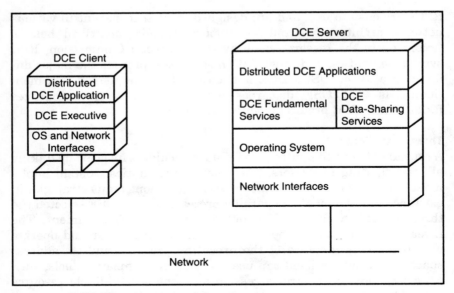

**Figure 1.7**   DCE Client/server model

integral part of the distributed computing model being developed by such standards bodies as ISO (International Standards Organization).

### 1.3.3  The complete picture

The Distributed Computing Environment represents a valuable contribution to the development of open distributed computing. To make the open computing environment architecture complete, two additional efforts are taking place today:

- To make applications easily available for a multitude of hardware and software platforms, vendors and organizations such as the OSF and the UI are working toward the development of the *Architecture-Neutral Software Distribution Format (ANDF)*. ANDF technology will increase the appeal and power of open systems by making available a rich set of applications for a broad range of computing platforms.

- As distributed computing becomes a reality, the need to define a consistent approach to managing networking systems, irrespective of the underlying hardware and software platforms, becomes more pressing. OSF's proposed solution to a uniform framework for the efficient, object-oriented, cost-effective management of open systems will be the development of the *Distributed Management*

*Environment (DME)*. DME and similar products will provide a solid foundation for the development of systems management applications. Since OSF submitted its DME Request For Technology, IBM, HP, DEC, NeXT and over 20 other vendors, research institutions, and government bodies are submitting technology to be considered as the DME foundation.

Standards-based architectures like the DCE, ANDF and DME should be used as a proper foundation for development of an open and standard client/server architecture. The various components and principles of the client/server architecture are the main subject of this book.

# Approach to Distribution

The evolution of computing environments, as described in the previous chapter, brought to life various forms of distributed processing. Distributed computing is the next evolutionary step beyond file sharing. A distributed computing environment such as Open Software Foundation's Distributed Computing Environment, or DCE (described in the previous chapter), makes a collection of loosely connected systems appear to be a single system. Distributed computing makes it easier to develop and run applications that use resources throughout a computer network. Applications can be distributed to run on the computers best suited for the task. Various tasks can be run in parallel, providing higher performance and better resource utilization. A client/server architecture is built on, and represents a special case of distributed computing—a cooperative distributed processing. Today's client/server requirements include the freedom to store data and run applications on a wide variety of interconnected platforms. Client/server implementations should be available in an open, flexible, standardized, multivendor computing environment. The importance of standards and open systems has already been described in the previous chapter. The next critical building block of the client/server architecture deals with distributed environment models, and is the subject of this chapter.

## 2.1   DISTRIBUTED MODELS

The development of a distributed computing architecture has been affected by two opposing forces that prevail in today's computing environment. The first force breaks up applications and pushes the resulting pieces (fragments) toward the end users. There are at least two reasons for this behavior:

- development and execution of applications on workstations and PCs that provide significant price/performance gains
- end users demands for local autonomy and additional functionality (such as flexible and consistent graphical user interfaces) that increase user's productivity

The second, opposing force, has its roots in the end user's need to access corporate data. This need affects systems integration requirements, and results in the centralization of applications on large, powerful mainframes. That second force increases the need for ever-higher levels of integrity, performance, and availability (see Fig. 2.1).

These requirements are rarely achievable on a single small system. The answer lies in the development of a distributed model consisting of a large centralized platform connected to a network of sufficiently powerful workstations operating in local area networks (LAN). The main architectural questions in such a model are:

- how and where in the model computing resources are distributed
- how to implement intercommunication facilities among all participating computing resources

To answer the first question, let's consider one of today's most popular distributed computing environment configurations—the multitiered approach.

### 2.1.1   Multitiered environment

Most large organizations have begun moving toward what has become known as a three-tiered architecture. The root of the three-tiered architecture is a familiar hierarchical, traditional master-slave computing architecture. Examples of this architecture are IBM's System/ 370 and the original implementations of the Systems Network Architecture (SNA).

The three-tiered architecture has added distributed and cooperative processing capabilities to the hierarchical computing model. In the most trivial implementation of such an architecture, the computing resources are distributed vertically. Specifically, the top tier is usually

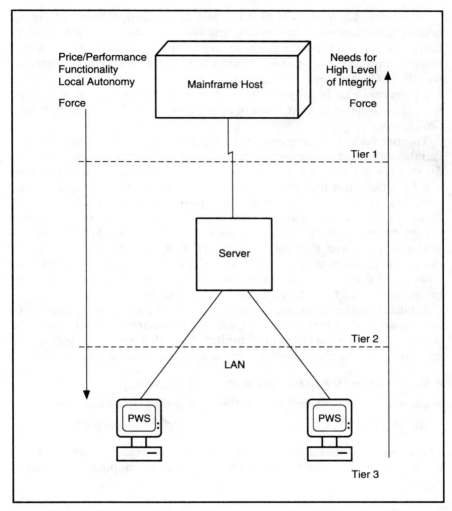

**Figure 2.1** Three-tiered architecture

occupied by the most powerful system and the source of corporate data, the mainframe. The second tier contains powerful LAN servers, which have dual properties: they act as top-tier clients that send appropriate requests to the mainframe. At the same time, they function as servers for the workstations and PCs that reside in the third tier.

An example of such a vertical three-tiered architecture would be an organization that extends its central single-host, data center capabilities by building LANs in each of its headquarters departments and connecting corresponding LAN servers to the host.

Of course, such an architecture can be expanded horizontally by adding mainframes to the top tier, and local area networks and servers to the second and third tiers. For example, an organization that desires to extend its East Coast operations by building a second data center on the West Coast, can put LANs into each regional sales office. Office LAN servers can be physically located in remote (relative to a host) locations, and can be connected to either host via a Wide Area Network (WAN).

The network management, system performance, data integrity and reliability in such an extended three-tiered model require some kind of an intratiered communication (intercommunication between hosts in the first tier, and between servers in the second tier). Therefore, the resulting architecture becomes more complex to build and manage. However, the resulting computing capacity has also increased, probably in orders of magnitude. Moreover, the resulting architecture is scalable. It means that as the number of workstations grows, additional local area networks, more powerful servers, and even additional tiers can be put into operation, without rebuilding the network or, more importantly for the end users, applications.

A multitiered computing model appears to be reasonably flexible to implement. In principle, it's a distributed cooperative application. In practice, however, to efficiently implement multitiered architecture for any given application, the following questions must be answered:

- On which tier (or tiers) should the data be placed?
- On which tier (or tiers) should the application logic be placed?
- On which tier (or tiers) should a user interface be placed?

These are the questions that reflect the intrinsic properties of the client/server architecture—interactions among application components.

### 2.1.2   Cooperative client/server processing

As was mentioned earlier, cooperative processing is the foundation and the driving force of the client/server architecture. The distinguishing characteristic of a cooperative processing application is the high degree of interaction between various application components (or application fragments). In a client/server architecture, these interactions are the interactions between the client's requests and the server's reactions to those requests. In order to understand these interactions, let's look at the general application components. A typical application consists of the following components:

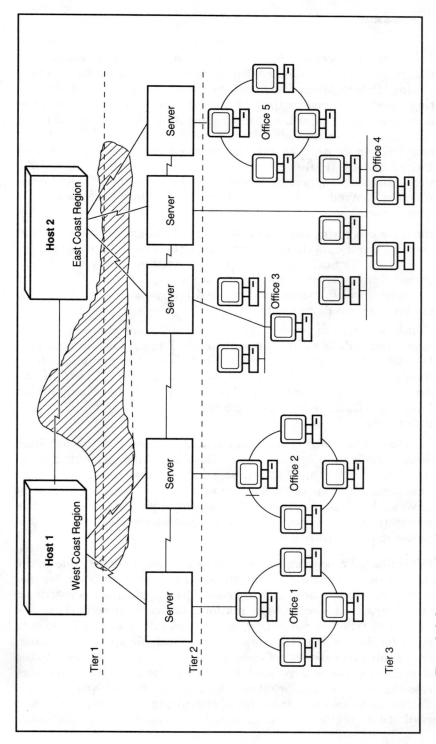

**Figure 2.2** Extended three-tiered architecture

- *Presentation processing logic.* This is a part of the application code that interacts with a device such as an end user's terminal or workstation. Presentations logic performs such tasks as screen formatting, reading, and writing of the screen information, window management, keyboard, and mouse handling. Some of the facilities that provide presentation processing logic are IBM's CICS, IMS/DC and TSO for centralized mainframe environment. Graphical User Interfaces (GUI) are provided by facilities such as the OS/2 Presentation Manager, Microsoft's Windows for the PC DOS environment, X Windows, OSF's Motif, and SUN's Open Look for a UNIX environment.

- *Business processing logic.* This is a part of the application code that uses the input data (from a screen and/or database) to perform business tasks. Typically, this code is user-written in any of the supported third-generation (3GL) languages (e.g., COBOL, C, PL/I), or in higher-level fourth-generation (4GL) languages (user-written or produced by a code generator).

- *Database processing logic.* This is a part of the application code that manipulates data within the application. The data is managed by a Database Management System (DBMS). Data manipulation in Relational DBMSs (RDBMS) is done using some dialect of the Structured Query Language (SQL). SQL's Data Manipulation Language (DML) is typically embedded into the 3GL or 4GL application code.

- *Database processing.* This is the actual processing of the database data that is performed by the Database Management System (DBMS). Ideally, the DBMS processing is transparent to the business logic of the application. However, from the architectural point of view, database processing is an essential part of the cooperative processing interactions, and should be considered as a component of cooperative application processing.

In host-based processing, these application components reside on the same system and are combined into one executable program. No distribution is taking place, and, in general, the application is restricted by the limited resources of the platform on which it runs. With the advent of distributed computing, new opportunities are being open to system developers and end users. Portable scalable applications capable of running on networks of open systems that are transparent to the end users can now be developed. By distributing computing resources across the network, significant cost-benefits can be achieved.

To distribute means to take something, divide it into fragments, and spread these fragments out. In distributed computing, to distribute

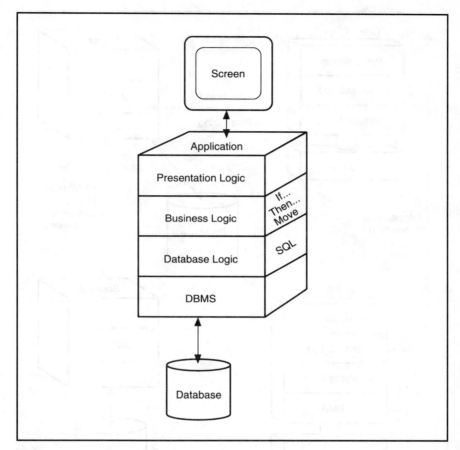

**Figure 2.3**  Typical application components

means to divide available computing resources into fragments and spread them across a network. The question is, what resources should be distributed, and what are the consequences of such a distribution?

When only data is distributed between several locations, a single application can conceivably access the data from any location, in a fashion totally transparent to the application. Certain benefits (such as placing data close to its source, data distribution for higher availability, etc.) can be derived from such a distribution. However, the singularity of an application can create a bottleneck, a limiting factor in achieving higher performance, portability, and cost-benefits of application scalability.

If, however, in addition to data, some application processing is also distributed across the network, various computing resources can be bet-

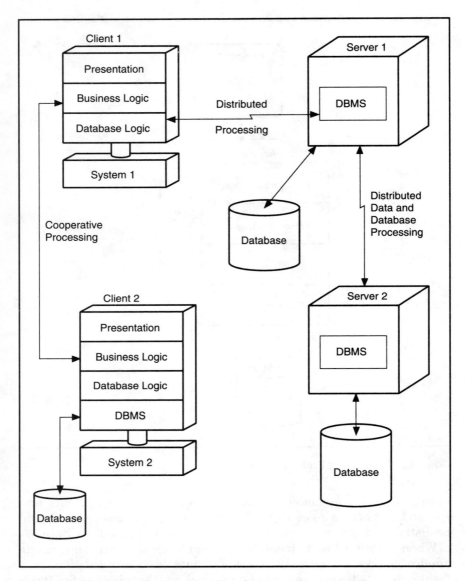

**Figure 2.4**   Client/server, distributed, and cooperative processing

ter utilized, especially considering the significant price/performance characteristics of modern workstations. Of course, once application components are distributed, they must cooperate in the processing of a business application. The client/server architecture employs distributed cooperative processing to:

- distribute application processing components between clients (typically presentation and some part of the business logic) and servers (typically some parts of the business logic, database logic and DBMS)
- support cohesive interactions between clients and servers in a cooperative fashion

One of the questions every client/server system designer must answer is how to distribute application components between clients and servers. In a multitiered architecture, this question is extended to the component's placement into various tiers. While there is no universal recipe to the proper distribution of application components, some general recommendations can be made:

- In general, a presentation logic component with its screen input-output facilities is placed on a client system, and these clients are typically placed in the lowest tier of the multitiered environment (PC and workstations).

- Given the available power of the client workstations, and the fact that the presentation logic resides on the client system, it makes sense to also place some part of the business logic on a client system. It should be true for at least that part of the application logic that deals with the screen-related editing, and maybe those pieces of the code that are specific to a particular client.

- If the database processing logic is embedded into the business logic, and if clients maintain some low-interaction, quasi-static data, then the database processing logic (such as local data manipulation) can be placed on a client system.

- Given the fact that a typical LAN connects clients within a common-purpose workgroup, and assuming that the workgroup shares a database, all common, shared fragments of the business and database processing logic and DBMS itself should be placed on the server.

Similar principals can be used to decide the placement of a client/server application component in a multitiered cooperative environment. To a large extent, the question of component placement should be decided by:

- the quantity of data relevant to any given application
- the number of active users running applications against this data
- the number of interactions between various application components

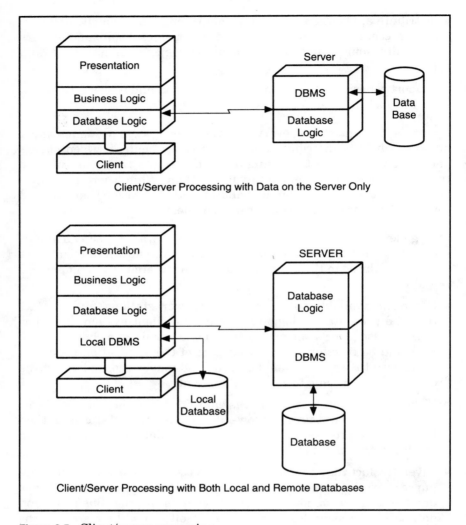

Client/Server Processing with Data on the Server Only

Client/Server Processing with Both Local and Remote Databases

**Figure 2.5**   Client/server processing

- the technical characteristics of the platforms selected for clients and servers

For example, if the application requires frequent read and write access to a large corporate database, that database and its processing logic are placed in the top tier. If the access is infrequent, or is mostly read-only, it may be feasible to place relevant copies of the data onto a second-tier server. The server-based DBMS (usually different from the host DBMS), database processing logic, and common shared parts of the business logic should be also placed there. In this case, every tier contains its own database, and system designers face the problem of heterogeneous data access (this problem is discussed in greater detail later in the book).

Figure 2.6 illustrates such an architecture where the top tier contains a mainframe IBM 3090 host that accesses IBM's DB2 database. The second tier is a database server running a relational DBMS such as Sybase SQL Server, and the third tier contains PS/2 running MS DOS, MS Windows and dBase III database.

### 2.1.3   Cooperative processing techniques

To make all the components of the architecture illustrated on Fig. 2.6 cooperate, certain intercomponent communication techniques must be employed. Theoretically, there are three basic types of cooperative processing communication techniques that a client/server architecture can use:

- Pipes
- Remote Procedure Calls
- Client/server SQL interactions

*Pipes* represent a connection-oriented mechanism that passes data from one process to another. Pipes are widely used in UNIX-based systems. A common water pipe, with the water going in one end and coming out in another place, is a good illustration of a communication pipe (in our description, data is the water). In principle, the processes can be on different machines, even running under different operating systems.

Various pipe implementations may support one or several concurrent transport mechanisms. The details of the supported transport mechanisms are hidden from a pipe user, and pipes impose minimal protocol and format restrictions on users. Basically, pipes provide facilities only to mark the boundaries between discrete messages, to determine the identity of the sender, and to perform verification of the receipt of a message. Pipe implementations vary from very simple to such complex architectures as IBM's Advanced Program-to-Program Communications (APPC). IBM's SNA and Sun's NFS are just two examples of the pipes mechanism.

A *Remote Procedure Call (RPC)* has been briefly described in Open Software Foundation's Distributed Computing Environment (DCE). An RPC is a mechanism by which one process can execute another process (subroutine) that resides on a different, usually remote, system, possibly running on a different operating system. Any parameters needed by a subroutine are passed between the original and the

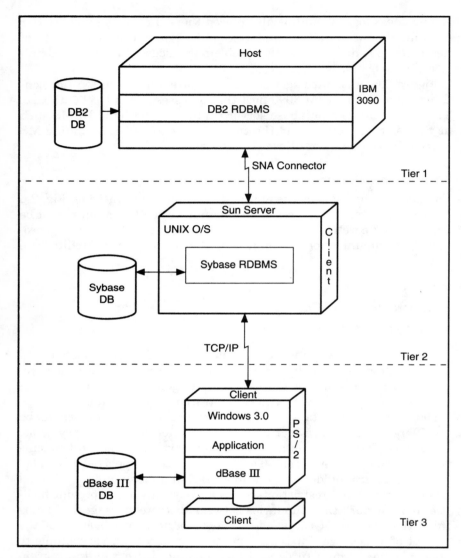

**Figure 2.6** Three-tiered architecture with heterogeneous data access

subroutine processes. As with pipes, the details of the transport mechanism used by the RPC is hidden from an RPC user. A specific RPC tool may support one or several different transport mechanisms. The main requirement for successful RPC implementation is the ability of a caller to find a server where the subroutine resides. One way to accomplish the search is to match the required subroutine name with those maintained in a special subroutines/servers database. The entries in this database can be modified so that the target server for the subroutine can be assigned dynamically. This assignment can change from one invocation of an RPC to another. RPCs impose some format restrictions on users. Examples of RPCs are OSF's RPC, Sun's Netwise, IBM's OS/2 Remote Program Link (RPL), and Sybase's RPC.

*Client/server SQL interaction* is a mechanism for passing the Structured Query Language (SQL) requests and associated data from one process (usually a client) to another process (server). Client/server SQL is a special case of client/server interactions, applicable to distributed relational database applications. In this case, the server is a relational database server. It can reside on a different system (remote relative to a client), possibly running under a different operating system. The majority of the client/server products implemented to date are based on client/server SQL interactions.

As with pipes and RPCs, many different transport mechanisms are supported. And, while the details of the transport mechanisms are hidden from application developers, client/server SQL interactions impose severe protocol and format restrictions on the users. SQL syntax, functionality, and supported data formats are the reasons for these restrictions.

Pipes, as a connection-oriented mechanism, can solve a large set of intercommunication problems in cooperative processing. RPCs can solve only a subset of problems solved by pipes. However, an RPC is a connectionless mechanism. The RPC connection exists only for the duration of the call. Theoretically, two successive RPCs to the same remote routine, identified by name, could be executed on different servers. Client/server SQL interactions, on the other hand, represent a connection-oriented mechanism similar to pipes. The connection here is made between the client (issuer of SQL requests) and the server. This connection is, in fact, a client/server conversation between partners.

The drawback of client/server SQL interactions is its data-oriented nature. Indeed, a client/server architecture that implements only the SQL interactions mechanism is limited to relational database (RDBMS) applications only.

Application requirements beyond the scope of an RDBMS application cannot be satisfied by client/server SQL communications. Therefore, any open client/server system should be designed to take advantage of various cooperative processing communications techniques as required by the business application logic.

## 2.2    SINGLE SYSTEM IMAGE

A successful client/server architecture takes advantage of network computing and price/performance advances in microcomputer technology by off-loading traditional mainframe processing onto powerful servers and workstations. In a client/server environment, the majority of the application processing is done on a client (workstation), and all common, shared tasks, such as database access, are performed on a mainframe or local area network server. The fact that certain functions needed by an application are performed on a different system, potentially miles away from the client site, should not affect the way applications appear to behave. In other words, distributing application components between clients and servers should not change the "look and feel" of an application. Many different systems may participate in the execution of a single client's request. To the end users, however, the entire distributed multiclient/multiserver environment should appear as a single-user, powerful system. To summarize: properly implemented, a client/server distributed environment should provide end users with a *Single System Image,* or *SSI.*

In practical terms, single system image means that all client/server interactions between distributed application components (presentation, business, and database logic) should be performed in a transparent, timely, and effective fashion. A single system image is obviously a highly desirable feature of a client/server architecture. However, its implementation requirements are quite different for the presentation, application processing logic, and data distribution.

The next sections of this chapter list important issues of a client/ server architecture implementation—the issues that are described in greater detail later in the book.

## 2.3    DISTRIBUTED PRESENTATION

The first application fragment that interacts with the end user is the presentation logic. The presentation logic is the application's window into the outside world. It is this logic that interfaces with the end user, and, at the same time, interacts with the business logic. In a stand-alone or host-based environment, presentation and business logic are bundled together. With the advances in workstation technology, new capabilities have been opened to presentation logic developers. Traditional character-based terminals are being replaced by high-resolution screens with an unlimited number of colors. Point-and-click devices such as a mouse, rich graphics, computer imaging, and even audio-video input-output facilities are now available. These innovations allowed application developers to design applications with visual, intuitive graphical user interfaces (GUI) that offer such features as windows, scrolling bars, pull-down and pop-up menus, and push-buttons. Use of these tools and point-and-click mouse devices not only increases end user productivity, but its ease of use allows for shorter training, thus providing better leverage for the investment in application development and training.

To illustrate the power of a GUI interface, let's consider a real estate application. Imagine a contemporary real estate office. When a new customer walks into an office and asks to see all new-construction houses in a particular area, a real estate broker enters all the parameters into a computer, and receives a display of a color map of the desired area, with all potential houses clearly marked. The broker uses a mouse to point to one of the candidate houses, and a color picture of the house appears on the screen together with pertinent information. Point and click on the entrance, and the next window displays a view of the foyer. A guided tour of a house can be accomplished by audio comments.

This illustration is not science fiction. Products that provide facilities and applications similar to the one described above exist, and are implemented using a client/server architecture. The presentation portion of such an application is distributed to a client site—a powerful workstation equipped with a high-resolution color monitor. The reasons for the presentation distribution are quite compelling:

- High-resolution graphics require significant processing power. Each individual picture dot on a screen (pixel) is controlled in its placement, intensity, and colors, and there may be over a million pixels in a high-resolution monitor. The entire screen is "painted," pixel by pixel, and a large number of floating-point calculations are associated with every new screen.

- All windowing environments are event-driven. Most of the processing is controlled by a mouse pointer moving from one window to another, by pressing a mouse button, or when a scrolling bar or a menu item are touched. This processing requires significant computing resources.

- Workstations are often designed to perform high-function graphics. Their on-board processors are enhanced to handle 2-D and 3-D graphics.

The computing power requirements for most of the currently used graphical user interfaces make it economically beneficial to off-load the presentation logic onto a platform that is designed specifically to handle such requirements. And, just by the nature of presentation, such a

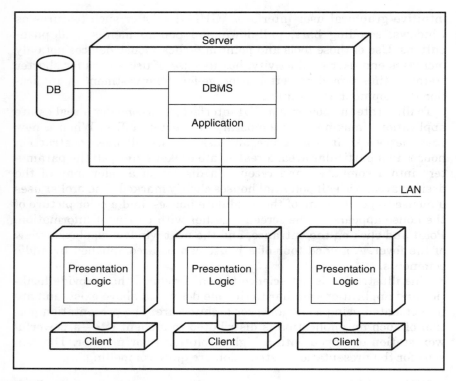

**Figure 2.7**  Presentation distribution

platform is designed for human interactions and should be at a user site. To satisfy the single system image requirements, interactions between the presentation fragments and the rest of the application logic should be accomplished in a user-transparent fashion.

The best known technology that allows applications to transparently access displays on a networked workstation was developed at Massachusetts Institute of Technology and was called *X Windows*. X Windows architecture is based on the client/server model. It provides a communication protocol between an application and its presentation logic, which may reside on a remote display workstation. X Windows and other presentation standards are described in more detail later in the book.

## 2.4  DISTRIBUTED PROCESSING

While presentation logic is on the forefront of the application-to-user interactions, it is really the business and database logic that represent the essence of an application. In a client/server environment, the presentation logic is typically placed on the client system. One of the critical design questions at this point is the placement of the business and database logic (together referred to as the application processing). Obviously, there are three possible solutions:

- Application processing logic is placed entirely on a client system.

- Application processing logic is placed entirely on a server.

- Application processing logic is fragmented, with the fragments distributed between the client and the server.

Each solution has its advantages and disadvantages.

*Case 1. Application processing resides on a client system.* There are several reasons to place application processing logic on a client system. Some of them are:

- Price/performance of the latest workstations is orders of magnitude higher than that of traditional mainframes; it is economically expedient to off-load expensive mainframe machine cycles onto significantly less expensive microcomputers. Remember, that in a three-tiered, client/server architecture the second tier is composed of microcomputer-based LAN servers that act as servers for the client workstations in the third tier and as clients for the first tier—mainframe.

- Assuming that at least a portion of the application processing logic deals with the terminal I/O performed by the presentation logic, it makes sense to place the application processing logic as close to the source of the terminal I/O data as possible. The alternative is to send screen data to the server for processing and back to display results over the network.

- If the entire application processing logic resides on a client system, network traffic between presentation and application processing logic can be significantly reduced.

- There is no need for the synchronization between application processing logic fragments, which would be necessary if the fragments are distributed between clients and servers.

Some of the disadvantages of this approach are:

- The need to maintain multiple copies of the same business logic on every client workstation represents a serious systems management problem.

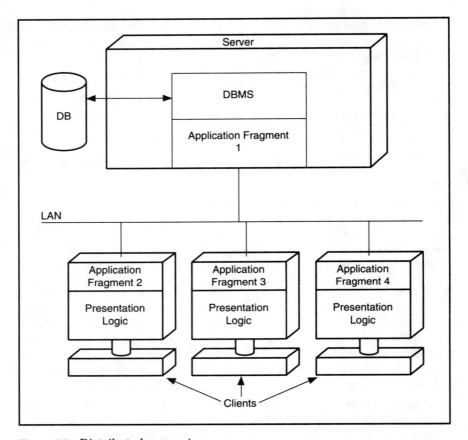

**Figure 2.8**   Distributed processing

- The benefits of a common shared modular code cannot be realized.
- The power of a server machine is not fully leveraged. At the same time, client systems could be overloaded, which might necessitate a hardware upgrade and additional investment in multiple workstations.

*Case 2. Application processing logic resides on a server system.* There are several reasons to place application processing logic on a server system. Some of them are:

- Placing common business logic modules on a central system eliminates code redundancy, simplifies systems maintenance, and allows for better leveraging of the investment in the server hardware.
- Placing business logic on the database server reduces network traffic between an application and a database.

- There is no need for the synchronization between application processing logic fragments that is necessary if the fragments are distributed between clients and servers.

Some of the disadvantages of this approach are:

- Placing entire application processing logic on the server system could result in overloading of the server resources, thus necessitating a server hardware upgrade. This is especially true when many different applications have to share the same server system.

- Interactions between the presentation and business logic can significantly increase network traffic and the response time for real-time applications.

- The power of client workstations could be underutilized, thus reducing the return-on-investment.

*Case 3. Application processing logic is distributed between client and server systems.* This approach can combine the advantages of the first two scenarios, while reducing the other approaches' disadvantages. Indeed, common fragments of the application processing logic can be placed on the server system, close to the database. Simultaneously, individual presentation-related fragments can be placed close to the presentation platform (client system). Redundancies can be eliminated, network traffic can be optimized, and the computing power of workstations and servers can be leveraged better. It is possible and desirable to fragment the application processing logic so that both server-resident and client-resident processes can be performed simultaneously, in parallel, as resulting overall computing time is reduced.

It appears that the distributed approach provides the most benefits. It is also the most complicated. Proper fragmentation is very important to the success of the distribution. The correct balance between client-resident and server-resident application processing logic is application-dependent.

The distribution of application processing logic is one of the critical client/server application design tasks. Today, it can be solved by using newly emerging distributed application design methodologies.

Another critical issue of application processing logic distribution is the issue of synchronization in distributed transaction processing. A client-resident application logic fragment interacts with the server-resident fragment in cooperative fashion by exchanging requests and responses. In general, interactions in the distributed transaction processing between a client and a server are synchronous. A client issues a request to a server and waits for the request to be processed. A positive or negative result is to be returned to the client before the next request is issued.

The problem arises when, in the course of the transaction, both a client and a server modify their respective resources. If both the client and the server have been successful in their parts of a transaction process, they can commit the changes to transaction resources, thus making the changes permanent. If one of the client/server interaction partners (a client process or a server process) fails, another partner should reverse the changes made in the course of the transaction to the original state the resources were in before the transaction started.

These rules are called a two-phase commit protocol. Even though it is often associated with distributed database processing, the two-phase commit protocol is an issue of distributed transaction processing. Two-phase commit protocol guarantees the integrity of the transaction resources. One of the best-known implementations of this protocol is IBM's CICS (Customer Information Control System) Distributed Transaction Processing (DTP). CICS DTP uses IBM's Logical Unit type 6.2 (LU6.2), also known as Advanced Program-to-Program Communications (APPC). APPC/LU6.2, two-phase commit, and interprocess synchronization are described in greater detail later in the book.

## 2.5   DISTRIBUTED DATA

So far, the analysis of the distribution of application components has concentrated on the presentation, business, and database logic. Each of these components, however, deals with data. Database logic accesses the data from a DBMS, business logic processes the data, and presentation logic displays the data to end users. In fact, the processing of data is the main purpose of an application. Several vital questions relate to the issues of the distributed data in a client/server environment. Some of these questions are:

- Is the data distributed or centralized?

- What role does a database server play?

- Where is the data located if distributed?

- How is the data fragmented if distributed?

- Is data replicated in multiple locations, and if so, how are all the copies kept current?

- How can data in multiple locations can be accessed in an application-transparent fashion?

- How can data integrity and availability be guaranteed?

- What are the data administration issues in a distributed environment?

These and other data-related issues are extremely important in understanding a client/server architecture and are analyzed in Part 4 of this book. However, the question of whether data is located on client or on server systems can be answered now.

*Direct and Indirect Connections.* As the client/server architecture evolved from shared-device processing, one of its main objectives was to allow a client-based application to access remote data efficiently. That access is provided by a *database server.* A database server contains the DBMS software and the data (database) itself:

- DBMS software, by its nature, is designed to be common, shared software.

- In a client/server environment the server is the focal point of all client requests.

- Advanced DBMS implementations allow for the placement of common procedures and even certain business rules into the server DBMS, which necessitates its central position in a client/server architecture.

- In a workgroup environment, the majority of the data to be processed needs to be shared among all clients.

- Advanced DBMS implementations include DBMS-resident data dictionaries that facilitate application development, support data location transparency, and provide for more efficient data administration.

- Placing data and the DBMS together on a database server makes it easier to implement facilities that provide data integrity and availability.

Therefore, the proper architectural decision would be to place the DBMS software and all shared data on a database server.

At the same time, if client applications require some unique, applications- and client-specific data, the proper place for it would be a data store located in a client system. These two situations would determine the way a client application could connect to a server running a DBMS. With the direct application-to-DBMS connection, the *client* application would use communication protocols and some kind of remote transaction processing to *request* a server-resident DBMS to access data. This situation can become more complicated if multiple servers have to be accessed.

- An application could use distributed transaction processing to establish sessions with multiple servers.

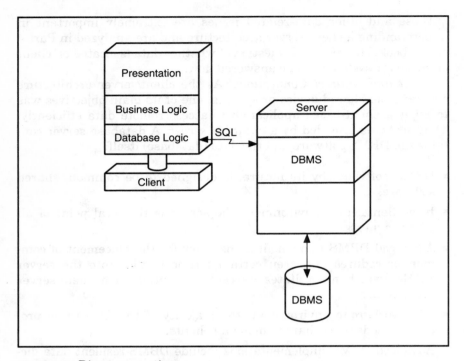

**Figure 2.9**  Direct connection

- One of the servers can propagate the client's requests to additional servers. Such a process can be based on remote server names, and the original server can either act as a coordinator of a distributed transaction, or send its request to a designated coordinator.

In either case, data integrity and administration issues would have to be resolved. For example, if the application data is spread across multiple servers (horizontally within a server tier or vertically between a LAN server and a host), distributed database management or *distributed request processing with the two-phase commit* will be required to guarantee data *integrity across servers.* Single System Image can be implemented by supporting data location transparency irrespective of the server on which the data resides.

With an indirect application-to-DBMS connection, the client requests remote data through an intermediary—local (client-resident) DBMS. The benefit of such an indirect connection is that the client can access both local and remote data, hopefully using the same data manipulation language.

One problem with the indirect connection is that, from an application point of view, the data is distributed between at least the client

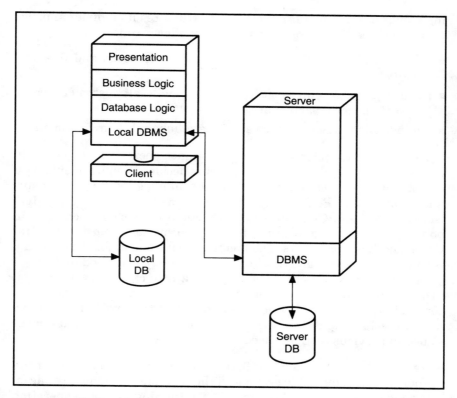

**Figure 2.10** Indirect connection

and the server. So, similar to the direct connection, distributed data integrity can be guaranteed by a distributed transaction management or *distributed request processing with the two-phase commit*. In addition, data location transparency should be supported to provide the single system image.

Another problem occurs when the client and server DBMSs are different products—this is the problem of the *heterogeneous* DBMS access. Differences in the dialects of the data manipulation languages could necessitate the development of DBMS-to-DBMS gateways.

Thus, both the direct and indirect connection between applications and DBMSs pose similar distributed data problems. The main difference is the assignment of the responsibilities for solving these problems. In the case of the direct connection, a server-resident DBMS should handle data requests, while for indirect connection, data requests could be distributed between the client and server DBMSs.

To illustrate the potential problems with data distribution in a three-tiered distributed client/server environment, consider the following scenario. A life insurance company structures its individual policy unit as a three-tiered organization in the following manner:

- Central Office, which maintains all corporate books and financial records
- regional service centers (RSC), which handle all customer service transactions for a particular region
- and insurance agents, which service a number of their customers

To improve customer service and to reduce operational expenses in the regional service centers, the company decides to equip agents with portable personal computers, capable of running several typical insurance applications. Periodically, agents should connect to the computers (servers) in the RSCs to off-load transactions (new clients, changes in policies, etc.), and to acquire current information from the Central Office and RSC computers. The business requirement for the company is that no change is valid until the corporate books are updated.

Architecturally, this scenario calls for a true client/server environment, with agent laptop computers in the third tier, RSC servers as a second tier, and Central Office's mainframe as the first tier. However, for successful implementation, all client/server-related issues mentioned in previous sections, need to be resolved.

- Agents take their laptop PCs to their customers and run appropriate applications. Thus, at least some of the customer data must reside on the agent's laptop PC. Laptop PCs are running MS-DOS operating system and dBase III database.
- RSC servers must handle all data related to the agents assigned to that RSC, plus some additional data necessary for an RSC management decision support system. In accordance with the open systems vision, and in order to achieve maximum price/performance, RSC servers are running a UNIX operating system and SYBASE relational database management system.
- The Central Office maintains corporate books and all relevant customer records. The Central Office mainframe is running IBM's MVS/ESA and DB2 and IMS database management systems.
- The updates performed by agents to the dBase III data must be propagated to the RSC server and Central Office DB2 and IMS databases. For some transactions, data integrity is mandatory—if the propagation fails on any tier, all changes must be backed out from databases on other tiers.
- To achieve application portability, an agent's applications must be designed in such a way that the required data can be accessed trans-

parent of its location or the underlying DBMS. Each DBMS involved in this environment uses its own data manipulation language, and two of the DBMSs (dBase III and IMS) are not even SQL-based (i.e., are not relational).

This example demonstrates some of the problems a designer of the client/server environment has to solve. In respect to distributed data issues, some of the problems and corresponding requirements had been formulated by C. J. Date, one of the first designers of relational databases. These distributed database requirements (C. J. Date's Twelve Rules) are listed in Appendix D and discussed in more detail in Chap. 11.

## 2.6  SOFTWARE DISTRIBUTION AND MANAGEMENT

Once a distributed architecture like a client/server is implemented, the issues of software distribution and management become extremely important. Indeed, there are networking issues, data administration and management issues, and little-talked-about information distribution issues. The latter are very important for the successful implementation of the client/server architecture. Consider that an agent's PC is running a company-supplied software—presentation logic (i.e., Microsoft Windows), application logic, and database logic (dBase III). Should any of these software components change (because of new release of purchased software, changes in in-house developed applications, or changes in business regulations), the agents expect to have their PC software upgraded. How should this upgrade be performed? Should the Central Office mail a set of floppy diskettes to each of its agents? Should every agent return his or her PC to the RSC for maintenance? Or is it better to distribute software upgrades using existing communication network facilities and taking advantage of the client/server architecture? These and other problems and issues of the client/server architecture are covered in greater detail in the remaining chapters.

## SUMMARY

Part 1 of the book looked at the evolution of the distributed systems. The client/server architecture was described as a special case of distributed cooperative processing. The importance of standards and open systems has been emphasized. Different views on a client/server environment have been given, and several critical questions of the client/ server architecture have been raised:

- What role should a client and a server play in the client/server architecture?
- What is the proper placement of the application components in the client/server architecture?
- How can the components interactions be implemented?
- What are the issues of presentation, application logic, and data distribution?
- What are the role and requirements for communications and networking, distributed transaction management, and software distribution?

These and other client/server related issues, as well as examples of the client/server implementations, are described in the next parts of this book.

# Client and Server Specialization in a Distributed Environment

*The client/server computing model, also known as the client/server paradigm, is becoming the dominant force that will influence computing in the 1990s. Demands for new systems capabilities follow, and are often ahead of, advances in computing technology. At the same time, computing environments are undergoing an evolution from general-purpose centralized systems towards architectures characterized by the collective power of many specialized systems interconnected via advanced networks. Indeed, even nature has successfully demonstrated similar trends. Consider single-cell organisms that evolved into more complex specialized multicelled creatures because more complex systems offer greater capabilities. Cells became specialized because relatively small specialized parts can evolve to achieve the desired functionality more successfully than large general-purpose parts. In a computing environment, cells are individual systems. Combining the specialized systems into a collective computing entity can be accomplished by interconnecting all system nodes in a network and allowing the nodes to enter into desired internode relationships.*

*In the client/server paradigm, the application components (presentation logic, business logic, database logic, DBMS) and data are distributed across the network. Network nodes can be classified as clients (those who request services) and servers (those who perform requested services). Clients and servers cooperate through a two-party relationship established for each client / server pair, even though there can be a many-to-one relationship between a collection of clients and their server.*

*In a client / server architecture, an individual system is designated as a client or a server depending on which activity (request a service or perform a service) the system performs in a given node-to-node relationship.*

*If the client / server designation is not permanent, then, theoretically, clients and servers should be designed as general-purpose systems with equal capabilities. This is true for a peer-to-peer computing environment. However, cooperative client / server processing does not entail interactions between equals. For example, it is a client who initiates the application, and, as a result, an interaction with its server. It is also true that client systems, not servers, interface directly with end users. Generally speaking, there are certain functions that clients perform best in a client / server environment. Similarly, there are other functions best performed by servers. For instance, database management systems (DBMS) are usually running on servers, not on clients. The optimum design should call for node specialization aimed at achieving the highest benefits from the cooperative processing between clients and servers.*

*Therefore, specialization requirements put clients and servers on different sides of the internodal relationship. However, another requirement for developing a complex client / server distributed networking system puts clients and servers close to each other. It is the requirement of the high-performance interoperability. As was discussed earlier, the best ways to achieve the desired levels of interoperability are standardization and open systems. Open systems are inspired by, and help to achieve, application portability, scalability and interoperability, which are also the goals and benefits of a client / server architecture.*

*In addition to the evolution of open systems, the client / server architecture is also influenced by node specialization in the complex client / server distributed environment. These two characteristics are reflected in the functionality of clients and servers, and the distributed environment in which they operate.*

*The focus of this and the next chapter is the functional and architectural specialization of clients and servers. This specialization is illustrated on examples of client's presentation functionality and server's hardware implementations. The discussion is rather detailed, so that designers of client / server computing environments can use these examples as a guide for proper selection of client / server implementation platforms.*

# Clients

Since client nodes are typically designed to interact with end users, their functionality and implementation can be specialized for these interactions. Similar to developing specialized sensory cells in humans and animals, client nodes must be designed to deliver such functions as high-resolution graphics and sound at acceptable performance levels. However, complete application requirements often exceed those of client node interactions, and can be satisfied only as a result of the collective performance of all system nodes.

## 3.1  CLIENT'S ROLE AND FUNCTIONS

The major functions performed by a client system in a client/server environment are presentation functions and some business logic (anywhere from none to all). End-user interactions with an application are performed through the presentation logic. The presentation logic is the application layer that, on one hand, interacts with the business logic of the application, and, on the other hand, interacts with end users. The latter includes all interactions with the physical device (terminal) and handling of actual end-user-performed input/output (screen I/O, keyboard I/O, mouse, etc.).

Traditional presentation functions dealt with character-based displays, where the processor sequentially displayed characters received from an application in a fixed font on a screen. Continuous evolution of presentation functions has been closely linked with high-performance workstations offering graphical display capabilities.

These displays allow the processor to control individual pixels on a screen by building a special "bit map." Each bit on a map corresponds to a pixel (picture element) on a screen, and the processor can paint any picture, be it characters, symbols, or drawings. Screen resolution is defined by the number of pixels available. Thus, the color, size, and placement of the objects on a screen is not limited by a particular character font or number of rows and columns. These display capabilities allow software designers to create uniquely effective, intuitive application interfaces that utilize rich graphics, computer imaging, and even audio-video input-output facilities. Imagine an office application that displays several pictures (called *icons*): a file cabinet to indicate file storage, a picture of an envelop for a single document, and a trash can. The end user can point and click on a document and the document text is displayed on a screen. Or, an end user can use the mouse to drag the letter icon to a trash can to discard the document. Even traditional character-based applications can utilize the power of graphical displays without changes to the applications. Software tools like Easel or Multisoft's Infront allow a character-based CICS (IBM Customer Information Control System) application to be presented to end users as graphical screens painted by the presentation logic on a workstation.

Obviously, the client system that has these display capabilities has to specialize in graphical presentations. The application logic of an application that uses electronic mail and server resource access control software, for example, can be developed separately from the presentation logic. Usually, it does not call for a client workstation specialization.

## 3.2   PRESENTATION MANAGEMENT

The specialization of client systems for presentation management must conform to the common goals of the client/server architecture in an open distributed environment. Presentation management should be based on standards to allow systems to interact with users in a consistent style; they should be portable across a wide variety of hardware platforms and able to interoperate with other open systems applications.

### 3.2.1   Why a standard GUI

Consistent interfaces between users and applications represent a key requirement for open systems. This requirement is extremely important since user interfaces affect both developers and end users alike. Indeed, while some program or database interfaces are hidden from the users, application presentation is visible to every developer and even to a casual system user. The presentation interfaces between users and applications are called *Graphical User Interfaces (GUI)*, and are designed to present information to users in graphic form. Graphics do not necessarily mean pictures. Word processor or a desktop publishing software with multiple text faces, sizes, and styles also requires a graphic presentation.

The wide variety of currently available interfaces (including character-based) may confuse users and developers. Each new interface requires users and developers to be retrained and applications to be modified. A new graphical user interface may cause the entire applications to be rewritten for a new platform which supports the desired GUI. Typically, applications written for one GUI are not portable to other GUI environments. Often developers must make difficult and costly decisions, limiting their product development to particular interfaces.

Examples include incompatible interfaces developed for the Macintosh, Microsoft Windows, and OS/2 Presentation Manager. Thus, a standard GUI with a single common application programming interface (*API*) and a standard "look and feel" will have a significant beneficial impact on developer and user productivity.

### 3.2.2 General requirements for standard GUI

Industry acceptance, support by hardware and software vendors, and end-user organization's preference for a particular GUI make that GUI a potential candidate for the GUI standard. However, a standard graphical user interface for open systems should also satisfy the following requirements:

*Portability:* Applications and user skills should be portable across various open system platforms. A standard GUI should maintain a stable API for every platform, thus allowing for quick and easy port from one platform to another. A standard GUI should maintain a consistent "look and feel" on all platforms, thus reducing the need to retrain, and easing the transfer of required user skills.

*Standards Compliance:* This requirement is the key open system requirement. It is also a necessary condition for a GUI to attract large corporate and government customers. A best-known de facto standard for an open system's GUI is the MIT X Window System. X Window System serves as a model for National Institute of Science and Technology (NIST), ANSI, and IEEE standards, and X/Open specifications. The MIT X Consortium has published a set of specifications that allow client applications to communicate and work together. These specifications are listed in the Interclient Communications Conventions Manual (ICCCM), and are important for enabling a high degree of applications interoperability.

*Development Tools:* Any GUI that is considered to be a standard must be accompanied by a comprehensive set of development tools. These tools can speed up application development, allow for developer-defined extensions, and build GUI applications for a wide variety of platforms.

*Flexibility:* A standard GUI must be flexible and extensible enough to accommodate new types of displays and other input/output devices that will become available in the future.

*Internationalization:* In today's global markets, internationalization is another way to achieve application portability. It includes other country's languages, numbers, monetary units, date and time formats, and special symbols and messages unique to that country's culture.

*Platform Independence:* To be truly open and standard, a GUI must be designed to operate independently of the operating system or hardware platform it runs on. Similarly, in a networking environment, a standard GUI should operate independently of the underlying networking protocols.

## 3.3   GUI FEATURES

In general, GUIs present information in rectangular areas on a screen called *windows.* Windows can overlap each other. Users are allowed to perform several manipulations on windows, such as changing their size and position. Windows can contain *objects* that can be selected by clicking a mouse pointer on small object pictures called *icons.* An entire window can be minimized in size to become an icon, and a user can restore an icon to its normal size (before minimization).

Advanced GUIs almost completely eliminate the need to type commands by allowing users to select commands from menus using a mouse or function keys. Windows can also contain other graphical entities (such as scroll bars, sliders, and buttons) that allow users to control the content of the window, and provide additional input to the application.

When compared to conventional programming, the most significant difference in the presentation logic that controls a GUI is the notion that the user must always be in control of the logic. Thus, the traditional structured programming with its housekeeping section, processing section, and an output section has to be modified. GUI programming should be able to accept and process asynchronous events initiated by a user or system at any time.

### 3.3.1    Event types

The set of supported user-generated input and system-generated events differs from one GUI implementation to another. Among the common types of events are the following:

- *Mouse events* occur when a user has moved the mouse pointer into or out of the entity, clicked on a mouse button within or without entity, or released the mouse button.

- *Keyboard events* occur when a user has pressed or released a keyboard key.

- *Menu events* occur when a user selects a command from the menu.

- *Window update events* occur when a portion of the picture of an application window has been damaged (possibly because it was overlapped by another window) and has to be redrawn.

- *Resizing events* occur when a user has changed the size of the window.

- *Activation / Deactivation events* are generated by the GUI to allow a user to change the current, active, window.

- *Initialize / Terminate events* occur when a GUI entity has been created or destroyed so that the application can perform necessary setup or clean-up logic.

### 3.3.2    Event distribution

These and other events should be processed by the presentation logic in cooperation with the application logic. The necessary processing is distributed among the GUI itself, the application logic, and the application programming interface (API) of a particular GUI. Typically, an API is a set of GUI-specific library routines that perform such functions as creating windows and displaying various graphics. There are several models for the event distribution processing:

- The *Event Loop model* specifies that an application must contain an event loop. The event loop calls a particular library routine to see if there are any pending events. Each pending event causes the application to dispatch an event handling routine before control is returned to the event loop. To preserve the user's impression of always being in control, the application must return to the event loop very quickly, even if event processing has not yet been completed.

- The *Event Callback model* requires the application to register an event handling function for each GUI entity that it creates, thus freeing the application from significant Event Loop overhead. When

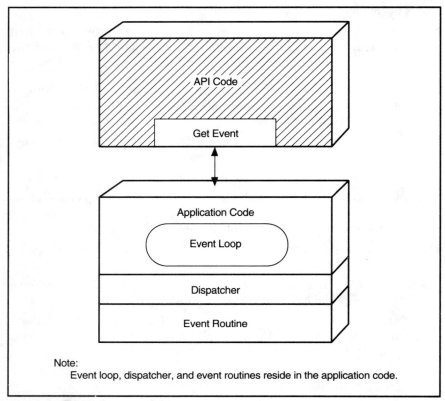

**Figure 3.1**  Event Loop model

a GUI detects an event (such as a menu command or keystroke) for the entity, it calls the appropriate application event routine. The application gets control only at entity initialization time and when one of its event handling routines is called.

- The *Hybrid model* combines an event loop model and event callback model. Microsoft Windows employs a model (where an application must contain an event loop) which calls a routine to get the next event. At that point, an application can call another API routine, which can, in turn, call the application's event handler.

### 3.3.3  GUI output features

There are many features of GUI output that distinguish one GUI from another.

*Coordinate spaces* describe the two-dimensional coordinate system that allows the GUI to address individual pixels on a screen by defining a starting point and the resolution of the drawing space. Most of

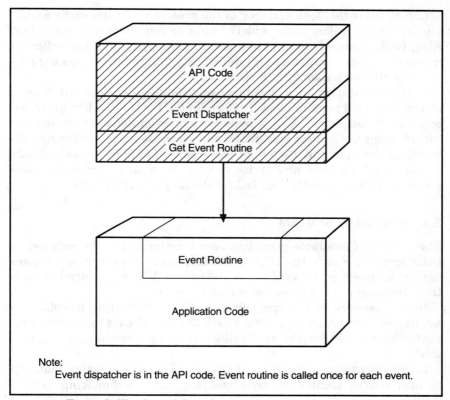

**Figure 3.2**    Event Callback model

the GUIs place the starting point at the upper left corner of the display, with the coordinate increasing downward and to the right. Some interfaces, such as OS/2 Presentation Manager, for example, differ in direction by placing the starting point in the lower left-hand corner, with coordinates increasing upward and to the right. Coordinate systems of different GUIs may also differ in resolution. Resolution is measured in dots per inch (*DPI*), and may be 75 DPI, 100 DPI, or, in the case of character terminals, a single character (DPI is not applicable in this case). Applications must be aware of coordinate spaces and resolution of a given GUI in order to paint the correct picture on a screen.

*Drawing algorithms* describe the way a particular GUI draws lines, centers lines, and connects lines. The difference often appears to be negligent. A three-pixel-wide line between two points, for example, can be centered on the end points, or below or above the end points. On certain low-resolution platforms the lines will look the same, but on higher-resolution display, lines may appear to be disconnected or overlapping.

*Color* affects the "look and feel" of the presentations drawn by a GUI. Unfortunately, colors differ widely from one display device to another. Also, GUIs themselves can treat colors differently, and use different numbers of bits to represent colors, which in turn determines the precision with which colors can be selected.

*Text* presentation in a graphical environment is different from a character-based presentation. Text under GUI is treated like graphics, and can be displayed with a wide variety of options. These options include colors, character size, fonts, and style. Desktop publishing software, for example, can use a high-powered GUI to allow users to create documents with fonts and styles varying from small script (for footnotes) to a 48-point Helvetica Bold Italic for a document title.

## 3.4   X WINDOW SYSTEM

The variety of available graphical user interfaces and the richness of their features justify the client's specialization in presentation management. However, some of the best-known GUIs do not need nor use the advantages of the client/server architecture.

In the network of the specialized nodes participating in collective application processing, the need arises to allow clients to perform presentation services for the applications running elsewhere in the network.

In the client/server distributed environment, presentation management requires technology that will support the following critical issues:

- Applications running on servers must be able to transparently access presentation logic that resides on client systems.

- Presentation logic on a client system performs services requested by the application running on a server. In effect, the client acts as a presentation server, while the server runs a client for that presentation server.

### 3.4.1   Description

The best-known technology for allowing applications to access displays on networked workstation transparently is the *X Window System,* also known as *X.* X was developed jointly by Massachusetts Institute of Technology, IBM, and DEC in an effort known as Project Athena. X architecture is based on the client/server model. It provides:

- network-transparent communication protocol between an application and its presentation logic, which may reside on a remote display workstation

- high-performance device-independent graphics
- hierarchy of resizable, overlapping windows

In the X Window System, multiple applications can display simultaneously, using one or many windows. X popularity starts with the fact that it is in the public domain and is therefore available for all vendors to use and develop in their own way. By exploiting a client/server computing model, X accomplished a breakthrough in distributed presentation. X is particularly useful in distributed heterogeneous environments where PCs, workstations, and minicomputers from different vendors need to run the same application. The X Window System allows developers to write programs that can display information and accept input on one node, while running on a different node on a network.

The following features of the X Window System deserve a more detailed explanation:

- The *X Model* is the architectural model of the X Window System. It consists of a display, a server, and client programs. The X display is the hardware that includes a bit-mapped screen, keyboard, and

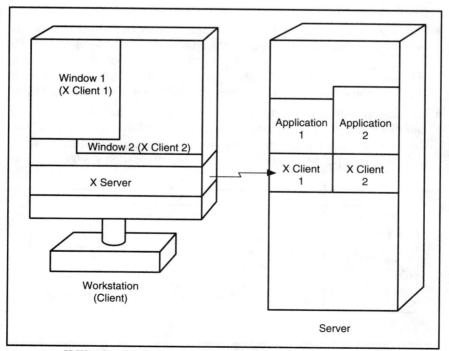

**Figure 3.3**  X Window System

mouse interfaces. An *X Server* program controls the display and provides an interface between itself and *X Clients,* which are usually application programs. The X Clients and X Server may be running on the same or different network nodes, and communicate with each other by exchanging specific messages. Different types of messages are collectively called the *X protocol.*

- X Window *hierarchy* consists of a "first," *root* window, with a tree of dependent, child windows below it. An X client usually has one or more "top-level" windows, whose parent is the root window. Below the top-level windows there may be many child windows used by applications.

- X is an *event-driven* system. After the initialization, X Clients are generally suspended until an event occurs on the X Server. X Clients are restarted when the X Server sends them special X protocol messages (i.e., window size has changed, a key has been pressed, etc.).

- *Window Manager* is a separate program that enables window movement, resizing, and iconizing. An X Window Manager is treated as an X Client in the X Model. It interacts with client applications through the X Server, controls the positioning and size of client's "top-level" windows, and determines the way input is directed to client applications.

- For an X Client to be able to communicate with an X Server, it needs to build X protocol requests for transmission to the X Server. To facilitate this procedure, a library of C routines was created. This library is called *Xlib* and is usually the lowest level interface available with the X Window System; Xlib is limited in its scope and capabilities.

- To alleviate the Xlib limitations, X Window System applications are usually written using another program layer built on top of Xlib—the *toolkit.* The toolkit provides high-level graphics functionality, including menus and special window objects called *widgets.* Some

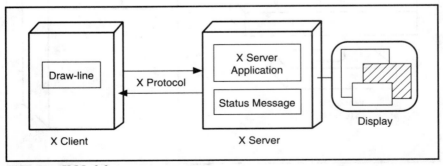

**Figure 3.4**   X Model

toolkits are conceptually split into two parts—Intrinsics Library and Widget Library.

- *Widget Library* contains widgets—abstract data objects such as buttons, scroll bars, and the like. An X Client can be easily constructed from a number of widgets, even though the X Client has direct control only over widget's general form, size, or contents. The widget appearance is determined by the toolkit itself.

- *Intrinsics Library* provides an object-oriented framework on which a Widget Library depends. It handles the creation, deletion, and management of widgets as well as event message handling.

- A fundamental concept of the X Window System is that it intends to provide functionality rather than policy. In other words, an X Server allows windows and graphics to be displayed without making any rules about the appearance of the windows or the GUI itself. The Window Manager determines the "look and feel" of the GUI, while X Clients should be written to function with any Window Manager (or none).

In client/server architecture terminology, the node that displays and accepts information, and interacts with the user, is the client node. However, in X terminology, the presentation logic that resides on a client is called an X Server. In order to communicate with its clients (X Clients), an X server must conform to X Window System X protocol, called *X11 protocols*.

X Clients contain the functional application logic written by a developer, even though they may reside on a "server" system in the client/server network. The X Clients are linked with the X Window libraries and the libraries of the specific X-based toolkit used to create an application. Although the designation of X Clients and X Servers seem to contradict the definitions of clients and servers in a client/server topology, it in fact follows the proper client/server computing model. Indeed:

- In the X Window System, X Clients initiate interactions with their server, the X Server.

- X Clients request an X Server to perform display or screen I/O functions.

- One X Server can service multiple X Clients.

- X Client and X Server can reside on the same machine.

### 3.4.2   X Terminal

From the environmental point of view, in the X Window System, X Clients can run on just about any UNIX host, and some non-UNIX ones as well. But when a hardware platform has to be chosen for the X Server, the choice is limited to:

1. UNIX workstation, which can support several users and applications simultaneously
2. DOS Personal Computer, which may allow users to leverage an existing investment in PCs and at the same time can provide access to both X Server and DOS applications
3. dedicated *X Terminal*

An X Terminal is the machine that runs only X Server software. Everything else, including an application, runs elsewhere on another system or systems. Using X Terminals simplifies centralized administration and security control, provides ease of maintenance and installation, and requires less power. Limited functionality leads to fewer microelectronics in an X Terminal, therefore allowing unassisted air cooling. And, of course, X Terminals are significantly less expensive than either workstations or PCs. A fully functional X Terminal can be obtained for under $2000. An example of an advanced X Terminal includes NCD17c from Network Computing Devices (NCD), with a 1,024x768 display resolution.

### 3.4.3   Motif

The X Window System is not a complete GUI. It is a package of windowing, graphics, and event handling routines that forms the basis for several popular GUIs—OSF's Motif, SUN's Open Look, and DECwindows. Even though the X Window environment may be sufficient for many applications, it is usually complemented by a Window Manager. It is a separate program whose exclusive purpose is to manage windows (move, resize, iconify windows) and to provide a GUI with a particular behavior and appearance.

For example, two popular GUIs—Motif and Open Look—although based on the X Window System, demonstrate different behavior and appearance because they employ different window managers and different programming interfaces. Both Motif and Open Look are strong contenders for becoming a GUI standard for open systems, and deserve a more detailed examination. These two products are described from the point of view of the general requirements for the standard GUI.

The Motif graphical user interface is the result of Open Software Foundation's Request For Technology process. The Motif GUI, released in July of 1989, is based on X Window System and incorporates the best features from DECwindows, HP's toolkit and window manager, and Microsoft's Presentation Manager.

*Portability.* The OSF/Motif GUI is implemented using a single API for all supported platforms. The API is based on DECwindows technology, extended to support Microsoft's Presentation Manager-style behavior and a unique three-dimensional appearance. Presently, OSF/ Motif runs on over one hundred platforms including IBM's RS/6000, DEC's VAX, SUN's SPARC, MIPS R2000 and R3000, Intel 80286, 80386, 80486, i860, and Motorola 68020, 68030, 68040 and 88000 architectures.

Due to OSF/Motif's use of Microsoft's Presentation Manager style and appearance, this GUI is familiar to a majority of computer users and developers. The similarity of appearance and behavior provides for consistent user interfaces and easy transition from one platform to another.

*Standards compliance.* OSF/Motif is based on the industry standard X Window System. Therefore, all applications based on OSF/Motif GUI are isolated from underlying system dependencies and require only a small portion of a code to be modified when an application is ported from one platform to another. In addition, OSF/Motif complies with the Interclient Communications Conventions Manual (ICCCM). ICCCM compliance enables OSF/Motif applications to share data and network resources with other ICCCM-compliant applications. It also allows OSF/Motif window manager to run all X-based, ICCCM-compliant applications even if they are not developed with OSF/Motif GUI. Conversely, OSF/Motif applications can run under any ICCCM-compliant window manager.

*Development Tools.* OSF/Motif is supplied as an enabling technology to hardware and software vendors and end-user organizations. OSF includes the following tools for the Motif's development environment:

- *User Interface X Toolkit* contains graphical objects (widgets and gadgets) built on the X Window System X11 Intrinsics.

- *User Interface Language (UIL)* is the specification language for describing the visual aspects of a GUI in a Motif application. UIL describes such objects as menus, forms, labels, and push-buttons, and the functions these objects should perform when user interaction events occur. The developers create a text file that contains a description of each object (widget) and associated functions. This text file is compiled by the UIL compiler into a resource file that is loaded at runtime. Thus, developers are provided with a flexible tool that allows the presentation characteristics (contained in the resource file) to be separated from the application itself.

- *OSF/Motif Window Manager* is a separate program designed to allow users to manage the windowing environment. Motif Window

Manager (MWM) allows windows to be moved, resized, and reduced into icons (iconofied), and supports OS/2 Presentation Manager's behavior and three-dimensional appearance.

- There are also a growing number of the third-party development tools that support OSF/Motif available. These tools include, but are not limited to, file managers, workspace managers, and interactive graphical interfaces design tools.

*Flexibility.* OSF/Motif's features (like the User Interface Language, which allows separation of the resource definition from the application code), provide for a high degree of flexibility and extensibility. Thus, new types of displays and other input/output devices can be accommodated with relative ease.

*Internationalization.* OSF/Motif complies with the X/Open's Portability Guide Issue 3 (XPG3) standards for Native Language Support (NLS). In addition to 8-byte character sets, OSF/Motif supports 16-bit and compound strings for use in European and Asian languages.

*Platform Independence.* Because of strict conformance with the X standard, OSF/Motif contains very few operating system and network protocol dependencies. The OSF/Motif GUI is supported by approximately 72 percent of worldwide computer hardware and software suppliers, including Data General, DEC, Dell, HP/Apollo, Groupe Bull, Hitachi, IBM, NEC, NCR, Siemens/Nixdorf, SCO, Sony, Unisys, Wang, and others. OSF/Motif is specified as the GUI of choice by major end-user organizations such as American Airlines, Boeing, European Economic Community, Lockheed, NASA, and Shell Oil. Over 70 percent of U.S. Government Requests For Proposals specify the OSF/Motif as the preferred GUI.

The list of operating systems that support OSF/Motif includes, but is not limited to, such popular environments as AIX, 4.3 BSD, Data General UX, Dell Unix System V, MS-DOS 2.0 or later, HP-UX version 6.5/7.0, Macintosh, MIPS RISC/OS, SCO UNIX, OS/2, SunOS 3.5/4.0, Ultrix, UNIX System V 3.2/4.0, and VMS.

### 3.4.4  Open Look

The Open Look graphical user interface was developed by Sun Microsystems and AT&T. It is very popular, especially among the users of SUN and AT&T systems.

Similar to OSF/Motif, the Open Look specifications are independent of any particular implementation.

*Portability.* There are three APIs that can be used to develop Open-Look-compliant applications. Sun's NeWS Development Environment (NDE) API for the NDE toolkit is supported on SUN's platforms.

SUN's XView provides an API to Xlib level of the X Window System and is supported on SUN SPARC and DEC VAX systems, Intel 80386 and Motorola 680x0 architectures. Xt+ API from AT&T is supported on various AT&T platforms. Open Look GUI provides users with a consistent and easy-to-use presentation, although the behavior and appearance of the Open Look GUI differs significantly from those of MS Windows, OSF/Motif, and OS/2 Presentation Manager.

*Standards compliance.* Open Look is based on the industry standard X Window System. Open Look's XView and Xt+ APIs are based on X Window X11 protocols. Therefore, these APIs are isolated from underlying system dependencies, requiring only a small portion of code to be modified when an application is ported from one platform to another. However, Open Look does not comply with the Interclient Communications Conventions Manual (ICCCM) for interclient communications. Therefore, Open Look Window Manager is required to ensure proper operations of Open Look applications.

*Development tools.* There are several toolkits that have been developed to facilitate the development of Open-Look-compliant applications:

- NeWS Development Environment (NDE), developed by SUN Microsystems, represents an emulated PostScript interpreter modified to support a windowing system. Similar to the X Window System architecture, the NDE consists of a client and a server portion interacting with each other to produce the Open Look GUI.

- XView, developed by SUN Microsystems, implements an Open Look API on top of the Xlib level of the X Window System. In comparison, OSF/Motif implements this API in the X toolkit built on the X Window System X11 Intrinsics level (higher level than Xlib).

- Xt+ toolkit from AT&T contains graphical objects (widgets and gadgets) built on the X Window System X11 Intrinsics.

- A separate development tool provides Open-Look-compliant powerful graphical file and desktop management facilities.

- Open Look user interface development tool—Developer's Guide—is available from SUN Microsystems to be used within SUN's Open Windows environment.

*Flexibility.* Open Look's X Window System foundation provides for a high degree of flexibility and extensibility. Thus, new types of displays and other input/output devices can be accommodated with relative ease.

*Internationalization.* Open Look implementations are currently limited to 8-byte character sets and are English-based, but can be expanded for European and Asian language support.

*Platform Independence.* Because of strict conformance with the X standard, Open Look contains very few operating system and network protocol dependencies.

*Note:* Much of the Motif vs. Open Look issue may become a moot point if a current X Consortium's effort to standardize methods for drag-and-drop window capability is successful. Such standardization will allow users to employ applications based on both GUIs (running on distributed, separate platforms) to exchange data by using a point-and-click methodology.

### 3.4.5   Other GUI implementations

In addition to the OSF/Motif and Open Look, there are literally dozens of GUIs on the market today. Several better-known GUIs:

- Macintosh is the oldest and most mature of the common GUIs. Significant efforts have been made to refine the Macintosh Interface. Despite its rather high entry price, Macintosh is very popular for graphics and publishing applications.

- Microsoft Windows is a comprehensive and mature GUI. Although limited to MS-DOS platforms, Microsoft Windows version 3.0 has expanded MS-DOS capabilities, and has practically eliminated most of the DOS drawbacks.

- Presentation Manager for OS/2 was developed jointly by Microsoft and IBM, and is strongly based on MS Windows. Running under OS/2, it provides a comprehensive and powerful GUI that avoids the limitations of MS-DOS.

- DECwindows is a GUI for DEC's Unix (Ultrix) and VMS systems. It is built on top of X Window System, and is the foundation for the OSF/Motif. DECwindows adds such useful GUI features as text fields, buttons, scrolling, and standard dialog boxes.

- NeXT GUI provides impressive gray-scale displays, and, through the use of optical disks, introduces a new dimension in GUIs capabilities. Lack of software and a rather high price are a few of the reasons for NeXT's slow acceptance.

- Character and block mode terminal displays certainly appear inferior to high-powered GUIs. However, it is still possible to provide some of the standard GUI facilities, such as windows, menus, text fields, and checkboxes on ordinary character terminals, especially given the large number of such devices installed to date.

A client/server architecture does not limit any particular implementation to high-resolution terminals. Therefore, it would be beneficial for developers and users alike to be able to develop and run applications on any and all of these platforms using the same presentation's "look and feel." Another benefit would be to be able to port an application from one platform to another without changing the look and feel of the GUI. One way to achieve this goal is to use tools that make the differences among different GUIs transparent to the applications.

## 3.5   COMPATIBILITY TOOLS

The goal of compatibility tools is to provide a common denominator to all GUIs. With such a tool, application developers will be able to master and use one tool to generate a desired graphical user interface on a given platform, rather than to learn several different interfaces. It means that, depending on a particular GUI an application decided to use, the application code would have to perform a set of GUI's API-specific functions. This set varies from one GUI to another.

For example, when an application that uses the OSF/Motif GUI needs to be ported to MS-DOS platform with MS Windows GUI support, the application would not have to be changed. All GUI interactions in this case will be handled through a common tool API. The tools that bridge differences in various GUI implementations should take into account differences in Application Programming Interfaces, event

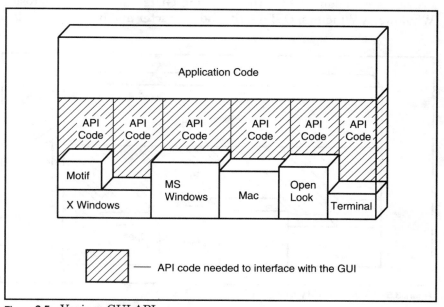

**Figure 3.5**   Various GUI APIs

handling logic, coordinate spaces, drawing algorithms, colors, text, and fonts used by various GUIs.

At the same time, these tools should retain as much of the native GUI look and feel as possible. Another requirement for such tools is to reject the "least common denominator" approach, which simply eliminates all the advantages of a particular GUI. Rather, such tools should provide a set of functions at least as rich as the most advanced of the supported GUIs, and, preferably, more so.

Given the widely differing levels of native GUI interface support, creating an API for such a tool is not a trivial task. There are several other requirements that should be supported by such a compatibility tool:

- Applications written using the tool should perform at least as well as if they were written to the native GUI's API.

- The tool or its reasonable subset should be able to support character or block mode terminals.

- The tool should be flexible and extensible in order to support future GUIs, new input/output and display devices, and media.

Given the need for, and advantages of, such a tool, it is no surprise that several vendors started development of compatibility products. One of them, Oracle Corporation, is working on its version of a compatibility tool—Oracle Toolkit. Currently, Oracle Toolkit is designed to provide a common API for the following GUIs: Macintosh, Microsoft Windows, X Windows, OSF/Motif, and character and block terminals.

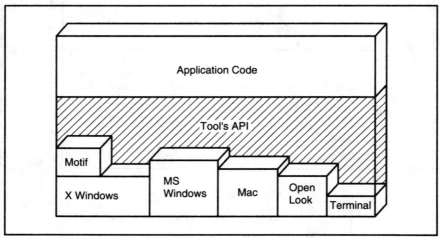

**Figure 3.6** Compatibility tool's API

Another example of such a tool is the XVT (eXtensible Virtual Toolkit) from XVT, Inc. XVT contains a set of libraries and "include" files, that comprise an additional layer on top of the native GUI. To isolate developers from the proprietary ways each GUI handles structures, fonts, and windows, and interprocess communication, XVT implements its own interfaces in a virtual toolkit, combined with a resource compiler.

Compatibility tools like Oracle Toolkit and XVT will allow developers to keep pace with advances in GUI technology and to facilitate applications portability and consistency of presentations while the GUI standards are being developed.

## 3.6   X WINDOW ALTERNATIVES

With the majority of vendors and standards bodies concentrating on X Window System, other window systems are often overlooked. However, X Window System is not the best technology for every application. Applications that require "What You See Is What You Get" (WYSIWYG) displays and high integration of display and printing images, require presentation capabilities over and above those a standard X Window System has to offer. Modern-day publishing applications, including desktop publishing, may benefit from such systems as Sun's NeWS. NeWS is based on a PostScript as one of the best imaging models for two-dimensional graphics.

PostScript provides device independence and printer correspondence that frees applications from the task of display-printer image reconciliation. Unlike X Window's pixel manipulation, PostScript deals with a stencil/paint model to describe a resolution independent image (the stencil defines an object boundary, the paint applies texture or color to the object).

Similar to X Window System, NeWS is designed to operate in a client/server architecture. In fact, NeWS uses X11 Protocol for the NeWS client/server communications.

One difference between X Window System and NeWS is that the NeWS server is extensible. To make a server extensible, NeWS is using lightweight processes that share the same address space with the server, and are scheduled by the server. Additional processes can be dynamically loaded from the client system into the server. Therefore, most of the interface management code can be moved from a client into the server. The developer decides how to distribute tasks between the client and the server processes. Thus, designed properly, NeWS PostScript application logic can be cleanly isolated from the interface logic. As a result, client/server network traffic can be significantly reduced.

The PostScript-based NeWS system has many advantages over the X Window System. With the combination of NeWS and X11 protocols, however, applications can be built that utilize the advantages of the client/server architecture, X Window System, and PostScript WYSIWYG features.

# Servers

One of the key principals behind the client/server computing model is the physical separation of the user's presentation management from other application services. In the complex client/server distributed environment, this idea is helping the evolution of client and server systems toward the specialization that is aimed at particular functional tasks in a unique way. This specialization has already been shown (in the previous chapter) to facilitate such client functions as client-user interactions, with the emphasis on presentation functionality.

Server nodes can also be specialized to perform server functions more efficiently. This chapter will examine typical server functions, certain specialized design features used to facilitate these functions, and several examples of specialized server implementations.

## 4.1 FUNCTIONS

Server specialization is best reflected in the functionality and design of database servers. Basically, database servers should be able to provide large amounts of fast disk storage, significant processing power, and the ability to run many applications (clients) simultaneously. However, as technology continues to evolve, specialization is extending to such functions as communications, terminal emulation, fax, library management, and electronic mail (E-mail).

Logically, a server is a logical process that provides services to requesting processes. In client/server computing, a client initiates the client/server interaction by sending a request to its server. The functions that a server should perform are determined, in large part, by the types of requests that clients can send to the servers. Conversely, if a server is unable to perform a function requested by a client, then this server cannot participate in a cooperative client/server interactions. Ideally, a client should not be sending an unsupported request to such a server.

In general, however, once clients and servers are interconnected in a network, the following functions may be required of servers by users:

- *File sharing*. In a workgroup environment, clients may have a need to share the same data file (for example, an insurance rates file in an insurance office). The rates file is placed in a shared file processor—*file server*—and clients send their file I/O requests to the file server. Usually, a file server provides a client with access to the entire file, so that when one client updates a shared file, no other clients are able to access this file. Another typical use of file servers is a file transfer between clients.

- *Printer sharing*. In a workgroup environment, one high capacity printer may replace all individual client printers. Then all clients may send file print requests to a *print server*. A print server maintains a queue of all files to be printed, sending each print file, in turn, to a shared printer (usually a high-output, high quality printer). Typically, all individual print files are printed with a special separator page indicating the client name and file name.

- *Database access*. In a client/server environment, application processing is divided between client and server systems. Servers may execute some portion of the business logic and database logic. Similar to file servers, *database servers* provide clients with access to data that resides on a server. However, database management systems (DBMS) are more sophisticated than basic file I/O access methods. DBMSs provide concurrent data access with various levels of locking granularity and data integrity. DBMSs eliminate data redundancy, allow for user-transparent data distribution, and even allow parts of application-specific data access logic to be incorporated into the DBMS itself. Clients request access to desired data (contrary to a file server's access to the entire file), and all necessary manipulation on the required data is performed at the database server. Thus, multiple clients can access a database concurrently.

- *Communication services*. In a workgroup environment that is connected to a remote host processor, all communications software and hardware can be concentrated on a special *communication server,* to which clients may forward their communication requests for processing.

- *Facsimile services,* that usually require special equipment and software, are now more frequently trusted to dedicated *fax servers.* Clients send and receive fax documents by requesting appropriate services from a fax server.

Other client-requested functions, such as electronic mail, library, network, resource and configuration management, are being handled in today's client/server environment by appropriate servers.

A server node in a client/server model can be specialized to perform its particular function in the most efficient way. However, besides individual, function-specific specialization, servers as a class of systems can be specialized to satisfy the following general-purpose requirements:

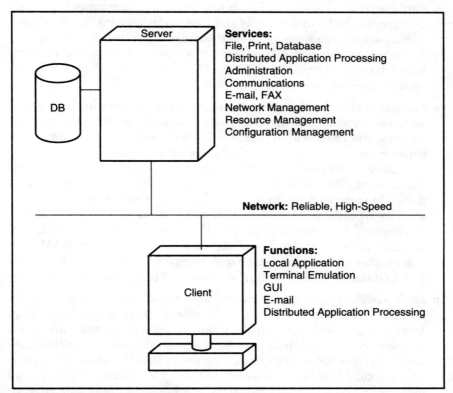

**Figure 4.1** Client/server functions

- *Multi-User Support.* Even in a small workgroup environment, a server should be able to service multiple concurrent clients. Clients running different tasks would expect a server to support preemptive multitasking processing. Note that multitasking can be implemented in a single-user system (like OS/2), and is a necessary but insufficient requirement for multi-user support (multitasking system is not equal to a multiuser system). Multi-user support requirements also include such important features as memory protection and multi-threading.

- *Scalability.* As the number of applications, their resource requirements, and number of users grow, a server should be able to satisfy these increasing demands on its resources (i.e., should provide scalable performance). Scalability does not mean that users should buy an overcapacity server system at extra cost. On the contrary, the system should satisfy current requirements and, at the same time, should be easy to expand (perhaps by upgrading a CPU or a DASD unit). A less attractive alternative to scalability would be to replace the system every time it reaches the limits of its capacity.

- *Performance.* A server system should provide performance levels satisfactory to the business needs and user requirements in a multiuser client/server environment. Even if business requirements do not call for subsecond response time for every business transaction, users would hardly appreciate a system that takes more than a few seconds to respond to every user action.

- *Storage.* As the number of users and applications running on a server increases, and as advances in storage technology drive the costs of physical storage down, the demand for extra storage and faster access times becomes one of the critical requirements for a server system. The storage demands come from operating systems that need additional storage to implement new advanced features, from users that desire to store various data files on a server, and from applications such as DBMSs and CASE tools that are some of the major storage consumers. For example, if a workstation running a CASE tool requires at least 16 Mbytes of Random Access Memory (RAM) and 300 Mbytes of DASD, a server may need 32–64 Mbytes of RAM and 1–1.5 Gbytes of DASD to support several of these workstations.

- *Multimedia.* As new applications and new technologies become available, the demand for multimedia storage support is increasing. Image, video, and sound applications are becoming more and more popular. So, the requirements for a server system may include the ability to store not only digitized images on DASD, but also hypertext on an optical storage device—Write-Once-Read-Many (WORM), and video/sound data on video cassettes, compact disks, and video disks.

■ *Networking.* Client/server communications happen over a communication network. Both client and server systems should have built-in networking capabilities. Without networking there is no client/server interaction, and therefore no clients and servers. If a system is designed with the networking requirements in mind, the system hardware and software architectures can be optimally integrated with the networking interfaces and protocols.

One conclusion that can be drawn from the analysis of these requirements is that mainframe systems appear to be the best candidates for the server platform. As far as capabilities and functionality are concerned, mainframes are certainly well suited to be servers in client/server computing. In fact, it is the stated direction of computer vendors like IBM that mainframe hosts are to play a server role in a client/server environment that supports multiple clients. Mainframe-supported clients may require and obtain access to large amounts of corporatewide data stored in various host DBMSs (DB2, IMS, IDMS, etc.). Indeed, mainframe-based transaction processing systems, such as IBM's Customer Information Control System (CICS), can today support thousand of users running on-line applications that can simultaneously access data stored in DB2, IMS, IDMS and VSAM files. If mainframe applications can be distributed in such a way that application processing is performed cooperatively by host-based and client-based application fragments, the result would be a two-tier, workstation-mainframe implementation of a client/server architecture. Such implementations exist today and, for example, can utilize a CICS-based application running on a CICS/MVS host, with front-end presentation logic performed by such tools as Easel running on graphical workstations.

Another example is a client/server architecture built on an OS/2 operating system that uses CICS for OS/2. Applications written for CICS OS/2 run on client workstations (IBM's PS/2) and are engaged in cooperative processing with CICS/MVS applications running on a host.

However, using hosts as servers can be disadvantageous from an economy-of-scale point of view. New, high-powered workstations allow end users to take advantage of the significant price/performance benefits of microcomputer technology. A typical mainframe costs orders of magnitude more than a workstation rated at the same processing speed.

Processing power is often measured in MIPS (millions of instructions per second), MLFLOPS (millions of floating point operations per second), or, more useful for end users, in the number of transactions per second (TPS) a given application can process on a given platform. If the transaction volume and throughput requirements are known, the TPS cost can help to determine how much has to be spent to support a particular business application.

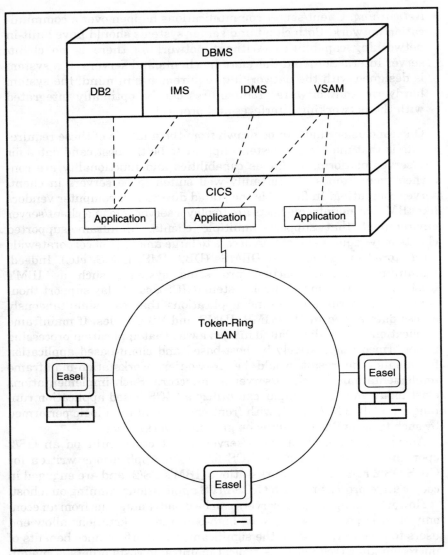

**Figure 4.2**  Mainframe as a server

Economy of scale becomes very important when users compare typical price/performance characteristics on large-scale systems (approximately $100,000–$200,000 per TPS on a IBM MVS DB2 environment)
to the cost of a similar capacity system built on IBM's RS/6000-520 or
SUN's SparcServer 490 system (approximately $1000–$4000 per TPS).
The same ratio can be observed on the cost per MIPS comparison
between a mainframe and an average 25 MIPS server.

The price/performance advantage of microcomputer-based servers is one of the reasons client/server architecture is being accepted by a growing number of businesses. The power and capabilities of mainframes assure their critical role as central corporate servers and the best platforms for central information repositories.

However, not all business needs require mainframe computing power and storage capacity. Nor can every business nor most applications justify a multimillion dollar mainframe and data-center-related expenses. Therefore, this chapter will look into several aspects of server platform specialization that allow hardware engineers to achieve the scalable high-performance characteristics of today's microcomputers.

## 4.2  SERVER HARDWARE ARCHITECTURE

The discussion of the high-performance aspects of server platform specialization will be concentrated on the specialization and advances in server hardware architecture. This analysis of server hardware architecture trends is intended to clarify often misused and misunderstood technological jargon employed by some hardware vendors, and, at the same time, give readers a reference point that can be used when a server purchasing decision is to be made. The focus of the discussion will be on two widely-popular hardware architecture features—Reduced Instruction Set Computer (RISC) and Symmetric MultiProcessing (SMP) architectures.

### 4.2.1  System considerations

The basic principals of computer design describe, among other things, the factors that affect computer performance. In general, these factors include CPU architecture, the size and implementation methods of the instruction set, the ability of compilers to optimize for performance, computer chip technology, and the operating system. From the application's point of view, CPU architecture, technology, and instruction set are less important than compilers and operating systems which, like applications, are today written in such high-level languages as C rather than Assembler.

Compilers and operating systems, therefore, should be capable of exploiting the hardware architecture to achieve the highest possible performance. Thus, the underlying instruction set becomes one of the critical performance factors. Indeed, computer performance can be described by the following symbolic formula:

Performance = 1/[(Cycle Time) × (Path Length) × (Cycles/Instruction)]

The Cycle Time is the opposite of the system clock rate, and is mostly limited by the underlying chip technology. Most of today's personal computers and workstations can operate at speeds from 12 to 33 MHz. Faster clock speed, especially over 50 MHz (50 million clock cycles per second), may require new, higher-density chip technologies. The shorter the cycle time, the higher the performance.

Path Length describes the number of machine instructions necessary to execute one command. The shorter the path length, the higher the resulting performance. CPU architecture, underlying instruction set, and optimizing compilers are the factors that can reduce the path length.

Cycles/Instruction factor describes how many computer cycles are necessary to execute one instruction. This number can vary from less than 1 (in Reduced Instruction Set Computer architectures) to greater than 1 in traditional architectures. If the number is less than 1, then more than one instruction can be executed in one CPU cycle. Thus, performance is better.

Other factors affecting computer performance include memory access times, external storage characteristics and I/O data transfer rates, and in a networking environment, communications and networks.

Some systems can be optimized best for commercial environments, which are generally characterized by integer processing, transaction processing, file and disk subsystems manipulation, and a significant number of attached low-to-medium-function terminals and workstations. Other systems may best be suited to scientific environments, which are generally characterized by very high floating point performance requirements, and few high-function graphical workstations attached to the central server via very high speed interconnections. Still other systems may be designed to achieve a careful balance between integer and floating-point performance, thus extending the system's applicability to both commercial and scientific worlds.

In any event, when system designers wish to address the performance issue, they may concentrate their efforts on one of the following:

- shortening the instruction path length
- improving the instructions per cycle ratio
- speeding up the system clock

The last option can be applied for integer processing or floating-point processing, thus limiting the applicability of the system to a particular environment. Conversely, the designers may attempt to achieve the desired performance for the mix of integer and floating-point instructions, thus creating a universal high-performance architecture.

### 4.2.2   RISC vs CISC

In the early 1980s, some system designers argued that the then current chip architectures could yield higher performance if new architectures would adopt the same principals as some of the best optimizing compilers. That is, optimizing compilers could produce almost as good code as the best programmers could write in Assembler language. Analyzing the compiled code, David Patterson of the University of California at Berkeley found that compilers used the simplest instructions of an available instruction set. These simple instructions could be used more efficiently than the complex instructions if the system hardware was optimized for this task. Unfortunately, the opposite was true. Traditional computer architectures were optimized for more complex instructions. The instructions in these architectures were decoded by the microcode which was placed in the microprocessor hardware. Patterson proposed the *Reduced Instruction Set Computer (RISC)*, as opposed to the traditional *Complex Instruction Set Computer (CISC)*. In RISC architecture, instructions are decoded directly by the hardware, thus increasing the speed of the processing.

Originally, a RISC processor contained only the simplest instructions extracted from a CISC architecture, and the hardware was optimized for these instructions. Not only did the RISC design contain the simplest instructions, but the number of available instructions was significantly lower than a comparable CISC design. Beginning in 1980, Patterson's group undertook the task of implementing RISC prototype processors, called RISC I and RISC II. RISC I, completed in 19 months, contained 44,000 transistors and outperformed a DEC VAX 11/780 by a ratio of 2 to 1.

An interesting historical fact is that the first RISC machine (though not identified by that name) was a result of a research project conducted by IBM from 1975 to 1979—the IBM 801 system.

Note that besides the performance, the apparent simplicity of RISC architecture provides another advantage—a designer can realize the RISC design in silicon chips more quickly. Therefore, time-to-market can be reduced and the latest technology can be used in a current design quicker than in a comparable CISC design.

The simplicity of RISC architecture is relative. Second-generation RISC designs introduced more complex instruction sets and increased the number of instructions (sometimes comparable to CISC design). Therefore, the real performance leverage in the second-generation RISC design is achieved by an optimized definition of the instruction set, machine organization, and processor logic design.

An important RISC feature is that each instruction is simple enough to be executed in one CPU cycle. In a "simple" RISC architecture, this may be true for a simple integer addition, but a floating-point addition may be simulated by several single-cycle instructions. To alleviate this and other similar problems, second-generation RISC architecture may be improved by a *superscalar* implementation (IBM's RS/6000 is an example of the superscalar RISC implementation). Superscalar design splits the processor into three separate units—the branch processor, which decodes instructions and assigns them to the other two units: the integer processor and the floating-point processor. Figure 4.3 illustrates the logical view of IBM RS/6000 superscalar RISC implementation.

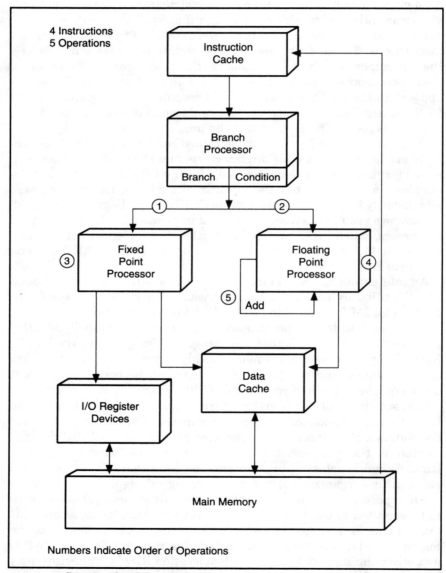

**Figure 4.3**  Superscalar RS/6000 RISC architecture

Each of the three units can perform several instructions simultaneously. Integer and floating-point units contain multiple buffers to handle new operations before old ones are completed; the branch unit can initiate multiple instructions. The resulting instruction "pipeline" can achieve up to four instructions (one fixed point, one floating-point, one branch, and one condition) or five simultaneous operations per cycle (three integer operations—fixed point, branch and condition—and two floating-point operations that constitute one floating-point instruction: "multiply and add"). That's why a superscalar RISC machine performs well in commercial, high-performance integer processing environments and in scientific, floating-point intensive applications.

Another innovation in the RISC architecture is *superpipelining*. Pipelining is a technique that allows more than one instruction to be processed simultaneously. A typical pipelined CPU, like Mips R3000, uses five execution steps, or stages, to execute one cycle-long instruction. As a result, five instructions may be at different stages of execution at the same time. To optimize the performance, designers increase clock rates and introduce higher granularity of stages—superpipelining. For example, Mips R4000 uses eight stages of pipelining instead of five.

A careful balance between superscalar and superpipelining RISC implementations will result in even higher performance levels of microcomputers, and desktop workstations capable of hundreds of MIPS will be available in the near future at the cost of a regular PC. The performance advantage of the RISC architecture has to be leveraged by optimizing compilers and operating systems. To date, only UNIX-based operating systems are capable of supporting RISC architecture.

In the last few years, several major vendors have announced RISC-based products, all of which support virtual memory and a UNIX operating system. The entries include MIPS Computers, SUN Microsystems' SPARC, Motorola's 88000, Intel's i860, HP's PRISM and the latest entry into RISC-based workstation market—IBM's RS/6000.

## 4.3  RISC IMPLEMENTATION
## IN IBM RS/6000

The RS/6000 system is a second-generation RISC machine, which uses superscalar RISC design with a high degree of parallelism. IBM dubbed its RISC System/6000 architecture as POWER (Performance Optimized With Enhanced RISC). In this implementation, RISC is viewed as Reduced Instruction Set Cycles, defined as minimal path length times cycles per instruction.

### 4.3.1   Technical highlights

The RS/6000 is a highly concurrent, superscalar, RISC machine, whose design is optimized to perform well in numerically-intensive engineering and scientific applications as well as in multiuser, commercial environments. The underlying circuit technology employs Very Large Scale Integration (*VLSI*), 1 micron Complimentary Metal-Oxide Semiconductors (CMOS), that allow 300,000 to 1,000,000 devices per chip. As the second generation of RISC architecture, the RS/6000 system defines the instruction set containing 184 instructions. Superscalar architecture allows multiple execution units for fixed point, floating-point, and branch processing. Some unique features of this design:

- Multiple sets of condition codes that are scheduled and managed by the optimized compiler much like the general-purpose registers are scheduled for load and store instructions. This increases the parallelism between the fixed point and floating-point units.

- Single-cycle, floating-point multiply, add/subtract, and multiply-add (multiply-subtract) double precision instructions are provided; at a

| Floating-Point Performance | |
| --- | --- |
| LINPACK (100x100) Double-Precision | |
| FORTRAN MLFLOPS | |
| SUN 370 | 2.8 |
| RS/6000 Model 320 | 7.4 |
| VAX 9000/210 (Scalar) | 8.0 |
| RS/6000 Model 540 | 13.0 |
| VAX 9000/210 (Vector) | 18.0 |
| Cray 1S | 27.0 |
| Cray X-MP (1 Processor) | 66.0 |

**Figure 4.4**   Compute-intensive performance (*Source: IBM RISC System/6000 Technology, RISC System/6000 Hardware Background and Philosophies, Page 4, Table 2.*)

clock speed of 25 to 30 MHz, this translates to a sustainable peak performance of 50 to 60 million floating-point instructions per second (MLFLOPS).

- Floating-point instructions can be executed at the same speed as the fixed point instructions.

To supply the high data rates required by a CPU capable of executing four instructions per cycle, separate instruction (8 kbytes) and data caches (32 to 64 kbytes) are implemented. To sustain cache reload bandwidth requirements, a 64- to 128-bit-wide memory interface with 160 to 480 Mbytes/s transfer rate is built into the system. Data integrity and error checking and correction are implemented throughout the processor complex. The I/O subsystem is based on IBM's Micro Channel Architecture (MCA). The performance of the CPU and the I/O subsystem is balanced to sustain a 20 to 25 Mbytes/s (with a peak of 40 Mbytes/s) I/O bandwidth. This high bandwidth is essential for high-performance I/O adapters such as graphics, Small Computer System Interface (SCSI), and local area network (LAN).

The resulting performance approaches that of a large traditional mainframe or the previous generation of supercomputers.

### 4.3.2    RS/6000 family

The RS/6000 family of workstations and servers contains several systems characterized by a common architecture, common hardware, common microchannel bus, and common operating system—AIX version 3. Each system is designated by a three-digit code. The first digit signifies the type of the system—desktop (2 or 3), deskside (5 or 7), or rack-mounted (9). The second digit varies from 2 to 6, and indicates the processor capacity. (There is a 25 percent increase in the processor power between the two consecutive processor groups.)

Examples of desktop systems include RS/6000 POWERstation 320 and POWERserver 320. Both allow for single or multiuser access and a respectable performance of at least 27.5 MIPS or 7.4 MLFLOPS. Examples of deskside systems include RS/6000 POWERstation/POWERserver models 520, 530, 540, 550, and 560. The processor power is increased by 25 percent from model to model. In addition, all models are upgradable (i.e., model 520 can be upgraded to the model 530, 530 to 540, etc.).

POWERstation 730 is a high-performance graphics deskside system. It supports real-time interactions to deliver up to 16.7 million colors, 1 million three-dimensional vector transformations, hardware shading, depth queuing, and graphics rotation. Rack mounted POWERservers

930 and 950 provide an expandable fixed disk storage, variety of internal I/O features, and extensive connectivity support. POWERserver 930 can be upgraded to a high-performance rack mounted POWERserver 950.

In addition to POWER stations and server, RS/6000 family includes low-cost workstations (mod 220), and X-server terminals (Xstation 120 and Xstation 130). Xstations support both Ethernet and Token Ring attachments, a variety of display devices, local printer, and mouse, and also act as X Window System servers by downloading X Server and TCP/IP software.

### 4.3.3   Overview of AIX version 3

The operating system for the RS/6000 family of products is IBM's Advanced Interactive eXecutive operating system version 3 (AIX version 3). This system is based on the UNIX operating system because of UNIX popularity in the technical computing market and its affinity with RISC architecture. AIX version 3 was built to achieve three major goals:

- Provide an operating system for the 1990s by creating a UNIX system that incorporates the latest in system software technology

- Support and take advantage of the RS/6000 RISC architecture and hardware

- Ensure that AIX structure and design supports portability to other widely used architectures, such as the Intel 80x86 and IBM System/370/390 architectures

The balanced solution required by the second and third objectives resulted in several trade-offs that allowed optimization for the RS/6000 hardware, yet kept specific RS/6000 support isolated and to a minimum.

To achieve the stated objectives, certain structural changes were required in the UNIX system. These changes included Virtual Resource Manager, Berkeley Software Distribution technology (BSD 4.3), X Window System, Network File System (NFS), and Network Computing System (NCS). The resulting operating system, while retaining UNIX system semantics and interfaces, proved to be a truly revolutionary solution, as indicated by the selection of AIX version 3 as one of the contributing technologies for the Open Software Foundation's open operating system—OSF/1.

AIX version 3 is characterized by the following:

- It adheres to open system and industry standards—ANSI standards, IEEE (Institute of Electrical and Electronic Engineers) POSIX standards, AT&T UNIX System V Interfaces, BSD 4.3, X/Open, X Window System, OSI X.25, TCP/IP, SNA, NFS and NCS.

- A system kernel provides support for single or multiuser environments, 10,000 processes, and appropriate hardware associated with any supported configuration. AIX provides a Virtual Resource Manager (VRM) and Virtual Memory Manager (VMM) to support full UNIX semantics and very large memory available on RS/6000 system.

- It has enhanced system reliability, availability, and serviceability (RAS) characteristics that are supported by an advanced journaling system, a Logical Volume Manager (LVM), and software mirroring capabilities.

- Enhanced system management, ease-of-use characteristics, and improved configuration and file system management are supported by a new data management architecture—Object Data Manager and Simplified Management Interface Tool (SMIT).

- Enhanced security includes conformance with the Department of Defense Trusted Computer System Evaluation Criteria, discretionary access control, user identification and authentication, auditing, trusted communication, and system administration.

- An advanced program development and management environment is supported by common compilers and development tools, shared library and page-mapped loading, and dynamic loading techniques.

- It supports various subsystems, such as a communication subsystem (TCP/IP, SNA services, OSI protocols including X.25, NFS and NCS are supported), relational database managers, transaction processing, and graphics subsystems (includes X Window System and OSF/Motif support).

- It supports distributed computing services and distributed applications in a heterogeneous computing environment.

In summary, AIX version 3 is an advanced UNIX-based and standards-compliant operating system optimized for superscalar RISC implementations. Chosen as one of the base technologies by the Open Software Foundation, AIX version 3 will continue to evolve into a truly open operating system.

### 4.4  SYMMETRIC MULTIPROCESSING

Multiprocessing is becoming an indispensable tool for improving the performance of computer systems struggling to support ever more complex and demanding applications. As CPU costs are decreasing, users find that adding processors to their existing multiprocessor hardware is significantly more economical than either adding computer systems or replacing existing systems with more powerful uniprocessor systems. Adding or replacing uniprocessors has its drawbacks:

- Adding processors usually results in addition of expensive peripheral devices.

- Stand-alone uniprocessors cannot share memory, unless they are networked at additional expense. Nor can they speed up applications, unless applications are distributed at additional cost and complexity.

- Adding faster uniprocessors is more expensive than obtaining the same performance by increasing the number of processors.

Thus, multiprocessor-based systems provide the ability to increase performance incrementally. The resulting *scalability* allows for future upgradability, and represents a cost-effective solution for such applications as DBMS, gateways, and transaction processing. Typically, these applications are composed of smaller, relatively independent tasks that can be assigned to numerous processors. Applications like these are ideally suited to be run on servers in a client/server environment. Therefore, multiprocessor-based servers represent another example of server specialization.

There are two generic types of the multiprocessor systems:

- A *Loosely-Coupled* or *Distributed Memory Multiprocessor* incorporates a large number of self-sufficient processors, each with its own operating system and resources (memory, disk, etc.). The processors communicate over networks and I/O channels, which makes interprocessor communication and cooperation dependent on network and I/O channel performance and throughput, and, therefore, relatively slow.

- A *Tightly-Coupled* or *Shared Memory Multiprocessor* consists of a relatively small number of processors that share a common memory, common operating system, common I/O, and various other system resources. Processors select tasks to be executed from a common task pool, and are interconnected via a high-speed common system bus, thereby providing extremely efficient interprocessor communications.

Of these two generic multiprocessor types, only shared memory multiprocessors provide true scalable performance at a low cost.

### 4.4.1   Scalable hardware architecture

Shared memory multiprocessing ensures that any processor completing one task is immediately put to work on another—the next available task. A shared memory multiprocessor typically incorporates a number of processors, called processing elements (PEs), that share a common memory, common I/O, and various other common system resources. All

PEs execute a single copy of an operating system, and each PE executes a task selected from a common task pool. Typically, in order to reduce the volume of shared memory traffic, each PE has one or more memory caches. One or more memory controllers may be included in this architecture to support the high memory access requirements of multiple PEs. The PEs and memory controllers are interconnected via a high-speed system bus, thus providing high efficiency interprocessor communication.

When all PEs in a shared memory multiprocessor have equal capabilities and can perform the same functions, it is called a *Symmetric Multiprocessor,* or *SMP*. Each PE in an SMP system can run user applications as well as any portion of the operating system, including such operations as I/O interrupt, operating system kernel functions, and I/O drivers. In addition, any task can be executed on any PE and can migrate from PE to PE as system load characteristics change.

SMP implementation has a significant positive effect on scalability. Indeed, if a system designates one PE to perform a particular task—service I/O interrupts, for example (non-SMP architecture)—this PE will become overloaded as the number of I/O requests increases, and overall system performance will degrade.

SMP architecture provides two high-level features:

- *Seamless Execution* is the ability of an SMP system to seamlessly, transparently to the user, support existing applications. In truly

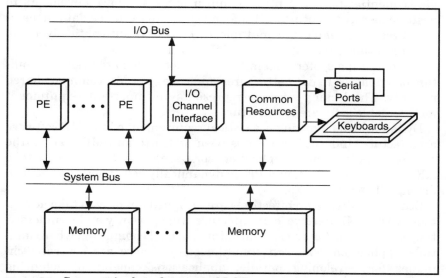

**Figure 4.5** Symmetric shared memory Multiprocessor

seamless implementations, all applications originally written for a uniprocessor will be able to run on an SMP system unmodified. By taking full advantage of multiprocessing, applications can achieve significant performance gains. This is especially important for servers running DBMSs and supporting transaction processing.

- *Scalable Performance* encompasses two components: computational growth and I/O growth. Computational growth can be achieved by adding processing elements, while I/O growth can be a result of adding peripherals and/or I/O buses. It is important to note that while the addition of a PE increases the overall system performance, the increase is not equal to the performance of the individual PE, but, rather, corresponds to a fraction of this PE performance. Factors such as system bus and memory subsystem design, and cache sizes, affect the resultant performance increase.

### 4.4.2   Scalable software architecture

Providing symmetry in shared memory systems has an impact on both hardware and software architectures. Software features supporting scalable SMP performance include capabilities to execute the operating system kernel, I/O interrupts, and I/O drivers on all PEs.

Operating system design becomes more complex on an SMP system. For example, Open Software Foundation's OSF/1 operating system supports SMP by implementing IEEE POSIX 1003.4 "P threads" standard-compliant threads. A thread, which is defined by POSIX as a single sequential flow of control within a process, allows developers to write cooperative routines, all sharing access to the same data in memory. Programs employing multiple threads will automatically make use of multiple processors on an SMP system.

The operating system locking strategy is designed to prevent simultaneous updates to data structures and codes in SMP common shared memory. The locking strategy represents an important requirement for a scalable software architecture.

Dynamic load balancing is a critical requirement of an SMP software architecture. Indeed, if a PE has been added to an SMP system, the operating system and application software should be able to take advantage of the additional PE by dynamically redistributing the load among all available PEs.

Scalable software architectures are designed not only to take advantage of the SMP hardware architecture transparently and seamlessly, they also provide for an easy entry into parallel computing, where multiple applications can run simultaneously. There are several techniques for developing parallel applications capable of achieving maximum performance in an SMP system. Among them are problem partitioning (dividing a problem into several smaller independent parts) and data decomposition for load balancing.

### 4.4.3   Examples of SMP implementations

High performance SMP systems offer comparable or higher performance than traditional uniprocessors, while promising near linear incremental performance scalability. Properly designed SMP systems allow for seamless execution and the ability of existing applications to execute transparently without modifications. That is why several SMP systems available today are used as DBMS servers, communication gateways, and transaction processing platforms.

Some popular shared memory systems include products like Pyramid Technology's high-end machines (which combine SMP implementation with RISC technology), Sequent Computers Symmetry series, and AT&T's StarServer E. Sequent Symmetry 2000 series are configurable general purpose computers that support simultaneous execution of commercial, technical, and transaction processing operations. Symmetry 2000 models 400 and 700 support from 2 to 30 tightly-coupled, 32-bit i486 microprocessors that share a common memory and a single copy of a UNIX-based operating system. Sequent's SMP implementation allows multiuser applications run as is, with transparent multiprocessing and dynamic load balancing. Hardware and software support for parallel programming combines user control and full UNIX operating system services compliant with POSIX, FIPS 151-1, AT&T's UNIX System V Interface Definitions (SVID), and X/Open Portability Guide Issue 3 (XPG3) standards. Sequent Symmetry series machines costing about $500,000 can achieve 82 TPS on an eight-processor system with a price/performance ratio of about $6000/TPS (transaction per second, using industry-standard TP1 benchmark).

AT&T's StarServer E is a shared memory symmetric multiprocessor that supports the Extended Industry Standard Architecture (EISA). The integral EISA I/O Bus supports numerous industry standard interfaces including SCSI and Ethernet, and is capable of data transfer rates of up to 33 Mbytes/s. StarServer E operates under the UNIX System V/386 Release 4.0. The system additionally supports MS-DOS and MS-OS/2 1.2 operating systems as guests. The StarServer E hardware architecture includes PEs built on Intel i486 CPU. In a single processor configuration, the StarServer E can achieve a performance of approximately 26.5 MIPS at a cost below $2000/MIPS. Due to its SMP implementation, StarServer E is expandable to up to 4-CPU configuration that is capable of producing 106 MIPS, supporting over 200 clients in a client/server computing model, and 64 to 160 concurrent users.

Scalable software support includes a symmetrical operating system with fine granularity locking, instrumentation, and tracing facilities for performance tuning. Parallel programming support is built into the C++ and Concurrent C programming languages.

Symmetry in StarServer E's operating system has been carried through all major subsystems: process subsystem, file systems, memory management, driver subsystem, stream subsystem, and scheduling subsystem. System management tasks are facilitated by StarServer E's advanced software Remote Diagnostics feature. In short, StarServer E provides the system's high reliability, administrability and serviceability. It is a powerful, deskside, SMP computer system with scalable performance for multiuser server applications.

The price/performance characteristics of specialized server systems (RISC-based and/or SMP-based) compare favorably with about $140,000/TPS for a loosely-coupled mainframe multiprocessor such as IBM 3090 model 400 (measured at 62 TPS). These price/performance figures justify architectural specialization for a server platform.

## 4.5    OTHER SERVER IMPLEMENTATIONS

Of course, while RISC and SMP solutions increase the price/performance of a microcomputer, there are other server implementations that can be successfully used in a client/server architecture. Among them are such well-known systems as IBM's Personal System/2 (PS/2) and Application System/400 (AS/400).

IBM's PS/2 is a family of widely used personal computers based on Intel microprocessor architectures. The models that possess the necessary power to act as servers in a medium-size workgroup environment are the top-of-the-line PS/2 Model 90 XP 486 (desktop) and Model 95 XP 486 (deskside).

Both models are built on IBM's Micro Channel Architecture (MCA) and Intel i486 processor. The systems are fast, reliable, expandable, and upgradable. Processor speed can grow from 25 to 50 MHz. Internal memory is expandable to 64 Mbytes, while 256 kbytes can be added to the memory cache. Internal storage can be expanded to 1.6 Gbytes of disk space. Both models offer the built-in Extended Graphics Array (XGA) graphics with 1024x768 resolution that supports Computer Assisted Design/Computer Assisted Manufacturing (CAD/CAM) scientific and engineering applications.

Extensive communication capabilities include support for Token-Ring and Ethernet, OSI's X.25, SNA 3270 and System/370 channel emulation, Async protocol, and fax. PS/2 Models 90 and 95 are well suited for database and communication servers in a LAN environment, and support DOS (version 3.3 or higher), OS/2 (Standard or Extended Edition 1.2 or higher), and AIX PS/2 operating environments.

AS/400 is a midrange platform in IBM's Systems Application Architecture (SAA). In SAA environments, AS/400 can be used as an enterprisewide application server. To achieve this goal, the AS/400 offers a wide range of connectivity options, including support for the Ethernet, 16-MBit/s Token-Ring, Transmission Control Protocol/Internet Protocol (TCP/IP), Telnet terminal emulation, connectivity with AIX clients, and bridges Token-Ring LANs over Integrated Services Digital Networks (ISDN).

As one of the supported SAA platforms (others include OS/2 on PS/2, MVS and VM on IBM mainframes), AS/400 can be very useful in SAA's cooperative processing environments, where applications are split between clients and servers. AS/400's support of Advanced Peer-to-Peer Networking (APPN) helps its role as a server in a cooperative client/server environment. What is more, IBM extends its platform's interoperability by providing the AIX AS/400 Connection Program that supports terminal emulation capabilities under SNA and TCP/IP for RS/6000 systems. For those users who desire to use Microsoft Windows GUI to access AS/400 databases, products like ShowCase (Rochester Software Connection, Inc.) allow Windows 3.0 and Microsoft's Excel to link with data stored in AS/400 databases.

*Important note.* This chapter did not discuss server operating systems. Such a discussion is beyond the scope of this book. However, in general, a "reasonable" server operating system should be multi-user, multi-tasking, multi-threaded, fully preemptive and secure, so that multiple users and applications do not interfere with each other. Such an operating system should provide robust performance and memory protection for its subsystems, users, and applications. Ideally, such an OS should be able to support hardware and applications scalability and portability. Several Unix implementation and forthcoming Microsoft's Windows NT are examples of a server operating system that satisfies most of these requirements.

# Networking and Communications

*Up to this point, the discussion of client / server architecture
has concentrated on the characteristics of clients and servers
as specialized nodes in a distributed computing environment.*
Client/server computing *was defined as a specialized form of
distributed cooperative processing. In client / server
architecture, various application components are distributed
between client and server platforms which cooperate to
perform the desired application functions.* Client/server
interactions *were defined as those where a client initiates the
interaction and requests a particular service from a server.
The server reacts to the client's request by performing the
desired service and sending the response back to the client.
Such interactions do not make any assumptions on a
topology of the client / server architecture. In fact, there is
nothing to prevent a client and server from existing on the
same physical machine. Nevertheless, these interactions
require reliable and robust communication facilities between
clients and servers. In very general terms, when clients and
servers are physically located on separate, potentially remote
nodes, client / server communications will have to be
performed over a suitable network. Such a network could be
a local area network (LAN) for a small workgroup or a wide
area network (WAN) for geographically dispersed nodes.
Traditional IBM Systems Network Architecture (SNA)
networks, popular Transmission Control Protocol / Internet
Protocol (TCP / IP) networks, public networks utilizing*

*packet-switching protocols, and networks based on the standard Open Systems Interconnection (OSI) protocols could all be used for client/server communications. Understanding these networks and communication protocols is critical to an understanding of the client/server architecture.*

# Communication Systems

In a distributed environment, various system resources (data, computing power, programs, etc.) are spread (distributed) across several locations. These resources utilize some kind of communication system to interact with each other. In this context, a communication system is a mechanism that allows the distributed resources to exchange control information and data. Communication systems, while essential for distribution, may be implemented in a way totally transparent to end users. Conversely, they may be visible enough for the end users to be aware of the network that provides actual resources interconnection. Whatever the implementation, communication between nodes is necessary, and this communication requires some kind of a physical network that connects all interacting nodes.

## 5.1 COMMUNICATION AND DISTRIBUTION

Client/server architecture is a special case of cooperative processing. Cooperative processing, in turn, is a special case of distributed processing. A distributed processing environment, however, is not motivated by client/server computing model needs alone. Among factors that contribute to current interest in distributed systems are:

- Technological advances in microelectronics that have changed the price-performance ratio in favor of multiple low-cost, high-performance systems

- Interconnections and communication costs that have fallen dramatically in the past few years
- User demands for more economical, faster, more sophisticated and reliable facilities

One objective and benefit of distribution is resource sharing. A number of resources, such as computers, peripherals, special-purpose processors, programs, data, etc., are interconnected by a communication system in order to allow the sharing of resources. The interconnected systems form a *network* which is used by a *communication system* to switch messages or packets of information between different sites, systems, terminals, and programs.

Here are some definitions that will be useful when discussing networks and communications. A *communication system* is the collection of hardware and software that supports intersystem and interprocess communication between software components in distributed nodes. The nodes are interconnected by a *network* which provides a physical *path* between nodes (see Fig. 5.1). The direct connection between two or more systems is sometimes referred to as a *link*. A system that performs main application functions and controls the communication system is sometimes called a *host*. In a distributed system, the *name* of an object indicates a system, a process, or a node, an *address* indicates where the named object is, and a *route* tells how to get there.

One of the most common shared resources in distributed systems is data. Many applications require the sharing of data among diverse users with different computing facilities. By distributing data, reliability may be improved by replicating data into multiple copies. Access times may be improved by maintaining local copies of data by replication and partitioning. The data communication system may be used to transmit both data and data requests between different sites, systems, and programs. While interconnected systems may or may not form a distributed processing system by themselves, the data communication system used for message and data interchange can itself be considered as a distributed system. Indeed, it is physically distributed, its components cooperate to provide common services, and it is controlled by a network management system.

## 5.2 COMMUNICATION SYSTEM FUNCTIONS

The following are some of the most important functions of a communication system.

*Naming and addressing.* A communication system has to manipulate names for objects such as processes, ports, mailboxes, systems,

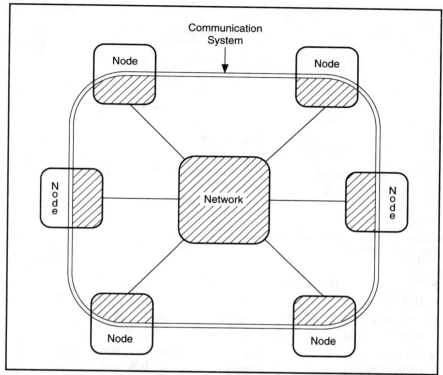

**Figure 5.1**    Network and communication system in a distributed environment

and sessions between users. Typically, users supply names in symbolic form (e.g., 'system1'), and the communication system must translate (map) that symbolic name into a network address. Therefore, a communication system must maintain appropriate translation tables (directories). Routes are related to the address translation—a destination address is mapped onto a path or an intermediate object, such as a gateway.

*Segmenting.* If user messages or files to be transmitted are too long, the communication system might have to fragment a single message into multiple segments (see Fig. 5.2). Of course, once a message is segmented for transmission, the communication network has to be able to reassemble the message from its fragments before delivery to the end user.

There are several reasons for segmentation.

■ Very long messages increase access delays for other users since they hold exclusive control over shared network resources for longer periods of time.

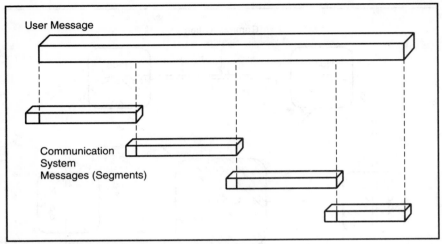

User Message

Communication
System
Messages (Segments)

**Figure 5.2**  Segmentation

- Shorter messages improve efficiency and reduce transmission error rates.
- Internal buffers, used by the communication system, can limit the transmitted message size.
- When various networks comprise a particular transmission route, each of the component networks can have a different message size.
- Breaking long messages into small segments may allow the use of parallel data links (in some networks), thus supporting parallel transmission and reducing overall delays.

*Blocking.* When a single message fragment is transmitted over the network, significant protocol overhead is incurred, especially when the message is short. Therefore, some communication systems use a blocking protocol to combine messages from different users into a single block for the transmission.

*Flow Control.* Many networks are designed to share limited resources among many users on the assumption that not all users will be active at the same time. In reality, however, communication networks may experience certain peak traffic scenarios where the resulting traffic exceeds the network throughput capacity (rush-hour traffic congestion is a good example). A network flow control function is designed to prevent transmission congestion and/or deadlock, and to optimize network performance by regulating the flow of information between a pair of communicating entities. For instance, *pacing* protocols are used to prevent the sender node from sending more information than the receiver can handle.

*Synchronization.* In order for a pair of entities to communicate with each other, their interactions must be synchronized. The receiver must be able to determine the start and duration of each signal, byte, and block. Indeed, if a receiver is faster than the sender (transmitter), it may gain and misinterpret extra information. Conversely, it may lose some information if it is slower than the transmitter.

During communication, entities maintain their state information via a communication protocol. The communication states must be synchronized at the initialization time and after a major failure.

Shared resources, such as shared data, require synchronization between processes to support resource integrity. An example of the multilevel synchronization protocol used in communication systems is IBM's Advanced Program to Program Communication protocol (APPC) which is described in Chap. 8.

*Priority.* A communication system can assign a priority to messages to allow preference handling when competing for resources. High-priority messages (alarms, alerts, interrupts) should have shorter delays. A communication system should be able to assign priority statically or dynamically (according to message content or based on a message source or destination).

*Error control.* One of the prime objectives of communication system functionality is to provide reliable, error-free communication. Error control functions include error detection, correction, and recovery. Error detection can be performed by including redundant information, by using control information that allows determination of information corruption, or by assigning sequence numbers to messages and detecting sequence errors. Redundant data can be compared to determine a possible error in the case of mismatch. Control information can use various algorithms to calculate a check digit or a check sum of all information bits. Comparing calculated results with the ones received, errors can be detected. Sequencing is used to determine lost, duplicated, or out-of sequence messages. Error correction and recovery are often implemented by automatic retransmission, possibly via a different route, although sometimes error-correction codes can be also used.

Other functions, such as session management and control, are also very important. Some of the communication system functions are described in greater detail in the next three chapters together with particular communication protocols.

## 5.3 LAYERS, PROTOCOLS, AND INTERFACES

A communication system is responsible for supporting communication between nodes in a distributed system. It allows any network node to communicate with any other node connected to the communication network. Computer network architectures should facilitate interconnectivity among homogeneous and (especially in an open systems arena) heterogeneous systems. To better understand how a communication system is architectured to support communications, let us consider a model of typical person-to-person communication. Three separate levels, or layers, can be defined:

- *Cognitive layer* includes concepts such as understanding, knowledge, and existence of shared, mutually agreed upon symbols. For example, if one person communicates a description of a book to another, then, at the very least, both persons must understand what a "book" is.

- *Language layer* is used to put concepts and ideas into words. Obviously, if people do not have a common, mutually agreed upon language, any communication will be impossible.

- *Physical transmission layer* provides the means for the actual communication, whether it is sound waves, paper for written communication, or any other media.

All three layers are independent of each other in function, and the upper layers require the support of the lower ones. To communicate ideas, the language and transmission are necessary, but the opposite may not be true. The same principals can be applied to the building of distributed and communication system architectures. At the very least, all network architectures should share the same high-level objectives:

- Connectivity to permit various hardware and software to be interconnected into a uniform, single system image, networking system

- Modularity to allow building of diverse networking systems from a relatively small number of general-purpose components

- Reliability to support communications in an error-free fashion with error detection and correction availability

- Ease of implementation, use, and modification by providing general, widely acceptable solutions for network installation, modification and management, and by supplying end users with network-transparent communication facilities

To achieve these high-level objectives, network architectures support highly modular design, where each module's functions are organized into functional, hierarchical, architectured *layers.*

Layers are composed of entities, which can be hardware components and/or software processes. Entities of the same layer but in different network nodes are called *peer entities;* the same level layers in different nodes are *peer layers.* Communication between layers is governed by a set of rules, or *protocols.* Protocols include, but are not limited to, formats and order of the information exchange, and any actions to be taken on the information transmission and receipt. The rules and formats for the information exchange across the boundary between two adjacent layers comprise an *interface* between layers.

For example, a typical distributed system architecture may consist of the following functional layers.

- The *application layer* is the topmost layer of the architecture. Typically, it performs management of application processes, distribution of data, interprocess communication, and decomposition of application functions into distributable processes. Application layer functionality is supported by lower level layers.

- The *Distributed Operating System layer* provides systemwide distributed services required by the application layer. It supports naming and addressing, the sharing of local resources, protection and synchronization, and intercommunication and recovery. The Distributed Operating System unifies the distributed functions into a single logical entity and is responsible for creating the Single System Image (SSI).

- The *local management and kernel layer* supports the Distributed Operating System in the individual nodes. It also supports local interprocess communications, memory and I/O access, protection, and multitasking. This layer supports higher-level layers by providing the services requested by the Distributed Operating System layer, and by communicating with its peer layer in other nodes.

- The *communication system layer* supports communication required by the application, Distributed Operating System and local management layers.

The layered architecture provides several important benefits:

- *Layer independence.* Each layer is only aware of the services provided by the layer immediately below it, but not of the implementation of the lower layers.

- *Flexibility.* An implementation change in one layer (for instance, new technology, different hardware, etc.), should not affect the layers above and below it.

- *Simplified implementation and maintenance.* This is due to the support of a modular layered design and architectured decomposition of overall system functionality into simpler, smaller sections.

- *Standardization.* Encapsulation of layer functionality, services, and interfaces into a precisely defined architectured entity permits standards to be developed more easily.

## 5.4   ISO REFERENCE MODEL

IBM Systems Network Architecture (SNA) is a layered architecture that was developed by IBM for data communication networks based primarily on the IBM and compatible hardware and software platforms. However, other vendors and organizations have also developed, or are in the process of developing, other architectures which can offer alternative methods of building data communication networks. Thus, two important trends can be found in the marketplace:

- Almost every major vendor offers its own proprietary network architecture, and these architectures are not compatible.
- If a business customer uses multiple hardware platforms for its DP operations, the task of connecting different networks is becoming more and more difficult.

Therefore, the need for a standard set of rules, or protocols, for the exchange of information between different, heterogeneous, network architectures becomes urgent. Various standards organizations are working on developing standard architectures, protocols and interfaces. The Consultative Committee on International Telegraphy and Telephony (CCITT) is an international standards organization that develops standards for various aspects of telephone and data transmissions (e.g., X.3, X.25, X.28, X.29, etc.). The Institute of Electrical and Electronics Engineers (IEEE) focuses on networking standards. In particular, IEEE has developed local area networking standards known as IEEE Project 802.

The realization that standards were needed to allow communication between different platforms, in conjunction with the potential benefits and advantages of layered architectures, led the International Standards Organization (ISO) to develop a reference model with the express purpose of providing a common basis for communication system standards. This set of standards, currently being developed, is called the Open Systems Interconnection, or *OSI*. The OSI model has adopted the best features of existing architectures. It also provides additional features which make the heterogeneous communication networks interconnection easier and more efficient to develop.

Even though the OSI model is still being developed, the OSI architecture is often used as a reference model by vendors and standards

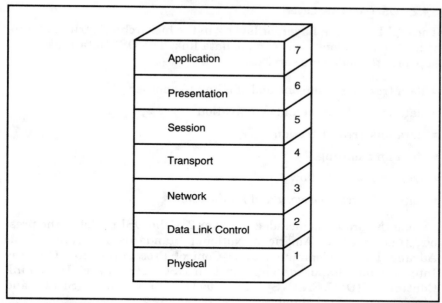

**Figure 5.3** OSI layers

organizations alike. Not surprisingly, it is a hierarchical layered structure, which consists of seven architected layers. Each layer performs a specific OSI network function, services the next higher layer, requests services from the next lower layer, and communicates on a peer-to-peer basis with the corresponding layers in other nodes.

In order to better understand the particular implementation of various communication systems, the next seven sections will briefly describe the basic functions of the seven OSI layers.

### 5.4.1 OSI Physical Layer

The OSI Physical Layer, or layer 1, is at the bottom of the OSI model. It deals with the physical implementation of a network. The OSI Physical Layer defines the electrical and signaling characteristics that are necessary to establish, maintain, and disconnect physical connections in the network. Currently, the Physical Layer of the OSI model includes these standards developed by the CCITT:

- V.35 and V.24 for analog transmissions
- X.21 for digital transmissions

The OSI Physical Layer describes how bits of information are to be sent and received, but does not provide for data recognition.

### 5.4.2   OSI Data Link Layer

The OSI Data Link Layer, or layer 2 in the hierarchical structure, provides transmissions over a single data link. The OSI Data Link Layer supports the following services:

- data transport from one end of a link to another
- data link activation and deactivation
- data link error detection
- data link sharing
- transparent data flow
- data link error recovery and notification

Among the protocols included in Layer 2 of the OSI model at the present time, are the American National Standards Institute (ANSI) Advanced Data Communications Control Procedures (ADCCP), the International Standards Organization (ISO) High-Level Data Link Control, or HDLC, SNA's Synchronous Data Link Control (SDLC), and a widely recognized standard called IEEE 802.2.

### 5.4.3   OSI Network Layer

The OSI Network Layer, or layer 3 in the hierarchy, provides control between two adjacent nodes. The following functions have been assigned to the OSI Network Layer:

- Network addressing (assignment, pairing and matching)
- Blocking and segmenting of the message units
- Data units sequencing
- Switching and routing
- Local flow control
- Optional expedited data transfer control
- Error detection control
- Congestion control
- Error recovery and notification

All of these functions of the OSI Network Layer are included in the CCITT recommended X.25—an international standard for the packet-switched data networks.

### 5.4.4  OSI Transport Layer

The OSI Transport Layer, or layer 4 in the hierarchy, is defined to provide the so called end-to-end control between two user nodes. This layer takes packets of data from the OSI Network Layer and assembles them into messages. The OSI model defines the operation of the Transport Layer as a multiphased procedure:

- *Phase 1—Establishment.* This phase establishes transport connections to lower layers.
- *Phase 2—Data Transfer.* The data transfer phase transports data between OSI layers.
- *Phase 3—Release.* The release phase disconnects transport connections.

### 5.4.5  OSI Session Layer

The OSI Session Layer, or layer 5 in the OSI hierarchy, provides network functions associated with the sessions. The following functions are defined in the OSI model for its Session Layer:

- Session initiation and activation
- Session termination and release
- Synchronization and resynchronization of the session connections
- Dialog control
- Normal and expedited data transfer

According to various trade publications, IBM's Advanced Program-to-Program Communication using Logical Unit type 6.2 (APPC/LU6.2) architecture will play a major role in developing OSI standards for the OSI Session Layer.

### 5.4.6  OSI Presentation Layer

The OSI Presentation Layer, or layer 6 in the OSI hierarchy, provides the data stream presentation protocols. These protocols should allow a network to determine and maintain track of the information, such as message syntax, contained in the user data stream. The following functions have been defined for the OSI Presentation Layer so far:

- transformation of data syntax, e.g., encryption of the data
- selection of a presentation image syntax

The following protocols are not completely defined for this layer:

- Virtual Terminal
- Virtual File
- Job Transfer and manipulation

### 5.4.7  OSI Application Layer

The OSI Application Layer is the topmost layer in the OSI hierarchical model. At the present time, the Application Layer is defined to contain all the protocols between systems that are not included in any other OSI layer. The OSI Application Layer consists of the three parts:

- *Common Application Services*. These are the services that can be used by all communicating parties. Common Application Services provide the protocols that can select the type of conversation to be held between users, or the structure of this conversation, such as a file transfer structure. Common Application Services also provide such control protocols as commitment, concurrence, and recovery.

- *Specific Application Services*. These services contain the protocols of all user information exchanges. These protocols may be private within a single communication, or widely accepted, even internationally recognized, communication standards. At this time, international communication standards for the OSI Application Layer include X.400 Message protocol, X.500 Directory protocol, and File Transfer, Access, and Management protocol (FTAM).

- *User Element*. In the OSI model, this represents the end points of the user information (e.g., final origination and destination points). If the user element is defined, there will be no need for a user interface above the Application Layer.

Chapters 6 through 8 discuss several specific network architectures and protocols. There, the OSI model is used as a reference to the network's features and architecture.

## 5.5  CLIENT/SERVER
## COMPONENTS CONNECTIVITY

In a client/server architecture, client and server systems are constructed from a number of interconnected components. Each component provides an interface through which it communicates with other components. Thus, communication between clients and servers can be viewed as the communication between relevant components. Two distinct classes of components can be defined:

- *Process components.* Typically, these are software components that actively perform some functions.

- *Resource components.* These provide the services requested by process components.

From the point of view of client/server interactions, an active resource component acts as a server, whereas the users of the resource component and process components act as clients.

Process and resource components, as well as clients and servers, enter into an association with each other for the purpose of communication. This association is the *connection* between a sender of information (request, message, etc.) and a receiver of that information. The client/server connections can be static or dynamic. Static connections are set up at compile or load time, or at system initialization time, and cannot be changed. Dynamic connection can be changed "in-flight," at run time.

### 5.5.1 Communication and synchronization

In a cooperative client/server distributed environment, coordination and cooperation between components (clients and servers) is provided by the communication system's communication and synchronization functions. Communication functions involve the exchange of information, and are supported by flow control, error control, naming and addressing, and blocking and segmenting. Synchronization functions involve the coordination of actions between two or more components.

Communication and synchronization are closely related. When communication is performed in shared memory closely-coupled systems (such as Symmetric Multiprocessing systems described in Chap. 4), software components such as semaphores or monitors are used for synchronization. In more traditional loosely coupled systems that are interconnected by communication networks, mechanisms such as message passing must be used for communication and synchronization.

In either case, the communication service provided by a communication system can be *connectionless* or *connection-oriented*. Connectionless services are those where each message transaction is independent of previous or subsequent ones. These are low-overhead services that are relatively simple to implement. An example is a *datagram* service, where the user is not provided with any form of response to a transaction. Typically, datagram services are used for broadcast or multidestination message transmission.

A connection-oriented service provides a relationship between the sequence of units of information transmitted by a particular communication layer. This is more complex than a connectionless communication service. Most connection-oriented services have three phases of operation: establishment, data, and termination. An establishment phase can be used to negotiate connection or session options and, thus, quality of service. A terminal session to a remote computer or X.25 packet-switched network protocols accepted by the CCITT are examples of connection-oriented services.

With respect to connections in general, the flow of information can be unidirectional (from a sender to a receiver) or the more complicated bidirectional. The latter involves a return message and synchronization in response to the initial request.

Bidirectional communications are an essential form of communication for the client/server architecture. A client component requests some service to be performed by its (possibly remote) server, then waits until the results of its request (if any) are returned. Bidirectional client/server interactions can be provided by a message-oriented communication implemented in such request-reply protocols as IBM's Logical Unit 6.2 (LU6.2), or by a procedure-oriented communication such as remote procedure calls (RPC).

### 5.5.2   Procedure-oriented communication—RPC

Procedure-oriented communication allows applications in a distributed computing environment, such as Open Software Foundation's Distributed Computing Environment (DCE), to run over a heterogeneous network. The basic technology that enables this functionality is the *Remote Procedure Call, or RPC.*

The RPC model is based on the need to run individual process components of an application on a system elsewhere in a network. RPCs use a traditional programming construct—the procedure call, the use of which is extended from a single system to a network of systems. In the context of a communication system role in a client/server environment, an RPC requesting a particular service from a resource component (server) is issued by a process component (client). The location of the resource component is hidden from the user (client). RPCs are highly suitable for client/server applications, usually providing developers with a number of powerful tools that are necessary to build such applications. These tools include two major components:

- a language and a compiler that simplify the development of distributed client/server applications by producing portable source code

- a run-time facility that allows distributed applications to run over multiple, heterogeneous nodes, thus making the system architectures and the underlying network protocols transparent to the application procedures

Among several RPC implementations and proposals competing for the role of standard RPC, DCE's RPC appears to be one of the strongest candidates and deserves closer examination.

To develop a distributed, DCE-compliant, client/server application, a developer creates an interface definition using the Interface Definition Language (IDL). IDL syntax is similar to ANSI C language with the addition of several language constructs appropriate for a network environment. Once the definitions are created, the IDL compiler translates them into stubs that are bound with the client and the server (see Fig. 5.4). The stub on a client system acts as a substitute for the required server procedure. Similarly, the server stub substitutes for a client. The stubs are needed to automate otherwise manual operations—copying arguments to and from RPC headers, converting data as necessary, and calling the RPC Run-time.

RPC Run-time should have the following features:

- Transparency and independence from the underlying networking protocols

- Support for reliable transmission, error detection, and recovery from network failures

- Support for a common method of network naming, addressing, and directory services, while at the same time being independent of network directory services

- Multithreading support for parallel and concurrent processing, and ability to handle multiple requests simultaneously, thus reducing the time required to complete an application

- Portability and interoperability with various system environments

- Support for resources integrity and application security

The DCE implementation of the remote procedure calls includes special semantics for both network transport independence and transparency. DCE RPC includes a pipe facility to eliminate such resource limitations as inadequate main memory. ISO's X.500 standard is used to provide global directory services. DCE RPC uses Kerberos authentication and authorization to support security service, and asynchronous threads to support concurrent and parallel processing.

## 5.6   NETWORKS

A *communication system* was previously described as the collection of hardware and software which supports intersystem and interprocess communication between software components in distributed nodes.

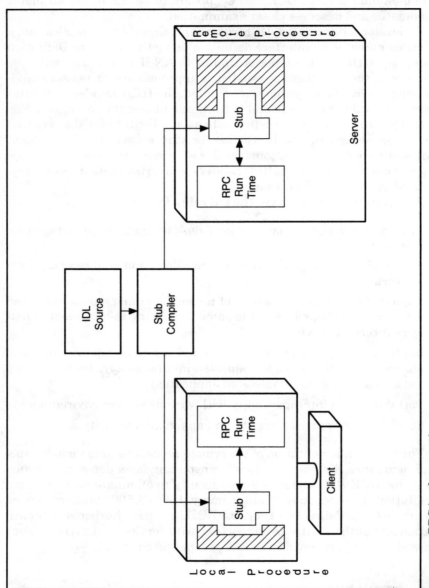

**Figure 5.4** RPC implementation

The actual links between nodes comprise a *network,* which represents an ordered collection of physical *paths* between interconnected nodes. This chapter will introduce readers to the following aspects of net-working—topology and basic network technologies.

### 5.6.1   Classification

Network communications can be classified by the ability of a network node to communicate directly with one or more nodes:

- *Point-to-point* communication allows one node to communicate only with an adjacent node. In its basic form, a point-to-point network consists of two directly connected nodes (see Fig. 5.5). Of course, a multinode network where each node is connected to its adjacent node also forms a point-to-point network. In this instance, adjacency is measured by how many logical steps it takes to get from one node to the adjacent node. For example, in Ethernet all nodes are one logical step from each other.

- A *multipoint* (multidrop) network is a network where all nodes share one line by sharing time on the line. Multidrop networks are similar to rural telephone party lines, where a user picks up a phone and checks to see if the line is occupied by someone else. If so, the user hangs up and tries again later. As the number of nodes grows, the possible delays become longer. Therefore, multidrop networks are useful where high-speed data transmission is not necessary, but where implementation costs are a factor.

Network communications can also be classified by the way in which messages are transmitted from node to node:

- *Broadcast networks* (mostly local area networks) are those where all nodes are connected to a common transmission medium, so that a single message can reach all nodes.

- *Store-and-forward networks* (mostly wide area networks) are those where a complete message is received into an intermediate buffer

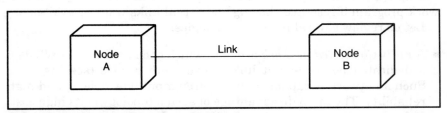

**Figure 5.5**   Point-to-point communication

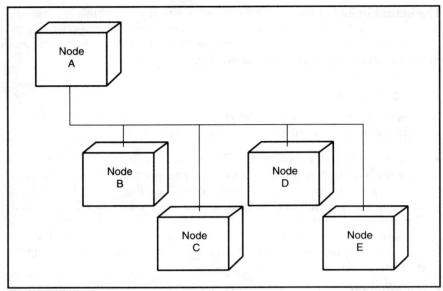

**Figure 5.6**   Multipoint network communication

before being retransmitted toward its destination. The nodes in store-and-forward networks are interconnected by independent point-to-point transmission lines.

### 5.6.2  Topology

Network topology defines the basic interconnection structure of nodes and links. Topology can be viewed as the architectural drawing of the network components—the nodes (any system on a network) and the links between them. Links can be phone lines, private lines, satellite channels, etc. Basically, links can be divided into physical (actual, real) links and virtual links. Networks use virtual links to allow sharing of the physical line by multiple network programs and data transfers. Virtual communications over physical lines are extremely valuable to providing cost-effective communications capabilities. Imagine, for example, the costs of providing a new physical line for every new network program if resource sharing via virtual links was not available.

Let us review several network topologies:

- A *Fully Connected network* is one in which each node is connected by a dedicated point-to-point link to every other node (see Fig. 5.7). Such a network is capable of high throughput, low delays, and high reliability. The main disadvantage of such a topology is its high cost. Indeed, $n$ nodes require $n(n-1)/2$ links, where each node must have

$n - 1$ interfaces. Adding a node requires every other node to be modified. A special case of a fully connected network is a mesh network. It has point-to-point links between some nodes. A store-and-forward transmission is required between those nodes not directly connected.

- A *Star network* consists of nodes that are connected to a single central switching node (see Fig. 5.8). This topology is often used when multiple terminals are connected to a central computer. The expansion costs of a star network are low, and delays should not exceed one intermediate node. The main disadvantage is poor reliability, since a central switch failure can stop all communications.

- A *Hierarchical* or *Tree network* is a topology where one focal point is occupied by a host (central computer), which acts as a master in a master-slave relationship with the network nodes. A typical example is IBM's Systems Network Architecture (SNA) terminal network. Tree networks are useful for process control applications, since they reflect the hierarchical, master-slave nature of a control system.

- A *Bus network* is an example of a broadcast network implementation, where a shared transmission medium interconnects all nodes. Hence, the length of links and associated costs are minimized. A single interface is required to connect a new node to the network, which results in low expansion cost. Ethernet is an example of a bus network.

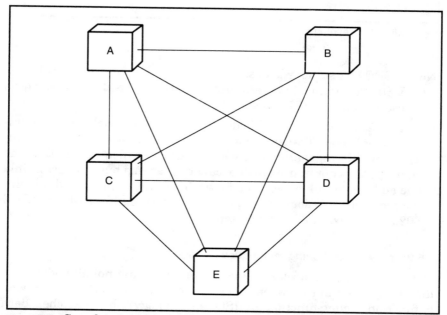

**Figure 5.7** Complete interconnection

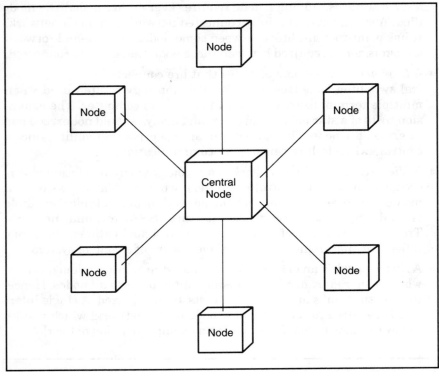

**Figure 5.8**  Star topology

Note: IEEE 802 standards describe protocols that control logical links (IEEE 802.2) and media access protocols. Ethernet-like bus networks are described by the IEEE 802.3 standard.

- A *Ring network* consists of nodes linked to their neighbors by a uni-directional loop. Transmission can be broadcast or point-to-point. The signal is regenerated at each interface, which means that the ring length is not limited by line capacity (as in a bus network). Only one additional link is required for each additional node, and communication software does not require routing. IBM's Token-Ring (IEEE 802.5) is an example of a ring topology.

### 5.6.2   Network switching techniques

Network topologies, discussed above, illustrate that not all nodes have direct physical links between them. Therefore, a network must provide a function (relay function in ISO terminology) that switches data between links to provide a point-to-point path between some nodes.

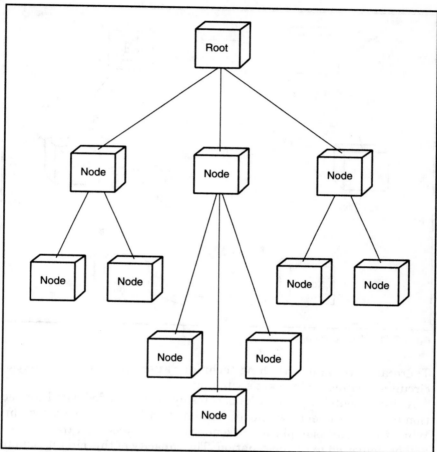

**Figure 5.9**   Hierarchical (Tree) topology

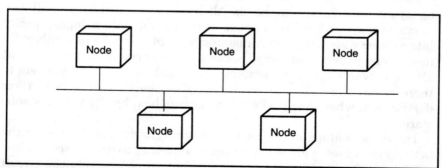

**Figure 5.10**   Bus topology

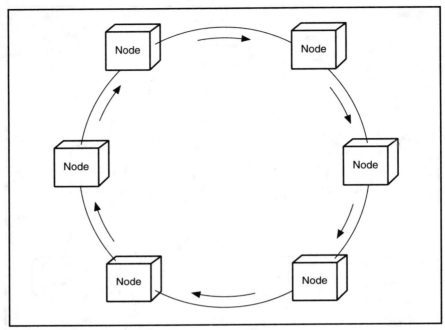

**Figure 5.11**   Ring topology

There are two main switching techniques used in modern networks: circuit switching and packet switching.

A circuit switching network operates by forming a dedicated connection (circuit) between two nodes (similar to a U.S. telephone system). While the circuit is in place, the sender is guaranteed that the message will be delivered to the destination. The capacity of this circuit is guaranteed (i.e., no other network activity should decrease the circuit capacity).

Packet-switched networks (usually used to connect computer systems) take a different approach. All traffic is divided into small segments (packets) that are mapped (multiplexed) into a high-capacity intersystem connection for transmission from one node to another. To implement packet-switching, packets must carry identification that allows network operating system (NOS) software to send packets to their destinations. The network hardware delivers packets to their destination, where the packets are reassembled by the network software.

The disadvantage of the packet-switching technique is that as the activity increases, a given pair of communicating partners receives less resource capacity from the network. That is, contrary to the circuit switching, the available capacity is not guaranteed. However, lower-cost and high-speed networking hardware provide for high performance and wide acceptance of the packet-switching networking.

Sometimes, a message switching technique is described as an alternative to both circuit and packet switching. It involves storing messages of any size (including files) in the switching node's storage. Messages can be stored for hours or days until the destination node wishes to receive the message. This type of packet-switching technique is often implemented in electronic mail applications.

The networking functions, architecture, techniques, and characteristics discussed in this chapter will be used as a foundation for understanding local, metropolitan and wide area networks, various standards, protocols, and particular implementations of client/server communications.

# Local Area Networking

A proliferation of personal computers throughout organizations has resulted in an increase of PCs used for a wide variety of business functions. It has also resulted in the ever-increasing need for personal computers to communicate. The communication needs include inter-communications among personal computers as well as communication with centralized data processing facilities and the sources of corporate data. Several networking technologies have been developed to support this intercommunication. Among them are Wide Area Networking, Metropolitan Area Networking, and Local Area Networking.

## 6.1  LOCAL AREA NETWORK CONCEPTS

Intelligent workstations, such as personal computers or UNIX-based technical workstations, can be used as stand-alone systems to support local applications. However, as workgroup environments become more and more popular, the reasons for interconnecting these intelligent workstations in a network are getting more apparent. Among them are:

- the need to access data stored in another, not local, system
- the need for the members of the workgroup to share devices that are

too expensive to be used by a single user only (a PostScript laser printer being one example of such devices)

- the need for the workgroup members to exchange information electronically

### 6.1.1  LAN, WAN and MAN

The distance between network users is one of the factors that determines the required network type and, therefore, the underlying technology. One situation includes user requirements to access processing and data storage capabilities typically available from mainframes. Similarly, interconnectivity may be required by users widely separated geographically. In this case, the networking solutions may involve public telecommunication facilities for fast data interchange. The networks that tie all these users together are called *Wide Area Networks* (*WAN*).

Sometimes, it is useful to distinguish between wide area networks that can span remote locations at very large distances, measured in hundreds and thousands of miles (e.g., users in New York, Los Angeles, and Tokyo), and networks that link users within a particular metropolitan area. Networks that operate within a city or those that can use physical telecommunications facilities typically associated with the city infrastructure (e.g., underground cabling system), are sometimes called *Metropolitan Area Networks* (*MAN*). A typical MAN provides voice, data, and video communications at speeds of 45–600 Mbits/s (million bits per second) at distances ranging from 1 to 50 miles.

Relatively short distance communications between intelligent workstations (such as personal computers) are supported by a networking technology known as *Local Area Networks* (*LAN*). The Institute of Electrical and Electronics Engineers (IEEE) defines a LAN as a data communication system that allows a number of independent devices to communicate directly with each other, within a moderately sized geographic area over a physical communication channel of moderate data rates.

Local area networks can be used for shared data, application and device access, electronic mail, process monitoring in a factory environment, and even for alarm and security systems. However, the most interesting feature of a local area network is its ability to support cooperative client/server applications in which an application runs partly on LAN stations and partly on a LAN server or even a mainframe host, as was described in the previous chapters. Also, the range of LAN applications can be significantly extended by interconnecting several networks. LAN interconnection can be implemented over wide area networks, thus extending the communication capabilities of local area networks far beyond the traditional distance limitations of a typical LAN. At the same time, the ease of use and direct interconnection typical of a LAN are still maintained.

### 6.1.2   LAN characteristics and components

The IEEE definition of a LAN provides LAN characteristics that distinguish local area networks from other networking technologies. Indeed:

- By allowing independent devices to communicate directly with each other, LAN supports peer communication between its nodes. This is in contrast with such centrally controlled hierarchical systems as, for example, IBM's Systems Network Architecture (SNA).

- By emphasizing a moderately sized geographic area, IEEE separates LAN from wide area networks. Typically, a LAN does not exceed a distance of about 6 miles, and often is limited to a single building or a group of buildings placed close together (as in, for example, a college campus environment).

- By defining a physical communication channel with moderate data rates, IEEE contrasts LANs with wide area networks, which often use public-switched communication facilities.

Moderate data rates used to imply that LAN data rates were to be slower than those of the direct mainframe links and channel-to-channel communication, measured in several million bits per second. However, with the advances in physical transmission technology, and especially the advent of the fiber-optics communications, local area networks can support data rates from 1 to 100 Mbits/s.

A typical local area network that corresponds to the IEEE LAN definition consists of two general types of components: nodes and links between nodes. In LAN terminology, though, nodes, which can be any device attached to a network, are known as *stations*. All LAN stations are linked, or interconnected via a *cabling system,* which includes physical communication channels (wire, cable) and any devices necessary to attach the stations to the network.

For example, to avoid the loss of a signal over the length of the wire, signal regenerators, or repeaters, are sometimes installed in a LAN. Each station must possess sufficient intelligence to handle the communication control functions. Thus, peripheral devices (such as printers and hard disk drives) are not LAN stations, but rather are attached to some of the intelligent stations.

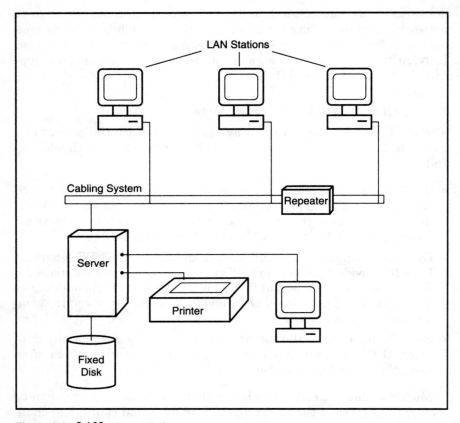

**Figure 6.1**  LAN components

As was illustrated in the previous chapter, networks, including local area networks, are characterized by the shape the cabling system takes—the network topology. In addition, different local area networks are characterized by:

- The *transmission medium*—the type of cable that is used in a given LAN

- The *transmission technique*—the technique that determines how the transmission medium is used for communication

- The *access control method*—the method by which LAN stations control their access to the transmission medium

These LAN characteristics are described in greater detail in the next section.

## 6.2   TRANSMISSION AND ACCESS CONTROL METHODS

The physical transmission of information over a local area network can be described by two main categories: the actual medium used for the transmission and the way this medium is used.

### 6.2.1   Transmission medium

A wide variety of physical communication links are used for the transmission of information. The telecommunication industry continues to expand the available transmission medium to achieve extremely high transmission rates while improving costs and availability of the new physical connections.

Even though traditional media employed in conventional telecommunication applications can be used in local area networks, today's LANs are often implemented by using twisted-wire pairs, coaxial cable, and fiber-optics links.

Twisted-wire pairs consist of two insulated and braided strands of copper wire. Usually, such pairs form a cable by grouping pairs together and enclosing them in a common protective jacket. The typical intrabuilding telephone wiring is an example of such a cable. Relatively low cost and high availability of such a cabling system have resulted in the popularity of the twisted-pair wire for LAN implementations. Twisted-pair wire can support transmission speeds of up to 10 Mbits/s.

To eliminate possible electrical interference, a twisted-wire pair cable can be enclosed in a special, high-quality protective sheath. Such cable is called a shielded twisted-wire pair cable and, even though slightly more expensive, it is used where higher reliability and higher transmission rates over longer distances are required. The IBM Cabling System Type 1 and 2 cables are examples of twisted-wire pair cables offered by a computer vendor.

Coaxial cable is familiar to television users, especially those with cable TV. Coaxial cable contains a central conducting core (usually copper) that is surrounded by the insulating material, another conductor (braided wire mesh or a solid sleeve), and yet another insulated protective and flexible jacket. Although more expensive, coaxial cable is better-isolated from electrical interference than a twisted-wire pair. Coaxial cable can support transmission rates of up to 100 Mbits/s. DECconnect Communication System's Thin and Standard Ethernet cables are examples of the coaxial cable used in LAN implementations.

Fiber-optic links are a relatively new transmission medium available for commercial LAN implementations. Optical fiber contains a core—an extremely thin glass cylinder surrounded by a concentric layer of glass, called cladding. Optical signals take the form of modulated light beams that traverse the length of the fiber-optic link at the speed of light. The cladding is made of a material whose refractive index is lower than that of the core. Therefore, the light signals traveling along the core are reflected from the cladding back into the core. A number of such optical fibers are bound together into one fiber-optic cable, surrounded by a protective sheath. Fiber-optic cables are characterized by weights lighter than coaxial cables but with significantly higher costs. However, the light signals transmitted over a fiber-optic cable are not subject to electrical interference. The optical transmission medium can support extremely high transmission rates—565 Mbits/s rates can be found in commercially available systems, and experiments have demonstrated data rates of up to 200,000 Mbits/s. IBM Cabling System's Type 5 cable is an example of fiber-optic cables used for computer network.

Various implementations of these physical links can be found in a large number of commercially available cabling systems offered by general purpose communication vendors as well as vendors of various computer networks. For example, IBM markets its own IBM Cabling System, and Digital Equipment Corporation offers DECconnect Communication System.

### 6.2.2   Transmission techniques

Whatever the transmission medium employed in a given LAN environment, the LAN designer must select a technique that LAN will use to transmit signals over a physical communication link. In general, there are two available transmission techniques for transmission over a physical communication channel: *baseband* and *broadband*.

Baseband transmission uses discrete signals (pulses of electricity or light that represent a binary 0 and 1) to carry information over a physical transmission medium. Such a signaling technique is called *digital signaling*. Baseband transmission uses the entire communication channel capacity to transmit a single data signal. Since multiple stations attached to a network must share a common communication channel, a technique known as *time-division multiplexing* (TDM) is usually employed to allow attached stations to transmit signals one at a time.

One of the concerns with digital transmission is that as a signal travels along a channel it may get weaker; its form gets distorted and the receiving station may have difficulty recognizing and interpreting the signal. In other words, the difference between a '0' and a '1' may be insufficient to distinguish between the two. Special devices—

repeaters—are strategically placed along the route of a signal to overcome the signal deterioration problem. Repeaters totally regenerate the signal and retransmit it toward its destination.

Broadband transmission typically employs nondiscrete (analog) signals that are continuously transmitted over a transmission medium in the form of electromagnetic waves. Discrete information is encoded into analog waves by using amplitude, frequency, or phase modulation of the base (carrier) signal. In radio transmission, amplitude modulation is known as AM, and frequency modulation as FM. In general, the higher the frequency of the carrier signal, the higher the volume of information that can be carried by this signal. The difference between the highest and lowest frequencies that are carried over the channel reflects that channel's information-carrying capacity, and is referred to as the channel *bandwidth*. The bandwidth is directly related to another measurement of channel capacity—the number of bits per second that can be carried over the channel, known as the *data rate*.

Similar to the time-division multiplexing of baseband transmission, analog broadband transmission employs frequency-division multiplexing (FDM), which divides available bandwidth into multiple communication channels. Some of these channels can be used for data transmission, while others can be employed for video, fax, or telephone transmissions simultaneously. The majority of information transmitted in LAN environments is data—digital, discrete signals. When a broadband transmission is used, the digital signals must be converted into analog form by modulating the analog carrier signal. At the receiving station, these signals must be converted back (demodulated) into the original digital form. The modulation-demodulation process is performed by devices known as *modems* (modulator-demodulator). Various encoding schemes are employed by LANs to represent discrete '0's and '1's. Some of the better known encoding schemes are the Electronic Industry Association's RS-232-C, and Zero complemented Differential Encoding used in IBM's high-performance Synchronous Data Link Control (SDLC).

### 6.2.3 Transmission control

In general, various transmission control methods can be classified as follows:

- *Centralized control* is that in which one station controls the entire network and gives other stations permissions to transmit.

- *Random control* allows any LAN station to transmit without being given specific permission.

- *Distributed control* gives the right to transmit to only one station at a time. The right to transmit is passed from one station to the next. All stations cooperate to control access to the network.

Each of these transmission control methods offers its own advantages and disadvantages, and has access control methods designed specifically to work best with that particular transmission control. For example, centralized transmission control provides for easier network coordination and management, and requires simple station-to-network interfaces. At the same time, centralized transmission control, by definition, provides a single point of failure, and the central control point can prove to be a bottleneck. Access control methods are designed to facilitate and employ various transmission controls.

Centralized control may employ the following access control methods:

- *Polling.* One station (master) sends a question-notification to all other (secondary) stations indicating that a given station is allowed to transmit. If the receiving (polled) station has a message to transmit, it sends the message to the master station. In turn, the master station forwards the message to its destination. While the polled station is being listened to, the secondary station is allowed to transmit more than one message, provided there are other messages and enough time to transmit them.

- *Circuit switching.* This can be used successfully in a centralized control LAN implemented by using a star topology. Here, a central station receives requests for a transmission from a secondary station and establishes a connection (circuit) between the sender and its intended receiver. Circuit switching is widely used in telephony, especially in private branch exchanges (PBX).

- *Time-Division Multiple Access (TDMA).* This provides a specific time slot for each station on a network. The station is allowed to transmit only during this time slot. The time cycle is started and synchronized by a master station. TDMA can be successfully used on a bus LAN topology.

One of the best known access control techniques for random transmission control is Carrier Sense Multiple Access with Collision Detection *(CSMA/CD)*. It is one of the most commonly used LAN access methods, is employed by the Ethernet, and is also defined as one of the IEEE LAN standards. In CSMA/CD, before a station can transmit, it must listen to the network to determine whether or not another station is transmitting (sense the carrier). If the network is silent, the station can transmit its message, which arrives at every other station.

Only those stations whose address is indicated in the message will actually receive the message.

It is conceivable, however, that two or more stations might transmit their messages simultaneously, resulting in message collision. If this happens, the receiving stations ignore the garbled messages, while the transmitting stations attempt to resend the messages. To avoid repeated collision, each transmitting station waits for a period of time (determined by a random number generated by the station) before it transmits again. In light message traffic, CSMA/CD is very efficient, and access to the transmission medium is fast. Heavy message traffic, however, leads to an increased number of collisions. As a result, access method efficiency and network performance deteriorate.

Distributed transmission control can be supported by such well-known access control methods as *token passing* and carrier sense multiple access with collision avoidance (*CSMA/CA*).

Token Ring passing is most widely used in ring topology networks (e.g., IBM's Token Ring). A token is a small message that is constantly circulating around the ring. Token passing can be used in a bus or a tree topology. Token bus methods are similar to a token ring, emulating the token ring method on a logical topology level.

When a token that is marked "free" is received by a station, the station can transmit a message. Whenever a station transmits a message, it appends the message with a token marked "busy." Each station that should receive the message copies the message and updates the token's bits to indicate whether or not the station received the message. Finally, the message gets back to the sender. The sender station resets the token to free and removes the message. Token passing guarantees that each station has a chance to transmit at least one message during a predetermined period of time. The main disadvantage of the token passing technique is its complexity and token processing overhead.

CSMA/CA is very similar to the CSMA/CD access methods. Each station listens to the carrier while a transmission from one of the stations is in progress (if any). When the line is free, the stations begin to transmit their messages in the order of the station priorities assigned to them. In order to avoid potential message collisions, each station waits for a specific period of time before it begins the transmission.

When designing local area networks, many interdependent factors should be taken into consideration—the transmission medium, transmission control and access methods, network topology, bandwidth, and data rates. All these factors affect network performance and cost. Decisions regarding network topology, transmission control, and access control methods should be made based on the processing and cost requirements of a particular LAN.

## 6.3    IEEE 802 ARCHITECTURE

The IEEE plays a major role in defining LAN standards. Specifically, IEEE has undertaken a special project, Project 802, that has as its goal the development of a flexible network architecture oriented specifically to local area networks.

### 6.3.1    LAN standards and IEEE Project 802

IEEE has attempted to define LAN architecture in conformance with the ISO's Open System Interconnection architecture, described in the previous chapter. However, the scope of IEEE Project 802 is limited to only the two lowest OSI layers: the physical layer and the data link layer (see Fig. 6.2). The functions performed by the higher OSI layers are left up to individual LAN vendors and even users. These functions are provided by a network operating system (NOS). NOS is typically implemented as a software product that is capable of performing print server, file server, and electronic mail support (functions of the highest—application—OSI layer), internetworking connectivity and network management support (functions of the OSI session, transport, and network layers).

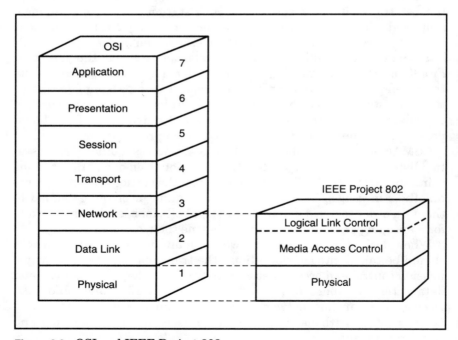

**Figure 6.2**    OSI and IEEE Project 802

Since a single standard capable of meeting all LAN requirements was very difficult to define, the approach taken by IEEE Project 802 was to develop sets, or families, of standards. These sets of standards are organized in a hierarchical, tree-like set of layers that correspond to the architected LAN layers. IEEE Project 802 defines a single standard for the logical link control layer: IEEE 802.2. Physical layer standards include twisted-wire pairs, coaxial and fiber-optic cables, together with the transmission types, encoding methods, and data rates. The media access control and physical layers are described by multiple IEEE 802 standards. Some of them are listed below.

### 6.3.2   IEEE 802.2: logical link control layer

The LAN logical link control layer is described by the IEEE 802.2 standard. This standard is a common element in all IEEE 802 standards. As the root of the IEEE 802 hierarchy, IEEE 802.2 isolates the higher layers of a network architecture from the specifics of a particular LAN implementation. The IEEE 802.2 standard defines both service interface specifications and peer-to-peer protocols. It is responsible for the exchange of protocol-specific control signals between LAN stations. Among the other functions defined by IEEE 802.2 are data flow organization, command interpretation, generation of responses, and error control and recovery.

### 6.3.3   Media Access Control layers and IEEE 802.3

Media Access Control (MAC) layers of the IEEE 802 standards are designed to support multiple devices that compete for access to a single physical transmission medium. The MAC layer defines the rules that stations must obey in order to share a common transmission medium. The media access control standard contains these functions:

- Medium access management functions are used to control the sharing of a transmission medium among all stations in a network.
- A framing function identifies the beginning and the end of a message by adding header and trailer information. Framing facilitates sender-receiver synchronization, routing, and error detection.
- An addressing function identifies devices participating in the sending and receiving of messages and determines the appropriate network addresses.
- An error detection function ensures that a message has been transmitted and received correctly.

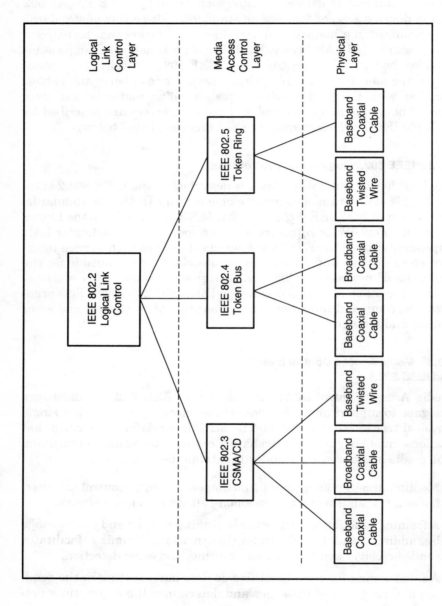

**Figure 6.3** IEEE Project 802 layers

IEEE Project 802 identified the carrier sense multiple access with collision detection (CSMA/CD), token bus, and token ring access control methods to support MAC standards. All three access control methods, described previously, interface with the same logical link control standard—IEEE 802.2. Project 802 has named its chosen access control methods as IEEE 802.3, IEEE 802.4, and IEEE 802.5, respectively. The first MAC method—CSMA/CD—is best known for its use in Ethernet networks.

### 6.3.4    Ethernet

Ethernet networks originated from the LAN development work performed by Xerox Corporation at its Palo Alto Research Center (PARC). The Ethernet design was very successful, and Ethernet specifications, jointly defined by Digital Equipment Corporation, Intel Corporation, and Xerox Corporation, provided substantial contribution to the IEEE 802.3 standard. Many vendors today offer Ethernet network products that are compatible with various operating systems and the IEEE 802.3 standard. For instance, both Ethernet and IEEE 802.3 offer data encapsulation/decapsulation and data encoding/decoding. IEEE 802.3's media access management and physical medium attachment functions correspond to Ethernet's link management and channel access management.

Ethernet is designed to provide network simplicity, low cost, flexibility and compatibility between different Ethernet implementations, high speed, low delay, stability, and maintainability of Ethernet-based LANs. Usually, Ethernet supports baseband transmission at a data rate of 10 Mbits/s, with a maximum cable length of 500 meters (approximately 1650 feet).

### 6.3.5    IEEE 802.4: token bus standard

The IEEE 802.4 standard is one of the two IEEE 802 token-passing-based standards. IEEE 802.4 defines a token passing standard for LANs implemented on a physical bus topology. In the IEEE 802.4 token bus control method, each station knows the address of the station from which a token is received (predecessor) and the address of a station to which it must transmit a token (successor). An IEEE 802.4 token is passed (transmitted) from one station to the next. When the token is received, the station is allowed to transmit messages for a predefined amount of time. When the time limit has been reached, or when a station has no messages to transmit, the transmitting station sends the token to the next station. Even though the physical topology of the IEEE 802.3 network takes the form of a bus, the logical operation is in the form of a logical ring (see Fig. 6.4). The IEEE 802.4 standard supports data rates from 1 to 10 Mbits/s. General Motors' Manufacturing Automation Protocol (MAP) is an example of a networking architecture based on the IEEE 802.4 standard.

### 6.3.6   IEEE 802.5: token ring standard

The IEEE 802.5 token ring standard uses a logical model similar to the IEEE 802.4 token bus architecture.

The IEEE 802.5 token ring architecture consists of a logical ring implemented using a physical ring topology. Transmission of tokens and messages flows in a single direction (see Fig. 6.5). Information units are passed from one station to the next, and each station acts as a repeater.

Similarly to the IEEE 802.4, the right to transmit in a token ring network is controlled by a token. It is said that a "free" token is the one that allows the station to transmit. When one of the stations that needs to send messages receives a free token, it changes the token to a "busy" state and is allowed to transmit messages for a predefined amount of time. The busy token is included by a transmitting station as part of a message. When the time limit is reached, the transmitting station transmits the token and a message to the next station. Each station receiving a message checks the message address to see if it has to process the message. As the message travels around the ring, its originator finally receives it, changes the token to a free token, and removes the message. Besides station addresses, tokens can contain

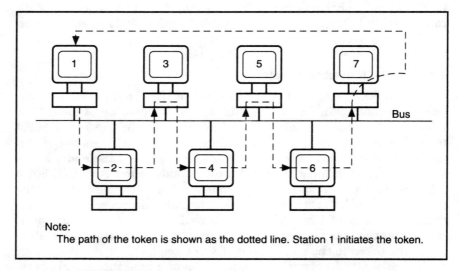

Note:
    The path of the token is shown as the dotted line. Station 1 initiates the token.

**Figure 6.4**   IEEE 802.4 Token passing bus

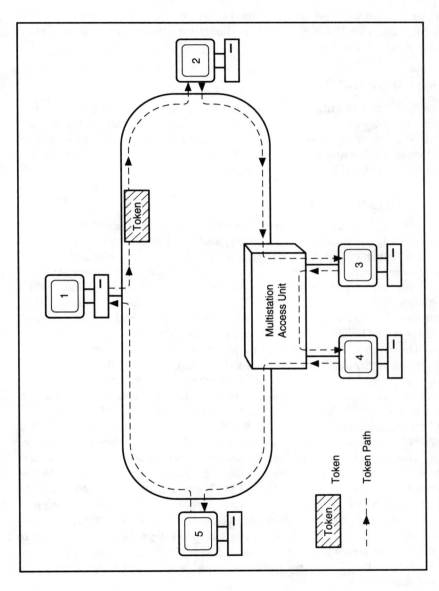

**Figure 6.5**  IEEE 802.5 Token passing ring

message priorities. The IEEE 802.5 standard specifies a baseband transmission technique over a twisted-wire pair with data rates of up to 4 Mbits/s, and over a coaxial cable with data rates of up to 40 Mbits/s. The IEEE 802.5 is the basis for IBM's widely used Token Ring local area networks.

## 6.4 LAN IMPLEMENTATIONS

The IEEE 802 standards define LAN architectures that provide a common set of communication functions. These standards have been widely adopted by vendors of LAN products. Standardization allows different (heterogeneous) types of equipment to be attached to the same network and interoperate successfully.

### 6.4.1 IBM LAN solutions

To meet the goals of heterogeneous connectivity, rapid data transmission, high reliability, availability, and serviceability, IBM has developed a variety of LAN products and services that support several LAN architectures and interfaces. The IBM implementation of the media access control standards includes IBM Token Ring network (IEEE 802.5) and IBM PC Network—both broadband and baseband (IEEE 802.3). A common interface and the logical link control level (IEEE 802.2) is offered via the IBM LAN Support Program and the higher level programming interface to the network—NETBIOS. In addition, IBM provides bridges that connect LANs of the same type (e.g., IBM Token Ring Bridge Program), and gateways that interconnect heterogeneous LANs, as well as LANs with host computers, and WANs (IBM Token Ring/PC Network Interconnect Program, IBM PC 3270 Emulation Program, APPC/PC, and APPC for OS/2 EE).

*IBM Token Ring Network.* This IBM LAN architecture is consistent with the IEEE 802.5 standard. It uses baseband transmission and data rates of up to 4 Mbits/s over a cabling system based on shielded or unshielded twisted-wire pairs. The logic and control necessary to implement media access control are provided by IBM's Token Ring network adapter cards, installed on PC-based LAN stations. Up to eight stations can be attached to a network Multistation Access Unit to form a star-wired subnetwork (see Fig. 6.5). Such access units can be connected together in a ring network capable of supporting more than eight stations.

*IBM PC Network.* This network implements the IEEE 802.3 standard (CSMA/CD) in two products: PC Network-Broadband and PC Network-Baseband. The baseband version uses a tree topology and transmission rates of up to 2 Mbits/s. The baseband PC Network uses a daisy chain or star topology, also with transmission rates of up to 2 Mbits/s.

*NETBIOS.* The logical link control layer interface, consistent with the data link layer of the OSI reference model, is provided by the IBM LAN Support Program. This interface corresponds to the IEEE 802.2 standard. At the same time, the LAN Support Program provides higher level OSI's session layer interface—NETBIOS. The NETBIOS's full-duplex transmission protocol supports reliable data transmission over a virtual circuit and a datagram service without acknowledgment. In addition to datagram service, NETBIOS performs control, name service, and session service functions. Although NETBIOS does not conform to a published standard, it represents a de facto LAN standard. Various LAN vendors offer network operating systems that emulate the NETBIOS interface.

*APPC Interfaces.* An alternative session layer interface for IBM's local area networks is provided by APPC/PC. This interface is based on the Advanced Program-to-Program Communication (APPC) protocols defined for the IBM SNA (Systems Network Architecture) Logical Unit Type 6.2 (LU6.2). APPC/LU6.2 is designed to provide a general purpose peer-to-peer communication between programs. The APPC protocol supports the synchronization between two programs (processes) that is necessary for distributed transaction processing and data integrity in a distributed database environment. APPC/LU6.2 is one of the most important communication mechanisms for the successful implementation of a client/server architecture. The role and features of the APPC/LU6.2 are described in more detail in Chap. 8.

In an IBM PC Network, the APPC/PC interface supports a session-level protocol with a synchronization level of CONFIRM. This level allows conversing partners to exchange confirmation/error signals on request, thus ensuring reliable data transmission. APPC/PC uses SNA facilities, and is well suited for interconnections between an IBM PC Network and an SNA network controlled by a host computer system.

### 6.4.2   Novell—NetWare

Novell's NetWare is one of the most pervasive LAN implementations, with either a direct support or a comprehensive protocol gateway on every major platform. NetWare can be used with Ethernet, CSMA/CD networks (e.g., AT&T StarLan and IBM PC Network) as well as with token ring architectures, including IBM Token Ring. NetWare emulates NETBIOS, supports file and printer sharing, electronic mail, remote access, inter-LAN communication via a NetWare Bridge, and a gateway to IBM's SNA (NetWare SNA Gateway) over a synchronous data link control (SDLC) line.

NetWare provides a number of utility and monitor programs that allow network administrators to easily add new users to the network, open/close files, and maintain system security. NetWare allows network administrators to change the user's password and to hide selected files from a user.

In addition to PC DOS vendors, UNIX vendors offer direct support for Novell's NetWare. A number of UNIX hardware vendors have released, or will soon release, versions of Portable NetWare. To provide more seamless links between standard NetWare and UNIX hosts, Portable NetWare is implemented as "not native" to its host hardware platform, but, rather, it runs as a guest under another operating system. As a result, a new, higher level of UNIX-NetWare connectivity can be achieved, with the support of all traditional NetWare clients (DOS, Windows, OS/2, Macintosh) available for the UNIX host.

Novell and third party vendors support NetWare not only on such platforms as Apple, DOS (including Microsoft Windows), OS/2, and UNIX, but even on IBM MVS, IBM VM, OS/400 and VMS. Novell NetWare licensees include Data General, Hewlett-Packard, ICL, Interactive, Intergraph, MIPS, NCR, Prime, Pyramid, Unisys, and Wang. In addition, IBM recently entered into an agreement to sell Novell's NetWare.

### 6.4.3    Banyan—Vines

Banyan Systems (Westborough, MA) offers one of the most technically advanced distributed network operating systems (NOS) on the market—Vines. Vines is designed to support large PC networks. One of the Banyan Systems' large customers—Compaq—runs its internal network of approximately 11,000 geographically dispersed PCs using Vines.

Vines distributed architecture integrates directory, security, and network management services on interconnected servers, each of which supports one or more PC LANs (see Fig. 6.6). A Vines server can run on Intel 286, 386, and 486 based PCs over a POSIX-compliant version of UNIX system V. Vines supports DOS, Windows and OS/2 client workstations.

Vines architecture supports multiple LAN types, including Ethernet and Token Ring, and virtually any LAN topology. Vines provides support for a variety of communication protocols, including 3270 Emulation, TCP/IP, and X.25 Packet Switching protocols. In addition, Vines can run over WAN server-to-server interconnections, thus providing a single, global view of an organizational network.

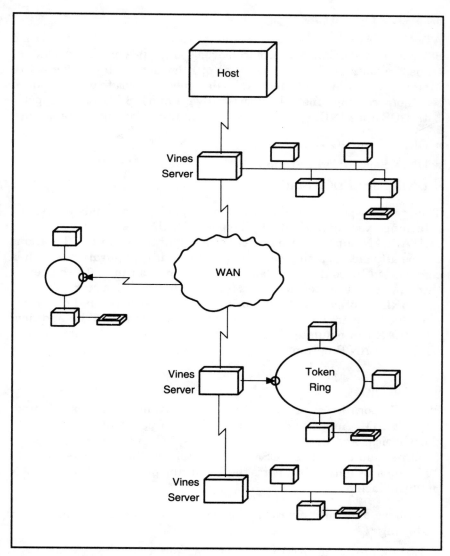

**Figure 6.6**  Vines network

Vines provides a user with a single, integrated view of the network. Vines uses an authorization mechanism to support network-wide security. Network administrators are provided with easily managed configuration and monitoring tools. Vines offers a set of standard services that include a file and print services as well as a popular Vines Network Mail.

### 6.4.4   AT&T—STARLAN

AT&T's STARLAN is a local area network that is based on the IEEE 802.3 standard CSMA/CD protocol, even though it typically operates at transmission rates lower than those of Ethernet (1 Mbits/s versus 10 Mbits/s). The STARLAN network is designed to operate over standard telephone cabling (unshielded twisted-wire pair). STARLAN supports both DOS and UNIX operating systems in the following combinations:

- DOS Server/DOS Station
- UNIX Server/UNIX Station
- UNIX Server/DOS Station

The last is especially useful when an organization builds a LAN by attaching existing DOS PCs to the powerful UNIX servers.

STARLAN supports a daisy chain configuration (up to 10 stations can be attached to a single cable), and the star configuration, which is constructed by connecting daisy chain segments (up to 11 segments) through network extension units (up to 12 units) into a star.

STARLAN provides file and printer sharing services and electronic mail facilities in both DOS and UNIX environments. In addition, STARLAN can emulate NETBIOS, thus providing compatibility with IBM's PC LAN Program.

### 6.4.5   3Com

3Com Corporation is one of the major LAN vendors that offers products for IBM, Apple, and compatible lines of personal computers. At the physical and data link control levels, 3Com supports the use of Ethernet and IEEE 802.3 CSMA/CD formats at the data rates of up to 10 Mbits/s. 3Com also supports the token ring protocol. The 3Com LAN products include:

- 3+Share network operating system, providing file and printer sharing
- 3+Mail, providing electronic messaging services
- 3+Route, 3+Remote, and 3+NetConnect products, allowing interconnection among 3Com networks
- 3+3270, allowing 3Com networks to access an SNA host as an IBM 3270 terminal

Recently, 3Com announced that the company will license all its LAN software technology to Microsoft Corporation.

### 6.4.6  Apple—AppleTalk

The AppleTalk LAN protocols are built into the Apple's Macintosh hardware and operating system, as well as into other devices such as Apple's laser printers. Therefore, users of Macintosh computers can build a network by simply plugging necessary devices together with the appropriate cabling system.

The Basic AppleTalk network is an inexpensive, easily managed LAN. It provides simple device-to-device communication and printer sharing services.

The AppleTalk network uses a bus or a tree topology, with the shielded twisted-wire pair as a preferred cabling system. CSMA/CA is the media access control protocol used by AppleTalk. Up to 32 devices can be connected on a single network, even though multiple AppleTalk networks can be interconnected. A typical AppleTalk LAN uses very slow data rates of 230 kbytes/s (as compared with 10 Mbps/s Ethernet, for example), which makes acceptance of the AppleTalk LAN for a client/server architecture more difficult.

## 6.5  OTHER LAN ARCHITECTURES

In addition to the LAN architectures described up to this point, there are other architectures that are developed to suit specific applications. These architectures are based on the variety of options allowed by standards as they are defined by such standard bodies as IEEE, OSI, and CCITT. Among these application-specific architectures are manufacturing LAN architectures (MAP and TOP) and the architecture based on the use of fiber-optics cable (FDDI).

### 6.5.1  MAP and TOP specifications

The Manufacturing Automation Protocol (MAP) addresses the area of factory automation. It has been developed by the task force sponsored by General Motors. To address the issues of engineering, manufacturing, and general office automation, Boeing has sponsored another task force, whose charter was to develop Technical and Office Protocol (TOP).

In general, both MAP and TOP use a hierarchically interconnected network structure. In the hierarchical MAP/TOP architecture, the lowest levels are occupied by local area networks. Depending on the distances involved, these LANs can be interconnected over a Campus Network, Metropolitan Area Network (MAN), and Wide Area Network (WAN) (see Fig. 6.7).

Both MAP and TOP use the seven-layer OSI reference model as the basis for their respective architectures. MAP and TOP specifications

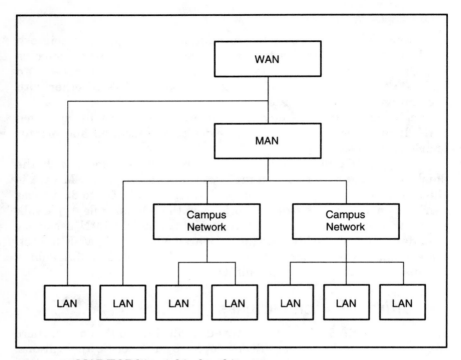

**Figure 6.7** MAP/TOP hierarchical architecture

include well-documented limited, but similar, sets of the OSI protocols, which allow for easy interconnection between MAP and TOP networks.

Both MAP and TOP use the IEEE 802.2 logical link control protocol but different access control methods. MAP uses the IEEE 802.4 token bus standard, while TOP has selected the IEEE 802.3 CSMA/CD standard. At the higher layers of the OSI model, both MAP and TOP support full-duplex transmission and error detection and recovery; they employ the File Transfer, Access and Management (FTAM) protocols, and a variety of application services protocols.

### 6.5.2 FDDI

The Fiber Distributed Data Interface (FDDI) standard was developed by the American National Institute of Standards (ANSI). Its X3T9.5 committee developed FDDI to meet users' requirements for high-performance networks and high-speed network interconnections.

The ANSI FDDI standard is based on the use of the token passing technique over optical fiber cables at data rates of 100 Mbits/s. The token passing protocol used in FDDI is similar to the IEEE 802.5 token ring standard, although there are some minor differences in token handling. The FDDI standard has been developed to satisfy the requirements of the following types of networks:

- *Backend local networks* are often used to interconnect mainframes and large data storage devices. Such interconnections require extremely high data transfer rates.

- *Backbone local networks* are usually used to interconnect local area networks. Backbone networks need high transmission rates to eliminate a potential bottleneck in inter-LAN communication.

- *High speed office networks* are required to support the high data transfer rates requirements for image and graphics processing. High resolution graphics and image are typically stored in so-called Binary Large Objects (BLOBs), which can be up to several gigabytes in size.

The FDDI standard provides a high-capacity, reliable networking specification, enforced by automatic optical bypass switches and dual-ring configuration.

## 6.6    INTER-LAN CONNECTIVITY

Local area networks allow a group of computer users to communicate with one another and to share data, services, and devices. LANs are ideal for workgroup environments and client/server implementation on a geographically small scale. However, in reality, users of different local area networks need to communicate and share information with members of workgroups other than their own. Therefore, it is often required to interconnect existing LANs.

Local area networks can be interconnected directly or through higher-level networks—MANs and WANs. When interconnecting local area networks or LAN segments, several methods can be used:

- *Repeaters* are the simplest method for network interconnection. A repeater's functionality is limited to interconnecting individual segments of similar smaller networks to form a larger network. Typically, repeaters are used in bus LAN topology.

- *Bridges* can interconnect networks that support different transmission protocols (i.e., CSMA/CD LAN and Token Ring LAN). A bridge between two LANs receives messages from both networks, checks their destinations, and transmits the messages to the required LAN. Since messages are stored in the bridge system before retransmission, bridges are said to implement a store-and-forward technique.

To properly handle messages, a bridge must know and understand the addressing scheme used on both networks. From the point of view of the OSI reference model, bridges operate at the physical and data link layers.

- *Routers* perform the network layer functions of the OSI reference model. A router routes the message from the source node to the destination node through intermediate nodes. In this case, two addresses—next node on the route and final destination node— should accompany the message. The first address changes from one station to another along the route, while the second address remains constant. For a router to be able to work, the interconnected networks must be compatible at network and higher OSI layers (layers 3 and above), but may be different at physical and data link layers. A key function of the router is determining the next node (station) to which a message is to be sent.

- *Gateways* are used to interconnect networks that may be built on entirely different architectures. Thus, gateways implement functions of all seven layers of the OSI model. Gateways handle any message, address, and protocol conversions necessary to deliver a message from one network to another. Gateways offer the greatest flexibility in internetworking communication. This flexibility comes at a cost of higher price and more complex design, implementation, maintenance, and operation of a gateway.

Routers, bridges, and gateways form the basis for inter-LAN networks. A backbone network, described as a candidate for the FDDI implementation, is a good example of an inter-LAN connectivity solution.

# SNA, TCP/IP, and DNA

Network architectures, such as ISO's OSI, IBM's SNA, and DEC's DNA and TCP/IP, are designed to make the logical view of the communications network independent of its physical implementation. The OSI model described in Chap. 5 deals primarily with the interconnection between systems, and provides a generalized view of a layered network architecture. Various local area network architectures use the OSI model as a reference, and therefore conform with OSI standards. In addition to the LAN standards and architectures critical for the client/server implementations in local area network environments, there are several network implementations so widely accepted that they have become de facto networking standards, and are often used successfully in client/server implementations based on these network architectures.

## 7.1 SNA COMPONENTS, LAYERS, AND FUNCTIONS

IBM's Systems Network Architecture recently turned 15 years old. SNA has dramatically changed since it was first introduced. It supports a variety of applications and is widely used—IBM claims that it has issued 40,000 SNA licenses. With the thousands of networks installed worldwide, SNA has emerged as one of the most accepted de facto networking standards. SNA provides a consistent set of communication rules, called protocols, and the communication access method, called ACF/VTAM.

SNA is designed to satisfy the network user requirements efficiently and cost-effectively:

- SNA provides resource sharing. It eliminates the need to install separate communication links for different types of workstations or applications, since networking enables access to an application on any host processor and from any workstation.

- SNA enhances network dependability. SNA protocols recognize data loss during the transmission, use data flow control procedures to prevent data overrun, avoid overload and congestion, recognize failures, and correct many errors. Network availability is higher due to such SNA features as the extended recovery facility, alternate routing, backup host, and built-in control procedures in workstations, modems, and controllers.

- SNA helps users with network expansion and maintenance by providing open documented interfaces, which are implemented in all SNA products. This reduces the amount of programming involved in system integration.

- SNA simplifies problem determination by providing network management services in each network component plus global management software, such as NetView.

- SNA maintains an open-ended architecture that helps to accommodate new facilities such as digital networks, digitized voice, distributed systems, electronic document distribution, fiber optics, graphics, satellites, Token-Ring network, Videotex, and Viewdata.

- SNA provides a network interconnection facility which allows the users in one SNA network to access information and programs in other SNA networks by using SNA gateways. Therefore, SNA network boundaries are transparent to the network users.

- SNA provides network security via its logon routines to prevent unauthorized users from accessing the network. For additional security, SNA provides encryption facilities.

To summarize, SNA handles connections between users in a network in such a way that the underlying physical aspects of how the information unit is routed between users through the network are transparent to the user. The end-points of a communication link are defined as *logical units*. A logical unit provides a set of facilities which isolate the user from the physical characteristics of the network devices.

Traditionally, an application program ran on a special network node—Host processor. The user used a terminal connected to the network's peripheral node, thus supporting a host-to-terminal, master-slave hierarchical relationship.

One of SNA's objectives, especially in the framework of IBM's Systems Application Architecture, or SAA, is to support distributed processing. SAA distributed processing implies a peer-to-peer relationship between applications, instead of the old, rigid master-slave communication. In SNA, peer-to-peer communications requirements caused the creation of a new logical unit type—Logical Unit type 6.2 (LU6.2), a new physical unit type—Physical Unit type 2.1 (PU2.1, now called SNA Node Type 2.1), and a new set of rules, called LU6.2 protocol. This new protocol provides peer-to-peer communication capabilities and is called Advanced Program-to-Program Communication (APPC), or APPC/LU6.2.

### 7.1.1 SNA components and links
### between them

An SNA network consists of many different hardware and software components connected via *links*. A link consists of a link connection and two or more link stations. A link connection is the physical transmission media connecting two or more nodes. Link stations use data link control protocols to transmit data over a link connection. The transmission media can be telephone lines, microwave beams, fiber optics, coaxial cables, etc.

Data link control protocols specify the rules interpreting the control data and providing the transmission across the link. In a LAN environment, SNA data link control protocols support IEEE 802.5—Token Ring. Other well-known SNA protocols include the following.

- *Synchronous Data Link Control,* or *SDLC,* describes the connection of network components using telecommunication links. SDLC transmits data serially, bit by bit, independently of the physical medium connecting the nodes. The main features of SDLC are:

  - It allows a number of messages to be transmitted in one direction on the link before receiving a response.

  - It increases the volume of data that can be transmitted on the link.

  - It reduces response times for transmission.

  - It detects errors and retransmits data automatically.

  - It allows any character to be included in the data stream.

- *System / 370 / 390* data channels are designed to connect the various network components directly to a host processor. System/370/390 data channels transmit data bits in parallel and provide superior speed of transmission.

In addition to the links mentioned above, SNA also provides products supporting other data link control protocols.

- Binary synchronous (BSC) protocols allow SNA networks to send and receive data from non-SNA workstations.
- X.25 interface is an international standard supported by the International Telegraph and Telephone Consultative Committee (CCITT). X.25 allows SNA networks to transmit data across packet-switched networks.
- Short-Hold Mode is a protocol used mainly with certain European circuit-switched networks.

### 7.1.2   SNA end users

End users use the network to obtain network services, which are mainly the exchange of data between two points or nodes. In discussing the System Network Architecture, the term *End User* is used to describe:

- individuals interacting with the network through workstations
- application programs requesting the network services

Thus, the SNA architecture describes the end users as both the source and destination of the information that is being transmitted on a network.

### 7.1.3   SNA Network Addressable Units and nodes

Network Addressable Unit (NAU) functions provide SNA end users with the ability to send and receive data through the network. Every SNA node contains a physical unit (PU) that provides physical connectivity between devices. SNA defines several types of physical units. They are listed in App. A. Every end user gains access to a SNA network through a logical unit (LU). LU types are described in App. B.

SNA defines a *node* as a portion of a hardware component and associated software components that implement a particular architecture-defined SNA function (see Fig. 7.1). There are three kinds of nodes:

- *Host subarea nodes.* These are processors that contain a telecommunication access method such as ACF/VTAM, and provide the SNA functions that control and manage a network.

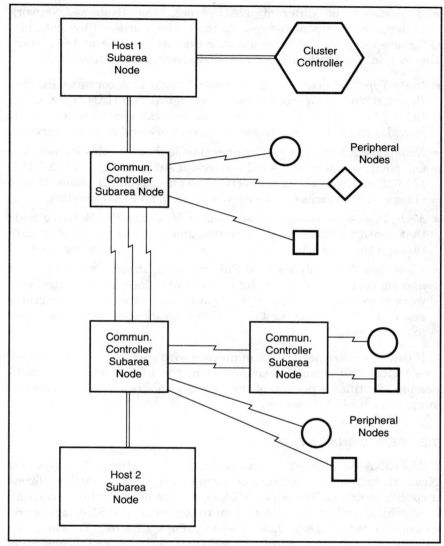

**Figure 7.1**  SNA nodes

- *Communication controller subarea nodes.* These are communication controllers (special communication processors) that contain a network control program, such as ACF/NCP.
- *Peripheral nodes* (all others).

Different SNA products support different SNA functions. To distinguish SNA nodes by their routing capabilities, connection capabilities, and presence of different NAU types, the Systems Network Architecture assigns node types to the various nodes. Physical units (PUs) are assigned the same numeric type as the SNA node in which they reside. Currently defined are the following node types:

- *Node Type 2.0* describes a Peripheral node that contains PU 2.0. Type 2.0 Node supports the following logical unit (LU) types: LU 2, LU 3, LU 6.2, and LU 1 (the last is for non-SNA interconnection). It provides end users with access to the network and end-user services.

- *Node Type 2.1* describes a Peripheral node that contains its own control point, which provides PU services. It supports LU 1, LU 2, LU 3, LU 6.2, and direct link connections to other type 2.1 nodes. It provides end-user access to the network and to end-user services.

- *Node Type 4* describes a Communication Controller Subarea node that contains PU Type 4. It routes and controls the flow of data through the network.

- *Node Type 5* describes a Host Subarea node. It contains PU Type 5, and supports all LU types. Its primary functions are to control network resources, to support application and transaction programs and end-user services, and to provide network operators with access to the network.

If two end users need to communicate with each other, their respective logical units must be connected in the LU-LU *session*. A half-session identifies a portion of the logical unit's resources allocated to support each LU-LU session.

## 7.2   SEVEN SNA LAYERS

IBM's SNA is a hierarchical layered architecture. The Systems Network Architecture consists of seven layers, each of which performs a specific function. The seven SNA layers are organized in a vertical, hierarchical architecture. In bottom-to-top order, the SNA layers are: *Physical Control, Data Link Control, Path Control, Transmission Control, Data Flow Control, Presentation Services,* and *Transaction Services.* Each SNA layer participates in the SNA hierarchy in the following fashion:

- It performs services for the next higher layer.

- It requests services from the next lower layer.

- It communicates with the corresponding layer in another SNA network.

- Changes to one layer do not affect the other layers.

Similar to the OSI reference model, the seven SNA layers are organized into a vertical hierarchy. The SNA layered structure can be divided into upper and lower parts as follows (see Fig. 7.2):

The upper four layers—Transmission Control, Data Flow Control, Presentation Services, and Transaction Services—provide the Network Addressable Unit (NAU) functions and boundary function.

The lower three layers—Physical Control, Data Link Control, and Path Control—define the path control network and provide the path

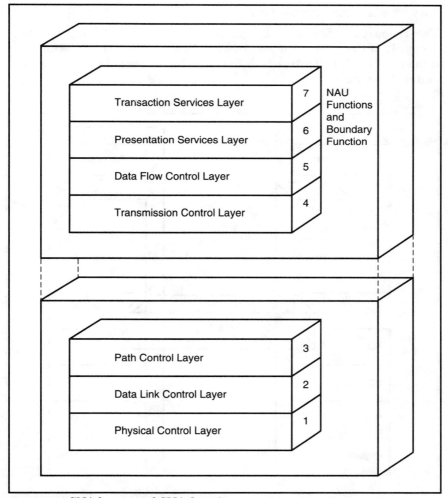

**Figure 7.2**   SNA layers and SNA functions

control network functions and services. The path control network transmits and routes data between Network Addressable Units.

Systems Network Architecture defines that half-session resources (these are the logical unit's resources allocated to support each LU-LU session) are managed by the two lower layers of the NAU function (Data Flow Control Layer and Transmission Control Layer), whereas the Transaction Services and Presentation Services layers provide services to the network's end users and network operation control (see Fig. 7.3).

### 7.2.1  Transaction Services Layer

The Transaction Services Layer is at the top of the SNA layered hierarchy. It is the layer in which SNA service transaction programs are implemented. The Transaction Services Layer provides the following end-user services:

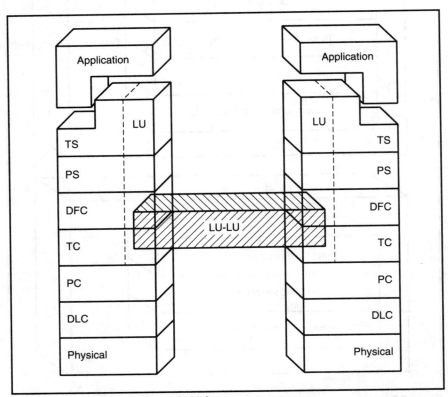

**Figure 7.3**  LU-LU session and SNA layers

- Operator Control of the LU-LU session limits
- Document Interchange Architecture (DIA) for document distribution between SNA-based office information systems
- SNA Distributed Services (SNADS) for asynchronous data communication between distributed applications

The Transaction Services Layer also provides certain services to control the network's operation. These services are Configuration Services, Session Services, and Management Services.

*Configuration Services*

- activate and deactivate links
- assign network addresses during dynamic network reconfigurations
- load and maintain the same-domain software

*Session Services*

- translate network names to network addresses during sessions
- verify both user passwords and access authority assigned to an end-user when an LU-LU session is about to be activated
- select session parameters based on the LU characteristics and type of the initiation requests

*Management Services* manage

- network problems
- network performance
- collection of accounting information
- network configuration
- changes and reconfigurations in the network

### 7.2.2   Presentation Services Layer

Transaction programs communicate with each other, in accordance with well-defined conversation protocols, by using conversation verbs. The Presentation Services Layer defines these protocols for program-to-program communication. It also controls the use of the transaction program conversation level verbs.

The Presentation Services Layer

- controls the loading and initiation of the transaction programs
- maintains and supports send and receive mode conversation protocols

- supervises the transaction program verb parameter usage
- enforces sequencing protocol restrictions
- processes transaction program verbs

### 7.2.3    Data Flow Control Layer

Data flow on an LU-LU session needs to be controlled according to the session protocols used. The Data Flow Control Layer provides that control. The following functions are performed by the Data Flow Control Layer:

- Assignment of the data flow sequence numbers
- Correlation of the requests and responses
- Support for chaining protocols by grouping of related request units into chains
- Support of bracket protocols by grouping of related chains into brackets
- Support and enforcement of the session request and response mode protocols
- Support and coordination of the session send and receive mode protocols

### 7.2.4    Transmission Control Layer

The Transmission Control Layer is the lowest of the upper four SNA layers that provide network addressable unit functions and boundary functions. This means the Transmission Control Layer provides basic control of the network's transmission resources. The Transmission Control Layer provides the following functions:

- Sequence number verification when a message is received
- Data encryption using enciphering and deciphering protocols
- Management of the rate at which the requests sent from one Logical Unit are received in another Logical Unit
- Support for the boundary function for peripheral nodes

### 7.2.5    Path Control Layer

The Path Control Layer is the highest of the three SNA layers that provide path control network functions. The Path Control Layer provides SNA protocols that route messages through the network. The Path Control Layer is used by all types of sessions to

- perform path selection through the network
- route data through the network
- support segmenting and blocking protocols to combine and/or divide message units
- control virtual routes and virtual route rate of the throughput—virtual route pacing
- control explicit routes in the network

### 7.2.6  Data Link Control Layer

As the name implies, the Data Link Control Layer provides functions for the data link elements of the path control network. The Data Link Control Layer provides protocols for message units transfer across a link, and for link level data flow and error recovery. The Data Link Control Layer supports SDLC, System/370 Data Channel, CCITT X.25, and Token-Ring protocols. The following functions are supported by the Data Link Control Layer:

- Transmission of message units across links
- Link level data flow management
- Error detection and recovery for transmission errors

### 7.2.7  Physical Control Layer

The Physical Control Layer provides a physical interface for any transmission media used as a physical connection in the network. This layer defines the electrical and signaling characteristics needed to establish, maintain, and terminate the physical connections on which the links in a network are built.

### 7.3  PEER COMMUNICATION BETWEEN SNA LAYERS

Peer-to-peer communication enables the networks to be designed from the top down or from the bottom up, which was not possible before peer-to-peer communication became available. Furthermore, real peer-to-peer communication makes possible the creation of the networks, connecting mainframes, minicomputers, and Programmable Workstations (PWS) into a cooperative computing environment. Distributed transaction processing and distributed databases can be implemented in such a network. Different hardware platforms can be used at different locations of the business enterprise, thus providing better leverage of the DP/MIS investment.

Peer communication is communication between equals. It differs from the hierarchical and master-slave types of communications in which the communication is always initiated by a higher-level party (master), where requests are sent from master to slave, but not the reverse. Older network designs did not permit peer communication, often resulting in communication bottlenecks. The Systems Network Architecture allows *peer communication* between the SNA layers residing at the same levels within the hierarchy. In fact, the most advanced SNA logical unit, LU6.2, is defined to provide the peer-to-peer communication capability between programs.

As was mentioned before, each SNA layer performs services for the next higher level, requests services from the next lower level, and communicates as a peer with equivalent layers in another node. To support peer communication, each layer must be isolated from the internal procedures that another layer follows.

For example, the Presentation Services layer performs services for the Transaction Services layer, requests services from the Data Flow Control layer (both in the same node), and communicates with Presentation Services layers in other nodes. The Presentation Services layer performs its functions independently of any other layer in the SNA architecture. Since the SNA layers are defined to be functionally independent from one another, any layer may be modified or enhanced without disruption of the functions and operations of the other layers in the SNA network. That, in turn, allows SNA networks to grow, change, and, when necessary, migrate to new technologies.

## 7.4    SNA AND OSI

The structures of the OSI model and the SNA model are very similar: both represent a hierarchical architecture consisting of seven layers. The layers of both models have the same properties. Each layer performs a specific model function (SNA function or OSI function); lower layers provide services for higher layers; and layers of the same level can communicate with each other as peers. Indeed, both models are built to formally describe how communication networks should be implemented.

However, the purpose of the OSI model is different from that of the SNA model. The goal of the OSI model is to bring "law and order" into the diverse world of network communication architectures—to provide standard information exchange protocols for communication between autonomous, possibly different, architectures.

IBM's Systems Network Architecture, on the other hand, is designed for the exchange of information between network nodes that belong to a single architecture. That single architecture is the one on which IBM

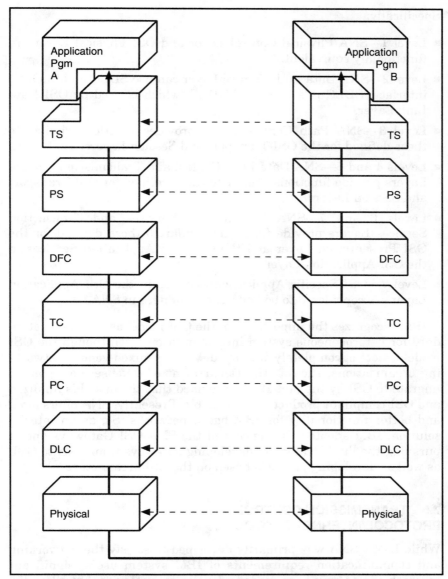

**Figure 7.4**  Communication between SNA layers

builds its various program offerings. The existence of a single architecture allows IBM to tailor both the hardware and software network components to achieve maximum efficiency and performance.

The functions of both SNA and OSI layers are similar, even though there is no one-to-one correlation between SNA layers and OSI layers.

Specifically:

- Level 1—SNA Physical Control Layer and OSI Physical Layer are functionally equivalent.
- Level 2—SNA Data Link Control Layer can use SDLC and the X.25 interface. SDLC is a subset of HDLC, which is used by OSI Data Link Layer.
- Level 3—SNA Path Control Layer provides functions similar to those defined for the OSI Transport and Session Layers.
- Levels 4 and 5—SNA Data Flow Control and Transmission Control Layers provide functions similar to those defined for OSI Transport and Session Layers.
- Levels 6 and 7—SNA Presentation Services and Transaction Services Layers provide functions similar to those defined for the OSI Presentation Layer and the Common Application Services in the OSI Application Layer.
- Level 7—OSI Specific Application Services in the OSI Application Layer are considered to be end-user exchanges in SNA.

IBM recognizes the importance of the OSI model as a common standard for heterogeneous system interconnection, even though the OSI model is not yet completely developed. Various mixed-vendor networking organizations, such as the Department of Defense, now plan to migrate to OSI by the mid-1990s, provided that the model is finalized and OSI-compliant products are available. Presently, SNA offers more and better functionality for IBM-based networks. So, as an interim solution, IBM adopted the concept of the SNA-OSI Gateways and is pursuing the dual strategy of developing gateways from SNA to OSI, as well as developing products based on the OSI architecture.

## 7.5    TRANSMISSION CONTROL PROTOCOL/INTERNET PROTOCOL

While IBM's SNA was primarily developed to satisfy the networking and communication requirements of IBM system users, significant research efforts have been made to develop technologies that allow disparate, heterogeneous physical networks to interconnect. The majority of this research was sponsored by various U.S. government agencies.

These organizations were first to realize and appreciate the importance and potential of network interconnection, sometimes called internetworking, or internet. The leading internet technology has resulted from the research funded by the Defense Advanced Research

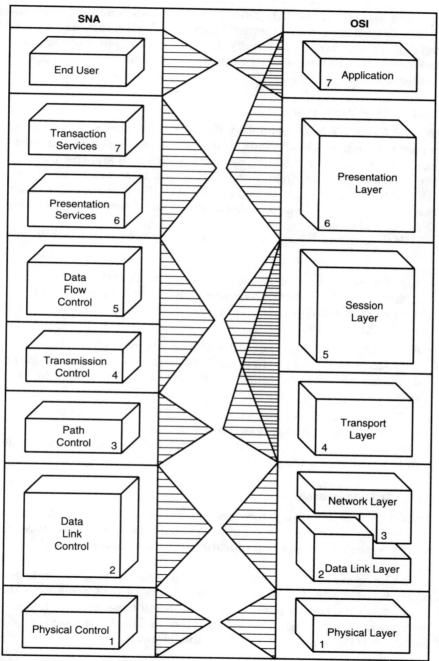

**Figure 7.5**  SNA and OSI layers

Projects Agency (DARPA). This technology, known as the Transmission Control Protocol/Internet Protocol (TCP/IP), includes a set of networking standards that specify the details of computer communications as well as conventions for networks interconnection and network traffic routing.

### 7.5.1  TCP/IP internetworking

TCP/IP forms the base technology for a large internet which connects major research establishments, universities, and government agencies. The result is the Internet, connecting such well known entities as the National Science Foundation (NSF), the Department of Energy (DOE), the Department of Defense (DOD), the Health and Human Services Agency, the National Aeronautics and Space Administration (NASA), and others.

TCP/IP features differ from other network protocols in the following ways:

- *Network technology independence.* By design, TCP/IP is independent of any particular vendor's hardware. The TCP/IP defines how information transmission units (datagrams) are to be transmitted on a particular network.
- *Any-to-any interconnection.* This allows any pair of computer systems to which it attaches itself to communicate by assigning a unique address, recognizable throughout the internet, to each system.
- *Source-destination acknowledgment.* TCP/IP protocols support end-to-end acknowledgment between the source and the ultimate destination of the message, even if the source and the destination reside in physically separate networks.

### 7.5.2  TCP/IP protocols

The TCP/IP is a four-layer communication architecture that can be conceptually described as a hierarchy, built on a physical network interface, that provides communication interfaces to the network hardware (see Fig. 7.6).

The layer above the network services is referred to as the internet protocol (IP) layer. It is a connectionless service that deals with the delivery of information packets. (It is connectionless because it treats each packet independently from all others.) The IP is essentially a datagram service designed to satisfy the following:

- definition of a basic unit of data transmission, used throughout the TCP/IP network

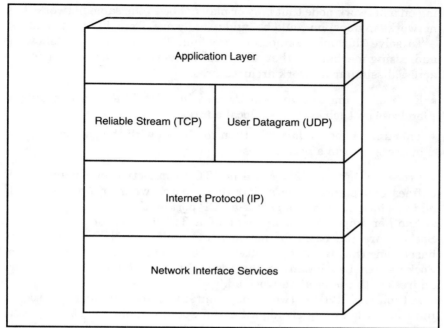

**Figure 7.6**   TCP/IP architecture

- routing of data packets, including routing between dissimilar network architectures (for example, between IEEE 802.3 LAN and X.25 WAN)

- best-effort (but not guaranteed) information delivery

The IP protocol includes rules on how packets should be processed, how and when error messages should be generated, and conditions under which packets should be discarded. However, the IP, by design, does not guarantee delivery of data.

Guaranteed delivery, data concurrency, and sequencing are the responsibilities of the transmission control protocol (TCP) layer. In addition, the TCP takes care of the error checking, retransmission, and connection to applications on other systems.

TCP is a connection-oriented protocol, which uses connections between two points, not individual end points, as its fundamental concept.

### 7.5.3   Addressing, sockets, and sequencing

TCP/IP was built primarily to allow a particular program on a particular node on a particular network to connect to a remote program residing on a network node that may or may not be in the same network. The networks in question could be (and usually are) from different vendors.

To solve this interconnection problem, TCP/IP uses the following addressing mechanism that allows for delivery of information packets across dissimilar network architectures:

- Each program (known as a Process in TCP) is assigned a unique address on each system—a local address.
- This unique local address is then combined with the particular node address to form a *port* address.

Processes by themselves are not TCP connection end points. TCP defines end points to be a pair (host, port), where a *host* is the IP address for a host, and a *port* is a TCP port on that host.

Another important component of a TCP/IP network is a *socket*. Sockets are the basis for network I/O built in UNIX environments based on the Berkeley Software Distribution operating system. Sockets can be viewed as the result of a combination of the port address with the local network address.

A typical TCP/IP network may contain a large number of sockets, but each socket uniquely identifies one specific application on a specific node on a specific network. Through the socket mechanism, the IP can get packets to the proper nodes where the TCP will then deliver the packets to the proper program (Process) on that node.

Two sockets that wish to connect to each other must use a particular mechanism to establish such a connection. TCP, being a connection-oriented protocol, provides several such mechanisms. One of the more common ways for TCP to establish a connection is by using an *active* or *passive* network *open*. When a socket that wishes to receive data declares itself open and available for incoming traffic, it is a passive open. A passive open may even be *fully specified,* which means that the socket that issued a passive open tells the network which socket may connect to it.

Unlike the passive open, the active open socket attempts to find a socket with which it wishes to connect. An active open can be successful only if the requested socket cooperates by being a passive or an active open. To establish a connection that supports correct synchronization between two end points, TCP uses a three-way *handshake.* The three-way handshake works as follows:

- The requestor of the connection sends a synchronization signal and an initial sequence number to the destination end point.
- A receiver receives the synchronization signal (segment), and sends back the acknowledgment, sequence number, and synchronization signals.

- On receiving both signals, the requestor sends the acknowledgment back to the receiver.

Since TCP is built upon unreliable packet delivery services (IP), messages can be lost, delayed, duplicated, or delivered out of order. The three-way handshake is both necessary and sufficient for the proper synchronization. It guarantees that both sides are ready to transfer data (and know it), and both have agreed on initial sequence numbers. TCP uses packet sequencing to ensure proper order of packet delivery. TCP uses checksum method for error detection, and further enhances the guaranteed delivery protocol by using retransmission of messages in the event of time-outs. Once the connection is established, TCP provides for transfer of data from one socket to another. The most popular methods for TCP data transfer are as follows.

- Segmented data transfer allows TCP to send data in segments across the network. Segment sizes can be adjusted to provide for the best efficiency.

- Push mode forces TCP to send all data without network efficiency considerations being involved. It is used when an immediate data transfer is required.

### 7.5.4   Internet services

From the user point of view, TCP/IP internetworking appears to be a set of application programs capable of communicating with each other over the network. The following are the most popular applications of the TCP/IP internet.

- *Electronic mail.* This allows users to prepare memos and documents and to send them to other individual network users and user groups. TCP/IP supports the Simple Mail Transfer Protocol (SMTP). SMTP provides for return receipts, message/mail forwarding, and other useful features.

- *File transfer.* TCP/IP supports file transfer programs which allow users to send large files (e.g., images or entire libraries) across the network. File transfer facilities are provided by a mechanism known as the File Transfer Protocol (FTP).

  FTP allows for a record transfer, a block (a group of records) transfer, or an image transfer (irrespective of the file content). FTP may support some character conversion (ASCII to EBCDIC, for example) before a transfer begins.

- *Remote access to a remote system* (remote login). This allows a user logged into one computer to connect to a remote computer and establish an interactive session with it. To a user it looks like the user's terminal (keyboard and display) is directly attached to the remote system. An example of the TCP/IP remote access application is TEL-NET—a virtual terminal facility that allows a user to connect to a remote system as though the user's terminal is physically attached to the remote system.

## 7.6 DNA

Digital Equipment Corporation (DEC) has been particularly support-ive of network connectivity for networks based on DEC products as well as for networks built by other vendors. Interconnection of DEC networks is based on DEC's proprietary network architecture—Digital Network Architecture (DNA)—and on the family of products that implement that architecture, known as DECnet.

### 7.6.1 History

In 1974, in order to help leverage machine sales to current and poten-tial customers by providing communication facilities between various DEC systems, Digital Equipment Corporation undertook the develop-ment of a communication and network architecture. The architecture was called the Digital Network Architecture (DNA).

The suite of communication products, called DECnet, were designed to offer cohesive, seamless communication capabilities between dis-similar processor architecture and dissimilar operating systems.

The resulting architecture—DNA—was created as a peer-to-peer net-work product. This means that no one node is the "master" node, a con-troller or owner of the network. All DECnet nodes may converse with all other DECnet nodes as long as they follow proper communication proto-cols—DNA protocols. Needless to say, such a peer-to-peer network archi-tecture makes networking very flexible. DNA is easy to configure for major hardware and software changes. However, the peer-to-peer design and the lack of a central control node make network administration a more difficult task. As a result, constant node polling may be required to obtain information about links, performance, bottlenecks, delays, etc.

### 7.6.2 DNA phases

When DNA was developed, it was recognized that keeping track of soft-ware version numbers on different systems could present a significant configuration problem. To resolve some of the issues, DEC introduced *phases* of network software release, with a certain level of functional-ity being imposed on each phase. Each phase of DECnet specifies

- the operating system(s) supported by the phase
- the communications hardware supported by the phase
- new features introduced in the phase

In addition, DECnet phases are designed to be downward compatible for the immediately previous phase, which allows two consecutive phases to coexist during a phase-to-phase migration period.

The phase mechanism allowed DEC to properly configure and activate dissimilar systems once the appropriate DECnet products for the given phase were available. To date, DECnet has evolved through five phases.

### Phase I

DECnet Phase I was originally offered in 1976, and was intended to supply basic file transfer functions and task-to-task communication. Phase I implementation was rather limited. Not only did DECnet Phase I not conform to the standards (of course, the major networking standards were started around 1978), it supported communication for only a few nodes via the simplest asynchronous communication hardware, supported few operating systems, and routing was not available.

### Phase II

DECnet Phase II was implemented to offer much better conformance to the ISO standard—OSI reference model. Manual routing was introduced, and many more operating systems had been supported, including DEC's VMS operating system.

### Phase III

DECnet Phase III provided full routing functionality, expanded file transfer, and task-to-task communications facilities. DECnet Phase III introduced several new features:

- Alternate link mapping allowed DEC nodes on dissimilar networks to communicate.

- The concept of the remote (virtual) terminal allowed a user to log into a remote system as if it were a local host.

- Transparent programming facilities (for DEC VAX systems) allow a programmer to simply "open" a remote communication facility similar to opening of a file. The remote program is then treated as a sequential file, and read and write operations are used in order to receive and send messages.

## Phase IV

DECnet Phase IV was introduced in 1984 and offered some enhancements to better conformance with the ISO's OSI standard. To expand its influence in the world of local area networks and personal computers, the support of Ethernet LAN, MS-DOS (from Microsoft Corporation), and Ultrix (DEC's version of UNIX operating system) was added in Phase IV. Thus, Phase IV marked a new era for DECnet by providing a DEC product on a non-DEC computer and non-DEC operating system. Phase IV opened the way for third-party vendors to offer DECnet Phase IV compatible systems for non-DEC supported hardware and operating systems (including various UNIX implementations and Apple's MacIntosh).

## Phase V

DECnet Phase V support was announced in December of 1987. Phase V is a new evolutionary step for the DNA, since it was designed to provide full OSI capabilities while maintaining the look and feel of the DECnet. DECnet Phase V expanded its support for the OSI standards, including usage of OSI protocols at all seven layers (where reasonable and supportable), thus allowing Phase V to communicate with other OSI-based systems. This complex and ambitious goal is being implemented in stages over the next several years.

In addition to full OSI capabilities, DECnet Phase V provides support for new features—distributed naming services, distributed file and queueing services, File Transfer and Management (FTAM), Virtual Terminal Protocol (VTP), domain networks, and other capabilities.

### 7.6.3    Architecture

The DNA is a layered architecture. Similar to the OSI reference model, DNA layers communicate with each other to provide desired communication functionality. Each of the layers uses a different type of protocol and has different functionality. Users gain access to the DNA from the top layers, and the packet of user information is formed and sent from the originating node to its final destination. Incoming packets travel up the layers until they reach their destination—a program or a user interface. Figure 7.7 illustrates Phase V DNA architecture and its relationship to the OSI model.

DNA's session control and transport layers are responsible for information packets routing. The three lower layers—network, data link control, and physical—perform all physical network functions, including interfaces to the communication hardware.

DECnet, the implementation of the Digital Network Architecture, maintains two databases that are critical to its functionality: the permanent database and the volative database. The permanent database

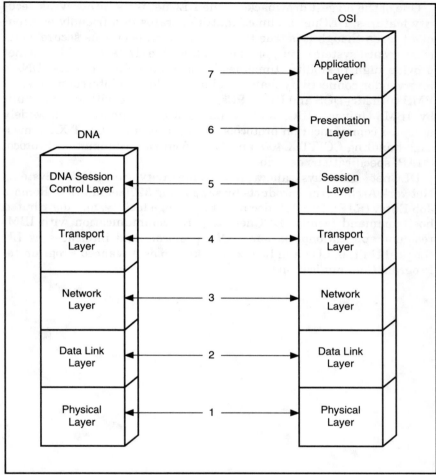

**Figure 7.7**   Phase V DNA architecture and OSI

stores static information about the node, its interfaces, and network program status (states) after the node is activated. The permanent database is read at DECnet initialization time, and its information is loaded into memory. The volative database is, in effect, a set of memory-resident tables that is created at the DECnet initialization time. The volative database is used to keep track of interface and adjacent node status, the routing matrix, and various counters. By definition, the volative database exists from DECnet initialization time until system shutdown or the network is stopped. Both databases can easily be modified by the network or system manager which facilitates network maintenance and administration.

One of the biggest drawbacks of the DECnet is its rather weak security features. DECnet assumes that it operates in a friendly environment (even though it is true that any network is only as secure as its least secure system). But, on the positive side, DNA and the DECnet provide high flexibility, timeliness, and robust functionality. DNA's intervendor connectivity features allow DECnet to interconnect VAX/VMS with MS-DOS and IBM's PCs, and to interface with systems built by IBM, Univac, CDC, and Wang. DECnet supports such widely accepted communication protocols as Ethernet and CCITT X.25, message-handling CCITT X.400, and Manufacturing Automation Protocol (MAP) specifications described earlier.

DECnet gateways allow interconnectivity to IBM's Systems Network Architecture products by supporting 3270 emulation, Remote Job Entry (RJE), DISOSS document exchange facility, and distributed host command facility. DECnet supports communication with IBM-resident applications via such SNA protocols and interfaces as LU (Logical Unit) 0, LU2 and LU6.2 (also known as Advanced Program-to-Program Communications, or APPC).

# Advanced Program-to-Program Communication Overview

As was stated previously, client/server computing is a special case of distributed processing. It is cooperative processing between clients and servers. Interestingly enough, Advanced Program-to-Program Communication (APPC) is a program-to-program communications protocol for IBM's cooperative processing strategy. While not the only architecture for program-to-program communication, APPC is probably the most complete and therefore the most complex architecture. It has been defined as a part of IBM's Systems Network Architecture and provides a rich set of interprogram communications services. APPC permits peer communications between distributed processing programs at SNA network nodes that support the APPC architecture.

APPC is the key communication component of IBM's Systems Application Architecture (SAA). SAA is a continuously evolving set of selected software interfaces, conventions, and protocols designed to provide a framework for developing integrated applications with cross-system consistency.

The APPC architecture is a set of protocols used by application programs in different processors to communicate with each other as peers in the execution of a distributed transaction. APPC facilitates the development of distributed applications by providing an architectural foundation for program-to-program communications independent of the type of processor or operating system in which these applications exist. As such, APPC is extremely important to the client/server architecture. It is widely used in various distributed and client/server implementations, especially those based on IBM products. Its architecture and features have been adopted into such standards as the OSI reference model and X/Open's XA architecture.

This chapter describes APPC and the SNA logical unit type 6.2 (LU6.2), on which the APPC protocols are based, as a functionally layered system. As was shown in the previous chapter, every SNA node contains a physical unit (PU) that provides physical connectivity between devices. Every end user gains access to an SNA network through a logical unit, or LU. Both terms—APPC and LU6.2—are often used interchangeably and referred to as APPC/LU6.2.

## 8.1 APPC DESIGN OBJECTIVES

The structure and functions of APPC/LU6.2 are defined to satisfy the following requirements:

- *Simultaneous Activation.* In a distributed transaction processing environment, APPC/LU6.2 allows the conversation partners to be active simultaneously so that the partners do not have to wait for each other for every action.

- *Efficient Allocation of Resources.* This includes not only local resources, but also sessions as communication resources. APPC/LU6.2 provides transaction programs with exclusive use of sessions in the form of conversations as part of their communication resources.

- *Minimum Conversation Overhead.* APPC/LU6.2 achieves this by session scheduling and conversation allocation over a pool of available sessions.

- *Various Conversation Life.* Conversations should only last for a period of time determined by the conversing programs. Thus, APPC/LU6.2 supports conversations varying from one short message to many-message multiple exchange conversations. If need be, APPC/LU6.2 allows conversations to continue indefinitely, terminating them only when failures occur.

- *Attention Mechanism.* APPC/LU6.2 provides an attention mechanism to handle asynchronous nonerror events.

- *Error Detection and Notification.* APPC/LU6.2 provides means to detect errors and notify conversation partners about them.

- *Commitment Protocol.* APPC/LU6.2 provides a Sync Point protocol to support error recovery and the distributed update capabilities of protected resources in a distributed transaction processing environment.

- *Mode of Service.* APPC/LU6.2 is designed to support a desired mode of transmission service (interactive or batch).

- *Flexibility via Subset Definitions.* APPC/LU6.2 functions are grouped into subsets. These subsets allow APPC/LU6.2 to support a base function set common to all implementations of LU6.2, as well as optional sets, which may contain additional APPC/LU6.2 functionality.

## 8.2  TRANSACTION PROGRAMS

APPC/LU6.2 is designed to provide application programs with support functions for program-to-program communication. Direct users of APPC/LU6.2 are application transaction programs. An *application transaction program* is a user-written program designed to perform communication requests and other functions of distributed applications. Utility and management services to application transaction programs (and SNA logical units) are provided by *service transaction programs*. Service transaction programs are different from application transaction programs. They are SNA-defined and are considered to be part of APPC/LU6.2.

A typical transaction program (TP) is different from a program in general by the way it is invoked and the communication functions it initiates. A transaction program is invoked by another transaction program or by the LU6.2 via an *Attach* mechanism. The invoking TP (invoker) can initiate a conversation with another TP, which in turn is *connected* with its invoker via a *conversation*. For example, consider a CICS (Customer Information Control System) application transaction program that is designed to participate in a CICS Distributed Transaction Processing. In this case, the first application TP (TP-1) initiates a conversation with another TP (TP-2) by sending some data and control information. TP-1 uses special commands that are a part of the CICS implementation of APPC/LU6.2. The invoking program, TP-2, gets started by TP-1 and receives data sent to it by TP-1 (see Fig. 8.1).

A transaction program uses APPC/LU6.2 to communicate with other transaction programs by issuing transaction program *verbs*. Sometimes, an LU6.2 may issue transaction program verbs on behalf of a transaction programs.

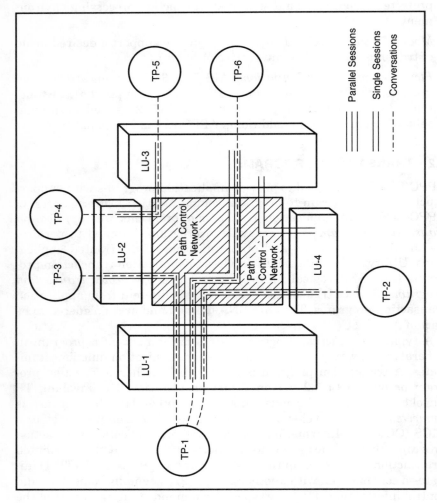

**Figure 8.1** LU and SNA network

## 8.3 DISTRIBUTED TRANSACTION PROCESSING

Distributed Transaction Processing, or *DTP,* is a process where two or more programs, usually residing in different systems, cooperate in order to perform certain required functions. That cooperation includes program intercommunication and local resource sharing. As a result, each program can use the other program's CPU cycles, data bases, queues, and interfaces, such as display and keyboard devices, to perform its portion of the required functionality.

APPC/LU6.2 participates in the DTP by acting as an interface between programs and the network control layer (for example, SNA's Path Control Network layer). In essence, APPC/LU6.2 allows a transaction program to invoke remote programs and to communicate with them. It is important to realize that APPC provides only one type of communication—*program-to-program.* Workstation operators, for example, do not communicate with LU6.2 or use APPC directly. They use local workstation programming support which is designed to interact with the LU6.2 (e.g., keyboards and display terminals appear as microcode, or fixed programs, to the LU6.2).

To be able to communicate with each other, two transaction programs must establish a logical connection, or *conversation,* between them. APPC/LU6.2 assists one transaction program in initiating a conversation with another transaction program over a *session* held between two logical units (an LU-LU session). The portion of a session allocated to each LU6.2 is called a *half-session.* An active conversation has exclusive use of a session, even though transaction programs cannot explicitly request use of a particular session. Sessions are not "visible" to transaction programs. Conversations, on the other hand, are. Successive conversations are allowed to reuse the same session.

While conversations, as logical connections between transaction programs, may be short-lived, session are long-lived, and may be used by more than one conversation. Two SNA LU6.2s are capable of supporting multiple active APPC sessions between them. These sessions are called *parallel* sessions.

Another feature of APPC/LU6.2 is its ability to support many transaction programs concurrently, serially, or both. Each transaction program may have multiple conversations with one or more other transaction programs. Each conversation connects a pair of transaction programs, and all active concurrent conversations constitute one *distributed transaction.* For example, consider that transaction programs TP-1 and TP-2 are connected by a conversation, and TP-2 has an active conversation with TP-3 concurrently (see Fig. 8.1). At the same time TP-3 is connected by a conversation to TP-4. Then TP-1, TP-2, TP-3, and TP-4 are all participants in the same distributed transaction.

An extremely important feature of APPC/LU6.2 in a distributed transaction processing environment is that APPC provides synchronization services for *protected* transaction resources. These are local resources whose state changes are logged. Therefore, any changes performed by a transaction can be backed out, and the resources can be restored to a consistent before-change state if a transaction fails. APPC/LU6.2 provides *SyncPoint* and *Rollback* functions for distributed transaction error recovery.

## 8.4   LU6.2 PROTOCOL BOUNDARIES AND COMPONENTS

APPC/LU6.2 is designed as a *universal* method for peer-to-peer, program-to-program communications. As such, it can be implemented on a variety of hardware/software platforms and transaction programs written for different environments and in different languages.

That is why the architectural definitions of APPC/LU6.2 are specified in generic terms, called the transaction program *protocol boundary,* and represent the APPC/LU6.2 interface-to-application transaction programs. The interfaces between different implementations of APPC/LU6.2 and transaction programs are dependent on the particular environment. Each programming environment that provides APPC/LU6.2 protocol boundary is called an *Application Programming Interface,* or *API.*

Depending on the implementation environment, APPC/LU6.2 uses various subsets of the protocol boundary to interface with transaction programs. One set of transaction program verbs, for example, may consist of the subsets of verbs for mapped conversations, basic conversations, and SNA Distributed Services (SNADS).

In terms of the layered APPC/LU6.2 architecture, the subsets of the protocol boundary represent sublayers within APPC/LU6.2. Protocol boundaries exist between layers or sublayers of the node, as well as between peer components of the same layer (see Fig. 8.2). A protocol boundary between two layers or sublayers of the same node defines data exchange rules called *layered protocols.* A protocol boundary between two peer components of the same layer is called *peer protocol.*

For example, the transaction program layered protocol boundary allows a transaction program to request LU6.2 services to communicate with other transaction programs. On the other hand, the transaction program protocol boundary can be viewed as a boundary between peers—two transaction programs. Actual exchanges between peers is accomplished by exchanges between layers (interlayer exchanges).

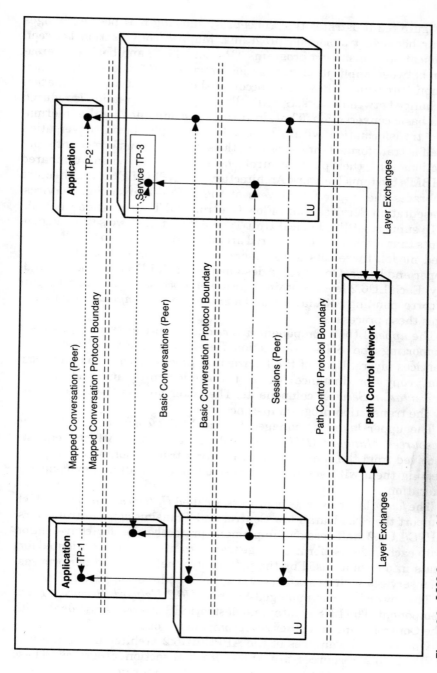

**Figure 8.2** LU6.2 protocol boundaries

Figure 8.2 illustrates that concept by showing how peer exchanges occur between transaction programs. Mapped conversation between application transaction programs TP-1 and TP-2, and basic conversation between application transaction program TP-1 and service transaction program TP-3, are accomplished by actual information exchange between layers. Specifically, mapped conversation is reduced to a basic conversation. That, in turn, is accompanied by the information transformation within layers. For example, basic conversation itself is transformed into a session, the session is transformed into connections in the path control network, etc. When compared to IBM's Systems Network Architecture, the APPC/LU6.2 architecture embraces the upper four layers of the SNA—Transaction Services, Presentation Services, Data Flow Control, and Transmission Control.

To support APPC, Logical Unit Type 6.2 contains two sets of components that implement the layered architecture. Similar to the SNA layered model, these sets of components are organized into two layers: upper and lower. One layer is designed for each LU6.2 protocol boundary. Each LU6.2 layer contains a group of *processes* that support a pair of corresponding SNA layers, and a *management component* that manages these processes.

The *upper* LU6.2 component layer consists of transaction processes supporting the SNA Transaction Services and SNA Presentation Services layers. Each of the transaction processes contains an execution copy (or instance) of a transaction program and certain *Presentation Services* components. The latter process the verbs issued by the transaction program instance.

The upper layer is managed by the LU6.2 component called the *Resources Manager (RM)*. The RM reacts to the Attach requests received from the remote LUs by creating transaction processes, connecting them with session, and destroying them after they complete executions.

The *lower* layer consists of processes called *Half-Sessions (HS)*, which support the SNA Data Flow Control and Transmission Control layers. APPC/LU6.2 half-sessions implement protocol rules for conversation data exchanges, perform message transformation from TP-oriented formats into formats used by the path control network, and perform session services such as session cryptography and session pacing.

The lower layer is managed by the *LU6.2 Network Services (LNS)* component. The LNS creates and destroys HS processes and deals with the Control Point and other SNA components outside LU6.2.

One of the advantages of the APPC/LU6.2 architecture is the way APPC/LU6.2 resources are known to transaction programs. These resources are referred to by a transaction program by installation-defined names, rather than by actual network addresses or line char-

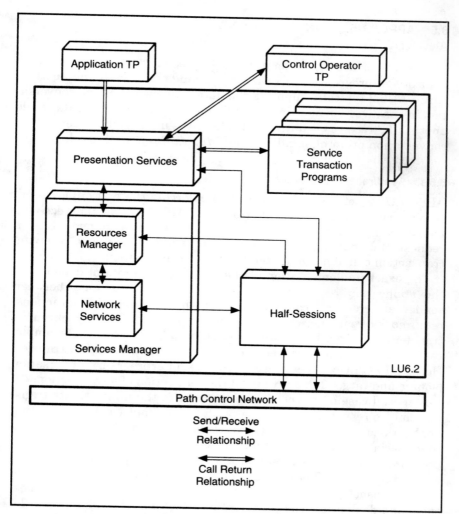

**Figure 8.3**  LU6.2 components

acteristics. Thus, a transaction program's interface with LU6.2 is transparent of the network's implementation and configuration details. One transaction program, for example, invokes another by a transaction program name, and uses an LU6.2 name to identify the partner LU. This approach makes APPC/LU6.2 very useful in implementing client/server architecture over a distributed network.

For clarification purposes, the following convention is adopted: the source or local TP (source or local LU) is the one which initiates the conversation with the target or remote TP (or target/remote LU).

## 8.5  APPC/LU6.2 CONVERSATIONS AND STATES

Conversations are logical connections between logical units over which transaction programs and LUs can exchange data with one another. APPC/LU6.2 typically supports the data exchange over the conversation in one direction at a time. One TP has the right to send data, while another TP receives it until the sender gives up its right to send. This conversation protocol, is called a *half-duplex flip-flop* protocol.

### 8.5.1  Send/receive protocols

APPC/LU6.2 acts as a "traffic cop" in enforcing the half-duplex send/receive conversation protocol. However, APPC allows the receiving transaction program to send an error indicator or a change-direction request, thus putting itself into the send state. Of course, a receiving transaction can abnormally terminate the conversation.

The exact implementation of the send/receive protocol depends on the application requirements. The degree of concurrency between sender and receiver can vary from high synchronous interactions, required by real-time on-line inquiry applications, to asynchronous transfers, required by certain distributed applications. For example, real-time on-line inquiry requires synchronous information transfer. Here, APPC/LU6.2 needs to keep the interprogram conversation (source and target TP) active until the completion of a transaction.

A special case of a synchronous transfer is the intermediate transmission no-response requirements of, for example, status reporting applications. APPC uses a *one-way conversation* as a way of handling that special case of synchronous conversation. The source transaction program initiates a conversation with the target transaction program, sends data and deallocates the conversation. A message reaches the target transaction program, which in turn is activated, receives a message, and deallocates the conversation. However, since the source TP does not expect any reply, it could have terminated itself while the message was in transit. Thus, the source and target transaction programs are allowed to be inactive at the same time.

When a distributed application requirement is to allow both sender and receiver to exchange data at their convenience, as in the document distribution applications, APPC/LU6.2 provides support for *asynchronous* transfers via a *store-and-forward* protocol. Here, the sender sends data to the destination via a local *service* transaction program, which can store the message in a queue until such time when the destination transaction program is ready to receive the message.

To alleviate the possible interpretation problems that may be encountered when different transaction programs use different internal data formats, APPC/LU6.2 provides common formats for data transmission, called mapping (discussed in more detail later in this chapter).

### 8.5.2 Conversation states

APPC conversations can exist in several architecturally-defined states. These states are the result of actions taken by participating logical units and transaction programs. Conversation requests issued by a local or remote transaction program, as well as network errors, may all cause a conversation state to change.

At the same time, the state of the conversation determines the actions that a particular transaction program is allowed to take (i.e., the commands that a TP is allowed to issue). If a communication request is issued for a conversation in the disallowed state, it causes state check ABEND conditions. For example, a send request issued for a conversation on which only receipt of data is allowed will generate such an error. The APPC/LU6.2 conversation protocol boundary defines the following conversation states:

- *Send state*—TP can send data, request confirmation or sync point.
- *Receive state*—TP can receive data from a remote TP.
- *Reset state*—TP can allocate the conversation.
- *Confirm state*—TP can reply to a confirmation request.
- *Defer state*—TP can request confirmation, sync point, or flush a send buffer, all in order to enter into Reset or Receive states.
- *Syncpoint state*—TP can respond to the sync point request.
- *Backed out state*—TP can respond to the "backed out" indication.
- *Deallocate state*—TP can deallocate the conversation.

APPC conversation states are clearly applicable to the client/server computing model. For example, in order to initiate a client/server interaction, the client must be in a Send state, while the server must be in the Receive state.

## 8.6  APPC/LU6.2 SESSIONS

Conversations between transaction programs are carried over sessions between their respective logical units. Therefore, one of the principal functions of APPC/LU6.2 is to provide session services between communication partners.

### 8.6.1    Session allocation

*SESSIONS.* A particular session is used by only one pair of conversing transaction programs at a time. In a multiprocessing, multiple-workstation environment, APPC/LU6.2 should allow for multiple concurrent transactions by supporting two or more sessions at a time, even with the same partner. Logical units that can support parallel sessions (multiple concurrent sessions with the same partner) are called parallel-session LUs, even if only one such session is currently active.

There are some logical units, however, that can have only one active session at a time. Such LUs are called single-session LUs. Any session they support, regardless of whether it is with a single-session or with a parallel-session LU, is called a single session. The session classification depends on the type of the participating logical units. All sessions between a pair of LUs are either single or parallel. In other words, a parallel-session LU6.2 can have one or more concurrent parallel sessions with one or more parallel-session LUs, and one single session with each single-session LU.

When a session is activated by an LU6.2, or a previously used session is freed, the LU6.2 places the session in a *session pool*. When a TP initiates a new conversation, LU6.2 allocates a session from the session pool, provided that one is available.

Thus, LU6.2 avoids the time- and resource-consuming session activation process by allowing sessions to be reused by successive conversations. The configuration and size of the session pool is specified by an operator.

*WHO IS FIRST.* When a session is allocated, each end of the session can try to start a peer level conversation at the same time, thus creating a session contention. To resolve this contention, the *session contention polarity* is specified for each session. A session for which a local LU6.2 is designated to win an allocation race is called a *contention-winner* session, or *first-speaker* session.

A session that a local LU6.2 is designated to lose to its partner is called a *contention-loser* session. The contention-loser LU6.2 will then *bid* the contention-winner to use the session. That is why contention-loser sessions are also called *bidder* sessions.

### 8.6.2    Session characteristics

There are certain session characteristics that apply to the actual session activation/deactivation and usage. While these characteristics are beyond the scope of this book, descriptions of a primary/secondary LU, session pacing, and BIND requests deserve a more detailed examination.

*PRIMARY AND SECONDARY LU.* When one LU6.2 activates a session with its partner, it does so by sending a BIND request message.

The logical unit that sends the BIND request (activates the session) is called the *primary* LU (PLU). The LU that receives the BIND is called the *secondary* LU (SLU). The same Logical Unit can be primary on one session and secondary on another. The PLU always has the first use of a session. That is, it can always initiate the first conversation on the session, regardless of the session contention polarity. The contention-winner LU "repossesses" its right to initiate conversations when the first conversation completes.

*PACING.* One LU may send data to another LU faster than the receiver can process it. To prevent that situation from happening, APPC/LU6.2 observes a *session-level pacing* protocol. At session activation time, communicating partners exchange the number and the size of the messages they can process at one time. The sending LU6.2 will not exceed the receiving LU acceptance limit until it receives an acknowledgment from the receiver that it is ready to receive another message.

*BIND REQUEST.* To activate a session between two LU6.2 units, a BIND request is sent from the PLU to the SLU. The BIND request carries the PLU's suggested session parameters that may be based on the PLU's implementation-dependent support or on the installation-specified values currently in effect.

The SLU receives the BIND and uses it to determine whether it can accept the requested session parameters. The SLU does not reject the BIND because of any incompatibility it may find with the parameters specified in the BIND. Instead, if the BIND format is valid, the SLU sends a positive response. This response includes a complete set of session parameters that can either match or not match the ones sent on the BIND request. The BIND session parameters for which the SLU may choose different options are known as *negotiable* parameters.

## 8.7  APPC SECURITY

An important feature of APPC/LU6.2 is its ability to provide installations with security functions. There are three security functions that APPC/LU6.2 can optionally provide: LU-LU verification, end-user verification, and session cryptography.

An LU-LU verification is a *session-level security* protocol which is invoked when the session is activated. It is performed by a three-step exchange between two LUs, with each LU using an LU-LU password and the Data Encryption Standard (DES) algorithm. One LU-LU password is assigned between each pair of LUs and is used for all sessions between these logical units.

This is how the LU-LU verification works:

1. At session initiation, the PLU sends random data (in BIND request) to an SLU.

2. The SLU uses the LU-LU password as input to a DES algorithm to encipher that random data, and returns the enciphered data along with its own random data to the PLU in its BIND response.

3. The PLU compares the received enciphered data with the original data enciphered by PLU using the same LU-LU password and DES algorithm. If the two do not compare, the verification fails, session activation fails, and a security violation is recorded.

*End-user verification* is the *conversation-level* security protocol that is used to confirm the identity of the partner transaction program (end-user). End-user verification can include a user-id and password supplied by the end user initiating a request. When LU6.2 receives such a request, it verifies that the security fields match the user-id and the password known to it. If a match is not found, the request is rejected.

Finally, to prevent the data from being interpreted and/or modified while in transit, LU6.2 can provide *session cryptography*. Here, all user data is enciphered at the source LU and deciphered at the target LU, using a cryptographic key known to both conversing partners.

## 8.8   APPC ERROR HANDLING

Transaction processing, like any other kind of data processing, can be affected by errors. Perhaps the biggest difference between errors in transaction processing and conventional batch processing is the variety of errors affecting transaction processing.

### 8.8.1   Types of errors

*APPLICATION ERRORS.* These are application processing-related errors, such as errors in the data processing and application processing logic. For example, application-specific handling of input/output errors, end-of-file, and record-not-found conditions can all adversely affect an entire application. However, since these errors are application-dependent, the responsibility for error detection and error recovery belong to the application transaction program.

*LOCAL RESOURCE FAILURES.* In a transaction processing environment, local resources are defined as nonnetwork resources (for example, disk and tape storage). Local resources can be protected or unprotected. The recovery of unprotected resources such as sequential files on a local DASD subsystem is the responsibility of a transaction program, Database Management System, or the operating system supporting these resources.

However, if the resources are defined as protected (such as a database file with logging turned on), then the transaction program can use the sync point function of APPC/LU6.2 to coordinate the protected resource recovery together with the nonnetwork operating system facilities. One good example of this is the use of APPC synchronization level 2 on LU6.2 conversations in the CICS/VS environment.

*PROGRAM, SESSION, and CONVERSATION FAILURES.* Some errors cause a transaction program to terminate abnormally. If there were any conversations active with the transaction program that were not deallocated by the error, APPC/LU6.2 attempts to recover from the error. This recovery is performed by deallocating these conversations, thus freeing the session for use by other transaction programs. Beyond these actions, error recovery can be performed by application programs and/or installation- or user-supplied error exits.

If an unrecoverable failure of a session occurs due to incorrect protocols received or link failure, the session itself fails, and LU6.2 is notified of the session outage. If there were no active conversations on the failed session, the transaction program is not affected. Otherwise, the transaction program is also notified of a conversation failure. Conversation failures are failures of the underlying session. These failures are reported to the transaction program in the form of the return codes. Even though the session and conversation cannot be recovered, the APPC/LU6.2 will attempt to activate another session, if desired, to another instance of a transaction program.

*LU6.2 FAILURE.* An LU6.2 can fail as a result of hardware or software malfunction. Often such failures appear to the remote LUs as session failures, and these remote LUs will attempt to recover as they would from a typical session failure.

### 8.8.2  Error recovery support

LU6.2 is architected in such a way that it supports error recovery protocols designed to assist transaction programs in their attempt to recover from application and local resource failures.

The program error recovery functions supported by LU6.2 allow application transaction programs to take certain actions in case of failure:

*Confirmation* protocols allow a transaction program to ask for positive or negative acknowledgment from the partner transaction program. Such acknowledgment is generated by a transaction program using special APPC-supported commands (CONFIRMED and SEND_ERROR verbs), and is application-logic-dependent.

*Program Error Indication* functions allow one transaction program to inform its conversation partner of an error.

*Sync Point* protocol is a distributed error-recovery function of APPC/LU6.2. It supports recoverability and consistency among distributed transactions and their resources.

*Abnormal Conversation Deallocation* function of APPC/LU6.2 allows a transaction program to terminate a conversation when the continuation of the conversation is either impossible or meaningless because of detected errors.

*LU6.2 RECOVERY FUNCTIONS.* For certain errors recovery is initiated by the LU6.2 itself, or by an operator. However, in the case of an unrecoverable session error, a deadlock, or a loop, LU6.2 is capable of terminating a session abnormally. The transaction program is then notified of the conversation failure.

## 8.9  APPC APPLICATION PROGRAM INTERFACES

Each APPC/LU6.2 implementation has one or more programming environments that support various APPC function sets. Each such environment is called an Application Programming Interface (API). There are two types of LU6.2 API implementations:

- *Open API* supports user-written transaction programs such as a Data Base Management System (DBMS). An Open API provides verbs and parameters which cover the base function set and, depending on API implementation, some optional function sets.

- *Closed API* implementations support only an implementation-defined set of service transaction programs (like the service transaction programs for the IBM's Document Interchange Architecture, or DIA). Closed API provides only a limited set of verbs and parameters required by a specific transaction, and user-written transaction programs are not supported.

### 8.9.1  Principal base and optional functions

The protocol boundaries of APPC/LU6.2 are organized into subsets which divide LU6.2 into hierarchical layers and support peer exchanges. One of the reasons for organizing APPC/LU6.2 functions and protocols into function sets is the desire to support implementation and environment transparency. Thus, the APPC/LU6.2 function sets consist of a *base function set* and a number of *optional function sets*.

The base function set provides basic communication functions common to all APPC/LU6.2 implementations, while optional function sets are implementation-dependent and serve to satisfy various additional requirements. By design:

- All APPC/LU6.2 implementations of a particular function set provide that set's functionality according to the protocol boundary.
- Any APPC/LU6.2 implementation that supports one function in an optional function set, supports all other functions in that optional function set.

This design principle of the APPC architecture defines an extremely critical feature of APPC/LU6.2 connectivity. Namely, all APPC/LU6.2 implementations can communicate with each other using the base function set, and any two APPC/LU6.2 implementations using the same optional function set can communicate with each other using that optional function set.

Optional functions can be divided into two groups:

- *Send options* define formats and protocols to be sent, but do not affect the receiving of data. Send options can be sent to all LUs.
- *Receive options* define what can be received as well as what can be sent. The receive options are described by the source LU6.2 and the source transaction program. They can be rejected by a receiving LU if it or its transaction program cannot support the requested receive options.

The most important base functions are called principal base functions. They include:

- *Basic Conversations* formats and protocols. Open API implementations support basic conversation verbs, but not necessarily in all programming languages. For example, CICS/VS supports both basic and mapped conversations, but the command level interface does not support basic conversations.
- *Mapped Conversations* are supported by all Open API LU6.2 implementations, but most of the implementations support high-level interfaces only. For example, mapped conversations support in CICS/VS is implemented for COBOL and PL/I.

The principal optional functions include:

- *Mapping.* This is an optional function for mapped conversations.
- *Sync Point.* This is an optional function for both basic and mapped conversations.

- *Security.* This is a set of optional functions designed to provide LU-LU verification, end-user verification, and data encryption protection for APPC/LU6.2 supported sessions.

- *Program Initialization Parameters* (PIP) functions. These are designed to set up a target transaction program and to give it a set of initial parameters.

There is also a set of performance options which provide the means to improve the performance of transaction programs for specific application transaction requirements. A good example of these options is an option to eliminate certain acknowledgments from conversation protocols. Note that these options belong to a class of send options. Therefore, if one transaction program supports them, but its partner TP and LU do not, the transaction program can still operate correctly.

### 8.9.2 APPC verbs overview

The LU6.2 protocol boundary is the structured interface that defines the formatted functions, called *verbs,* and the protocols, or rules, for the allowed sequences of verbs. The verb protocols are defined in terms of resource *states* as follows: *A transaction program can issue a particular verb only when the resource affected by that verb is in a proper state for that verb.*

Knowledge of the verbs and states of the APPC/LU6.2 protocol boundary not only allows users to design distributed application and distributed transaction programs, but also eases the design and coding process. APPC/LU6.2 verbs are designed to allow programs to communicate as peers with each other, independent of the underlying network configuration. The verbs are issued from transaction programs that follow the same general structure as that shown on Fig. 8.4. Of course, a particular APPC/LU6.2 implementation may provide a programming language that uses syntax and statements different from those used in this chapter. Complete list of LU6.2 verbs can be found in App. C.

In general, a transaction program:

- has a name

- begins with a list of resources and their parameters, called program initialization parameters (PIP)

- contains APPC verbs and other program statements that comprise the transaction processing portion of the transaction program

- terminates by an implementation-defined statement (RETURN in our example), that ends program execution by returning control to

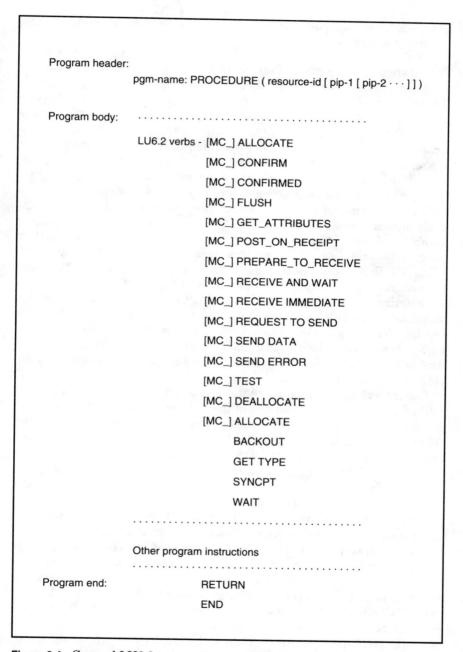

Program header:

        pgm-name: PROCEDURE ( resource-id [ pip-1 [ pip-2 · · · ] ] )

Program body:    · · · · · · · · · · · · · · · · · · · · · · · · · · · · · · · · · ·

        LU6.2 verbs - [MC_] ALLOCATE

                   [MC_] CONFIRM

                   [MC_] CONFIRMED

                   [MC_] FLUSH

                   [MC_] GET_ATTRIBUTES

                   [MC_] POST_ON_RECEIPT

                   [MC_] PREPARE_TO_RECEIVE

                   [MC_] RECEIVE AND WAIT

                   [MC_] RECEIVE IMMEDIATE

                   [MC_] REQUEST TO SEND

                   [MC_] SEND DATA

                   [MC_] SEND ERROR

                   [MC_] TEST

                   [MC_] DEALLOCATE

                   [MC_] ALLOCATE

                      BACKOUT

                      GET TYPE

                      SYNCPT

                      WAIT

        · · · · · · · · · · · · · · · · · · · · · · · · · · · · · · · · · ·

        Other program instructions

        · · · · · · · · · · · · · · · · · · · · · · · · · · · · · · · · · ·

Program end:           RETURN

                     END

**Figure 8.4**  General LU6.2 transaction program structure

LU6.2 (at which point LU6.2 may deallocate all conversations and other resources)

A transaction program that communicates with another, partner transaction program must identify its partner to the network. Therefore, one of the resources named in the input parameter list is the resource-id of the conversation that connects the transaction program with its partner. During program execution, the transaction program issues APPC verbs, one at a time, and LU6.2 executes them. Generally speaking, while LU6.2 executes a verb, transaction program execution is suspended. It is resumed when LU6.2 completes the APPC verb processing and returns control to the transaction program.

Conversations between transaction programs use two-way alternate (half-duplex flip-flop) data transfer. A send/receive relationship is established when the conversation is allocated and one transaction program sends data while another transaction program receives it. When the first transaction program finishes sending, it gives the right to send data to its partner, and prepares to receive data.

To optimize transmission traffic, APPC/LU6.2 at each end of the conversation uses buffers for sending and receiving data. LU6.2 at the sending TP places data related to each sending verb into its *send buffer,* thus accumulating data until the amount is sufficient for transmission, or until the transaction program explicitly requests data transmission.

The receiving LU6.2 accumulates incoming data in its *receive buffer* and makes the required portion of the data available to its transaction program when the program issues a verb to receive data. To sum up, APPC/LU6.2 minimizes the actual number of transmissions through the network and provides the receiving transaction program with the data accumulated in advance of the verb issuance, thus reducing processing delays.

The APPC verbs are divided into two major categories— *Conversation* verbs that define the means of the program-to-program communication, and *Control-Operator* verbs that define how the program or operator can control LU6.2 resources. All verbs in this chapter are described from the point of view of the issuing transaction program and its LU6.2—*local* TP and local LU6.2. The other end of a conversation is referred to as a *remote* TP and remote LU6.2.

*CONVERSATION VERBS.* SNA defines two types of LU6.2 conversations: *basic* conversations and *mapped* conversations. Based on a conversation type, the conversation verbs are divided into mapped conversation verbs, type-independent conversation verbs, and basic conversation verbs. *Mapped Conversation Verbs* are used by application transaction programs typically written in high-level programming language. *Basic Conversation verbs* are mostly intended for use by LU6.2 service TPs, even though they can be used by application TPs. The basic and mapped conversation verbs are similar. The difference is in the level of LU6.2-provided support and the processing details. State transitions, conversion of data records into logical records conversation, ABEND conditions, and similar details are all provided for in the logic of a basic conversation program. A mapped conversation program, on the other hand, is isolated from these details by the mapped conversation support of APPC/LU6.2.

The full description of the APPC/LU6.2 verbs can be found in App. C. A list of these verbs and their short description follows:

- ALLOCATE allocates a basic or mapped conversation.
- CONFIRM and CONFIRMED are used to synchronize distributed transactions.
- FLUSH transmits the content of the send buffer.
- SEND_DATA sends data in a logical record format to a remote TP.
- SEND_ERROR informs a remote TP of an error detected by local TP.
- RECEIVE_AND_WAIT waits for information to arrive into the receive buffer.
- RECEIVE_IMMEDIATE attempts to receive information without wait.
- DEALLOCATE deallocates a conversation from the TP.
- PREPARE_TO_RECEIVE changes the conversation state from send to receive.
- REQUEST_TO_SEND asks for a change of direction and permission to send.
- GET_ATTRIBUTES makes information relevant to the conversation available to the transaction program (LU name, mode name, etc.).
- POST_ON_RECEIPT requests posting of the conversation when the information is available to be received by the transaction program.
- TEST tests whether the preceding POST_ON_RECEIPT or REQUEST_TO_SEND posted the conversation.

*Type-Independent Conversation verbs* can be used with both mapped and basic conversations. They are as follows:

- SYNCPT directs all participants in sync point processing to take a sync point.

- BACKOUT is the sync point verb that restores all protected resources in the distributed transaction to the last consistent point (as of the last logical unit of work).

- GET_TYPE returns the resource type (MAPPED CONVERSATION for mapped conversations, BASIC CONVERSATION for basic conversations).

- WAIT waits for a special event (posting) to occur on any mapped or basic conversation.

*CONTROL-OPERATOR VERBS*. These verbs are designed to be used by control-operator transaction programs to perform functions related to the control of LU6.2. The control-operator verbs are divided into three categories: Change-Number-Of-Sessions (CNOS) verbs, Session-Control verbs, and LU6.2 Definition verbs. The last are used to define or modify local LU6.2 parameters.

Incorrect specification or execution of the verbs can cause a transaction program to end abnormally or to generate an ABEND condition. When a transaction program terminates abnormally, it deallocates all active conversations with which it is involved. In order to avoid ABEND conditions, a transaction program must strictly adhere to the verbs specification and continuously monitor states of the conversation.

## 8.10  ADVANTAGES OF APPC

APPC/LU6.2 plays a critical role in providing distributed transaction processing and client/server interactions in a client/server environment. To emphasize the importance of APPC for the distributed transaction processing and the client/server architecture, a brief list of the major advantages of LU6.2 follows:

- APPC provides for application conversations on a peer-to-peer level within an SNA network.

- APPC/LU6.2, combined with SNA Node Type 2.1, supports the Advanced Peer-to-Peer Networking (APPN). APPN allows applications to communicate directly with their partners on remote systems or on other systems that implement the base SNA Low-Entry Networking architecture.

- APPC shields application programmers from system and network considerations by providing a common architecture for general purpose program-to-program communication.

- APPC provides access to a wide variety of systems and concurrent support for a wide range of network configurations.

- APPC allows for distributed transaction processing within the network.

- APPC provides for data format and session protocol transparency.

- APPC provides users with advanced communication functions, such as security.

- APPC/LU6.2 is the session services and program-to-program communications standard defined by SAA. As such, it is included in SAA's Common Communications Support (CCS) and Common Programming Interface for Communications (CPI-C).

- Since APPC is based on the LU6.2 standard, which is IBM's strategic communications architecture for synchronous program-to-program communications, APPC applications written today will be able to communicate with any new hardware and/or operating systems that will support APPC in the future.

- APPC architectural principles are adopted into such open systems standards as ISO's Open System Interconnection and X/Open's XA.

Indeed, APPC is supported in all major IBM platforms, from Personal Computers (APPC/PC and OS/2 Communications Manager) to mainframes (CICS/VS, CICS/ESA, ACF/VTAM, APPC/MVS), and such distributed applications as Distributed Data Facility of IBM's DB2. Independent software vendors (ISV) successfully use APPC for their implementations of efficient data transfer products. APPC is used by IBM and ISVs for the distributed transaction and database processing applications, especially those designed to work in a client/server environment.

Among non-IBM products worth mentioning are XCOM6.2 (Spectrum Concepts, New York, NY)—high-efficiency file transfer software based on APPC/LU6.2, and Sybase's Open Server/CICS (Sybase, Emeryville, CA). The Sybase DBMS is a good example of a client/server architecture implementation. It uses Sybase's database Remote Procedure Calls (RPC) on the client side of the Sybase client/server model, and APPC/LU6.2/CICS on the mainframe database server. In effect, Sybase has put an RPC front-end onto the APPC protocol. Such developments confirm the important role and the applicability of APPC in the client/server architecture.

# 4

# Cooperative Processing and Data Management in a Client/Server Environment

*The first three parts of this book have described the evolution of the computing environments that lead to the emergence of a client/server computing model. Client/server interactions have been defined as the cooperative interactions of various computing components in a distributed environment. This cooperation was shown to promote a particular kind of specialization of client and server nodes in a distributed networking environment.*

*Client/server interactions were described as data communications between clients and servers across network nodes and even networks. And, therefore, the basic principles of data communication and networking and their roles in a client/server architecture were illustrated. This included local and wide area networking and such communication techniques and protocols as Advanced Program-to-Program Communications, Transmission Control Protocol/Internet Protocol, and Remote Procedure Calls.*

*The advantages and potential benefits of a client/server architecture have been linked to the ever-growing role of standards and open systems. Now, the analysis of a client/server architecture can be directed toward specific issues and the significant difficulties associated with the distribution of application components. These are the questions that client/server environment designers should answer:*

- *What is the proper distribution of the application components in the client / server architecture? Where should each of these components (presentation logic, business logic, data logic, and database processing logic) reside?*
- *How should the data be distributed, accessed, and managed?*
- *How can component interactions be implemented?*
- *What are the roles of, and requirements for, distributed transaction management?*
- *How can software distribution and management in a distributed environment be implemented?*
- *How should data and program access security be implemented in a client / server environment?*

*The answers to these questions represent a central part of the client / server architecture. Cooperative client / server processing, distributed data management and distributed transaction processing, software distribution and management, and several particular client / server and distributed environment architectures, are described in Chap. 9 and succeeding chapters.*

# Client/Server and Cooperative Processing

Conceptually, the client/server architecture can be defined as a special case of cooperative processing where an entire application is divided (not necessarily equally) between a client system (typically, a programmable or intelligent workstation) and a server system. Both client and server components are engaged in the processing of an application in such a fashion that software components interact with one another to jointly, cooperatively perform the desired application functions. Both client and server hardware components are specialized to facilitate the cooperation of the software components. This definition puts the emphasis on cooperative processing.

## 9.1 CLIENT/SERVER COMPUTING MODEL—EXPANDED DEFINITION

Client/server computing is inseparable from the idea of cooperative processing. In fact, cooperative processing is a necessary condition for the creation of the client/server architecture. But it may not be sufficient to identify a cooperative processing as the only requirement characterizing a client/server architecture. Indeed, if two software components (two programs, for example) are engaged in cooperative processing, they do not necessarily represent a client/server computing model. Specifically, even if one of the two programs always initiates interactions with its partner in the form of sending requests and receiving responses, two points deserve close attention:

- Interactions between the two programs may be short-lived and their "client/server" relationship may be terminated as soon as the interactions stop.

- Cooperative processing between two software components can be implemented in a way that does not take advantage of the evolutionary specialization of client and server hardware platforms. By definition, software-only cooperative processing is hardware-platform-transparent.

While none of the above points imply that cooperative processing of software components is "bad," it is important to remember that some of the major benefits of a client/server architecture are the power and price/performance advantages of microcomputers. Significant productivity, ease-of-use and ease-of-learning gains associated with the advent of graphical user interfaces are also closely related to client/server computing. These client/server benefits are realized through the specialization of the hardware components of the client/server architecture.

Therefore, we can now expand the definition of the client/server architecture to include not only cooperative processing between software components, but also cooperative interactions between hardware components. Thus, the term *client/server* often has two meanings—one being cooperative processing between client and server software components, and another being a relationship between a hardware "server" system and a "client" workstation.

When the hardware components are removed from consideration, cooperative processing between software components is sometimes called server-requester computing (see Fig. 9.1). Contrast this model with the client/server computing model (Fig. 9.2), where hardware specialization plays an important role.

The server-requester computing model does not include any hardware dependencies, but the differences between client/server and server-requester computing models go beyond the role of hardware:

- Both the requester and the server programs may run on the same computer system, and may not need communication facilities for their interactions. For example, the server-requester relationship could be a relationship between calling and called programs.

- The server-requester relationship exists only for the duration of the time it takes the server to process and reply to the request.

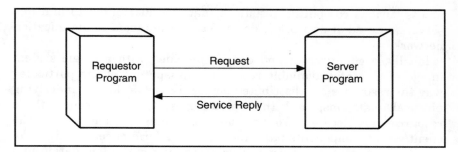

**Figure 9.1**   Server-requester computing

- In general, a server-requester computing model does not specify that the relationship has to be a variation of cooperative processing.
- Server-requester interactions do not even have to be synchronous, although more often than not these interactions are performed in a synchronous fashion.

The client/server computing model, on the other hand, offers a view of the environment from the perspective of the client workstation (Fig. 9.2). An end user of the client/server computing environment can

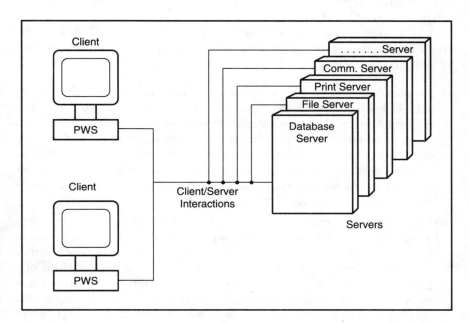

**Figure 9.2**   Client/server computing

access various computing resources that are distributed to multiple servers, located at network nodes and connected via a communication network.

Ideally, a client/server end user is provided with a single system image of the total available resources transparent of the particular way the resources are distributed across the network, the underlying physical platforms, and the operating systems on which these resources are located. To provide this single system image, the client/server components participate in some form of cooperative processing between them. Cooperative processing is the foundation and the driving force of the client/server architecture.

## 9.2   COOPERATIVE PROCESSING STRUCTURE

The cooperative processing is a special case of distributed processing. In this case, typical application functions and corresponding application components—presentation logic, business processing logic, and data management logic—are (a) distributed among two or more computing systems, and (b) characterized by the high degree of interaction between them. These interactions are performed in a cooperative fashion with a major goal of achieving a desired application functionality. In the client/server architecture, these interactions take the form of client's requests and server's reactions to the requests.

The principle application functions are analyzed in Part 1 of the book, and are summarized here for the purpose of continuity (see Fig. 9.3).

- *Presentation logic.* This is a part of the application code that interacts with a device such as an end user's terminal (character-based or a graphics-capable workstation). Presentation logic performs such tasks as screen formatting, dialog management, reading and writing of the screen information, window management, and keyboard and mouse handling. Advanced presentation logic can handle such functions as data type and range validation, cross-field editing, context-sensitive help, message logging, and access control (security).

- *Business processing logic.* This is a part of the application code that is not directly related to end-user and/or database I/O. Instead, business logic processes the input data (from a screen and/or database) according to the requirements, rules, and algorithms of a particular business task it is designed to perform. Typically, business processing logic code is user-written in any of the supported third-generation (3GL) languages (e.g., COBOL, C, PL/I), or in higher level fourth-generation (4GL) languages (user-written or generated by a code generator).

■ *Data management logic* typically consists of two components:

*Data processing logic*—a part of the application code that manipulates data within the application. A data manipulation language (DML) is typically embedded into the 3GL or 4GL application code. Data residing in Relational DBMSs (RDBMSs) is accessed using some dialect of the Structured Query Language (SQL).

*Database processing*—the actual processing of the data that relates directly to the requests formulated in the DML (physical I/O, buffer, log and lock management, etc.). It is performed by the Database Management System (DBMS). This low-level data management is hidden from the business logic of the application. From the architectural point of view, however, database processing is an essential part of the application logic that is to be distributed in a cooperative processing environment.

Note that the separation of application logic into these categories is not always straightforward and the boundaries between the components are not always clearly defined. However, applications developed with structured programming techniques and proper software engineering guidelines can help separate these components.

In host-based processing, these application components reside on the same system and are typically linked into one executable program. The absence of distribution leads to reliance on a single-host system. In general, the application is limited by the limited resources of the platform on which it runs. In a distributed environment, multiple systems are connected into a network of resources, all of which are conceivably available to the application.

To make all these resources available and useful to the application, the application components should be distributed in such a way that cooperative processing between them becomes possible. The client/server architecture employs distributed cooperative processing to

■ distribute application processing components between clients (typically presentation and some part of the business logic) and servers (typically some parts of the business logic, database logic and DBMS)

■ support cohesive interactions between clients and servers in a cooperative fashion

The high-level view of cooperative processing, given in Part 1 of the book, provides general scenarios for the distribution of application

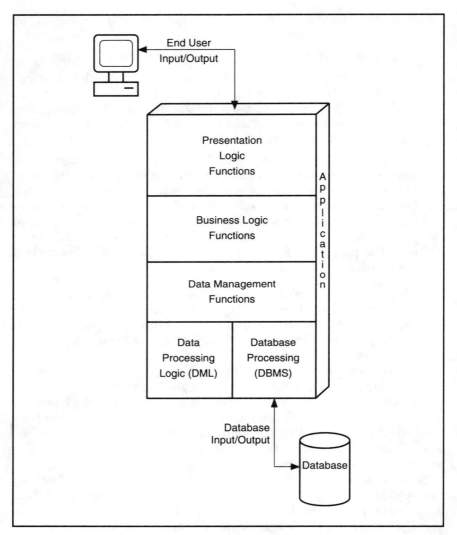

**Figure 9.3**  Typical application components

components—distributed presentation, distributed business logic, and distributed data management. However, a closer look reveals that a finer granularity in application components distribution exists. This new view in turn leads to several possible styles of cooperative processing between various distributed applications (Fig. 9.4).

Depending upon the distribution points (or lines) chosen for a particular application structure, the following *atomic* cooperative processing styles can be defined:

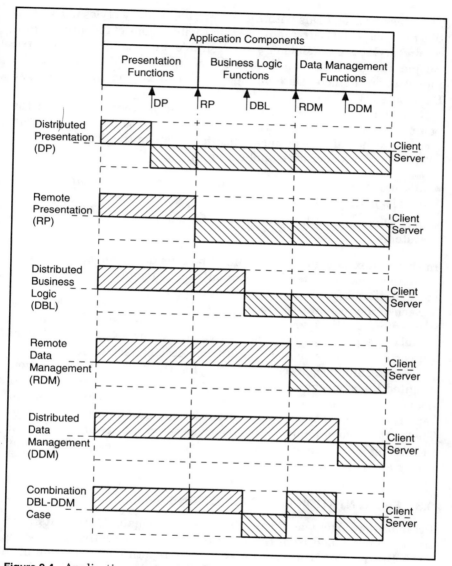

**Figure 9.4** Application components distribution points

- Distributed Presentation (DP)
- Remote Presentation (RP)
- Distributed Business Logic (DBL)
- Distributed Data Management (DDM)
- Remote Data Management (RDM)

This classification deals with the atomic, elementary styles of coopera-
tive processing. Of course, only certain combinations of cooperative pro-
cessing styles are possible or even desirable. For example, Distributed
Business Logic (DBL) can include Distributed Data Management (see
Fig. 9.4), or Remote Data Management can be combined with the
Distributed Business Logic styles.

Note that the classifications above should be considered from the
point of view of the application core—the business function. It is, in
fact, the principal reason the application exists in the first place.

Therefore, a cooperative application can be split

- to separate presentation logic, data management logic, and/or business logic from each other
- to combine and/or distribute parts of the application across multiple
  systems

In this context, business logic cannot be considered remote. Indeed, it
cannot be remote to itself, but can only be distributed between two or
more platforms.

Each of the cooperative processing styles defined above can be implemented in a client/server architecture. A client/server computing
model corresponding to each of the cooperative processing styles can be
supported by one or more cooperative processing techniques.

These techniques, described in Part 1 of the book as the connection-
oriented Pipes mechanism, the connectionless Remote Procedure Call
(RPC) mechanism, and the client/server SQL interaction mechanism,
can also be refined to support a particular cooperative processing style.
The next sections analyze the five cooperative processing styles and
techniques that can be used to implement a corresponding client/
server environment.

## 9.3  PRESENTATION LOGIC FUNCTIONS

Presentation logic was already described in Chap. 3. Here, its functions are examined from the point of view of cooperative processing.
Even though this discussion may appear repetitious, it is helpful to
briefly revisit the subject of the presentation logic functions here,
rather than continuously referring readers to Chap. 3.

Presentation functions are those directly related to end-user input/
output. Therefore, presentation logic functions are designed to interact
with such devices as end users' character-based terminals or graphics-
capable workstations. Presentation functions perform such tasks as
screen formatting, dialog management, reading and writing of the
screen information, window management, and keyboard and mouse

handling. Advanced presentation functions can handle general input editing, data type and data range validation, cross-field editing, context-sensitive help, session transcripts, message logging, and user access control.

In a general client/server architecture, presentation functions are said to be distributed and are typically performed on a client system—a workstation. The scope and capabilities of presentation functions are enhanced by, and lead to, client system specialization.

X Windows System is a useful example of the client/server implementation of the presentation functions.

From the cooperative processing point of view, the way the presentation functions are separated from the rest of the application determines the two styles of cooperative presentation: distributed presentation and remote presentation.

### 9.3.1  Distributed Presentation

In the context of a cooperative application structure (see Fig. 9.4), Distributed Presentation corresponds to the DP split point of the application. Thus, presentation functions are distributed when the presentation part of the application code is split between two or more network nodes. Figure 9.5 illustrates Distributed Presentation where a portion of the user interface logic is located on one node, while the rest of the presentation, together with the remainder of the application logic, is located on another node.

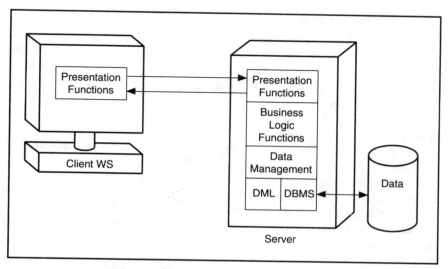

**Figure 9.5**  Distributed presentation

The typical Distributed Presentation model consists of front-end and back-end components. Front-end components handle the physical part of a user interface—screen displays, graphical user interfaces, window management, color, fonts, mouse, and keyboard. Therefore, the Distributed Presentation front-end is located on an end-user interface device—a terminal, a personal computer, or a workstation. In the client/server terminology, the front-end presentation component resides on a client node.

The back-end presentation components reside on a node different from the front-end's node, and perform some common, shared presentation functions. In the client/server architecture context, the back-end presentation components reside on a server system.

The important feature of Distributed Presentation is the fact that the cooperative processing is performed between the front-end and back-end of the presentation components, and both the nodes' hardware and software are responsible for this cooperation.

The front-end/back-end processing of Distributed Presentation represents one of the techniques used to develop cooperative applications. The X Window System for UNIX-based platforms, Easel and Infront graphical user interfaces (DOS and OS/2), and OS/2 Presentation Manager, are just a few implementation examples of Distributed Presentation. Distributed Presentation is especially beneficial when used in conjunction with personal computers (PC) to deliver graphical user interfaces to mainframe applications (e.g., CICS). It leverages existing investments in host applications and databases, as well as in PCs and LANs.

### 9.3.2  Remote Presentation

In the context of the cooperative application structure (see Fig. 9.4), Remote Presentation corresponds to the RP split point of the application. Therefore, presentation functions are said to be remote (from the business logic component) when a presentation part of the application code is placed, in its entirety, on one node, while the rest of the application is located on another node (see Fig. 9.6). The Remote Presentation style of cooperative processing is best suited for certain types of nonconversational applications where end-user interactions are predetermined.

Such predetermined interactions can lead to fully-specified, static user interfaces. The presentation functions can thus be limited to a single message being sent from the end-user node (where Remote Presentation functions are placed) to the application code residing at another node, with a single reply coming back.

Remote Presentation processing is cooperative processing between presentation functions and other application functions. This mode of

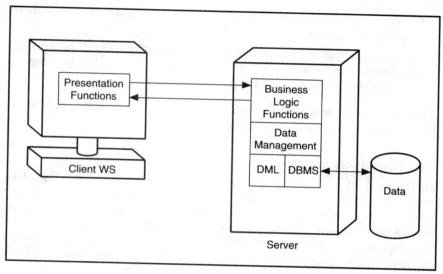

**Figure 9.6**  Remote presentation

cooperative processing can be supported by Remote Procedure Calls (RPC) or by some form of a program-to-program communication (for example, APPC). An example of Remote Presentation is DEC's transaction processing system (DECtp) running on VAX. The presentation is performed by the DECforms software (screen generation, input validation). Once the input is received, the transaction request is sent to the VAX server for processing.

## 9.4  APPLICATION LOGIC FUNCTIONS

Application logic functions are designed to fulfill the business reasons for which the application exists. In the most trivial case of a distributed environment, application functions are contained in a single system—a single node in a network. Presentation functions for this application, as well as data management functions, may be distributed, but the application business logic is not divided into pieces (components). This type of approach can be justified for certain low-activity, limited-access applications in relatively small networks.

However, such a design, while relatively simple, creates at least three significant problems:

- A single application location can result in a throughput bottleneck, especially in a high-volume transaction processing environment.

- A single application location makes the entire system less reliable by creating a single point of failure.
- Distributed computing resources are poorly utilized and the application-hosting node may need to be constantly upgraded to keep up with the ever-increasing transaction workload.

The natural way to alleviate these problems is to distribute application logic functions across several nodes.

### 9.4.1  Distributed functions

In the context of the cooperative application structure (see Fig. 9.4), Distributed Business Logic corresponds to the DBL split point of the application. The business logic functions are split so that they can be placed on different systems (nodes). In this way, the execution of the business transaction is performed as a cooperative effort between all business logic components with the cooperative participation of both presentation and data management functions.

A typical split of the business logic functions is done in the familiar front-end/back-end fashion (see Fig. 9.7). The front-end/back-end cooperation usually includes the front-end component's initiation of the interactions and the back-end component's reaction to the front-end's requests. This mode of operation resembles client/server interactions and is reflected in a client/server architecture implementation of Distributed Business Logic functions. In this scenario, the front-end

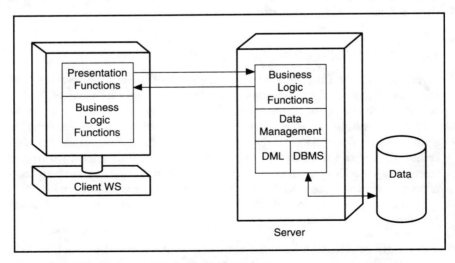

**Figure 9.7**  Distributed business logic functions

components are logically placed at client nodes, while the back-end components reside on a server system.

Distributed Business Logic functions are particularly well suited for complex, highly interactive and database I/O-intensive client/server applications. Indeed, the portion of the business logic related to the presentation functions typically resides on the end-user node (i.e., client workstation). The database-related business processing is ideally placed on the node containing database management system (i.e., DBMS server). As a result, the number of messages that the application fragments must exchange during a cooperative transaction can be seriously reduced, thereby improving response time and better utilizing available computing resources.

The underlying technology to support Distributed Business Logic applications includes various RPC implementations, as well as conversational program-to-program communication mechanisms such as IBM's APPC. Distributed Business Logic functions are typically the most difficult cooperative processing applications to design and develop. Even in its simplest form, a Distributed Business Logic application consists of two separately compiled programs, which must nevertheless be designed to be aware of each other and capable of working together in cooperative fashion.

Obviously, as the number of cooperating programs and the nodes they reside on grows, the complexity of application design and management grows as well.

Another complication of Distributed Business Logic applications arises from the power and flexibility of the client/server architecture. Consider, for example, the variation of the distributed functions that allows one node (client) to include some local database and self-contained functionality together with the distributed functions. It is not an uncommon situation considering the capabilities of modern workstations and the frequent desire of end-users to store/process some data at a local site. Examples of such local data may be word processing of private or sensitive documents and spreadsheets (e.g., a manager might want to keep employee evaluations and salary records at his/her workstation rather than at a shared facility). The design of such a distributed application must allow for different types of processing and, possibly, different DBMS access, depending on the input received from the presentation component of the application.

### 9.4.2  Transactions and distributed transaction processing

Distributed Business Logic functionality is closely related to the notion of transactions and distributed transaction processing. A transaction can be defined as a sequence of predefined actions, performed on behalf of an application, that take a computing system and its resources from one consistent state to another in order to accomplish the desired business functionality. This predefined sequence of actions represents a logical unit of work (LUW) performed by a transaction. Both terms—transaction and logical unit of work—are therefore used interchangeably throughout this chapter.

The information affected by transactions is stored in a computing system and can be accessed and/or changed in real time by executing these transactions. Such a computing environment is referred to as an OnLine Transaction Processing system, or OLTP. Transaction processing (TP) systems are most commonly used in controlling access to such computing resources as databases by interacting with the corresponding resource managers (e.g., database management systems). Transactions and LUWs possess the following properties:

- *Atomicity.* The entire LUW must be either completed or aborted. (The sequence of actions cannot be partially successful.)

- *Consistency.* A transaction takes a computing system and its resources from one consistent state to another.

- *Isolation.* A transaction's effect is not visible to other transactions until the transaction is committed.

- *Serialization.* As long as a transaction in progress depends on certain information, this information is locked to prevent any other transaction from changing it.

- *Durability.* Changes made by the committed transaction are permanent and should tolerate system failures.

To support these properties, transactions, as atomic units of work, require some kind of recovery and concurrency mechanisms to be in place. Another requirement is that the execution of a transaction must be controlled by a transaction processing (TP) management system, sometimes called a TP Monitor (TPM). TPM ensures consistency and data integrity in the event of a program or system failure. For example, IBM's Customer Information Control System (CICS) is the most widely used TP Monitor for the mainframe OnLine Transaction Processing (OLTP) environment.

In a nondistributed environment, TPM performs its functions by running on the same system as the application functions, presentation functions, and DBMSs. An example would be a CICS running on an IBM mainframe together with such database management systems as IBM's IMS/VS and DB2, and Computer Associates's IDMS.

The picture becomes much more complicated when the business logic functions, and therefore the work they are designed to do, are distributed among several systems. Each distributed node performs its share of the work in its portion of the still atomic "local" transaction.

While all local transactions maintain their properties for their local systems, the cooperative processing in which distributed business functions participate requires a new concept of distributed atomicity, consistency, isolation, and durability. This new concept is the concept of distributed transactions and distributed transaction processing (DTP). TP Monitors, recovery and consistency mechanisms, and all transaction management issues now have to deal with the realities and complexities of the distributed environment and cooperative processing.

Support for data integrity, recovery, and consistency (including two-phase commit protocols) on a transaction basis are among the most complex in a distributed transaction processing environment.

## 9.5  DATA MANAGEMENT LOGIC FUNCTIONS

One important conclusion that follows the definition of a transaction is that the transaction concept is absolutely critical to applications that change data resources (databases). It becomes even more critical when dealing with remote and distributed data management environments.

In general, data management functions allow users and applications to manage data storage and retrieval of information critical to the business enterprise. Therefore, data in general, and corporatewide critical data in particular, becomes a critical resource for the enterprise. Reliability and timely availability of this critical information may improve the overall corporate position, assist in critical tactical and strategic decision-making processes, reduce time-to-market for new products and services, and give a corporation a significant competitive advantage.

### 9.5.1  Distributed data and data management architecture

There is a distinction between data as an information resource and data management functions that help store, maintain, and retrieve data. In computer systems, data can typically be stored in two classes of data storage:

- *Files* are low-level operating-system- and often hardware-dependent entities. Files store data in records and blocks of records, are managed by the operating system's utilities, use the operating system's input-output subsystem, and usually are not transparent to the application. A typical file access is coded in the application's 3GL or 4GL code itself and is rather difficult to port from one file access type to another.

- *Databases* are designed to provide independence between applications and data. Databases can be viewed as operational administrative entities, unified by a common business purpose and a common access method—database management systems (DBMS). A DBMS implements a particular data model (hierarchical, like IBM's IMS; networked, like CA's IDMS; relational, like IBM's DB2, etc.) and insulates applications from the intricacies of actual data input-output. A DBMS provides applications with a consistent means of data access by supporting data definition and data manipulation languages throughout various implementations of a given DBMS on all supported platforms. A DBMS can provide data independence, consistency, integrity, security, and recovery. A DBMS provides interfaces between the network software and the application, and can therefore help to develop applications that can be used in distributed heterogeneous environments.

The advantages of DBMSs over traditional files have resulted in wide acceptance of various DBMSs (especially, Relational Database Management Systems, or RDBMS) on practically every computing platform. Therefore, the data storage and distribution issues in this book are illustrated on database access and distribution. Data Management logic functions are designed to be able to

- store, retrieve, and update large volumes of data

- maintain the integrity and security of data stored in the database

- provide a consistent user and programming interface to the application

- support multiple users and provide reasonable response time to user requests

In general, a cooperative distributed environment architecture is characterized by

- the data being distributed among several computing systems (nodes)

- the processing being distributed among several nodes and managed by a distributed transaction manager (network control, processes coordination, synchronization, and scheduling)

- the distributed data access being provided by such multilayer functions as application and user language interfaces, data input/output controllers, data dictionary, directory, catalog

- the data management systems (database and file management systems) being distributed alongside the data

The environment satisfying these requirements is illustrated in Fig. 9.8, which represents the conceptual view of the distributed architecture developed by the American National Standards Institute (ANSI).

This conceptual architecture can be implemented in many ways. Several database vendors have already implemented a distributed environment corresponding to the ANSI model. These implementations typically contain components that support functions performed by transaction controllers (at least to a certain degree), data I/O controllers, data dictionary/directory, and query/report processing (performed by the User Language Interfaces component of the ANSI model).

The components of the ANSI model can be also found in client/server environments, where data can be distributed among several servers, and "local" data may even reside at a client's workstation, although the client/server terminology is rather different than that of the ANSI architecture.

A distributed database architecture is discussed in more detail in the following chapters. Here, the discussion of distributed architectures is limited to their role and characteristics in cooperative processing environments. In particular, this section deals with the issues of distributed data in distributed environments.

Distributing data is an important step in designing distributed systems, not only because it allows data to be placed closer to its source, but also because it provides for greater data availability. For example, by placing multiple copies of the critical data at different locations, a potential single point-of-failure can be eliminated.

When data is placed among several nodes (distributed data), or placed on a remote node (remote data), all or part of the data management logic must accompany it. Two different styles of data management in a cooperative distributed environment can be defined: Remote Data Management and Distributed Data Management. A particular style depends on whether the data is distributed among several nodes or is remote (relative to the application logic), and on how much of the data management logic is actually distributed (relative to the application business logic).

### 9.5.2  Remote Data Management

In the context of the cooperative application structure (see Fig. 9.4), Remote Data Management logic corresponds to the RDM split point of the application.

Remember that data management logic typically consists of two components: data processing logic (a part of the application code that

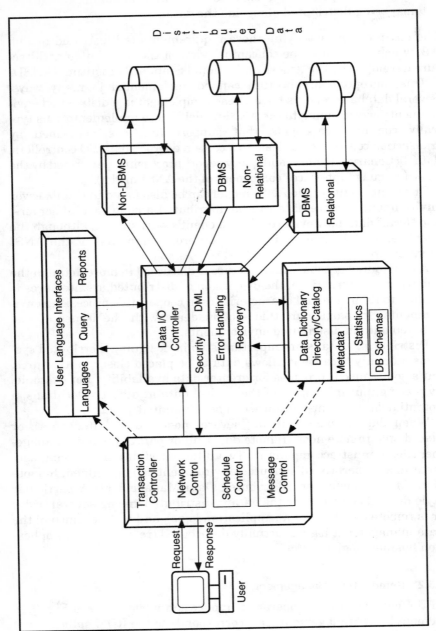

**Figure 9.8** ANSI distributed architecture

manipulates data within the application) and database processing (the actual processing of the data that relates directly to requests formulated by the database processing logic).

The database processing functions must reside on the same system as the database itself, while the data processing logic—functions of the Data Manipulation Language (DML)—may be placed close to the DBMS or close to (embedded within) the application business logic.

When all data, data processing logic, and DBMSs for a *given* application reside on a single system separated from the application node, it is considered to be Remote Data Management (see Fig. 9.9). In this case, *an application transaction deals with a single data location* at a time.

Architecturally, Remote Data Management is implemented via a front-end/back-end processing model, where the front-end system contains the business logic portion of the application, while the back-end contains the database and runs the DBMS itself.

Remote Data Management represents a classic file or database server approach, reflected in a simple (many clients, single database server) client/server architecture.

Essentially, since Remote Data Management in a single-server/many-clients environment assumes that data is *not* distributed, such an architecture represents a traditional, central database design that can be found in any nondistributed environment. Many commercial database management systems are capable of supporting remote data management (i.e., DB2, Oracle, Sybase, Informix, Ingres, Gupta, just to name a few).

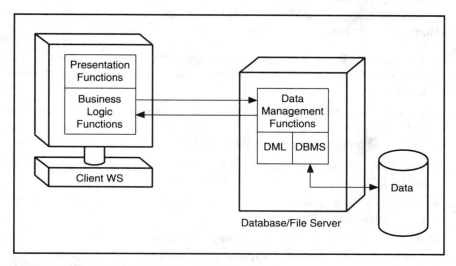

**Figure 9.9** Remote data management

In the case of relational databases (RDBMS) remote data management is implemented by a special type of cooperative processing technique: SQL client/server interactions.

These client/server interactions are based on the power of the relational data model and the Structured Query Language (SQL). SQL client/server is well suited for decision support applications, simple queries, and dynamic (ad hoc) requests, especially those requests that result in a simple, single reply.

The actual client/server interactions in a Remote Data Management environment can be implemented by such mechanisms as remote procedure calls (RPC), program-to-program communications (i.e., APPC), or any communication protocols supporting reliable message exchanges between the front-end and the back-end nodes. The last is especially true for nondatabase access to remote data (files).

Remote Data Management can also be implemented in a non-client/server environment. For example, IBM's CICS (Customer Information Control System) allows for data access functions to be shipped (the facility is called *function shipping*) from one mainframe CICS application to another. The other CICS application may reside in a different address space of the same system, or even on a different system. CICS function shipping allows data access to remote files, queues and IMS databases.

The Remote Data Management style of cooperative processing is relatively easy to implement. An application transaction deals with a single source of data; therefore, the issues of distributed data consistency and integrity do not have to be dealt with. In many cases, Remote Data Management provides end users with totally data-location-transparent access, which makes it ideal for application and/or database portability. However, Remote Data Management has its drawbacks:

- The Remote Data Management architecture places databases on a single system (i.e., database server), thus creating a performance bottleneck.

- Remote Data Management requires all data requests and responses to be transmitted by the network between a server and the application, thus creating a potentially significant communication overhead.

- The database server is limited in its functionality to the processing of the DML requests sent from the front-end.

- A single source of data and a single DBMS location create a single point-of-failure.

- While by design, considerable computing resources are available in a cooperative distributed computing environment, the singularity of a database server prevents it from taking advantage of all available resources.

To eliminate potential communication overhead in the network, Remote Data Management is best suited for applications characterized by low-volume, infrequent, user-directed ad hoc query processing (decision-support applications), that produce simple, small data volume results. The drawbacks of Remote Data Management are dealt with in Distributed Data Management.

### 9.5.3    Distributed Data Management

The Distributed Data Management style of cooperative processing is intended to eliminate problems introduced by Remote Data Management. In the context of the cooperative application structure (see Fig. 9.4), Distributed Data Management logic corresponds to the DDM split point of the application.

Distributed Data Management deals with data (databases) distributed among multiple nodes. Such distribution allows us to place data closer to its source, provides for higher data availability by placing multiple copies of the critical data at different locations, and eliminates a potential single point-of-failure.

When data is distributed among several nodes, all or part of the data management logic must also be distributed, accompanying the data. Thus, at least some portion of the database processing logic (DBMS) must reside on the same system as the database itself.

The Distributed Data Management environment is characterized by two-way distribution:

- The data and DBMS are distributed among multiple nodes, including the node with the application logic.
- Data management functions are distributed between a front-end system (data processing logic, or DML) and the back-end server (database functions, or DBMS) (see Fig. 9.10).

Such an architecture can reduce the network traffic due to the fact that data access requests (DML requests) are sent from an application business logic to the data processing logic on the same node. Data processing logic performs initial syntax checking, parsing, compile, and determination on the required data location. If the local data is required, the DML request is satisfied without being sent to the remote database server. Similarly, invalid DML requests are rejected before being sent into the network.

Distributed DBMS (DDBMS) employs such cooperative processing techniques as Remote Procedure Calls (RPC), program-to-program communications (i.e., APPC), front-end/back-end synchronous distributed transaction processing, and such special mechanisms as stored procedures and triggers. Distributed data management is ide-

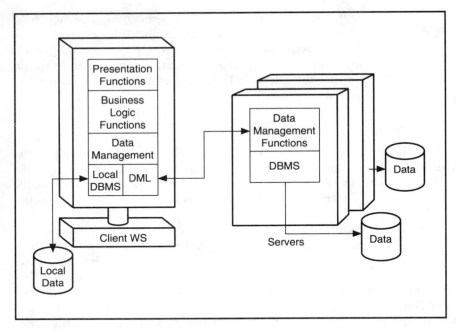

**Figure 9.10**    Distributed data management

ally suited to be implemented in a client/server architecture. There are several products available today that implement a distributed DBMS in a client/server architecture (Sybase, Ingres, and Oracle are just a few examples).

Properly designed, a DDBMS provides end users with data location transparency, data integrity, consistency, and reliability. However, the Distributed Data Management style of cooperative distributed processing introduces many serious issues associated with the distribution of data and data management. They include the ways data should be distributed, issues of data synchronization, consistency, locking, integrity, transparency, reliability, and administration. These issues are analyzed in the following chapters.

# Distributed Data Management

Traditionally, most large organizations develop applications to reside on central, mainframe computers. As a result, the data these applications access is also stored in central locations in corporate databases. However, the use of large, centrally located computers for such centralized application processing is becoming more and more expensive, especially when compared with the price/performance advantages of microcomputers. Today, businesses are becoming more and more interested in implementing distributed databases. Some of the reasons for doing this are:

- desire to reduce operating costs and to decentralize operations, in order to be more competitive and responsive to customer demands
- advances in the area of distributed and client/server computing
- availability of enabling technology for distributed processing, including products implementing distributed databases in client/server architecture

The main advantage of Distributed Data Management is the ability to access data located at multiple sites (network nodes) in a fashion transparent to end users. At the same time, Distributed Data Management includes keeping most data local to the sites that actually use the data. Of course, a properly implemented distributed database allows each node to be configured in such a way that it can handle the amount of data residing at that node, the complexity of user applications, and the number of users. As the number of applications and users grow, the corresponding data requirements grow as well. The resulting upgrades to a distributed environment tend to be less expensive than a corresponding centralized system upgrade, and can often be implemented in a fashion totally transparent to end users.

As was demonstrated in the previous chapter, Distributed Data Management is one of the styles of cooperative distributed processing implemented in client/server architecture. Indeed, client/server architecture offers an ideal solution to the requirements of Distributed Data Management. Most of the client/server architecture implementations available today are implementations of distributed database management systems, or DDBMS. Distributed Data Management environment is characterized by two-way distribution:

- The data and DBMS are distributed among multiple nodes, including the node with the application logic.

- Data management functions are distributed between a front-end system (data manipulation logic and language, or DML) and the back-end server (database functions, or DBMS).

While one of the most popular applications of the client/server architecture, distributed data management, deals with a lot of complicated issues, some of these issues have not been resolved to date.

The issues of data distribution, methods of distributed data access, data integrity, consistency, and concurrency are described in this chapter.

## 10.1  METHODS OF DATA DISTRIBUTION

Distributed data management deals with data (databases) distributed among multiple nodes. Distributing data among multiple sites offers the following benefits:

- placement of data closer to its source
- higher data availability by placing multiple copies of critical data at different locations, thus eliminating a potential single point of failure
- more efficient data access, thus improving data management performance
- application load balancing as it relates to data access
- ease of application and user growth

There are several methods of distributing data in a distributed environment. Some of these methods are rather simple, while others may appear more complex. The important fact in Distributed Data Management is that the method selected for data distribution affects the way the data can (and sometimes should) be accessed.

While the data distribution methods described in this section apply to any data organization, be it sequential, hierarchical, networked, or relational, the relational data model makes the illustration of the data distribution methods easier to understand. Therefore, most of the examples deal with data organized in a relational data model. The following is a very brief and *informal* description of the relational data model.

### 10.1.1    Relational data model

A relational data model views all data as being organized into tables. Table rows represent records of data, while table columns (attributes) represent fields in the record. There are no duplicate rows in a given table, and the order of rows is not significant. Tables reflect facts and values of the real world. Therefore, each table contains data about some real fact. For example, a bank's Individual Customer Table contains data about noncorporate customers, while an Employee Table contains data about bank employees (see Fig. 10.1).

The column (or a combination of columns) that uniquely identifies a particular fact upon which the table is based represents a *unique, primary key* for this table. Typically, each table contains a primary key. For example, a Customer Table may have a customer's social security number as the primary key (it is unique and identifies the customer). To eliminate data redundancy, designers perform the *normalization* process, which aims to put *all* data about *the primary* key in the same table where the key is defined.

To illustrate the relational data model, consider a Bank Application which deals with customers, employees, and checking and savings accounts. Let's look at the customer information. It consists of customer's social security number, name, address, account number, and account information (balances, last deposits/withdrawals, etc.). All these data elements can be organized into one table. However, since a customer may have many accounts, and several accounts may consist of more than one customer (e.g., customer's spouse or children), such a table will contain a fair amount of redundant (duplicate) data. Redundancy can cause a data integrity problem when such a table has to be changed. After the normalization process is completed, the resulting, *normalized* relational customer-account data model will consist of three tables: Customer, Checking Account, and Savings Account

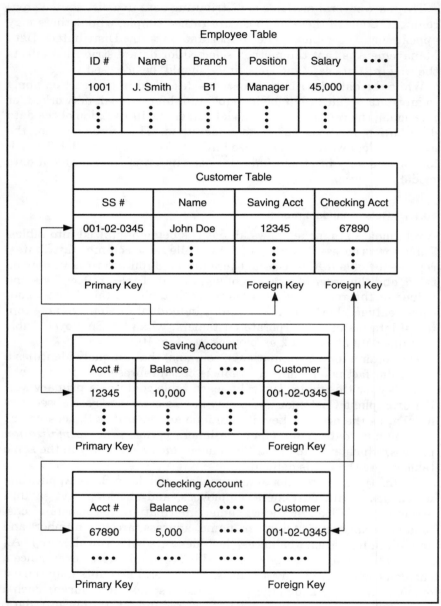

**Figure 10.1**   Relational data model

(Fig. 10.1). Similar to the facts of the real world, all three tables should be related. For example, the Customer Table may contain a column with the savings account number and another column with the checking account number.

It is important to note that the savings account number column in the Customer Table must point to an existing savings account number (primary key) in the Savings Account Table. Otherwise, the customer will have a nonexistent savings account. The same logic applies to the checking account column in respect to the Checking Account Table. Columns in one table that represent a reference to the matching primary key values in another table are called *foreign* keys. An example of a primary key-foreign key pair is the Social Security Number (SS #) column in the Customer Table and the corresponding customer column in the Savings Account Table. The relationship between primary and foreign keys presents an interesting problem when one (or more) of the related tables is updated. Consider, for example, that a row containing a primary key value, referenced by a foreign key, is deleted (e.g., a row of the Customer Table with SS #101-22-3333). Then the foreign key for this primary key (e.g., the customer column of the Savings Account Table) has to be either changed to point to the existing primary key value or deleted. Otherwise, the corresponding savings account will lose its owner. Similarly, if a new row containing a foreign key is inserted (added) in the table, the value of the new foreign key must match one of the primary key values in the related table. These rules describe the special type of constraints that exist between primary and foreign keys—the *referential integrity* constraint.

Relational databases support the relational language, *Structured Query Language (SQL)*. This language is used to formulate operations that define and manipulate data in relational form. The subset of the SQL that defines data is called *Data Definition Language (DDL)*, while *Data Manipulation Language (DML)* supports data manipulation in the relational data model.

SQL is the sole means of providing access to data in a relational database. SQL contains only a handful of operators and appears to be easy to learn and to use. This ease is deceptive, although it may be true for simple applications. To design a complex relational database and provide efficient data access to it, SQL requires a knowledge of relational algebra as well as an understanding of a particular RDBMS.

One of the main advantages of SQL and the relational data model is *nonnavigational* data access. In nonrelational database management systems the user has to tell the DBMS not only *what* data is needed, but also *how* to get to it. The *how* is done by selecting a data access path and navigating along it in the relevant data model. For example, in the hierarchical data model a programmer uses the appropriate procedural DBMS language (DL/I) to move from top to bottom and from left to right to reach the desired data destination.

In a Relational DBMS, use of SQL allows users to tell the RDBMS *only what* data is needed, and what manipulations are to be done, but *not how* to perform these manipulations. Relational DBMSs and SQL are based on relational theory. Therefore, users familiar with the theory should expect to access data with fewer errors and fewer unpleasant surprises.

Since users do not tell the RDBMS how to satisfy data requests, the database management system itself should be intelligent enough to figure out the best access path to the required data. By design, RDBMS provides for better data independence by isolating end users from the underlying physical structure of the database. SQL applications are, in theory, independent of a particular RDBMS implementation. A familiar tabular form of data representation, relative simplicity of SQL, lack of procedural data access coding, and data access portability across any RDBMS result in increased application developers productivity and are the main reasons for the wide acceptance of relational technology.

### 10.1.2   Manual extract

In a centralized, nondistributed environment, all data is concentrated in one central place (e.g., corporate databases on a mainframe). In a distributed environment, the data is distributed among multiple locations. Logically, however, distributed data still belongs to a centralized corporate data repository. Distributed Data Management environment designers must decide

- *how* and *when* data should be "taken" from the conceptual, central repository for distribution
- *what* the optimum locations are for data element placement

The latter question involves various data access methods as well as network throughput characteristics. The former question, however, applies equally to any data location configuration, and is dealt with in this chapter.

One of the simplest ways to distribute data is to allow the user to manually copy the data from one central location to other locations. This method of data distribution is called a manual extract. It is simple enough to be controlled by the user as requests for the data arrive at the data administrator.

For example, consider the Bank Application described above. The central Bank Information Repository is located in New York, and contains all customer, checking, and savings account data in corresponding tables. In addition, it contains a currency Exchange Table. In the distributed environment, bank branches maintain their own customer and account repositories corresponding to their customers (see Fig. 10.2). If a new branch is opened, the data administrator can make a complete or partial copy of the Exchange Table and load it in the Exchange Table for a given branch.

Such an operation can be performed as a manual extract. It can be done in one of two ways:

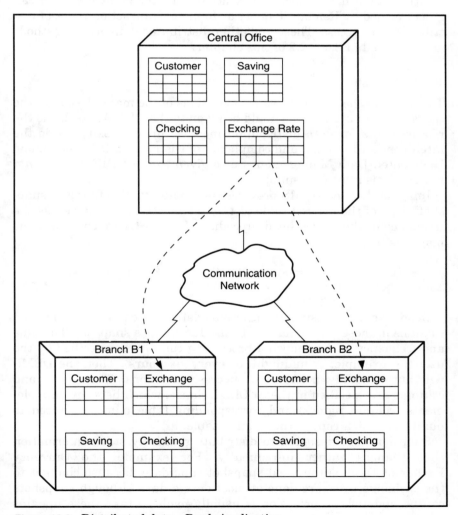

**Figure 10.2**  Distributed data—Bank Application

- from the central site (the extract is performed against the local table, and the load against the remote table)
- from the new branch (the extract is executed against the remote table, and the load against the local table)

In the case of the relational data model, extract and load can be done via appropriate SQL statements (e.g., SELECT and INSERT).

In fact, the manual extract would be satisfied by limiting each group of SQL statements (SELECTs and INSERTs) to a single data location (central site or new branch). More accurately, the manual extract can be performed by Remote Request or Remote Transaction types of distributed data access. These and other distributed data access methods are described in Sec. 10.2 of this chapter.

### 10.1.3    Snapshot

To automate the user-performed operations of the manual extract, the tasks of data distribution should be given to the DDBMS itself. As the requirements for data distribution increase in complexity, so do the intelligence, capability, and complexity of Distributed DBMSs. Among Distributed Data Management tasks given to the DDBMS, *snapshot* processing is relatively simple.

Imagine that the DBMS provides the capability of defining a "snapshot" copy of the desired table at the needed locations, as well as the frequency of the extract-load procedure. Using SQL, such definitions may look like:

```
CREATE SNAPSHOT <name> AS SELECT .... TIME <hh:mm:ss>,
INTERVAL <hh:mm:ss>
```

In snapshot processing, the user may define which tables (and which columns in these tables) have to be used to create a snapshot. The time and frequency of the snapshot processing can also be specified by the user (for example, at midnight, or every six hours). Then the DBMS will automatically perform all necessary actions. The tables and columns are specified in the SELECT clause, which lists the data elements (column names) and corresponding table names required to build a snapshot copy of the original table.

Snapshots are designed to distribute relatively static information that changes rather infrequently. For example, the Currency Exchange Table is the ideal snapshot candidate, because changes to the exchange rates are done at most once a day. Although snapshots can be updated, no provision is usually made to take these updates back to the original source of data. Therefore, snapshots are typically limited to read-only access.

### 10.1.4 Replication

For those applications where the distributed data can be updated at multiple locations, snapshot processing is not sufficient. Such an application may require that a copy of the same table be maintained at multiple locations.

The DDBMS is capable of supporting an advanced data distribution method, *replication,* when this DDBMS can:

- create and maintain copies (replicas) of a given table at multiple required locations

- maintain data consistency among all replicas (either synchronous or asynchronous processing)

In the Bank Application example, let's assume that customers can transfer their accounts from branch to branch. If a customer record and relevant account information is not found in a given branch, the required information can be copied from the branch that used to maintain the customer's accounts. In an extreme case, the entire Customer Table could be replicated, with replicas placed at every branch. In order to maintain accurate records, all replicas should have consistent information about customers and their accounts.

Synchronization of updates between all replicas is not the only problem that a Distributed DBMS must solve. When multiple copies of the same table exist, applications that access this replicated data in a distributed environment should not be aware of the location of the replicas. Otherwise, applications have to be changed depending on the location of the systems on which they currently reside, and on the number of replicas currently maintained. Indeed, if every branch of the bank maintains a Customer Balance Sheet program, the program should not be aware of the location of the Customer Table replica it accesses.

Besides table replication, distributed data requirements may include the need for the row level replication, where only particular rows of a given table are replicated by DDBMS. If only those rows that are subject to update are replicated, row level replication may simplify data synchronization.

Replication, data consistency, and location transparency are among the tasks that Distributed DBMS should perform to be able to support distributed replicated data. Each of these requirements represents a serious design and implementation problem. As will be demonstrated later in the book, some of these problems can be solved only by limiting the functionality of the access to distributed data.

### 10.1.5    Fragmentation

Data replication appears to be rather difficult to implement, even though it deals with entire tables. It may be more efficient to replicate only parts (fragments) of the data. Data fragmentation, however, is the most complicated method of data distribution.

Fragmentation is best illustrated in the relational data model, where data tables can be fragmented either horizontally or vertically.

To illustrate horizontal fragmentation, let's expand the Bank Application by adding the Employee Table, which contains one row for each employee (see Fig. 10.3). In a distributed environment, the Employee Table is to be distributed to different branches based on the list of employees for every branch. To do this, the entire Employee Table is fragmented *horizontally* by creating a subsets of employees—rows in the Employee Table.

To illustrate vertical fragmentation, let's assume that the Employee Table contains employee medical history records, which can be viewed only by the centrally-located medical department. These medical records represent a subset of the Employee Table columns. To distribute medical records (certain columns of the Employee Table) to the medical department, the Employee Table is fragmented *vertically,* and the appropriate fragments are placed at desired locations (see Fig. 10.4).

Of course, both the horizontal and vertical fragmentation methods can be combined to obtain subsets of rows and columns to be distributed. Regardless of the method, fragmentation, by being more selective, allows only the needed data to be distributed physically close to where it is used.

However, the main drawback of fragmentation is the complexity of its implementation. It becomes evident in light of the application requirement of full transparent access to data in the distributed environment. Consider the Employee Table that is distributed by fragmentation (horizontally, vertically, or both). If a management appraisal application requires access to all employee records in their entirety, such an application will have to access employee data in all branches of the bank, and then combine it with that portion of the employee data kept at the medical department.

Employees can transfer from one branch to another, and branches can be merged into bigger branches. Therefore, the application should be able to access distributed data that is totally transparent from the data location and the fragmentation method. This can be achieved by viewing the fragmented data as residing in a single table. The alternative is to rewrite the application every time an employee is transferred.

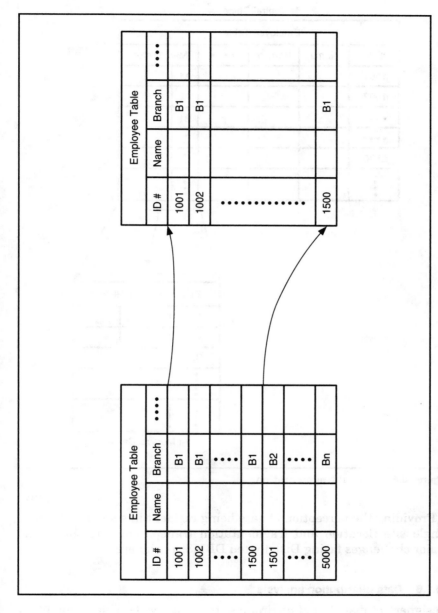

**Figure 10.3** Horizontal fragmentation

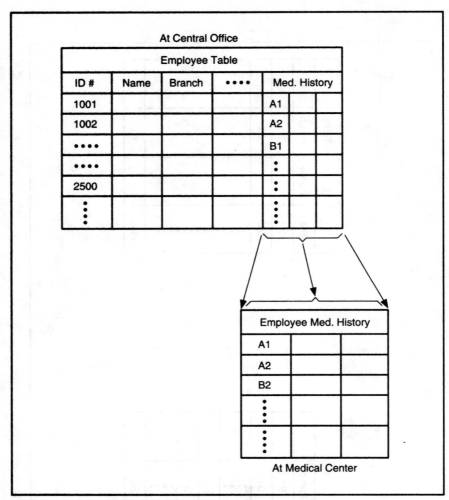

**Figure 10.4**   Vertical fragmentation

Providing the perception of data being resident in a single table at a single site (location and fragmentation transparency) is one of the major challenges facing Distributed DBMSs designers.

### 10.1.6   Data distribution analysis

Designers of distributed environments must decide which computing resources have to be distributed, as well as at which locations. Decisions about data locations are among those required in order to implement a truly distributed environment. There exist several methods designed to facilitate this decision process.

One simple but reliable method often used to perform a distributed data placement analysis is based on a simulation of interactions in a distributed environment. The following example is offered as an illustration of such a simulation. Let's assume that the distributed environment for the Bank Application consists of only two locations: the central site (location S1) and one branch (location B1). Assume further that the Customer Table, kept in its entirety at the central site, is partially replicated (e.g., horizontally fragmented, as described in the previous section) in the branch B1 location. In order to maintain consistent customer information, every update to the Customer Table at either location must be duplicated at another location, while read-only operations can be performed locally.

Let's assume, that the Customer Table at location S1 contains 10,000 records, is read 2000 times and updated 500 times daily. The branch B1 Customer Table contains 1000 records, is read 1000 times and updated 100 times daily (see Fig. 10.5, top).

If all customer data is placed at one particular location, all data access from another location must be sent over the network connecting these locations. If all customer data is placed at S1, then the data traffic from/to branch B1 would be equal to 1100 messages (1000 reads plus 100 updates). Conversely, if all customer data is placed at B1, the total traffic would be equal to 2500 messages (2000 reads plus 500 updates). This consideration appears to indicate that leaving customer data at the central site would be the best solution. However, it is easy enough to prove that distributing data between these two sites can be even more beneficial to the network traffic. Consider the matrix of possible data locations and the resulting traffic figures (see Fig. 10.5, bottom). Remember that traffic results from reading data not found at the given location and from the need to keep the updated data synchronous with its copy.

Out of the three possible configurations (all data at S1, all data at B1, data distributed between S1 and B1), the third configuration is optimum from the network traffic point of view (traffic equals 600 messages—500 updates from the S1 location plus 100 updates from the B1 location).

While not totally accurate, such an analysis can be expanded to include multiple data objects (e.g., Savings Account Table and Checking Account Table), costs-per-transmission (especially if there is a choice of networks), cost and requirements for data storage, and other characteristics of data distribution.

The important conclusions of this analytical approach are:

- Regardless of the data distribution method, distributing data appears to be beneficial to the distributed system throughput.

- The placement of the distributed data can be decided based on the logical data and process (read/update) models and the number and characteristics of the available data locations.

| Operation | Location | |
|---|---|---|
| | S1 | B1 |
| Read | 2,000 | 1,000 |
| Update | 500 | 100 |

Assignment of Read/Update Operations Between Locations

| Configuration Number | Data at Location | | Message Traffic |
|---|---|---|---|
| | S1 | B1 | |
| 1 | Y | N | 1,100 |
| 2 | N | Y | 2,500 |
| 3 | Y | Y | 600 |

**Figure 10.5**  Distributed data placement matrix

## 10.2  DISTRIBUTED DATA ACCESS

When data is distributed among several locations, all or part of the data management logic must be also distributed to accompany the data. As was already discussed, at least some portion of the database processing logic (DBMS) must reside on the same system as the database itself.

Regardless of the data distribution methods employed, the data access provided by the Distributed DBMS must be performed in such a fashion that location of the data is transparent to users and applications. In fact, in a truly distributed database environment, users and applications should not be aware that the data is distributed.

Distributed data access, while required wherever data is distributed among several network nodes, is not only appropriate but absolutely necessary in the client/server architectures which support data distribution between clients and servers. Any client/server implementation that allows data (and a local DBMS) to be maintained on client systems, as well as on the database server, must provide for distributed data access.

Therefore, various types of distributed data access are discussed in terms of the client/server architecture where an application resides on the client workstation and issues data requests for either local (client-resident) or remote (server-resident) data. These types of distributed data access are described below in order of increasing capabilities, and the relational data model is used for the illustration. Note that some of the Distributed Data Management issues had been formulated by C. J. Date, one of the first designers of relational databases. C. J. Date's Twelve Distributed Database Rules are listed in App. D and discussed in more detail in Chap. 11.

### 10.2.1  Remote request

Consider a simple one-client/one-server environment. One of the simplest tasks that the client application can issue is a data request to the server. When an application issues a single data request to be processed at a single remote site, it is called a remote request (see Fig. 10.6).

In the case of the relational model, such a single request is a single SQL statement which refers to data resident at a single remote site (server). Again, consider the Bank Application. If the Customer Table

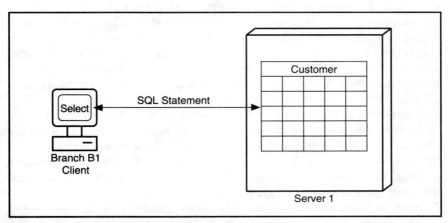

**Figure 10.6**  Remote request

is located centrally on Server 1 rather than distributed, (remote) bank branch B1 can issue a remote SQL request to read the customer's information. Such a request contains references only to the remote data. The Distributed DBMS can support remote requests transparently if the DDBMS maintains data locations. Conversely, the DDBMS can support remote requests if the application specifies data locations.

In the case of a Relational DDBMS, a sample remote SQL request to retrieve New York customer data from the Customer Table in the bank database (BANKDB) residing at the remote Server 1 can be specified as follows:

```
SELECT * FROM SERVER1.BANKDB.CUSTOMER
        WHERE SERVER1.BANKDB.CUSTOMER.CITY = "New York"
```

Remote requests can be used to perform the manual extract method of data distribution. In the same scenario, when the Customer Table is to be manually distributed to a local branch, the branch computer can issue a remote request for all customer data, and can then copy the data into the local DBMS.

### 10.2.2    Remote transaction

The definition of a remote request can also be formulated from the point of view of transactions and logical units of work. In the previous chapter, a transaction was defined as a sequence of predefined actions, performed on behalf of the application, that take a computing system and its resources from one consistent state to another in order to accomplish the desired business functionality. This predefined sequence of actions represents a logical unit of work (LUW) performed by a transaction. Therefore, a remote request can be redefined as a data processing *transaction,* or *logical unit of work,* which consists of a *single* data request that refers to data residing at a *single* remote location (server). By definition of the LUW, when a remote request is completed successfully, the remote data is in a new, consistent state, and all work done in the remote request is committed.

A remote transaction capability allows a transaction to contain *multiple* data requests, all of which refer to data residing at a *single* (remote) location (see Fig. 10.7). If a remote request represents a simple, single-action logical unit of work, a remote transaction may consist of multiple actions, all dealing with the data at a single location, and all comprising a single logical unit of work.

Therefore, a remote transaction is sometimes called a *Remote Unit of Work* (RUW). From the client/server architecture point-of-view, the

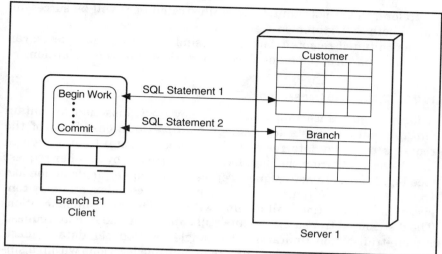

**Figure 10.7** Remote transaction

remote transaction capability implies that the remote data is placed at a single server and accessed from a client workstation in a single logical unit of work. In the case of the relational data model, a remote transaction may consist of several SQL statements, each of which refers to data resident at a single remote site (server).

In the Bank Application, the remote request to read customer information in the Customer Table from any branch can be expanded by adding an update action. For example, a remote branch B1 (Server B1) not only needs all the information about New York customers, but also needs to update the Branch Table's POSTED indicator (both tables reside on Server 1). Both of these actions represent a remote transaction that must be performed as one logical unit of work. If the application is required to specify data locations by using fully-qualified table names, such a remote transaction may look like this:

```
BEGIN WORK
SELECT * FROM SERVER1.BANKDB.CUSTOMER
          WHERE SERVER1.BANKDB.CUSTOMER.CITY = "New York"
UPDATE SERVER1.BANKDB.BRANCH
          SET POSTED_IND = 'YES'
COMMIT WORK
```

Note that the two SQL statements (SELECT and UPDATE) are surrounded by LUW brackets (BEGIN WORK and COMMIT WORK).

Therefore, the remote unit of work illustrated here will be successful only if both SQL statements are successful.

User-initiated remote transactions, similar to remote requests, can be used to perform the manual extract method of data distribution.

### 10.2.3   Distributed transaction

A distributed transaction capability allows a transaction to contain *multiple* data requests for data at *multiple* locations. Each of the requests refers to data residing at a *single* (remote) location, which may be *different* from the data location referred to by another request (see Fig. 10.8). A remote request represents a simple, single-action logical unit of work. A remote transaction is more complex, and may consist of multiple actions, all dealing with the data at a single location. The distributed transaction, while still supporting the remote-request/remote-transaction limitation of a single location per data request, goes even further by allowing access to multiple locations within a single logical unit of work. In a client/server architecture, the distributed transaction capability implies that the data, distributed among multiple servers, can be accessed from a client workstation in a single logical unit of work. A distributed transaction represents a *Distributed Unit of Work* (DUW). In the case of the relational data model, a distributed transaction may consist of several SQL statements, one for each data location among the available server locations.

In the Bank Application, the central office (Server 1) may need information about employees having an advanced educational degree (M.B.A.) who work at remote branch B1. Simultaneously, the central office may need medical history of all employees of that branch. All medical records are kept at the medical department (Server M).

Both of these actions represent a distributed transaction, since they deal with multiple locations in the same logical unit of work. If the application is required to specify data locations by using fully-qualified table names, such a distributed transaction may look like this:

```
BEGIN WORK

SELECT * FROM SERVERB1.BANKDB.EMPLOYEE
          WHERE SERVERB1.BANKDB.EMPLOYEE.EDLEVEL = "MBA"
SELECT * FROM SERVERM.BANKDB.EMPL_MED
          WHERE SERVERM.BANKDB.EMPL_MED.BRANCH = "B1"


COMMIT WORK
```

Note that even though the two SQL statements deal with different data locations, they are surrounded by the LUW brackets (**BEGIN WORK**

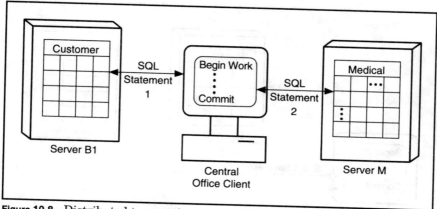

**Figure 10.8**  Distributed transaction

and COMMIT WORK). Therefore, the distributed unit of work illustrated here will be successful only if both SQL statements, executing at different locations, are successful. Similarly, if any one of the SQL statements fails, the entire logical unit of work is considered a failure.

### 10.2.4  Distributed request

The distributed request represents the most complex method of distributed data access. Distributed requests allow a transaction consisting of multiple requests to be processed by a distributed database server. A transaction consisting of multiple requests can be processed at multiple sites, and each request can reference data residing at multiple sites.

To summarize, a remote request represents a simple, single-action logical unit of work. A remote transaction is more complex and may consist of multiple actions, all dealing with the data at a single location. A distributed transaction, while still supporting the remote-request/remote-transaction limitation of a single location per data request, goes even further by allowing access to multiple locations within a single logical unit of work. Finally, the distributed request does not contain this single site per request limitation. Each request of the distributed request can access data from multiple locations, and, therefore, can be processed by multiple locations. Moreover, all actions performed within the distributed request comprise a single logical unit of work. In a client/server architecture, the distributed request capability implies that data can be distributed among multiple servers either by replication or fragmentation, and can be accessed transparently from a client workstation in a single logical unit of work (see Fig. 10.9). In the case of the relational data model, a distributed request

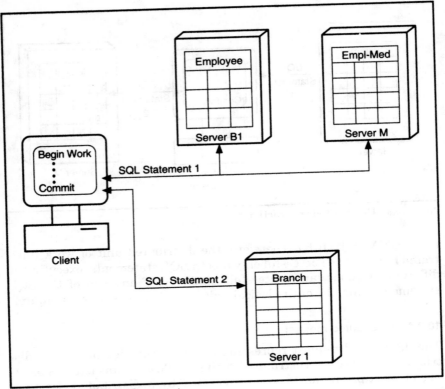

**Figure 10.9**  Distributed request

may consist of several SQL statements, each referencing data located at multiple server locations.

In the Bank Application, the central office (Server 1) may need to report all employees who have an advanced educational degree (M.B.A.), are working at remote branch B1 (Server B1) and, at the same time, include their medical history, kept at the medical department (Server M).

In addition, the Branch Table for the branch B1, kept at the central site (Server 1), has to be updated to indicate that the report has been completed. Such a business requirement can be satisfied by:

1. joining the two tables—the Employee Table at the location "Server B1," and the Empl_Med Table at the location "Server M"

2. updating the Branch Table at location "Server 1"

This is how such a distributed request may be coded in SQL:

```
BEGIN WORK

SELECT * FROM SERVERB1.BANKDB.EMPLOYEE B1,
             SERVERM.BANKDB.EMPL_MED M
        WHERE B1.EMPL_ID = M.EMPL_ID        AND
        WHERE B1.EDLEVEL = "MBA"


UPDATE SERVER1.BANKDB.BRANCH
        SET REPORTED = "YES"
        WHERE SERVER1.BANKDB.BRANCH = "B1"

COMMIT WORK
```

Note that the first SQL statement joins two tables from two different locations, while the third SQL statement updates data at yet another location. And all these actions are performed as one logical unit of work, even though multiple physical DBMSs at multiple locations are involved. All four types of distributed data access are required to support a distributed DBMS. But only distributed request processing may be considered to support the concepts of a truly distributed database management system.

Remote requests and remote and distributed transactions all permit access to remote data, as well as allow users to perform application (client) processing at locations different from the database (server) processing. Thus, these three types of distributed database processing all support some form of the client/server computing model. However, these three types of distributed database processing all impose restrictions on *how* the data should be accessed and *what* can be done by the application. In addition, remote request and remote and distributed transaction processing often require the application to know the physical location of the data. Ideally, the distributed request capabilities allow users to distribute data among multiple locations without applications having to know where the data is physically located. Therefore, distributed requests, by imposing no restrictions on application's data access logic, support the complete cooperative client/server processing in a distributed computing environment.

An example of such an environment is a fully distributed database application implemented in the client/server architecture (see Fig. 10.10). Here, the DDBMS provides both data replication and fragmentation. Because data is closer to applications using it, the DDBMS supports faster read-only operations and ensures data integrity when updates are performed on portions of the distributed data.

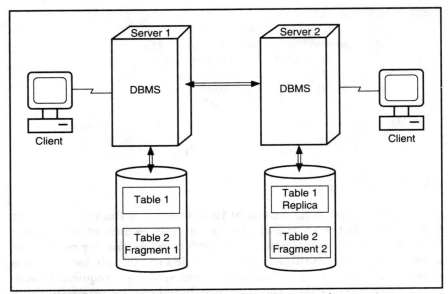

**Figure 10.10**   Distributed database in the client-server environment

## 10.3 DATABASE TRANSACTION MANAGEMENT

A truly distributed database management system should support distributed requests by providing data location and fragmentation transparency to the applications and end users. However, transparency requirements are only the beginning of a long list of features that a Distributed DBMS must have. One of the most important issues of the Distributed DBMS is the integrity of updates applied to the distributed database. Distributed data integrity and consistency of databases are based on the previously mentioned fundamental concept of transactions. This means that a truly distributed DBMS is responsible for maintaining the database in either of the two consistent states—before the update transaction begins and after the update transactions have been *successfully* executed. Partially completed transactions should not be allowed. Specifically, update data integrity is supported by the concept of the database transaction management.

### 10.3.1 Database transactions

As applicable to Distributed Data Management, the database transaction can be defined as a sequence of one or more data manipulation statements that together form an atomic, logical unit of work. Either all statements in the transaction will execute successfully, or none of the statements will be executed. Formally, a database transaction should possess the following properties:

- *Atomicity.* An entire transaction is either completed or aborted.

- *Consistency.* A transaction takes databases from one consistent state to another.

- *Isolation.* A transaction effect is transparent to other transactions, applications, and end users until the transaction is committed.

- *Durability.* The changes to recoverable resources made by a committed transaction are permanent.

In general, a transaction, or logical unit of work, is said to be committed when it completes all processing successfully. A database transaction is committed when all data manipulation statements have been executed successfully. In this case, all changes made by the transaction to recoverable data become permanent. Transactions can be committed implicitly, by successfully terminating, or explicitly, by issuing special commitment statements.

If any of the data manipulation statements fails, the entire database transaction fails, and all partial changes to the database made before the data manipulation statement failure (if any) must be rolled back in order to bring the database to its before-transaction consistent state. In a relational database, a database transaction that consists of one or more SQL statements is committed when all SQL statements are completed successfully; it is aborted if one of the SQL statements fails. SQL supports database transactions through two SQL transaction processing statements: COMMIT and ROLLBACK.

The ANSI/ISO SQL standard defines a SQL transaction model and the roles of the COMMIT and ROLLBACK statements. Most commercially available RDBMS products (for example, IBM's DB2) use this transaction model. Briefly, this transaction model specifies that a SQL transaction must automatically begin with the first SQL statement executed by a program or user, and continues to execute the subsequent SQL statements until one of the following occurs.

- COMMIT statement explicitly ends the transaction successfully, making changes to the recoverable data (e.g., databases) permanent.

- ROLLBACK statement explicitly aborts the transaction, backing out (rolling back) not committed database changes.

- A program executing the transaction terminates successfully (implicit commit), making the database changes permanent.

- A program executing the transaction terminates abnormally (implicit ROLLBACK), backing out all partial, uncommitted changes to the database.

When the transaction processing environment is localized (not distributed), and the only recoverable resource in question is a database, the DBMS itself can handle database transaction processing.

Usually, the DBMS uses a sophisticated transaction logging mechanism. Before-the-change and after-the change images of the changed database records as well as COMMIT indications are written in reliable, nonvolatile storage, before the database record itself is changed and written back to disk storage.

The picture changes drastically as the environment becomes distributed, and additional resources (e.g., databases, files, etc.) come into play.

### 10.3.2    Two-phase commit protocol

To better illustrate the complexity of database transaction management in a distributed environment, consider the Bank Application.

Assume that the business requirements caused the Savings Account Table for all customers to be placed in the Central Office located in New York, while all checking account records reside at the Checking Processing Center, located in Chicago. A money transfer (MT) transaction, which debits the savings account (in New York) and credits the checking account (in Chicago), deals with two physically remote databases and resource managers (DBMSs). As with any database transaction, the MT starts with the first SQL statement to subtract the required amount from the savings amount value and proceeds to add this amount to the checking account. For example, the MT transaction may look like this:

```
BEGIN WORK
UPDATE SERVERNY.BANKDB.SAVING
        SET SAV_AMOUNT = SAV_AMOUNT - <money amount>
        WHERE SERVERNY.BANKDB.ACCT_NO = <customer account
    number>
UPDATE SERVERCH.BANKDB.CHECKING
        SET CHK_AMOUNT = CHK_AMOUNT + <money amount>
        WHERE SERVERCH.BANKDB.ACCT_NO = <customer account
    number>
COMMIT WORK
```

If both of these actions are successful, the transaction should commit the changes to the appropriate databases. If any one of the SQL statements fails, the transaction should abort and the changes made before the point of failure should be rolled back. Indeed, neither debiting the savings account without crediting the checking account, nor crediting the checking account without debiting the savings account, satisfies a business's or customer's requirements.

The DBMS at each of the processing sites can take care of the local COMMIT/ROLLBACK processing. The issue here is the coordination between the actions taken by multiple participants (in this case, the local and remote DBMS resource managers). That's when the transaction manager services become extremely important. These transaction services can be performed by a distributed DBMS itself, or by a separate transaction processing manager (TPM), which then also becomes a participant in the transactions it manages. In order to decide whether to make the changes to the distributed databases permanent (i.e., to treat the COMMIT request as global), or to roll them back, the DDBMS or TPM must follow a special set of rules, called the *two-phase commit* protocol.

The two-phase commit protocol is the process by which a *global commit* request is performed. It works as follows:

- When an application attempts to commit a multiple-participant transaction, one of the participants is first designated as the *coordinator* of the two-phase commit process.

- In Phase One, which is called the *Prepare Phase,* the coordinator requests that all participants in a global transaction *prepare* to commit their local resources and signal their readiness back to the coordinator. Once the participant is prepared, its log file is marked accordingly and this participant can no longer attempt to abort the transaction.

- If all participants are ready to commit, the coordinator brings the transaction into Phase Two—the *Commit Phase*—by broadcasting the COMMIT signal to all participants. At that point all local resource managers commit their local recoverable resources.

- If any of the transaction participants fails to prepare to commit, the coordinator is notified. In this case, the coordinator broadcasts the ROLLBACK signal to all participants and the entire global transaction is rolled back.

Logging both the Prepare and Commit phases of the two-phase commit protocols allows all participants to determine the same outcome of the global, distributed transaction. It is either committed, thus placing the distributed resources into a new consistent state, or rolled back, nullifying the effects of the transaction as if it never happened. One of the better known examples of the two-phase commit implementation is the transaction management performed by IBM's CICS in coordination with such resource management as DB2, VSAM, or IMS/VS.

The two-phase commit protocol is just one of a long list of Distributed Data Management issues. RDBMS distributed query optimization, distributed DBMS administration, concurrency and locking, heterogeneous and homogeneous DDBMS implementation, access control (security), and other issues are described in the next chapter.

# Designing Distributed Data Management Systems

Distributed data and database management systems represent an interesting phenomenon. On the one hand, they appear to be one of the most popular, easily justifiable, and readily available implementations of client/server architecture. On the other hand, distributed databases are among today's most complex and misunderstood technologies. Their complexity is reflected in the variety of access standards, as well as in the multitude of definitions and vendor implementations in client/server environments.

An analysis of data distribution and access methods in cooperative client/server environments was done in Chap. 10. Also demonstrated was the need for complex distributed DBMS features such as data location, replication and fragmentation transparency, and distributed data integrity. The discussion and analysis of distributed database features and the issues with which the DDBMS designers have to deal, continue in this chapter.

## 11.1 DISTRIBUTED DATA DICTIONARIES

The difficulty with implementing truly distributed databases becomes obvious when DDBMS designers begin considering the ramifications of particular DDBMS requirements.

The main problem, which is unique to a distributed system, is the need for global, or centralized, knowledge about the entire system. Even from a communication point of view, it is difficult for one node to know everything about the rest of the network.

The problem becomes even more acute when the distributed system supports a distributed database. In such a case, the system must not only answer questions like "Where is Node A?" and "Where is Program B?," but must also have a knowledge about the structure and location of every file, database, table, column, and their possible replicas. Moreover, there are other questions related to DDBMS processing that a distributed database system must solve. Questions about distributed (two-phase) commit and deadlock detection in a remote node are just two examples.

Some of these questions can be answered by a database dictionary, directory, and catalog. A data dictionary/directory/catalog plays an important role in distributed system architecture. In general, a database system keeps all necessary information about the resources it manages (data elements, attributes, entities, rules, indexes, statistics, etc.) in a database dictionary. With the advent of the distributed DBMS, database dictionaries have been expanded to include references to remote data, control information about the network, and nodes characteristics. Data location references are typically stored in database directories. In a client/server environment, database dictionaries and directories are usually stored and maintained by the DBMS server.

In order for relational DBMSs to support nonnavigational data access typical of RDBMSs, all pertinent information about the relational objects is usually kept in a set of internal, relational system tables called System Catalogs.

The need to distribute and maintain a database dictionary has some serious implications for the implementation of truly distributed databases.

If a dictionary is not distributed in a database system, then it is *centrally* located. Every data request, regardless of the location of the requester, must be matched against this particular server-resident database dictionary in order to validate the request and determine the location of the requested data.

One drawback of such an approach is obvious. A centralized dictionary becomes a bottleneck for all data requests, as well as a strong candidate for the single point of failure.

Another reason for a distributed database dictionary is the nature of distributed database systems. Again, consider the Bank Application. Imagine that a centralized (nondistributed) database dictionary resides at the bank's New York headquarters. Every request for London customer data initiated by the London branch must first be routed to New

York for validation and a data location search, only to be returned to London for processing—a practically unacceptable solution. If the dictionary was distributed between New York and London servers, however, such a request would be satisfied within the London branch.

Such a distributed dictionary becomes "global." It contains a global view of the distributed database. However, the global dictionary itself is a distributed database. As such, the distribution of the database dictionary introduces a consistency problem. All database dictionary copies must be kept in sync, even as data locations and network node characteristics change. Indeed, a local copy of the database directory points to a particular location at a specific node. If the data moves or the node becomes unavailable, the data request cannot be satisfied. As a result, the transaction, or even the entire system, may fail.

In the ideal distributed database management system, the task of database dictionary synchronization is given to the DDBMS itself. Such an ideal distributed database system can be defined to satisfy a set of rules developed by C. J. Date.

## 11.2   C. J. DATE'S RULES AND DISTRIBUTED DATA MANAGEMENT ISSUES

In 1987, C. J. Date, one of the first designers of relational databases (together with Dr. E. F. Codd, the author of the relational theory), proposed 12 rules that a fully distributed database management system should follow (C. J. Date's rules can be found in App. D).

These rules do not represent absolute requirements. They were proposed in order to bring some clarity to heated debates on DDBMSs. However, C. J. Date's rules are now widely accepted as the working definition of distributed databases. This chapter analyzes the requirements, features, and feasibility of distributed databases in terms of Date's 12 rules.

### 11.2.1   Rule 1—local autonomy

The first rule defines the DDBMS requirement for local autonomy. The rule states that in a truly distributed database environment, the sites (DBMS locations) should be autonomous, or independent of each other. This rule assumes that each site where a distributed database resides is characterized by the following:

- A local database (for a given site) is processed by its own DBMS.
- The DBMS at every site handles the security, data integrity, data consistency, locking, and recovery for its own database.
- Local data access operations use only local resources (e.g., local DBMS).

- Even though each site is independent of other sites for local operations, all sites cooperate in accessing distributed data from multiple sites in one transaction.

Date's first rule is quite logical, considering the architecture of distributed database. For an example of a distributed database environment implemented as client/server architecture see Fig. 11.1. This particular client/server implementation consists of three client sites connected to two database servers. This environment is designed to support the already familiar Bank Application, in which client sites represent bank branches B1, B2, and B3. Each branch maintains a local customer database (to a given branch), together with local savings and checking account data, all managed by the local DBMS. Servers S1 and S2 represent the bank's data processing centers that maintain the checking and savings account databases accordingly for all customer accounts, as well as central copies (replicas) of all customer records.

Date's first rule, for example, allows one of the branches to open customer accounts when another branch is closed, even if one or both data processing centers are not operational (e.g., undergoing weekly maintenance). Moreover, each local transaction retains all database transaction properties of atomicity, consistency, isolation, and durability.

Conversely, violation of the first rule forces all bank branches and service centers to be on-line continuously, even if a customer decides to use a cash access machine in a local branch.

### 11.2.2    Rule 2—no reliance on a central site

Date's second rule is designed to complement the first rule. The second rule states that the truly distributed database system should not rely on a central site. This means that no one DBMS site (DBMS server) is more important and necessary than any other.

This rule dictates that a distributed DBMS environment should not be built to rely on one (and only one) particular site. Dependence on one central site can become a bottleneck for the entire system's throughput and performance. Also, one central site may become a single point of failure for the entire distributed system.

Date's second rule is sometimes misinterpreted to mean that a distributed DBMS should not have a central site, even from the point of view of global control. On the contrary, even the example of a two-phase commit in a distributed transaction environment illustrates that there exists a need for a "central" coordinator to manage the distributed commit process. This "logical" central point may exist only for the duration of the distributed transaction, but it must exist.

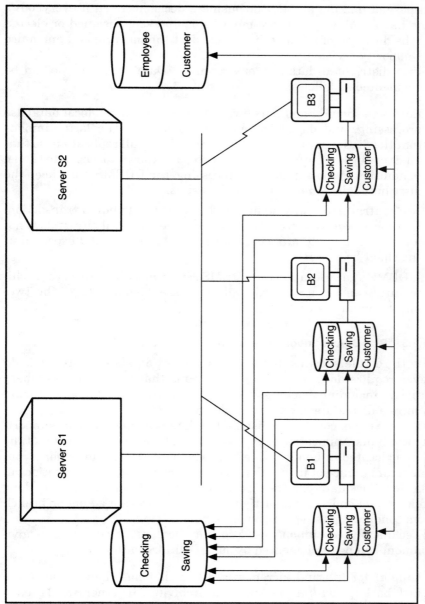

**Figure 11.1** Client/server distributed database

Imagine a group of people, all of whom are peers, meeting for the purpose of making a policy or business decision. Even if everybody's vote has equal weight, there must be one person, assigned or elected for the duration of the meeting, to conduct the meeting and announce the majority decision.

In a distributed database environment, Date's second rule can be implemented as follows:

- Each site should handle its own concurrency control, local database processing, and data dictionary management. The latter implies that the dictionary is distributed, probably by full replication, so that all data objects, both local and remote, are known to each site. Thus, in addition to the application processing, the DDBMS must keep the distributed dictionary current at all sites.

- No "central" site must be involved in every distributed transaction. In other words, if server S1 is chosen to be a central site, it does not have to participate in a customer inquiry initiated and executed at the client branch B1.

- A DBMS at any location (any DBMS server in the client/server architecture) can act as Distributed Database Manager (e.g., the two-phase commit coordinator).

### 11.2.3    Rule 3—continuous operations

The third rule specifies that the distributed database system should never require down time. The rule means that no planned database activity, including backing up and/or recovering databases, should require a distributed system shutdown.

For example, consider a distributed database environment supporting the Bank Application. Let's assume that one of the branches of the bank is located in London, England. The bank decides to perform routine maintenance of its databases (e.g., backup and reorganization) in the New York data processing center (Server S1) on a Friday of a long holiday weekend. Such an activity should not prevent a London branch from conducting its regular business.

Technically, continuous operations in the distributed database environment can be implemented by such DDBMS features as:

- support for full and incremental (data that has changed since the last backup) on-line backup and archiving. In other words, each database server should be able to backup its databases on-line, while processing other transactions.

- support for fast (preferably on-line) database recovery. One way to speed the recovery is to keep a mirror image of the database available. Some database servers have a disk-mirroring feature implemented in their hardware architecture. Some DBMSs implement software disk mirroring, thus providing DBMS fault-resistance.

- support for DBMS fault-tolerance (fault-tolerant DBMSs usually require fault-tolerant hardware).

### 11.2.4   Rule 4—data location independence

This rule describes a highly desirable, even critical, feature of a truly distributed database system. The rule defines an environment where data is distributed among multiple sites, but users and applications do not need to know that the data is distributed, nor where it is.

A truly distributed DBMS that satisfies Date's fourth rule provides users and applications with a single image of the database, which is "local" to the user and application in its appearance and behavior. Therefore, the fourth rule is sometimes called the rule of data location transparency. In a client/server architecture, where a client application is typically remote to the DBMS server, support for the data location independence rule is extremely important.

Some implications of this rule have already been described in the discussion of the methods of data distribution (see Chap. 10). Consider what would have happened if the fourth rule was not implemented in the Bank Application. If a customer transferred all accounts from one branch to another, all programs dealing with this customer's accounts would have to be modified to reflect the new data location.

Moreover, lack of data location transparency would require every application to be aware of the location where this application (and every program) exists. Without data location transparency, the local data has to be distinguished from the remote data. Therefore, if an application has to be moved from one system to another, it has to be changed accordingly.

That's why the data dictionary/directory plays a critical role. To implement data location transparency, designers of the distributed DBMS could use the following approach:

- Users and applications should refer to data by aliases.
- The distributed data dictionary must maintain a table of data elements, their aliases, and their locations.
- The distributed DBMS should be able to automatically maintain and use this data dictionary, even when a particular data object has been moved from one location to another.
- In order for every user and application to perceive the distributed database as a single local database, the DDBMS must distribute

(replicate) the data dictionary to every site, maintain all replicas of the data dictionary, and synchronize them among all distributed system locations.

Often, data location transparency refers to data entities. In the case of the relational data model, the data location transparency rule deals primarily with the databases and tables.

Indeed, it makes sense to keep New York customers in the Customer Table in the New York branch of the bank, while the London branch keeps its customers in its own local table. In this scenario, the majority of data access operations deal with one location at a time (per transaction). Data access is usually done via remote requests or remote transactions (remote units of work), and rarely requires distributed tables to be logically combined into one conceptual table.

Many DBMS vendors today implement at least some degree of the data location transparency by supporting remote requests/remote transactions that use different variations of the data dictionary approach.

### 11.2.5    Rule 5—data fragmentation independence

As illustrated in the methods of data distribution, data can be divided into fragments. In the case of the relational data model, the table can be divided into horizontal or vertical fragments, which can be distributed among multiple locations. This method of data distribution is called data fragmentation.

Date's fifth rule specifies that in a truly distributed database, a table that has been fragmented must appear as a single table to users and applications. In other words, the fragmentation must be transparent to the users and applications.

Data fragmentation transparency is closely related to Date's fourth rule on data location transparency. However, the data location transparency rule deals mostly with objects such as databases and tables, while data fragmentation transparency handles, for example, the situation when a single table is broken into several portions, each of which resides at a different site (see Fig. 11.2).

The difficulty of supporting data fragmentation transparency is in the reconstruction of the original table from fragments. Typical access to fragmented data may require the "logical" combination of data from two fragments into one unfragmented table. For example, if an employee table is fragmented into personal and medical fragments (each fragment at its own server location), an employee benefits department may need a complete, combined view of the employee record. Such a join between two fragments may look like the following SQL statement:

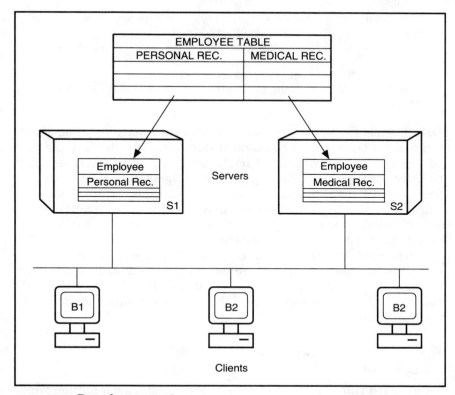

**Figure 11.2**   Data fragmentation

```
†BEGIN WORK
 SELECT * FROM SERVERB1.BANKDB.EMPLOYEE,
              SERVERM.BANKDB.EMPL_MED
         WHERE SERVERB1.BANKDB.EMPLOYEE.EDLEVEL = "MBA"  AND
               SERVERM.BANKDB.EMPL_MED.BRANCH = "B1"
 COMMIT WORK
```

When data from one table is distributed by fragmentation, data access to fragments may require conceptual table reconstruction. Depending on the type of fragmentation (vertical or horizontal), the application may request the DDBMS to join two tables (as in the case of the vertical fragmentation of the employee table in Fig. 11.2). Horizontally fragmented tables may be reconstructed using a SQL operation of UNION (e.g., the Customer Table is horizontally fragmented into New York and London parts). Fragmented table reconstruction using a UNION operation may look like:

---

†The naming convention here specifies that data element names consist of "location," "database," "table," and "column" names.

```
BEGIN WORK
SELECT * FROM SERVERNY.BANKDB.CUSTOMER
        WHERE SERVERNY.BANKDB.CUSTOMER.BALANCE GREATER 10000
UNION
SELECT * FROM SERVERUK.BANKDB.CUSTOMER
        WHERE SERVERUK.BANKDB.CUSTOMER.BALANCE GREATER 10000
COMMIT WORK
```

Data fragmentation transparency requires the implementation of data location transparency in the context described. But just using a data dictionary is not sufficient to implement data fragmentation transparency. Regardless of the type of data fragmentation, access to the fragmented data may require data from multiple locations within a single transaction. The data access may be a distributed transaction or a distributed request. And that is in addition to the need to synchronize distributed database dictionaries!

Distributed transactions and requests present several serious problems, among them the coordination of distributed updates, distributed data integrity, and consistency. Only a handful of DBMS vendors (e.g., Ingres, Informix) claim to support data fragmentation transparency.

### 11.2.6    Rule 6—data replication independence

Date's sixth rule expands the data location and fragmentation transparency requirements into the data distribution method of replication. The rule requires a distributed database system to be capable of updating replicated, redundant data, transparently from applications and users. As the name implies, replicated data is a copy of data that exists elsewhere in the system (at other servers, and even with some clients). Since the replicated data is one type of distributed data, Date's sixth rule requires the implementation of the data location transparency rule. But the data replication transparency rule has far-reaching implications.

In the Bank Application, an example of the replicated data may be a savings account database, kept in its entirety in the savings account processing center (see Server S2, Fig. 11.1). Each branch (B1, B2, and B3) keeps its own subset of the Savings Account Table for all of the branch's customers. For a given customer from branch B1, therefore, there exists a savings account record maintained at the customer's branch (client B1). At the same time, the exact copy of this record is kept at Server S2. If this customer withdraws money from the savings account, both the local (B1) and the remote (S2) copies of the database records must be updated. This is a classic case of the need to synchronize distributed resources by employing the two-phase commit protocol with either a distributed transaction or a distributed request.

The need for the two-phase commit is clear when the implications of unsynchronized updates are considered. If a customer withdrew all available funds and the local savings account record was updated (debited), but the central (S2) copy remained the same, the bank's books would show no change in the customer's account. Therefore, withdrawals (from other branches, cash access machines, etc.) would be possible. Thus, both update actions (local and remote account records) must either be committed or the transaction must be rolled back if any one of the updates fails.

The main issue in this scenario is not just the proper execution of the two-phase commit logic, but the need to perform such a synchronization *transparently* from the users and applications.

Ideally, a Savings Account Debit Program should not be aware of the existence of other copies of the data it updates, and may contain a simple single-site SQL update statement (using aliases):

```
UPDATE BANKDB.SAVINGS_ACCOUNT
    SET SAVINGS_AMOUNT = SAVINGS_AMOUNT - WITHDRAWL_AMOUNT
    WHERE BANKDB.CUST_ACCT_NO = 12345
```

Therefore, the DDBMS itself should initiate additional updates within the now expanded original unit of work. The DDBMS should conform to the two-phase commit protocol to ensure consistency between two copies of the savings account record. All these actions should be performed automatically by the DDBMS, without any user or application being aware of the replicated data. In effect, the DDBMS should transform the update statement into something like:

```
BEGIN WORK
UPDATE SERVERB1.BANKDB.SAVINGS_ACCOUNT
    SET SAVINGS_AMOUNT = SAVINGS_AMOUNT - WITHDRAWL_AMOUNT
    WHERE SERVERB1.BANKDB.CUST_ACCT_NO = 12345
UPDATE SERVERS2.BANKDB.SAVINGS_ACCOUNT
    SET SAVINGS_AMOUNT = SAVINGS_AMOUNT - WITHDRAWL_AMOUNT
    WHERE SERVERS2.BANKDB.CUST_ACCT_NO = 12345
COMMIT WORK
```

Of course, the DDBMS is made aware of the existence of replicas by searching through the distributed database dictionary, which must be kept synchronized among its own multiple copies as well.

As a result of adhering to Date's sixth rule, the DDBMS is becoming ever more complex and must perform increasingly involved, complicated tasks. Look at the task of adding records into the replicated table, for instance. Inserting rows causes the DDBMS to enforce referential integrity constraints in a distributed environment, where multiple copies of the foreign keys must be checked against multiple copies of the primary key.

Another complicated issue is locking. Even though a detailed discussion of locking is beyond the scope of this book, it is a good illustration of how difficult data replication transparency is to implement. Locking is the technique a DBMS uses to support consistency of data. While one transaction is updating a particular record or group of records, the data being updated is held by an exclusive lock, i.e., locked from updates (and sometimes from read access, in order to prevent a view of inconsistent, "dirty" data) by any other transaction. In a distributed environment, where multiple replicas are to be updated, how should a DDBMS ensure that all copies of a given record are locked in every data location?

And when two or more applications wish to exercise exclusive control over the same resources, such as database records that are already locked by these or other applications, they are in a deadlock. The DDBMS must resolve the deadlock condition, even though the locked resources reside in multiple remote nodes. Global deadlock detection is a serious problem that a truly distributed database system should be capable of solving. Typically, a DDBMS detects and resolves deadlocks by timing and terminating a transaction that timed-out while waiting for a resource.

In addition, some DDBMS products maintain a fixed, limited number of requests that can be active at any given time. Sometimes, a DDBMS employs a deadlock detection algorithm (e.g., terminate or interrupt the shortest-running task, terminate a task with fewer updates, etc.). In practice, some of the data replication transparency implementation problems could be solved by carefully designing applications, compromising, and imposing restrictions on the database processing. Some vendors implement a disk-mirroring technique, which they inaccurately describe as support for data replication transparency. Nevertheless, serious implementation problems, especially if a "truly" distributed DBMS is needed, still remain unsolved. Consequently, many vendors choose not to support replicated data transparency rules.

### 11.2.7    Rule 7—distributed query processing

Date's seventh rule deals with performance issues of distributed database systems. To fully understand these issues, let's look at how a query is processed in a nondistributed, centralized, relational database. (In a nonrelational DBMS, the performance of the query depends on the DBMS access path selected by a user or program.)

Remember that nonrelational DBMSs are navigational. That is, the access is directed by the user, and the DBMS itself follows the user's directives.

A relational DBMS (RDBMS) provides for nonnavigational data access where users request *what* data they need, and not *how* to access it. Generally speaking, a RDBMS contains a navigational brain—an optimizer—that is "intelligent" enough to select the best access path for a given query, which is totally transparent to the users and applications. Different RDBMS products offer different optimization techniques, which can be divided into two major classes—cost-based optimization and rule-based optimization.

Rule-based optimizers select an access path based on certain rules. For example, when processing a query to join two tables, the rule-based optimizer may decide that the table coded first (from left to right) in the SQL statement should be searched before the second table. The drawback of such an approach is demonstrated by the following example. Suppose that the bank's central office (Server S1) maintains a table of all bank employees and a table of managers. The query in question should look up all employees that are managers who hold M.B.A.s. Such a query may look like:

```
SELECT * FROM BANKDB.EMPLOYEE A, BANKDB.EMPL_MGR B
        WHERE A.EMPL_ID = B.MGR_ID         AND
              A.EDLEVEL = "MBA"            AND
              B.EDLEVEL = "MBA"
```

Usually, there are more employees than managers. Assume that the EMPLOYEE Table contains 100,000 rows and the manager table contains 1000 rows. If the rule-based optimization processes the leftmost-referenced table first, the RDBMS will search 100,000 rows of the EMPLOYEE Table to find all those with M.B.A.s, and then compare them with the 1000 rows in the Manager Table. Obviously, such an approach is not very efficient.

Cost-based optimization selects the access path for a given query based on the estimated cost of the query processing. Typically, the optimizer calculates the cost in units such as the number of I/O operations and/or CPU cycles. A cost-based optimizer may take into account the number of rows needed to be processed to satisfy the query, availability of indexes, and various statistical information about data organization, accumulated and maintained by the RDBMS in the System Catalog. Such a catalog must be active, since any additions or deletions to the database (relational objects as well as data records) may change the statistical information.

When a cost-based optimizer processes the query described above, it can calculate the least expensive access path based on the row statistics. Therefore, the query processing should start from a smaller table (EMPL_MGR), and compare the selected managers to the list of employees who hold M.B.A.s.

Performance becomes a major issue in *distributed* query processing. Imagine that the Employee Table and the Manager Table are distributed to two different locations. The size of each node's databases and relevant tables, the network speed, and the processing and I/O power of each node are among the major factors that affect the performance of a distributed query. In the client/server architecture, the DDBMS should maintain the list and processing characteristics of every available server.

In order to find the proper data location and obtain all necessary node characteristics and statistical information about remote databases, distributed query optimization requires access to a "global" database dictionary. A global dictionary can be implemented by replicating all local dictionaries on all nodes (database servers) where the query is performed. And to perform cost-based optimization based on real-time statistics, a truly distributed DBMS must maintain all dictionary replicas current.

In distributed query processing, one DBMS server must coordinate optimization and synchronization efforts among all participating databases. Such a coordinator is usually called a Distributed Data Manager (DDM), and is elected dynamically by the DDBMS based on various criteria. In the client/server architecture, the DBMS server that receives the query first can be elected to be the DDM.

Date's seventh rule specifies that in a truly distributed database system, optimization must take into account not only local, but also global factors, including distributed nodes and network characteristics. Consider an example that illustrates the issue of distributed query optimization and the role of the DDM.

Let's assume that the bank's central office (Server S1) maintains a table of all employees, while the processing center (Server S2) holds a separate table of managers. The query in question should look up all employees who are managers with M.B.A.s. Here's how such a query can be processed in a truly distributed database system:

- The server that first receives the query is elected to become the DDM (in this example, Server S1).

- The DDM knows that the tables in question reside at different locations (S1 and S2) and modifies the original query accordingly.

```
SELECT * FROM SERVERS1.BANKDB.EMPLOYEE A,
        SERVERS2.BANKDB.EMPL_MGR B
    WHERE A.EMPL_ID = B.MGR_ID          AND
```

```
A.EDLEVEL = "MBA"                 AND
B.EDLEVEL = "MBA"
```

- The DDM accesses its own system catalog to assign costs to the local join component (EMPLOYEE Table).

- The DDM connects to the remote server (S2) and accesses the S2 system catalog to assign costs to the remote components of the join (see Fig. 11.3).

- Based on the estimated costs and server characteristics, the DDM decides *where* the join is to be performed and *which* table is to be joined to the other.

- The DDM selects server S1 as the site for the join execution, since the S1 is the more powerful server. The DDM decides that the smaller table (EMPL_MGR) will be joined to the EMPLOYEE Table, since it requires fewer I/O operations and less network data movement between servers.

- The DDM initiates the selection of the proper rows from the smaller table and sends the filtered records (managers with M.B.A. degrees) across the network to server S1.

Without distributed query optimization, the DDBMS may choose an extremely inefficient alternative—sending all 100,000 employee records to remote Server S2 for selection and join, then sending the results back to S1. Clearly, joining data between two tables is the simplest possible case. Each additional table and/or database increases the number of choices for the optimizer and the complexity of the DDM. Therefore, a complete implementation of the distributed query optimization is a rather difficult task that only a handful of DBMS vendors attempt to undertake. In addition, remote data access standards, such as the Remote Data Access (RDA) standard from ISO, and full-function ANSI SQL standard, are still emerging. Products like Informix and Ingres support Date's seventh rule with certain limitations, and even then the quality of optimization decreases with the complexity of the query.

### 11.2.8    Rule 8—distributed transaction management

Date's eighth rule is intended to provide data consistency, integrity, concurrency, and recovery in a distributed database system.

Updating a distributed database introduces a new set of complicated problems. First of all, distributed update complications can cause different parts of the database to be out of sync if any one of the local

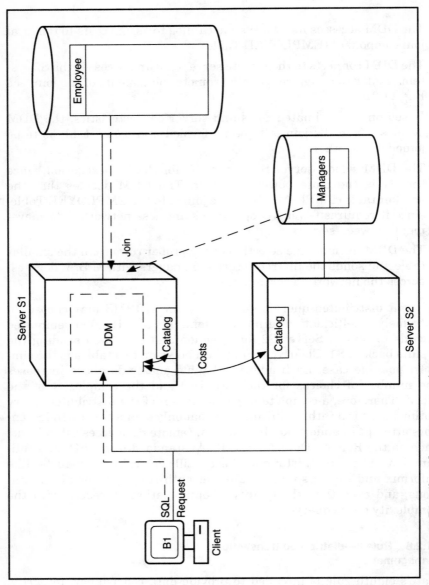

**Figure 11.3** Distributed query processing

updates fails. Two-phase commit protocol must be used to guarantee consistency of updated data.

Two-phase commit allows a commit/rollback process to be implemented in a distributed environment (distributed commit/distributed rollback). In essence, two-phase commit protocol supports the atomicity, consistency, and durability of database transactions in a distributed environment. By supporting consistent rollback, two-phase commit protocol also supports distributed database recovery from a transaction failure. However, two-phase commit protocol requires a coordination of efforts among all participating parties during the Prepare and Commit phases of the process. The synchronization task is assigned to a transaction coordinator. A DDM often acts as such a coordinator.

Often, it is not enough that the DDM supports two-phase commit protocol. Distributed transaction management guarantees that proper actions (COMMIT and/or ROLLBACK) take place automatically, without user or application intervention. Some DDBMS vendors (e.g., Sybase) offer a set of commands and procedures that allow applications and users to implement a two-phase commit protocol, while others (e.g., Oracle) avoid the problem completely by restricting updates to a single site. Very few vendors offer products that support automatic two-phase commit protocol, although some do in a restricted environment (e.g., InterBase and Ingres-Star).

Distributed commit is not the only problem that transaction management has to solve in a distributed environment. Other issues include distributed locking, deadlock detection, local backup/global recovery, logging, administration, and security. Each one of these issues represents a serious DDBMS design problem.

The difficulty of distributed transaction management resulted in the emergence of transaction management products developed by non-DBMS vendors. What's more, as demonstrated by transaction management implementation in mainframe On-Line Transaction Processing (OLTP), processing benefits when transaction management is separated from DBMS. Some of these products, such as IBM's CICS, offer a proprietary solution, which provides distributed transaction management across various proprietary platforms (e.g., OS/2, MVS). Other products are designed to be more open by operating in various UNIX environments (AT&T's Tuxedo, NCR's Top End, and Transarc Corporation's Transarc). The benefits and appeal of Open Systems force all vendors to promise to adhere to the still emerging distributed transaction management standards, such as the XA and ATMI standards from the X/Open. CICS, Tuxedo, Top End, and Transarc are discussed in more detail later in the book.

### 11.2.9    Hardware, software, networks and DBMS independence

Satisfying the desire for database management systems to work inter-dependently across networks is complicated by the fact that computing environments are increasingly heterogeneous. Date's last four rules—rules 9, 10, 11, and 12—deal with the heterogeneous nature of distributed systems. These rules specify that a truly distributed database system should not depend on underlying hardware platforms, operating systems, networks, or even individual database management systems. The aim of the last four rules is to support the goals of Open Systems by allowing the implementation of distributed database systems in practically any networking environment, including existing networks, databases, and equipment.

### 11.2.10    Rule 9—hardware independence

Date's ninth rule states that distributed database systems should be able to run on different hardware platforms, with all systems participating as equal partners. This rule allows designers to build distributed environments that consist of computer systems from different vendors and hardware architects. This rule is essential to developers of client/server computing systems. The rule actually reinforces the notion of client and server specialization. And it is easy to picture a distributed database (e.g., Oracle) in a client/server environment (see Fig. 11.4), where client B1 is Intel's i486-based personal computer, Server S1 is a RISC-based machine (e.g., IBM's RS/6000), Server S2 is a Symmetric Multiprocessor (SMP) from Sequent Corporation, and Server S3 is an IBM mainframe. In fact, many DDBMS vendors (e.g., Oracle, Sybase, Informix, Ingres) support Date's ninth rule by providing the DDBMS support for a wide variety of hardware platforms.

### 11.2.11    Rule 10—operating system independence

Date's tenth rule supplements and expands rule 9. Rule 10 allows DDBMS designers to choose a hardware platform, and at the same time, not be limited by a single operating system. Adherence to rule 9 by itself does not guarantee support for multiple operating systems. This rule can be supported by selecting a DDBMS solution designed according to international and industry-wide standards, i.e., designed to operate in an open system environment.

Today, the marketplace offers DDBMS solutions designed for particular proprietary operating systems (e.g., OS/2 Database Manager, Microsoft SQL server, IBM DB2), as well as solutions designed for various implementations of the best candidate for open systems—the

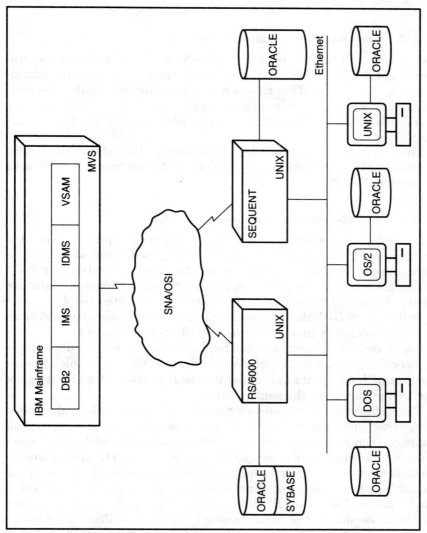

**Figure 11.4** Hardware/software/network independence

UNIX operating system (e.g., Sybase, Informix, Ingres, Oracle). The client/server environment shown in Fig. 11.4 supports both rule 9 and rule 10. Indeed, the Oracle DBMS shown here runs under MS-DOS, UNIX, and MVS.

### 11.2.12     Rule 11—network independence

Date's eleventh rule supplements rules 9 and 10 by adding a requirement for the DDBMS not to depend on particular network implementation and protocols. This rule is natural for any distributed network environment, especially in a client/server environment. Adherence to standards (OSI, TCP/IP, IEEE) allows many DDBMS vendors to support rule 11.

The client/server architecture shown in Fig. 11.4 allows the Oracle DDBMS to operate within an Ethernet LAN and across a wide area network (SNA/OSI).

### 11.2.13     Rule 12—DBMS independence

Date's rules, discussed up to this point, have been implicitly applied to distributed database systems, where every node was supporting a homogeneous DBMS. In other words, the intention of Date's rules 1 through 11 appears to be the transformation of an existing database system (such as DB2 or Oracle) into a truly distributed DBMS.

In fact, most DDBMS implementations available today support some of Date's rules only in a homogeneous DBMS environment.

Date's twelfth rule expands the horizons of homogeneous data access by specifying that a truly distributed database should be able to interoperate with different kinds of databases, regardless of whether or not the DBMSs are from the same vendor.

The variation of homogeneous data access that satisfies rule 12 is a distributed environment where all databases are not the same, but all support a common data model—the relational data model—and a common, standardized data access language—Structured Query Language. Unfortunately, the implementation of a heterogeneous distributed relational DBMS environment is not a simple task. The SQL standard is not finalized. Not every RDBMS vendor fully supports the currently available version of the SQL standard. Every RDBMS vendor implements its product differently, with different name lengths, different return codes, and proprietary SQL extensions.

The truly heterogeneous DDBMS system, however, is even more difficult to develop. Indeed, the real world is much more complicated than a single, homogeneous, or strictly relational DBMS environment.

As illustrated in Fig. 11.4, a business enterprise may adopt a DOS operating system and an Oracle DBMS for its client platform, Oracle and Sybase DBMSs for the UNIX-based servers, DB2, IMS, IDMS and VSAM for the mainframe MVS platform. In fact, the majority of data today usually resides in legacy databases and files (i.e., IMS, IDMS, VSAM), although a number of databases have been steadily migrating to IBM's DB2. This trend is true for many IBM and compatible mainframe sites. The problem of implementing a DDBMS in such an environment is complicated by the fact that each local DBMS "speaks" its own data access language and the translation of a SQL query, for example, into a hierarchical IMS data access is not a trivial task. Sometimes, it simply cannot be done without rewriting a query or an entire application.

Many vendors attempt to provide heterogeneous data access. Almost every RDBMS vendor provides access to IBM's DB2 as well as to its own RDBMS (for example, by building DB2 mainframe gateways utilizing Advanced Program-to-Program Communications protocol).

Sybase DBMS goes one step further by allowing access (APPC and Remote Procedure Calls, or RPC) from Sybase's SQL Server to IBM's CICS and all CICS-accesible resources (VSAM, IMS, IDMS, DB2). However, accessing heterogeneous data introduces complications into DDBMS issues such as heterogeneous data integrity, locking, administration, and security. Notwithstanding the difficulties of heterogeneous data access, however, it is easy to see that support of rule 12 is a real business requirement for the truly distributed database system. The key to such a solution is support of industry data access standards— Remote Data Access from the ISO, SQL from ISO, SQL Access Group and ANSI, XA Interfaces from X/Open, and others as they develop.

## 11.3   OTHER DISTRIBUTED DATA MANAGEMENT ISSUES

Even though they have become widely accepted as the working definition and the criteria for distributed databases, Date's 12 rules are not the perfect recipe for truly distributed database systems. However, adherence to Date's rules causes designers of distributed database systems to solve other important, even critical, issues.

### 11.3.1   Administration

Database administration in a distributed environment can be a potential nightmare for database and system administrators and has to be designed with extreme care.

Indeed, in a distributed database system, where every node is equal, how does a Database Administrator (DBA) perform backup, recovery, creation and deletion of database objects, modification at remote sites, change and version management, etc.?

Ideally, a properly implemented DDBMS should provide a central database administration facility and tools for distributed DBA support. If distributed DBA administration features are not implemented, then the administration of the DDBMS can be performed by local DBAs. That means that additional, highly qualified staff is required, and the synchronization of DBAs efforts has to be controlled. Of course, a "central" DBA can travel to each remote site that needs intervention. Obviously, it is not the most efficient or timely solution, especially if the remote sites are really remote—New York and Tokyo, for example. These are just a few issues demonstrating the importance and complexity of database administration in a distributed environment.

### 11.3.2   Security

Data security may be defined as protection of data from deliberate or inadvertent disclosure, modification, or destruction. Data security can be implemented by utilizing access control, assigning user privileges for data access and data object creation, deletion, or modification, creating password protection or data encryption, and other similar techniques. Data security can be enforced and validated by maintaining active, on-line auditing. These data security techniques and methods must be expanded to be operational in a distributed database system. In a distributed environment, data security issues are closely related to administration issues and require a high level of coordination between all participating controllers. Participants include data administrators, security administrators, and network managers.

One of the security problems in a distributed environment is the development of procedures that allow a user access to a table, for example, that is fragmented between three different nodes. At the very least, this user must be able to access the three network nodes and have access privileges to all three table fragments. If password protection is in effect, then all three nodes must recognize the same password. If the data is encrypted on one of the nodes, then the decrypting facility should be employed at this node to process the required data.

Of course, in a distributed database environment, especially in a client/server architecture that employs DOS PCs as client systems, totally secured, critical data can be downloaded into an insecure PC environment—a security administrator's nightmare. The rule calling for each node to be responsible for the protection of its own data might not be sufficient in this case.

In a client/server environment, many vendors attempt to solve security issues by placing all security procedures, rules, validations, and checks at the server itself. Then, the server becomes a place where all necessary security measures are implemented, including government standards of C1, C2, and B1 levels of security (discretional and mandatory access control, user verification and authentication, etc.). For example, Informix DBMS supports B1 mandatory access control security.

### 11.3.3  Currency control

Currency control issues can arise when a distributed database system is implemented according to Date's 12 rules. An extension of data consistency issues presents a potential problem when a database transaction updates two or more resources located at different sites. Database consistency issues are solved by employing a two-phase commit protocol that makes database transaction atomic, consistent, and durable. Currency is not related directly to a single database transaction. Currency in a distributed database environment is a DDBMS state in which all related databases in a network are consistent relative to a particular version and/or date and time. Specifically, consider the distributed client/server architecture shown in Figure 11.4. Assume that Server S2 developed a serious hardware problem and has to be brought off-line. The distributed database environment in Figure 11.4 is designed to satisfy Date's 12 rules, and a failure of one node does not bring the system down. Moreover, any transactions that were active when Server S2 failed are rolled back, thus ensuring data integrity and consistency. Assume that Server S2 keeps a management summary database of the bank account activity. This summary is continuously updated by certain transactions initiated from Servers S1 and S3, and client B1. If it takes 12 hours to repair Server S2 and bring it back on-line, the data residing there is no longer current and, for some critical applications, may not be useful. Now, the DDBMS, its administration, and the currency control team must perform certain procedures to make the S2 database current. To do that, S1, S3, and B1 updates have to be captured and reapplied to Server S2. The point here is that currency control is a real issue, one of the many critical issues a truly distributed database system should be designed to handle.

The discussion of Date's rules demonstrates the importance and complexity of truly distributed database implementation. One practical implementation of Date's rules is architecture designed to implement distributed data access across IBM system platforms—Distributed Relational Database Architecture (DRDA).

# Distributed Relational
# Database Architecture

The main goal and advantage of distributed data management is the ability to share and access data located in multiple systems in a fashion transparent to end users, while keeping most data local to the locations that actually use the data.

Distributed data management has been demonstrated as one of the styles of the cooperative distributed processing often implemented in the client/server architecture. In the context of the client/server architecture, distributed data management operates in environments where the data and DBMS are distributed among multiple systems. Data management functions are distributed between a front-end system (data processing logic, or DML) and a back-end server (database functions, or DBMS). Distributed data management, already implemented in several client/server and distributed mainframe environments, deals with many complicated issues, not all of which have been resolved.

Some of the issues of distributed data management are being addressed by the emerging industry standards, including ANSI SQL standard, X/Open's XA architecture, ANSI and ISO distributed computing models, and Remote Data Access (RDA) architecture. In addition to standard organizations, major DBMS vendors are also involved with distributed data management. Prominent among these vendor solutions is IBM's Distributed Relational Database Architecture (DRDA). In answer to the still unfinalized RDA standard, DRDA is IBM's strategy for providing distributed data management and inter-operability for its two major computing environments—Systems Application Architecture (SAA) and the Advanced Interactive eXecutive, or AIX (IBM's version of the UNIX operating system).

Today, traditional customer loyalty to a vendor of choice is being replaced by the desire to reduce operating costs and to decentralize operations in order to be more competitive. Advances in the area of distributed and client/server computing, and the availability of enabling technology for distributed databases in a client/server architecture, force users to look very seriously into open systems, distributed computing, and distributed databases. These trends affect even such major vendors as IBM. Given the challenges of open systems, and facing increasing pressure for higher interoperability and "openness" from its customer base, IBM has chosen to evolve both SAA and AIX as two complementary environments. The SAA-AIX interoperability efforts include increased connectivity, network management, distributed database and shared files, presentation services, mail exchange, and common languages on all SAA and AIX systems.

The Distributed Relational Database Architecture (DRDA) is intended to satisfy the needs of applications requiring access to distributed *relational* data in IBM operating environments—SAA and AIX—as well as in non-IBM environments conforming to DRDA. Given the large installed base of various SAA platforms and the success of IBM's AIX offerings (especially AIX version 3 running on RS/6000 computers), the DRDA goal is twofold. On one hand, DRDA is designed to facilitate the development of new distributed and client/server applications within and across SAA and AIX platforms. On the other hand, DRDA is intended to help migrate existing environments into the distributed and client/server world by leveraging investments already made in existing systems, networks, LANs, DBMSs, and transaction managers.

## 12.1   DRDA OVERVIEW

The Distributed Relational Database Architecture is designed to provide the necessary connectivity to and from relational database management systems (RDBMS), that can operate in homogeneous ("like") and heterogeneous ("unlike") system environments. In the DRDA framework, heterogeneous environments are those supported by the Systems Application Architecture (SAA), by the Advanced Interactive eXecutive (AIX), and by any non-IBM RDBMS products that conform to DRDA (see Fig. 12.1).

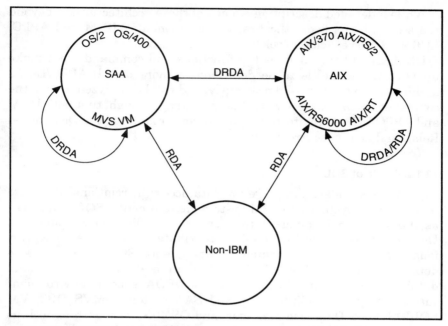

**Figure 12.1**   DRDA environments

By limiting its reach to relational databases, DRDA can standardize a single data access language—the Structured Query Language (SQL)—as the common language that all applications must use to access distributed relational data.

### 12.1.1   Relationship to other architectures

From a structural point of view, DRDA is built on other architectures: architectural building blocks. These building blocks represent the following IBM architectures:

- Distributed Data Management Architecture (DDM)
- Logical Unit Type 6.2 (APPC/LU6.2) Architecture
- SNA Management Services Architecture (MSA)
- Formatted Data Object Content Architecture (FD:OCA)
- Character Data Representation Architecture (CDRA)

DRDA ties these architectural blocks together into a common protocol that supports the distributed cooperation typical of distributed databases and client/server environments.

While a detailed description of each of these architectures is beyond the scope of this book, the first two components—DDM and APPC/LU6.2—deserve a closer look.

DDM architecture defines the functions and commands that make up DRDA, and needs to be described in more detail. APPC/LU6.2 architecture was discussed previously, and will be analyzed here in the context of DRDA connectivity. It is safe to say, though, that both DDM and APPC/LU6.2 architectures are the cornerstones of the Distributed Relational Database Architecture.

### 12.1.2    Role of SQL

SQL is the standard language for data access in relational database management systems. In IBM system environments, SQL is adopted as the standard language within Systems Application Architecture. Due to its consistency, SQL enables distributed data access across various relational database management systems. SQL allows users to define, retrieve, and manipulate data in a distributed relational database environment. In the context of DRDA, such an environment can be comprised of interconnected SAA systems—MVS DB2, VM SQL/DS, OS/2 Database Manager, and OS/400 Database—as well as any non-IBM RDBMS that conforms to DRDA rules and protocols. DRDA supports SQL as the standard Application Programming Interface (*API*) for execution of applications. DRDA uses SQL to define logical connections (*flows*) between applications and a Relational Database Management System (RDBMS). Program preparation processes use these flows to *bind* SQL statements to a target RDBMS.

DRDA specifies that applications use SQL to access an RDBMS. If the requested data is remote, the DRDA requires that a special mechanism be used to determine where the data resides and to establish connectivity with the target remote RDBMS. In SQL, an application can use the SQL CONNECT statement to establish connectivity with the named RDBMS. DRDA uses the term RDB_NAME to represent the name of the target relational database. To support subsets of data managed by a RDBMS (data fragmentation), DRDA allows each subset to be known by a separate RDB_NAME.

### 12.1.3    DRDA as the connection
### architecture

A distributed environment, including a client/server environment, is characterized by a collection of (possibly specialized) nodes intercommunicating over a network. Such an environment requires a connection architecture that defines specific flows, protocols, and interactions that are designed to support the intent and results of distributed data management. DRDA is the architecture that provides the necessary connections between applications and RDBMS in a DRDA-supported (SAA and AIX) distributed environment.

Even though DRDA's intent is to allow connection between IBM and non-IBM products, DRDA is primarily designed for IBM system environments and uses appropriate IBM communication architectures to describe:

- what information should flow between participants (clients and servers in a client/server computing model) in a distributed relational database management system (DRDBMS)
- responsibilities of all DRDBMS environment participants
- when the interactions (flows) should occur

In other words, DRDA provides the formats and protocols required for data access in a distributed database system. However, DRDA does *not* provide the application programming interface (API) for applications accessing data in a distributed RDBMS environment.

The distributed database processing formats and protocols supported by DRDA depend on the type of distributed database processing supported by the distributed database system.

There are four types of distributed database processing. They were described in previous chapters as remote request, remote transaction (remote unit of work), distributed transaction (distributed unit of work), and distributed request.

In IBM DRDA terminology, the four types of distributed database processing are called *degrees of distribution*. DRDA defines three degrees of distribution of database processing:

- *Remote Unit of Work* (RUW) includes remote request and remote transaction types of distributed database processing, and is described in the current level of DRDA.
- *Distributed Unit of Work* (DUW) is equivalent to the distributed transaction type of distributed database processing. This degree of distribution will be described in future levels of DRDA.
- *Distributed Request* is the same for DRDA and non-DRDA definitions. This is the highest degree of distribution, and will also be described in future levels of DRDA.

Within the framework of the remote unit of work (DRDA Level 3—current level of DRDA), an application program running on one system can use SQL to access relational data at a remote system. The SQL is provided by, and executed at, this remote system. This model is symmetrical—an RDBMS running on a system where an application is executing can be accessed by applications running on other remote systems.

As was illustrated previously, DRDA support of the remote unit of work limits data access to a single RDBMS per unit of work, even though an application may perform multiple SQL statements within this transaction. Typically, all processing performed within a remote unit of work is committed (or rolled back) by the *application* at the end of the transaction. From the client/server point of view, the current level (Level 3—RUW) of DRDA defines connections between an application process residing on a client system with the application/DBMS server.

That is in contrast with the distributed unit of work or a distributed request, where the *transaction manager* (TPM) is required to *coordinate* the commit/rollback process between multiple units of work executing at multiple locations (two-phase commit protocol). Future levels of DRDA should describe the responsibilities of participants in the distributed unit of work and the distributed request, as well as formats and protocols required by a transaction coordinator. For example, future levels of DRDA will define interconnections between two or more RDBMSs, which can be homogeneous (i.e., two DB2 systems), IBM heterogeneous (i.e., DB2 and SQL/DS), or a mix of IBM and non-IBM products, as long as all participants support DRDA.

### 12.1.4    DRDA protocols and functions

The DRDA model describes connections between application processes and server processes (application servers and DBMS servers) that support the application's requests. Therefore, the DRDA model can be described in general terms of the client/server architecture. However, since the DRDA model emphasizes the interactions between different processes irrespective of the platform on which they are running, the server-requester computing model (described in Chap. 9) can be used to describe DRDA protocols and functions more accurately. The DRDA server-requester computing model is illustrated in Fig. 12.2.

In this model, DRDA defines three major components: application requester (AR), application server (AS), and database server (DS). To support connections between an application client process (application requester), application server, and RDBMS server, DRDA provides two types of connection protocols and three basic types of functions. The connection protocols provided by DRDA are:

- *Application Support Protocol* provides the connection between application requester (AR) processes and application servers (AS).

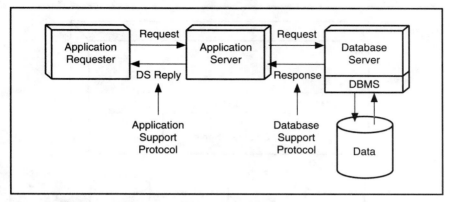

**Figure 12.2** DRDA computing model

- *Database Support Protocol* provides the connection between application servers (AS) and database servers (DS).

DRDA defines the server-requester relationship between AR, AS, and DS as follows:

- The *application requester* (AR) supports the application end of the DRDA connection by requesting services from the application server (AS).

- The *application server* supports the DBMS end of the DRDA connection by requesting data services from the database server (DS) and delivering the DS replies back to the AR.

These AR-AS-DS interactions correspond to client/server interactions in a three-tiered client/server architecture which can be implemented entirely in SAA environment. OS/2 clients, where application requestors (AR) reside, are connected to the OS/400 server, running the application server AS, which in turn is connected to the IBM mainframe system (e.g., IBM 3090), running MVS and DB2 (see Fig. 12.3).

For each of the DRDA components, DRDA provides the following basic functions:

- *Application Requester Functions* include SQL support and program preparation services from applications. These functions correspond to those client functions of a client/server architecture that deal with issuing source SQL statements.

- *Application Server Functions* support AR requests by transforming them into calls to the RDBMS and routing these calls to the appropriate DBMS servers. These functions correspond to the data

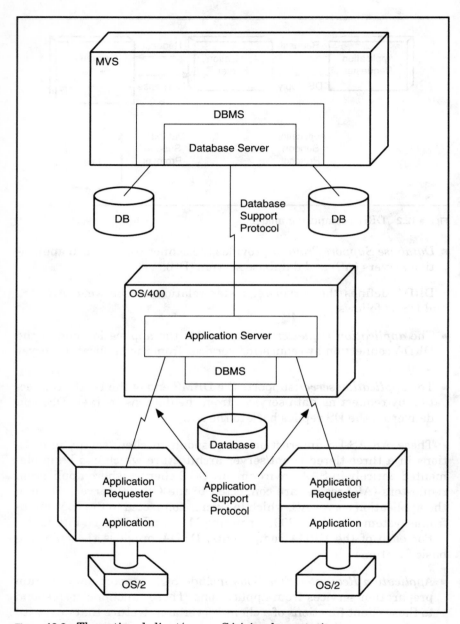

**Figure 12.3**  Three-tiered client/server SAA implementation

processing logic portion of the distributed application in a client/server environment.

- *Database Server Functions* support requests received from application servers (AS). In a client/server architecture, these functions correspond to the database processing functions performed by the DBMS portion of an application on the server system.

These DRDA functions can be implemented on separate systems, as illustrated in Fig. 12.3. Or, all functions can be implemented in a single system—a mainframe, for example—if an application is running on a mainframe and accessing DB2 data. Or, some of the functions can be performed on a single system, while the rest of the functionality is placed on a different system. For example, the DRDA implementation shown on Fig. 12.4 uses an OS/2 system to perform AR functions for the OS/400 system running the RDBMS. Here, OS/400 acts as both the AS and the DS. The MVS system, running DB2, also performs the AS and DS functions, but does it for a different requester—AS functions for the AIX requester, and DS functions for the MVS AS as well as for the OS/400 AS.

## 12.2 DRDA AND DDM

Distributed Data Management (DDM) architecture provides a conceptual model for building common data management interfaces that are used for data exchange between homogeneous (like) and heterogeneous (unlike) systems. DDM commands, parameters, objects, and messages constitute the DDM data stream, which accomplishes the data interchange between various systems. DDM describes the common data interchange interfaces for various data models, including the relational data model. There are more DDM commands, parameters, objects, and messages than DRDA requires to implement a distributed relational database management system. Thus, DRDA uses an appropriate subset of DDM in its references and definitions.

### 12.2.1 DDM architecture

DDM architecture makes possible the sharing and accessing of data between different computer systems by providing a common language and set of rules that enable different systems to communicate and share data. DDM architecture allows developers to build cross-system data management functionality into new, as well as existing systems. DDM architecture is designed to satisfy the following objectives:

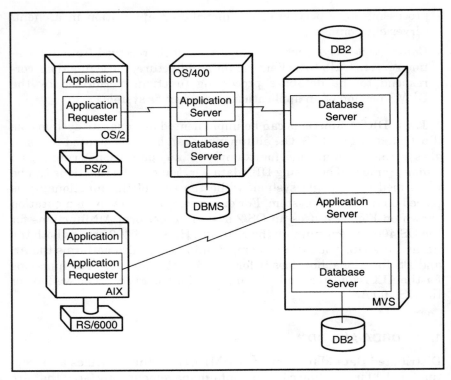

**Figure 12.4**   DRDA implementation example

- standardize data management facilities for new system development
- provide data interchange among different systems
- increase efficiency of data exchange among homogeneous systems

The DDM components that allow the architecture to achieve these objectives include:

- *Data Connectivity Language.* This is a DDM-provided vocabulary of terms and set of rules (a language grammar) for accessing data from remote files and relational databases.
- *Standardized data structures.* These are file models that describe how data is organized and managed within a file.
- *Standardized data access methods.* These are mechanisms that provide a consistent way of accessing data stored in a file.
- *Standardized relational database model.* This is a description of data organization within a relational database (RDB).

- *Standardized Structured Query Language Application Manager.* This is a mechanism that provides a consistent way of requesting SQL services from a relational database.

The main goal of DDM components is to allow applications and users to access data without concern for where the file or the RDB is located. In terms of Date's twelve rules for a truly distributed database system, one of the DDM goals is to provide data location transparency. DDM architecture is designed to be independent of an underlying system's hardware architecture and its operating system. In other words, DDM is designed to satisfy the hardware and operating system independence requirements specified by Date's Distributed Database rules.

DDM architecture can also be viewed as a language that is used for data exchange between different computer systems. The DDM language is composed of the *vocabulary* that contains DDM words (defined terms, such as *class* and *object*), *grammar* that describes the word order and rules which the words have to obey, and *protocols* that are sets of rules used to ensure the proper exchange of data between two interconnected systems.

### 12.2.2   DDM benefits

As the architecture designed to allow the sharing and accessing of data between different computer systems, DDM is designed to provide significant benefits to applications, users, and businesses.

These benefits are better illustrated on the example of the Bank Application (see Fig. 12.5).

The bank's Central Office keeps the master copies of all customer and account records on its mainframe system (Server S1). The Central Office is connected to two bank branches—B1 and B2. A balance report program runs at the Central Office (S1) and needs to access both branches (B1 and B2) in order to verify the balances. Without DDM, this application would require two interface programs to allow access to two different, heterogeneous systems. But with DDM implemented on each system, the following benefits are obtained:

- The development, programming, and maintenance costs are reduced since DDM provides all necessary interfaces (see Fig. 12.6).

- Data redundancy can be reduced if DDM-supplied shared data access is preferred to data replication. For example, all customer records can be kept at the Central Office, thus helping to prevent a potential loss of data integrity.

- DDM provides for data location transparency by supporting local data management interface (LDMI). DDM LDMI can handle

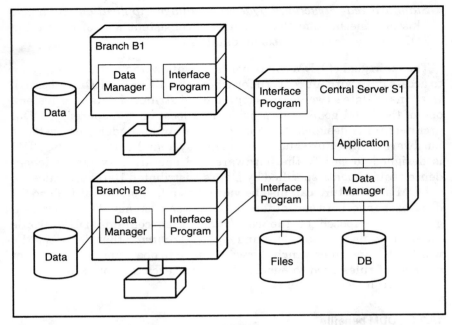

**Figure 12.5**    Bank Application without DDM

requests for data stored locally by passing them to the local DBMS or file system, while routing remote data requests to DDM to handle communications and necessary data access at remote locations.

- DDM improves data integrity in non-RDB environments by providing various file and record locking commands.

- DDM provides better resource management by facilitating a shared data load balancing between multiple available storage devices.

- DDM provides standardization, which is important for open systems, as has already been discussed in considerable detail. By providing standard access methods, language, communication protocols, commands, and messages, DDM helps ensure connectivity, portability, and interoperability of applications and systems.

### 12.2.3    DDM components interactions

DDM architecture is designed to provide data sharing and data exchange between two interconnected systems. In this context, DDM differentiates between the source system (the system containing the application program that requests data from a remote system), and the

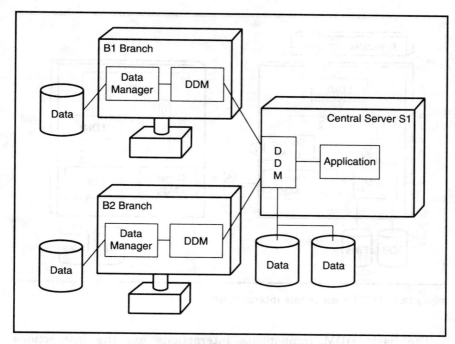

**Figure 12.6**   Bank Application with DDM

target system (the system that contains data requested by the source system). To support data exchange between the source and the target systems, DDM architecture defines two types of components:

- *DDM Data Management Services.* This is the software that performs bidirectional request-reply conversion. An application's data requests, directed to application files or relational databases, are translated into DDM commands, and DDM reply messages are translated into data formats that applications can use. Typically, DDM Data Management Services on each system (source and target) consist of the Local Data Management Interface (LDMI) and a DDM Server (see Fig. 12.7).

- *DDM Communications Manager.* This is the software that handles the communications protocols and procedures necessary to exchange data with another, interconnected system. DDM architecture includes specifications for the use of IBM Systems Network Architecture's Advanced Program-to-Program Communications (APPC/LU6.2), even though other communications facilities could also be used.

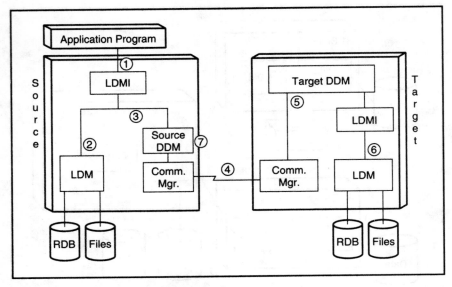

**Figure 12.7**   DDM components interactions

The basic DDM components interactions are the interactions between requesters and servers shown in Fig. 12.7:

1. The application program on the source system requests data from a DDM-supported data management facility (files or RDBMS) by sending a data request to the local data management interface (LDMI). LDMI determines whether the requested data is stored locally or on the remote system.

2. If the data is on the local system, the LDMI sends the request to the local data manager (LDM) for processing.

3. If the requested data is located on the remote system, LDMI routes the request to the source DDM server, which translates the request into DDM commands, and gives it to the source Communications Manager.

4. The source Communications Manager transmits the request to the target Communications Manager.

5. The target Communications Manager gives the request to the target DDM server, which interprets the DDM commands, locates the requested file or RDBMS, translates the DDM commands for the target's LDMI, and requests execution of the appropriate data management function.

6. The LDM of the target system retrieves the data and sends it back through the target LDMI to the target DDM server. DDM server translates the reply into DDM form and gives it the target Communications Manager, which sends it back to the source Communications manager.

7. The source DDM server receives data from the source Communications Manager and translates it into the format required by the source's LDM. In turn, the source LDM passes the data to the application program.

In addition to these steps, there are many other important tasks the DDM components must perform. Among them are resource management tasks (e.g., locating and locking resources, translating DDM data and commands), communications tasks (e.g., initiating and terminating communications, negotiating connectivity, controlling the flow of requests and replies), and common tasks (error handling and recovery, checking authorization).

### 12.2.4  DDM file models and access methods

DDM architecture considers three basic file forms:

- *Record-oriented files.* These contain data as an organized collection of records (basic, atomic unit of data for record-oriented files).

- *Stream files.* These contain sequence of bytes organized into a byte stream.

- *Directories.* These contain directory entries.

Based on these three basic file forms, DDM defines and supports the following file models:

- *Record-oriented models,* such as Sequential (SEQFIL), Direct (DIRFIL), Keyed (KEYFIL) and Alternate Index (ALTINDF)
- *Stream model* (STRFIL)
- *Directory model* (DRCFIL)

Every record-oriented file contains a set of records. DDM allows records to be:

- fixed length
- variable length, where the user can change the length of the record after it has been written to a file

- initially variable length, where the user can establish the length of the record before it has been written to the file
- inactive, where DDM uses inactive records to indicate empty file record positions

DDM *sequential* files start with the beginning of the file (BOF—one record position before the first record), contain records stored in the order in which they have been placed in the file, and end with the end of the file (EOF—one record position after the last record). DDM allows multiple alternate indexes to be built over a sequential file.

DDM *direct* files contain records that have a direct relationship between their content and their stored position (record number). Direct files also contain BOF and EOF attributes, but the first record position in a direct DDM file points to the first *active* record. Similarly, the last record position points to the last active records. DDM allows multiple alternate indexes to be built over a direct file.

DDM *keyed* files maintain an index that keeps track of the location of each record within the file. Each active record of the keyed file contains a key field that identifies the record. A key can be composed from multiple fields within the record. A separate index file containing an entry for each active record (each key) is also maintained. This index allows users to access keyed files sequentially or directly by a key value. In addition to the primary index, DDM allows multiple alternate indexes to be built over a keyed file.

DDM *alternate index* files support keyed access to the records of a base file (the one which contains the key fields). Alternate index files have the same BOF and EOF position as the underlying base files. Various access methods—Relative (by record number and/or by key), Random (by record number and/or by key), and their combinations, are provided by DDM to access record-oriented files.

DDM *stream* files do not contain records. Instead, data is represented as a consecutive sequence of bytes. The byte is the atomic unit of data. DDM stream files are accessed via the DDM-defined Stream Access Method (STRAM), where a substream of bytes of the specified length is dynamically mapped over the file stream. The BOF position is represented by the byte 0, while the EOF position is the one after the last byte in the stream. Logical records are mapped onto the stream by applications.

DDM allows a file shadow to be created when a stream file is opened. The file shadow is a working copy of the stream file, created and maintained for recovery purposes. (Commands intended to alter the main file are redirected to operate against the shadow.)

A DDM *directory* is a special file that maps the names of other files and directories to their locations. Directories are accessed via the

DDM-defined read-only Directory Access Method (DRCAM). Directory records, known as entries, are created, deleted, and modified by local data management functions.

### 12.2.5 DDM relational database models

The DDM relational database model consists of a single system model and a distributed system model. Both models describe a relational database (RDB), which represents data as a collection of tables and employs the Structured Query Language. A single system RDB model contains an SQL Application Manager (SQLAM) that provides a consistent method (interface) for requesting SQL services from an RDB (see Fig. 12.8). The SQLAM uses other system services (i.e., Dictionary, Directory, and Security Manager—SECMGR), to access the RDB and present the data returned by the RDB to the application.

In a distributed RDB model, DDM specifies that SQLAM services need the assistance of SQL agents and the Communications Manager (CMNMGR). According to the DDM definitions, the SQLAM, agents,

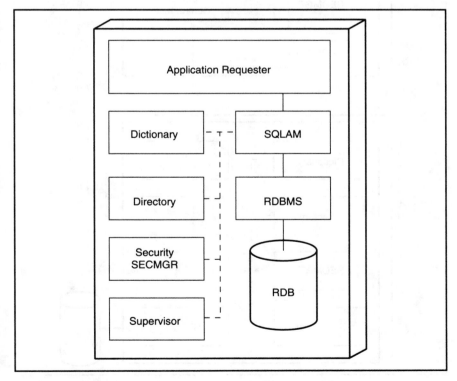

**Figure 12.8** DDM single system relational database model

and CMNMGR are to be split between the source and the target systems (see Fig. 12.9). The distributed RDB components are physically connected via corresponding CMNMGRs, even though logical connectivity exists between the application (source) and the RDB (target), as well as between source and target SQLAMs and Agents.

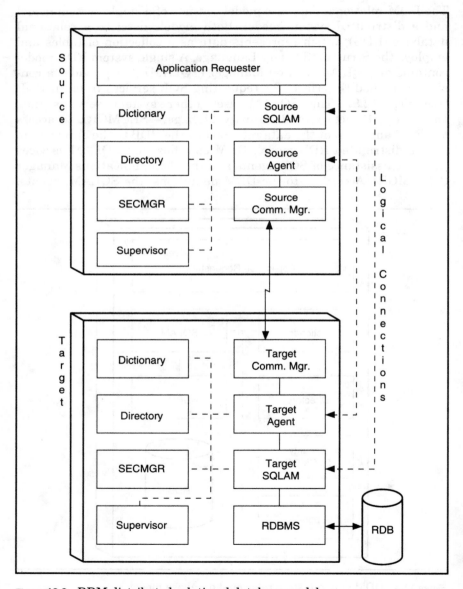

**Figure 12.9**   DDM distributed relational database model

In this model, the source SQLAM receives application requests for SQL services from the RDB, uses source directory to determine the location of the required RDB, and routes the request to the source Agent. The source Agent uses the source Communications Manager to send requests to, and to receive replies from, the target system.

DDM does not describe the internal functions (i.e., logging, locking, etc.) of the RDB. However, DDM defines that in the distributed RDB model, both source and target SQLAMs must cooperate to efficiently process SQL queries. DDM allows for multiple queries to be processed simultaneously, and requires source and target SQLAM to perform all necessary bidirectional data conversions if the source and target systems use different data representation.

## 12.3   DRDA PROCESSING MODEL

The DRDA processing model describes the interchanges required between applications and a remote relational database (RDB) to implement a distributed relational database management system. DRDA uses an appropriate subset of DDM architecture (namely its RDB model) and the APPC/LU6.2 architecture to support the following functions:

- Establish and terminate a connection between an application and a (remote) RDB

- Bind application's embedded (static) SQL statements and host language variables to a RDB

- Execute these bound SQL statements as well as dynamic SQL statements on behalf of the application and return results to the application

- Maintain a consistent logical unit of work (remote unit of work) between an application and a remote RDB

The DRDA processing model describes these functions in terms of commands and command replies, as well as in terms of the correct flows of these commands and replies.

The DRDA processing model is shown on Fig. 12.10, and its processing flows are described below:

1. An application contains previously bound (to the remote RDB) SQL statements that are transparent to the location of the target (remote) RDB. The remote RDB is represented by the local source SQLAM, residing on a source system (Application Requester, or AR), which is called whenever the application issues a SQL statement. Note that calls to the SQLAM interface are generated by the

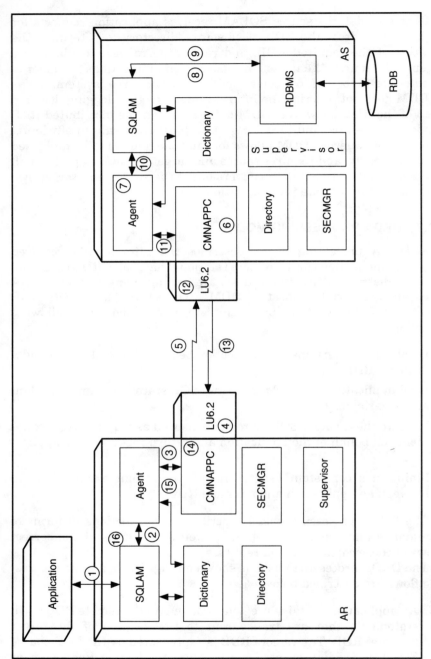

**Figure 12.10** DRDA processing model

program preparation process and may be different in each DRDA implementation.

2. SQLAM checks the SQL request's parameters and translates it into DDM commands. It does so by using the DDM function models stored in the Dictionary. SQLAM is also responsible for any required data representation conversion. SQLAM passes generated DDM commands to the source Agent. The function of the Agent is to represent a requester to a server by interfacing with other DRDA managers.

3. Source Agent receives the DDM commands, parameters, and data objects, and routes them to the DDM Communications Manager. It also keeps track of each command until the reply to that command is received.

4. DDM communications manager (CMNAPPC) uses APPC/LU6.2 protocols to communicate with the remote system. CMNAPPC receives DDM commands and objects, and creates DDM data streams for commands and data objects. Then CMNAPPC invokes the local source system's LU6.2 facilities.

5. LU6.2 of the Application Requester (AR) establishes an LU-LU session with the remote system (AS), and sends the request through the network to its partner LU6.2 over an LU6.2 conversation. AR and AS LU6.2 facilities utilize APPC protocols to maintain the conversation between the AR and AS intact, as well as to support session and conversation error recovery.

6. When AS's LU6.2 receives the data, the target DDM Communications Manager decomposes the DDM data stream into original commands, parameters, and data objects, and passes them on to the target Agent.

7. The Agent validates commands and parameters, and returns error messages (if any) to the DDM communications manager. If a command is valid, it is packaged together with received data objects and passed to the target's SQLAM.

8. The target SQLAM transforms DDM commands into calls to the supported RDBMS. All necessary data conversion from the AR format into the AS format is also performed here.

9. The target RDB processes calls from the SQLAM and returns any data, codes, and messages back to the target SQLAM.

10. The AS's SQLAM transforms received responses into DDM commands, parameters, and data objects, and sends them to the target Agent. All necessary AS-AR data representation conversion is also performed here.

11. The target's Agent checks the received data, assigns proper correlation identifiers to it, and sends it to the target Communications Manager.

12. The AS's communications manager creates a DDM data stream and invokes the target's LU6.2, which is still in session with its partner (AR's LU6.2).

13. The target LU6.2 sends replies over the network to its partner LU6.2 as a response to the conversation request initiated by the AR's LU6.2 facilities. APPC/LU6.2 protocols maintain a conversation between the AR and AS intact, as well as provide for session and conversation error recovery.

14. The AR's CMNAPPC invokes its LU6.2 to receive the reply, decomposes the data into DDM commands, parameters, messages, codes, and data objects, and passes it to the source Agent.

15. The Agent verifies the receipt of the data against the commands sent to the AS, and passes it to the source SQLAM.

16. SQLAM converts the DDM data formats into the SQL-compliant representation and returns the reply to the application.

The DRDA processing model described above employs several DRDA managers: SQL Application Manager, Communications Manager, Agent, Supervisor, Security Manager, and Directory and Dictionary Managers. Most of these managers' functions have already been described. However, DRDA managers not described as part of the DRDA flows also play an important role in DRDA processing model.

- The DRDA Supervisor manages various managers within a particular operating environment: Resources Manager, Directory Manager, Dictionary Manager, and Security Manager.

- The DRDA Security Manager ensures that the Application Requester (AR) represented by its agent accesses only those resources and managers it has been authorized to access, and only in the authorized fashion. The Security Manager works with the LU6.2 communications facilities, which perform all necessary requester's identification and verification, and with the RDBMS, which performs user's authorization to objects and operations with the RDB.

- The DRDA Directory Manager (DIRECTORY) maps the names of managers and their managed objects to their locations.

- The DRDA Dictionary Manager (DICTIONARY) provides interfaces to object descriptions (including valid DDM commands and messages) that are stored in the dictionary.

## 12.4   DRDA COMMUNICATIONS MANAGER AND APPC

DRDA communications are built on APPC/LU6.2 architecture and are supported by the DDM communications manager. The DDM Communications Manager interfaces with local communications facilities (LU6.2) to route DDM requests and replies to appropriate agents, to send and receive DDM requests, replies, and data, and to participate in communications error detection and recovery.

### 12.4.1   LU6.2 communications

The DRDA Communications Manager is designed to use APPC/LU6.2 protocols and the base and optional LU6.2 set functions that provide the robust program-to-program communications necessary to implement a distributed database. APPC/LU6.2 architecture was already discussed in previous chapters. Among the advanced features of the LU6.2 architecture:

- Sync point processing supports synchronous distributed transaction processing by implementing COMMIT/ROLLBACK coordination between participating LU6.2 nodes. DRDA uses relational database manager's COMMIT and ROLLBACK features rather than LU6.2 verbs.

- There is support for security, authentication, authorization, and accounting processing on LU6.2 sessions and conversation. In addition, APPC/LU6.2 permits propagation of security, authentication, authorization, and accounting information to the DRDA resource and control managers that participate in a distributed user transaction.

- Timely node, session, and conversation failure notification, as well as communication error handling is inherent in the APPC protocols of the LU6.2 architecture.

Remember that LU6.2 supports two categories of commands (or verbs). Conversation verbs consist of mapped, basic, and type-independent conversation verbs. These verbs are used by application transaction programs. Control-operator verbs provide for program or operator's control over the LU6.2 resources. LU6.2 verbs are listed in App. C. DRDA application requesters and servers (AR and AS) use *basic conversation* verbs.

All LU6.2 functions (verbs, parameters, return codes, and indicators) can be divided into two major groups: a base set that all LU6.2 implementations support, and optional function sets that a particular

LU6.2 implementation may support. Due to the complexity of distributed database processing, DRDA requires both base and option set functions of LU6.2. The following base LU6.2 function set is supported in DRDA:

- Basic conversation verbs such as ALLOCATE, DEALLOCATE, GET_ATTRIBUTES, RECEIVE_AND_WAIT, SEND_DATA, and SEND_ERROR
- Type-independent conversation verb (GET_TP_PROPERTIES)

Option set for DRDA includes the following:

- User ID verification for conversation level security (implemented in the ALLOCATE verb)
- Program supplied User ID and Password for conversation level security (implemented in the ALLOCATE verb)
- Logical Unit of Work (LUW) identifier (implemented in the GET_TP_PROPERTIES verb)
- Asynchronous receive capabilities, implemented by basic conversation verbs such as PREPARE_TO_RECEIVE, POST_ON_RECEIPT and TEST.

The LU6.2 base and option sets used by DRDA support current level of DRDA distributed capabilities—the Remote Unit of Work (RUW) method of accessing distributed data.

### 12.4.2    APPC/LU6.2 and DRDA
#### remote unit of work

DRDA uses APPC/LU6.2 architectured flows to initialize and terminate conversations and process DRDA requests that allow the implementation of a remote unit of work. Remember, that even though an RUW may contain multiple SQL statements, only one DBMS is accessed per UOW, and the application itself controls the commit/rollback processing.

*Initialization of a Conversation.* Only a DRDA application requester (AR) can start a conversation. During the initialization process, the conversation is allocated and the required LU6.2 conversation level security is used to perform end user verification. An end user is thus cleared to use the conversation and requested DRDA database management functions. This authentication procedure between the AR and AS is performed once per conversation during LU6.2 ALLOCATE verb processing. At the same time, basic accounting information—User ID and name, Logical Unit of Work ID (LUWID), remote logical unit name (LUNAME), and transaction program name (TPN)—is specified in the LU6.2 ALLOCATE verb and propagated through the DRDA environment.

*Processing of a DRDA Request.* DRDA requests are created to process SQL statements at a single remote location (as per RUW definition) and to prepare an application program. Only the AR can initiate a remote unit of work.

SQL is a set-level language (that is, one SQL statement can operate on a set of relational records at a time). Therefore, DRDA defines two data transfer protocols to support RUW: Single Row Protocol and Limited Block Protocol. Single Row Protocol is used in the processing of an SQL query that may be formulated with the single row clause (e.g., WHERE_CURRENT_OF) of the SQL UPDATE or DELETE statements. Single Row Protocol guarantees that the AS returns exactly one row to the AR.

Limited Block Protocol is used for queries that contain cursors for read-only operations. This protocol is optimized for the transfer of a minimum amount of data in response to a cursor DRDA request. LU6.2 SEND_DATA, PREPARE_TO_RECEIVE, RECEIVE_AND_WAIT, POST_ON_RECEIPT and TEST (AS only) verbs are used to transmit DRDA remote unit of work requests and responses.

*Commit and Rollback.* As was already mentioned, a DRDA remote unit of work is not under LU6.2 sync point control. Instead, an application program normally initiates commit or rollback processing by executing SQL COMMIT/ROLLBACK statements. (Both static and dynamic requests are supported.) If the application program does not request an explicit COMMIT but terminates normally, the AR must invoke the COMMIT function before terminating the conversation. Conversely, the AR invokes the ROLLBACK function if the application terminates abnormally. Both COMMIT and ROLLBACK functions are handled as normal DRDA requests, and LU6.2 synchronization protocols are not involved.

*Termination of Conversation.* Terminating a conversation makes the conversation resources, including the underlying session, available for reuse by both the AR and AS. Normally, only the AR can request conversation termination. The AS can terminate the conversation if it detects an appropriate error. The conversation is terminated by issuing the LU6.2 DEALLOCATE verb. Under normal circumstances, the application program should issue an SQL COMMIT/ROLLBACK statement prior to conversation termination.

*Conversation Failures.* In case of conversation failures, LU6.2 notifies both the AR and the AS. The AS must then implicitly roll back the uncommitted changes and deallocate all the resource managers supporting the conversation. At the same time, the AR must report the failure to the application via SQLAM.

At this point, the AR can either reject any subsequent SQL requests from the application, or it can treat the next SQL request as the beginning of a new unit of work. In the latter case, the DRDA processing sequence (i.e., initialization, DRDA request processing, termination) is repeated.

*Conclusion.* The Distributed Relational Database Architecture is the connection architecture for IBM's relational database management system products. DRDA is designed to provide the necessary connectivity to and from relational database management systems operating in homogeneous and heterogeneous system environments. DRDA can be used today to build a distributed database system in environments that are supported by the Systems Application Architecture (OS/2, OS/400, MVS and VM), by the Advanced Interactive eXecutive (AIX-PS/2, AIX/RT, AIX-RS/6000, AIX/370), and by any non-IBM RDBMS products that conform to DRDA. Even though DRDA's scope is mostly limited to IBM RDB implementations and currently supports only remote units of work, this very brief description of DRDA features and protocols, and the relationship of DRDA to other architectures demonstrates the complexity of distributed data management environments. It confirms the importance of database management systems and access methods, file and relational data models, and communication architectures, protocols, and components. Finally, DRDA demonstrates the power and convenience of the client/server computing model for building distributed computing environments.

# Distributed DBMS Implementations

Database management systems are the information backbone of today's organizations. Changing technology and business requirements make it increasingly clear that distributed systems and distributed database management systems will play a major role in the advanced computing environments today and in the future. Client-server computing, network computing, and peer computing are just several examples of such environments. The role of the distributed DBMS in the client/server architecture, design principles, and complexity of distributed database management systems have been described in the previous chapters from a theoretical point of view. DDBMS architecture and design goals (together with such communication architectures as Advanced Program-to-Program Communications) have been illustrated in the example of IBM's Distributed Relational Data Architecture.

So far, the emphasis was on the general theoretical criteria of an ideal DDBMS formulated by C. J. Date in his 12 Distributed DBMS rules. Today, evaluating and choosing a database management system is steadily becoming one of the first system decisions MIS managers must make. Therefore, this chapter is intended to discuss some practical, technical DDBMS implementation trends and features of which DDBMS designers and users alike should be aware. In addition, this chapter illustrates both the theoretical DDBMS foundation and technical features of distributed data management in a client/server computing environment with examples of several popular distributed database implementations.

## 13.1   IMPLEMENTATION TRENDS AND FEATURES OF DISTRIBUTED DBMS

Distributed database systems make special demands not only on the data base logical and physical design, but also on the database management system itself. A distributed DBMS must maintain data integrity by providing local and global locking mechanisms, and by supporting database commit/rollback transaction integrity.

A distributed DBMS must automatically detect deadlocks and perform transaction and database recovery. A distributed DBMS must be intelligent enough to optimize data access for a wide variety of application requests. The traditional DBMS bottleneck—Input/Output—must be tuned for specialized high-capacity handling and support for optimum space management techniques. This is especially true if the underlying platform is a limited resources microcomputer. Database security and administration facilities must be able to support distributed data/applications locations, preferably from a single, centralized location. And all this must be done by a DDBMS reliably and within acceptable throughput parameters, especially in a multiuser distributed OnLine Transaction Processing (OLTP) environment.

Therefore, even if every distributed DBMS implementation is designed to support some or all of C. J. Date's 12 distributed database rules, the users must take a close look at the actual technology of a given product. It is important to see how each particular rule is implemented, regardless of the hardware platform, in respect to the selected hardware/software platform, and what advanced features (if any) a given DBMS product offers to satisfy and possibly exceed customer expectations. In other words, when implementing a distributed environment, customers will benefit from and therefore should demand:

- A Relational DBMS (as opposed to nonrelational DBMS) and standard SQL support
- Support for referential integrity
- Support for data location, fragmentation, and replication transparency
- Support for local autonomy, hardware, operating system, and network independence
- Support for distributed data consistency delivered by a distributed two-phase commit protocol

- A cost-based optimizer for the data access path selection
- Support for distributed transaction management

Any DBMS chosen must provide users with appropriate levels of data and access security. Discretionary and mandatory security features such as authorization, authentication, access control, and automatic audit trails should be supported by a production OLTP-grade DBMS.

In addition to these attributes, a distributed DBMS user should examine implementation features sometimes not advertised by a prospective vendor and often overlooked in the product selection process. Some of these features and their benefits are described below.

### 13.1.1  DBMS server architecture

In a distributed multiuser client/server environment, a database management system resides at the database server and should be architected as a server component of the client/server computing model. As such, the DBMS server should be designed to receive and process multiple concurrent database requests from multiple remote users.

Operating in a limited resource environment (server system) under the control of an operating system, the DBMS designers can follow different strategies.

*Threads.* One strategy is to create an operating system server process (task) for every DBMS client, which can result in, among other things, additional operating system overhead (e.g., context switching) and additional CPU and memory requirements (see Fig. 13.1). This is called a single-threaded architecture.

Another approach is to launch a separate thread (subtask) for each client. Such a "lightweight" task is controlled by the DBMS server rather than the operating system (see Fig. 13.2).

Threads do not incur operating system overhead after being launched, and threads can share memory space with other threads. In general, a multithreaded DBMS server architecture is preferable to a single-threaded one. Among Unix-based DBMS server implementations, Sybase and Ingres are examples of the multithreaded server architecture. Sybase's latest release of SQL Server—Release 4.8—extends the concept of the multithreaded architecture to Symmetric Multiprocessing hardware platforms.

*Server-Enforced Integrity and Security.* Data integrity and security are critical requirements for database management systems. Integrity features, such as referential and domain integrity, assure the accuracy and consistency of data, while database security refers to authorization and control of data access. Integrity and security can be implemented in

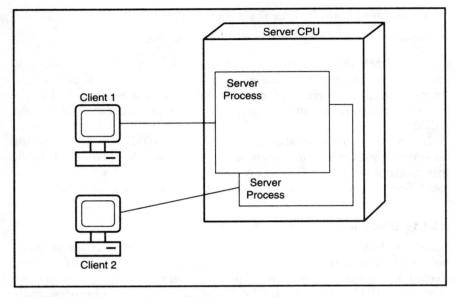

**Figure 13.1** Single-threaded architecture

several different ways. For example, integrity constraints and security procedures can be included in every application. In the client/server computing model, it may mean duplication of the relevant code on every client running these applications. However, a more efficient approach would call for implementation of the integrity and security features centrally, directly at the DBMS server level. Such DBMS server architecture will provide for higher application reliability, reduced development and maintenance costs, and increased database security.

### 13.1.2 DBMS server performance features

DBMS server performance is usually measured by using standard benchmarks, as well as some proprietary application transaction mix. Because many external factors affect DBMS performance (operating system environment, hardware platform, etc.), benchmarks usually demonstrate some particular small aspect of the performance picture as a whole, and can be unreliable as a predictor for any specific environment or configuration. However, there are certain DBMS design features that quite definitely affect DBMS performance. Some of these features are applicable to the performance of the individual DBMS, while others (like Global Optimization) affect the performance of the entire distributed database system.

*Global Optimization.* C. J. Date's seventh distributed database rule specifies that in a truly distributed database system, the optimization

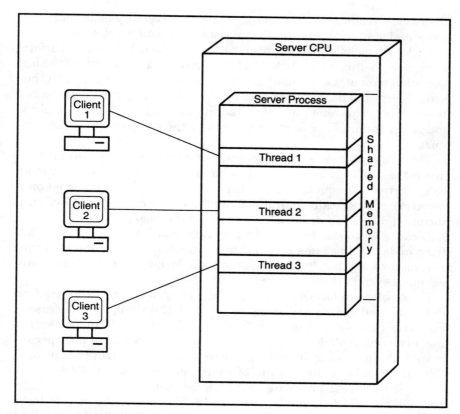

**Figure 13.2** Multithreaded architecture

must take into account not only local, but also global, factors, including distributed nodes and network characteristics.

Typical cost-based optimization selects the access path for a given query based on the estimated cost of the query processing. Usually, the Optimizer calculates the cost in such units as the number of I/O operations and/or CPU cycles, and takes into account the number of records needed to satisfy the query, the availability of indexes, and various statistical information about data organization. These statistics are accumulated and maintained by the DBMS in its internal System Catalog. Optimization becomes even more critical in distributed query processing. Consider an application that attempts to join two database tables that are distributed to two different locations.

The size of each node's databases and relevant tables, the network speed, and the processing and I/O power of each node are among the major factors that affect the performance of a distributed query. The distributed (global) query optimization requires access to a global database directory/catalog in order to obtain necessary node character-istics and statistical information about the remote databases.

Without global query optimization, a DDBMS may perform extremely inefficiently. Such a DDBMS may send all records of the big-ger table to another (remote) location, for selection and join, and then send the results back. As the complexity of the queries exceeds the two table join requirements, each additional table and/or database increases the number of choices for, and the complexity of, the opti-mizer.

Therefore, an efficient implementation of global query optimization is a rather difficult task that only a handful of DBMS vendors attempt to undertake. Products like Informix and Ingres support global opti-mization with certain limitations, and even then the quality of opti-mization decreases with the complexity of the query.

*Locking Granularity.* Locking prevents multiple users of a DBMS from updating the same records simultaneously. Some servers permit manual locking, but, in reality, automatic locking in a database man-agement system is imperative.

Users who are locked out from access must wait until the required data is freed (locks are released). When this happens, the user's response time and, thus, a perception of DBMS performance suffer. For instance, table level update locks, as a rule, result in poor perfor-mance. While locking, in itself, preserves data from corruption, it could limit the number of users simultaneously accessing the DBMS.

If a DBMS locks an entire database for each user, then the DBMS becomes, in effect, a single-user DBMS. Therefore, the size of locks that the DBMS can impose on a database (locking granularity) becomes very important. Ideally, the DBMS should lock only those records that are being updated. It is called *record-level* locking. Oracle DBMS, for example, supports record-level locking. However, since each lock requires a certain amount of memory and/or disk space, the num-ber of locks imposed on a database (and, therefore, the number of users) may be limited by the amount of available space. "Smart" DBMS servers can escalate locks from one level (e.g., record) to a higher level (e.g., data page or a table), and release lower-level locks when their numbers exceed the user-defined limit. For example, IBM's DB2 sup-ports lock escalation.

*Deadlock Detection.* Locking is associated with another performance problem: deadlocks. A deadlock occurs when Program A locks a record that Program B needs, and Program B locks the record that Program A needs. Each program must wait until the other completes, which is impossible. Thus, a deadlock, also known as a deadly embrace, has occurred. The DBMS server should automatically detect deadlocks and use appropriate algorithms to resolve them. As with global optimization, deadlock detection becomes much more complicated in a distributed environment. The time criterion might not be sufficient, since network delays and slow response time may be confused with a lock at a remote site. A truly distributed DBMS server should be capable of resolving "distributed" deadlocks, even though the majority of the available DBMS implementations use some simple, timeout-based rules to resolve deadlocks.

*Clustered Indexes.* Indexes usually represent separate data structures (e.g., various B-tree structures) that contain record keys and pointers to the corresponding records. Indexes can be used to access records directly by the key values, and can also guarantee uniqueness of the keys (if the keys are defined as unique). Indexes should be constantly maintained—kept in sync with the key values of the records when the data is updated, added, or deleted. Even though index maintenance can negatively affect the DBMS performance, lack of indexes could result in serious performance degradation in direct (by full or partial key) data access. In this respect, clustered indexes are most important. Clustered indexes are usually built on a primary (as opposed to a foreign) key, require the data to be sorted in ascending or descending key order, and are also sorted in the same order as the data (see Fig. 13.3). Thus, clustered indexes can significantly improve record search and sequential retrieval in key order by reducing the required number of input/output (I/O) operations.

*Note:* Some DBMS products (e.g., Ingres, Gupta) reduce or completely eliminate index I/O by supporting hash tables, where records can be found by a key stored at locations calculated by a special algorithm. Hash tables facilitate direct access and can coexist with indexes in the same DBMS.

A relational database management system's optimizer can improve the access path by automatically determining whether an index should be used for a given query. This is because index I/Os also consume resources and affect performance. Advanced optimizers, such as the one found in DB2, maintain index statistics and can actually determine whether a clustered index is still clustered after heavy insert/delete activity, before the decision is made to use the index. Despite the importance of clustered indexes, to date only few products support them (for example, Sybase SQL Server and IBM's DB2). In fact, clustered indexes are often crucial to the success of DB2 and Sybase in transaction-oriented benchmarks.

*Asynchronous I/O.* DBMS input/output is potentially a source of performance bottleneck. Properly designed DBMSs should minimize the number of actual physical disk I/O and spread the cost of I/O operations across many users. One technique that allows a DBMS to minimize the number of disk accesses is asynchronous I/O.

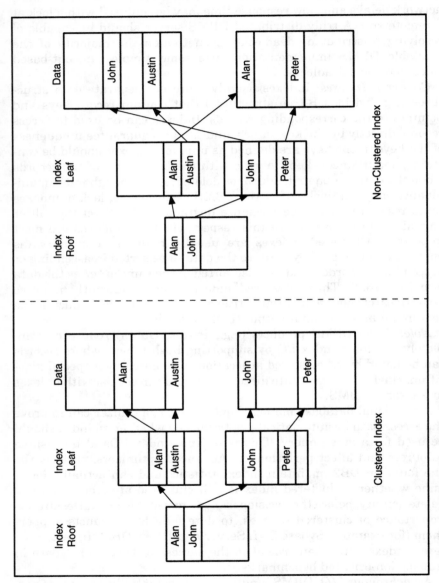

**Figure 13.3** Clustered and nonclustered indexes

This technique involves overlapping I/O operations with other work the DBMS server has to perform. In this case, the server does not wait for the completion of the I/O. Such an overlapping can be improved even further when the data is updated in shared buffers and the data writes are forced to disk only when the data buffers are full. The consistency of data in this case is guaranteed by write-ahead logging to a shared transaction log. In IBM system environments, asynchronous I/O is frequently implemented on an operating system level, as well as by a DBMS itself (e.g., DB2). Unix-based databases, however, must be designed to implement asynchronous I/O. Oracle, Ingres, Sybase and Informix all offer asynchronous I/O capabilities in Unix environments.

*Stored Procedures.* Stored procedures are collections of SQL statements and flow-control directives (e.g., IF, THEN, ELSE, etc.) that are parsed, verified, compiled, bound, and stored at the DBMS server. Stored procedures allow for the input and output parameters, user-declared variables, and conditional execution typical of any programming language. Stored procedures can call other procedures and can be executed on remote DBMS servers. Stored procedures not only enhance the efficiency and flexibility of SQL, but also dramatically improve DBMS performance. Indeed, due to the nonnavigational nature of SQL, the access path selection is performed by the relational DBMS optimizer when an SQL statement is bound (parsed, verified, etc.). This process is resource-intensive—the corresponding instruction path length may be measured in several thousand machine instructions. If it has to be performed every time an SQL statement is executed, the resulting performance will be greatly decreased (this type of SQL access is called *dynamic* SQL).

The SQL statements are *static* when they are parsed, verified, compiled, bound, and stored in the DBMS server before they are executed, or the first time they are executed. If SQL statements are static, the consecutive executions will be done at much smaller expense and, therefore, more rapidly. Some DBMS systems (e.g., DB2) implement static SQL in such a way that the SQL statements are parsed and compiled before the execution, during the program preparation process. The resulting objects are stored in appropriate DBMS libraries (Database Request Modules and DB2 Plans), from which they can be recalled. Other products (e.g., Sybase) parse and compile SQL statements the first time they are executed, and may store the results in memory (usually, in a shared procedure cache). Of course, even though there is no need to recall procedures from the libraries, one drawback of the latter technique is the possibility of the compiled stored procedure being paged out in a very active environment.

Regardless of the implementation technique, stored procedures improve the performance of SQL statements by eliminating costly preprocessing overhead. They also reduce network traffic by eliminating the need to send lengthy SQL statements from applications to DBMS servers. In a typical Unix-based client/server environment, for example, a stored procedure can be processed in one-fifth the time it takes to process a single embedded SQL command.

### 13.1.3    DBMS reliability and availability

*Transactions Recovery and Consistency.* A database transaction treats one or more SQL statements as a single unit of work, which is the atomic unit of database recovery and consistency. Consistency in DBMS prevents simultaneous queries and data modification requests from interfering with each other and prevents access to partially changed and not yet committed data.

A DBMS should provide for automatic database consistency by implementing the proper levels of locking, validating logical and physical database consistency, and supporting two-phase commit protocols.

Consistency checking should be performed automatically during transaction and database recovery. There are two major types of recovery: transaction recovery from a system/application failure and system recovery from a media failure.

Transaction recovery means that in case of system or application failure all committed changes must be made permanent—committed data must be written to a database device (disk). At the same time, data affected by this transaction, but not yet committed, is recovered (rolled back) to the pretransaction state completely and automatically. The direction of the recovery process is backward—from the point of failure to the last point of consistency.

In case of media failure (i.e., disk crash), a DBMS must be designed to perform nonautomatic recovery, which includes restoration of the lost data using the most current backup, and forward recovery of data from the point of the latest backup to the point immediately before the media failure. Transaction logs are usually used to store changes to the database and perform recovery procedures—before-change image (for backward recovery) and after-change image (for forward recovery). Often, a DBMS uses an automatic checkpoint mechanism to maintain the currency of the transaction log. The majority of the DBMS products available today support various degrees of database consistency and recovery.

*On-line Backup and Recovery.* The database backup and recovery mechanisms should be able to operate dynamically, on-line, while the DBMS server continues to operate. Indeed, in a multiuser, multidatabase environment, a backup of one database should not prevent users from accessing other databases, even on the same physical sys-

tem. That is especially true when many organizations authorize
database owners to be responsible for backing up their databases and
corresponding transaction logs. On-line recovery should allow a
database to recover automatically from an application or transaction
failure (i.e., perform automatic rollback), and support a forward recovery procedure. On-line backup and recovery should be a mandatory
feature for DBMS products selected for real-time, OLTP environments
(e.g., banking, brokerage, ticket reservation, air traffic control, etc.).

*Disk Mirroring.* One way to achieve database reliability and availability is to use fault-tolerant hardware and software platforms.
Hardware fault-tolerance requires a physical system implementation
where all (or the majority of) components are duplicated, so that when
one component fails, the "hot" standby takes over immediately. There
are several vendors that supply hardware fault-tolerant solutions (for
example, Tandem and Stratus computers). Unfortunately, these solutions are rather expensive and lock DBMS developers and users into a
particular vendor/product. Several DBMS vendors offer software-
based fault-tolerance by providing disk mirroring for transaction logs
and/or databases. For example, Sybase supports disk mirroring for
either the transaction log or the database itself.

Mirroring a transaction log protects against the loss of any committed transaction (see Fig. 13.4), while mirroring a database guarantees
continuous operation in the event of media failure. Indeed, mirroring a
database means nonstop recovery (see Fig. 13.5).

Disk mirroring requires availability of a separate physical disk drive
device on a DBMS server, and actually duplicates all writes to the pri-

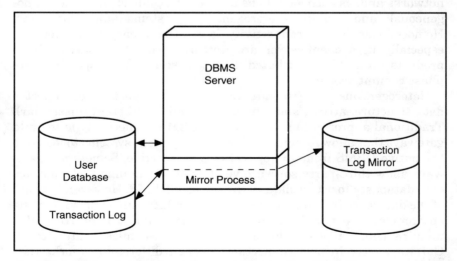

**Figure 13.4**  Disk mirroring—minimum guaranteed configuration

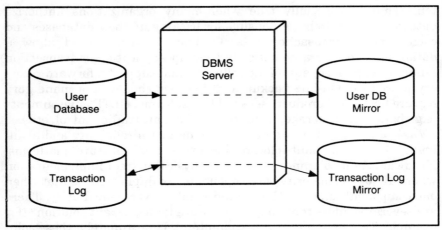

**Figure 13.5**   Disk mirroring on multiple disks

mary device on the mirror. Disk mirroring has the added advantage that both disks (the primary and the mirror) are available for read operations. Some DBMS products take advantage of this fact by routing read requests to the disk drive that provides better response time.

### 13.1.4   DBMS connectivity

*Heterogeneous Data Access.* An advanced DBMS implementation should be able to support the distribution of applications and data over networks and, as such, should be able to interconnect with like (homogeneous) and unlike (heterogeneous) systems and databases. Homogeneous DBMS connectivity is relatively easy to implement, especially in a client/server architecture. Some distributed DBMS products even offer distributed data consistency by supporting two-phase commit protocols.

Heterogeneous databases are much more difficult to interconnect—data structure, access, and language can all be different (dissimilar). Traditional approach to heterogeneous DBMS connectivity is to build gateways that allow foreign database management systems to look like the native DBMS from an application's perspective. Sometimes, gateways allow third-party software vendors' programming tools and foreign databases to access data in the selected DBMS. However, because of the difference in heterogeneous DBMS architectures and supporting environments (e.g., Sybase on a UNIX server and DB2 on IBM MVS mainframes), gateways do not provide for seamless data access. Gateways may involve connection between different networks (i.e.,

Ethernet and SNA), different communication protocols (i.e., TCP/IP and APPC), different data representation (i.e., ASCII and EBCDIC), etc. Therefore, gateways are rarely used to support database transactions that span multiple heterogeneous environments, where all data consistency is guaranteed by a distributed heterogeneous two-phase commit protocol. Such implementations will require a cross-platform transaction manager that can interface with all participating heterogeneous databases. Such TP managers are being designed within the guidelines of open systems. For example, X/Open has proposed XA interfaces for open systems TP managers, and OSF's Distributed Computing Environment, among other products, has selected these interfaces for its TP manager.

Nevertheless, today gateways solve a critical need to interconnect new and existing DBMSs. Gateways play an important role by providing access to heterogeneous systems, especially when critical business data and legacy applications all reside on an organization's mainframes. Almost all gateways available today offer access to IBM's DB2. Better gateway implementations use Advanced Program-to-Program Communications (APPC/LU6.2) to provide real-time read-write access to mainframe data. Some gateways, like those from Sybase, are DBMS-extensible, and allow Unix-based DBMS to interactively access *any* mainframe data available via CICS/VS (IBM's transaction monitor for IBM mainframes).

*Remote Procedure Calls.* If gateways represent one of the most popular ways to access heterogeneous data from one hardware/software platform to another, server-to-server and client-to-server DBMS connectivity is best supported via the mechanism of Remote Procedure Calls (RPC). Remote procedure calls represent a message-based, connectionless mechanism by which one process can execute another process residing on a different, usually remote, system, possibly running a different operating system. Any parameters needed by a subroutine are passed between the calling and called processes. A database RPC is a clearly defined request for a service or data issued over a network to a DBMS server by a client or another server. Unlike traditional remote procedure calls, database RPCs (e.g., Sybase DBMS RPC) can call stored procedures and allow the DBMS server to return multiple records (rows) in response to a single request. Since database RPCs eliminate the need for a client to send lengthy SQL statements and to receive individual records separately, they greatly reduce network traffic. In addition, RPCs can help to implement heterogeneous DBMS connectivity by solving the language incompatibility problems. One system can call remote procedure on another system without concern to the remote system's language syntax.

### 13.1.5  Advanced DBMS features

*DB Triggers and Rules.* Advanced DBMS implementations should provide users with the ability to initiate (trigger) certain user-defined actions based on a particular data-related event. Triggers, which can be viewed as a special type of stored procedures, are often used to implement referential integrity constraints. For example, a user may attempt to insert data into or update a table field which represents a foreign key (see discussion on referential integrity in previous chapters). The appropriate trigger can be designed to check the new field value against the values of the primary key. Similarly, delete actions can be controlled (e.g., prevented or cascaded) using user-developed delete triggers. In general, triggers can call other triggers or stored procedures, and are powerful tools for application development. Centrally located on the server (in Sybase and Ingres, for example), triggers can improve DBMS performance, although they require programming efforts, especially when implementing referential integrity. Therefore, dictionary-based declarative referential integrity implementations are preferable to those using triggers. Declarative referential integrity provides better documentation and clarity by using standard nonprocedural SQL statements to define referential integrity constraints. DB2 and OS/2 Data Manager both support declarative referential integrity.

If triggers are often used to support referential integrity, DBMS rules are used to implement user-defined domain constraints. For example, a database rule may say that the state code must be one of the approved two-character codes: NY, NJ, or CA.

DBMS products that support database-resident rules facilitate the development of applications by implementing many business rules centrally as DBMS rules. Ingres and Sybase are just two examples that implement DBMS-resident rules.

*Image Support.* Today, business requirements often include the need to support multimedia—in particular, image applications. Ideally, a DBMS selected for a client/server, distributed environment, should also support special IMAGE data types—BLOBs. BLOB stands for Binary Large Objects, and represents very large (up to several MB) fields that are used to store images, graphics, long text documents, and even voice recordings. Ideally, the DBMS should be capable not only of storing and retrieving BLOBs, but also of making BLOB fields available through the use of standard SQL like any other data element. Several DBMS available today (e.g., Informix, Ingres, Sybase) provide BLOB support.

*Graphical Front End Development Tools.* Users of distributed DBMSs all demand an advanced graphical suite of application development tools. Today, users can see two trends in the front-end tools for DBMS application development. Some DBMS products (like Ingres,

Informix, Gupta, and Oracle, to name just a few) integrate graphical application development tools as an integrated DBMS solution. Oracle even offers Computer Aided Software Engineering, or CASE, tools. Other DBMS vendors rely on third-party front-end tools vendors to supply application development tools that can construct applications efficiently for a given DBMS. Examples of such tools are JAYCC, Uniface, and Neuron Data. Intimate knowledge of the underlying DBMS often results in better application performance when integrated front-end/DBMS solutions are used. On the other hand, independent front-end tool vendors often offer better and more open graphical user interfaces (GUI), and allow users to be more flexible about choosing the best database management system. Whatever the case, front-end tools must be considered when selecting a DBMS.

### 13.1.6  Remote administration

Users looking for a distributed DBMS solution should want the selected DBMS to support database administration (DBA) functions from any site. Database administration includes installing the DBMS software, managing disk storage, creating and managing database objects, performing backup and recovery, providing database security, managing database users and their permissions/privileges, controlling database/table access, monitoring and tuning system performance, and determining and solving system problems. In a distributed environment, these tasks may have to be done at each DBMS location. Thus, users should require that DBMS vendors provide database administration facilities that allow limited DBA staff to perform the necessary administration functions rapidly, conveniently, and from any (preferably centralized) location. Indeed, if remote database administration is not available, an organization faces two unattractive choices: send DBAs to the DBMS location as the need arises, or maintain qualified DBA personnel at each location. If a network contains hundreds or even thousands of nodes, neither choice is economically feasible. Most DBMS products available to date, especially products that operate in Unix-based environments, provide at least some degree of remote database administration. Examples can be found in such database implementations as Oracle, Ingres, Sybase, and Informix DBMSs.

## 13.2  IBM DISTRIBUTED DBMS SOLUTIONS

Advances in client/server architecture and distributed computing, the emergence of open system standards and wide acceptance by users of open system goals continue to change the computing environment and information systems market directions and trends.

One of the most noticeable changes in the computer industry today is that the market for traditional mainframe and even minicomputers is shrinking, while the market for microcomputer-based solutions and local area network is expanding. These market changes, along with customer demands for the availability of distributed, open, client/server products, have led IBM to accept and embrace the client/server computing architecture and ideas of interoperability and support for open systems. As a result, IBM intends to extend the range of available services by providing connectivity, network management, distributed database, shared files, presentation services, mail exchange, and common languages not only among its two major operating environments—SAA and AIX—but also interoperability among multiuser, multivendor systems. The open interoperability goals set by IBM include multivendor networking, transparent data access, remote application access, enterprise system management, platform flexibility, distributed enterprise-wide applications, and consistent, standards-based user interfaces. These interoperability goals are based on OSF's Distributed Computing and Distributed Management Environments, active participation in standards organizations, and focus on open systems and client/server computing model. In the context of distributed data management, however, the discussion of IBM products is concentrated on distributed databases and several popular IBM DBMS interoperability solutions.

### 13.2.1 DB2 and SQL/DS

To date, IBM supports relational databases on all Systems Applications Architecture (SAA) platforms—MVS, VM, OS/400, and OS/2.

IBM's premier relational database for the mainframe MVS environment (DB2 and its VM counterpart, SQL/DS) supports distributed data access. DB2 distributed data management allows organizations to access the required data from multiple locations and consolidate the data at various levels to improve customer service, increase user productivity, and, in general, help the organization gain a competitive edge.

Architecturally, distributed DB2 is compliant with IBM's Distributed Relational Database Architecture (DRDA), described in the previous chapter. In general, DB2 RDBMS is a robust, features-rich product that offers production-grade OLTP performance, reliability, availability, and serviceability. DB2 boasts standards-compliant SQL implementation, declarative referential integrity, cost-based optimization, clustered indexes, reliable multilevel locking, static and dynamic SQL, support for the two-phase commit protocol, various service utilities, backup and forward recovery with archiving and multiple image copies, access from such diverse environments as CICS, IMS/DC, TSO and batch, asynchronous I/O, and many other useful features.

With respect to distributed database implementation, since version 2 was announced DB2 has supported Remote Request capability (one SQL statement per request, one location per statement) via its Distributed Data Facility (DDF). DB2 version 2.3 implements DRDA-defined Remote Unit of Work (multiple SQL statements per unit of work, single DBMS at a single location per unit of work) to access other DB2 or SQL/DS via static or dynamic SQL for read and update. (The latter is for TSO, batch and Call Attach Facility only.) In addition, DB2 version 2.3 implements a Distributed Unit of Work (multiple SQL statements and multiple DBMSs per unit of work, single DBMS per SQL statement), although only between homogeneous databases (DB2 to DB2).

DB2's Distributed Unit of Work supports multisite read/single site update, and does not support a distributed two-phase commit—a major limitation. DB2's implementation of distributed databases uses IBM's Systems Network Architecture (SNA), Virtual Telecommunications Access Method (ACF/VTAM), and Advanced Program-to-Program Communications (APPC/LU6.2).

As illustrated in Fig. 13.6, distributed DB2 V2.2 functions are provided through a separate address space (Distributed Data Facility, or DDF) and a special database (Communication Database, or CDB). A DDF is defined to ACF/VTAM as a SNA Logical Unit type 6.2 (LU6.2). Thus, it can establish and implement peer-to-peer communications between multiple DB2 subsystems using APPC/LU6.2 protocols and services. The CDB contains information required by the DDF to control

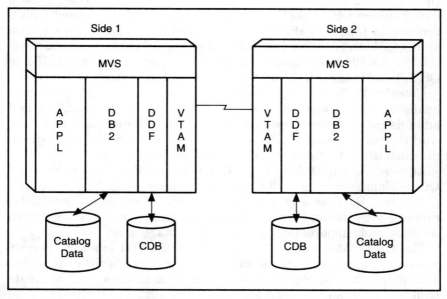

**Figure 13.6** Distributed DB2 V2.2 implementation

communications between DB2 subsystems (e.g., mapping of DB2 location names to network LU names, defining session and conversation parameters, users authorization/password verification for a given location, etc.).

Distributed DB2 V2.3 implementation provides such remote administration features as creating/deleting remote objects, granting/revoking remote user privileges, and interfacing with the network management software—NetView. Although DB2 is still far from C. J. Date's ideal distributed database, its remote and distributed unit of work features, high-quality optimization, high availability, and reliability make DB2 a good choice for a mainframe-based DBMS server in a distributed client/server environment.

### 13.2.2    OS/2 Database Manager

The OS/2 Database Manager (DM) is a relational database management system for Operating System/2 Extended Edition. The OS/2 DM is an RDBMS in its own right, and together with DB2 is one of the DBMS platforms defined in IBM's Systems Applications Architecture.

SAA is IBM's blueprint for consistency, connectivity, and interoperability among various IBM systems environments. SAA presents an infrastructure for distributed and cooperative processing, and is the IBM platform for the entire application development life cycle. In other words, SAA is IBM's architecture for enterprise computing. As part of the SAA, OS/2 DM is destined to play a significant role in distributing data between OS/2-based clients and OS/400- and DB2-based DBMS servers. In fact, it is IBM's intent to provide reliable remote update access for both DB2 and OS/2 EE DM as part of IBM's strategic direction for distributed databases. IBM is working to implement DB2 to OS/2 Data Manager links within the scope of the DRDA.

*Note:* IBM's Personal Computer Node Manager (PCNM) product is available today, and enables data and resource distribution and administration control from an IBM mainframe processor to a PS/2 workstation running OS/2 or DOS, where workstations can be attached to the host directly or via LAN Server.

As a relational DBMS, OS/2 DM consists of Database Services, Query Management, and Remote Data Services.

Database Services is DM's database engine. It manages stored data, provides integrity and concurrency control, security and configuration services, and supports OS/2 transaction management.

The Query Management component of the DM enables users to access and manipulate the database and provides facilities to define and alter database objects, insert/delete/update data, and to create panels, menus, and procedures.

From the relational database implementation perspective, OS/2 DM resembles its mainframe counterpart, DB2, although the DM lacks several important features found in DB2. Mainly, the DM supports a single database log (DB2 maintains dual logging) and does not support an archival log.

From the concurrency point of view, the DM does not support page level locking, but instead supports row-level locking (not implemented in DB2). The OS/2 DM allows reads of uncommitted data ("dirty read"). Like DB2, the DM's SQL support includes both static and dynamic SQL embedded in application programs, as well as declarative referential integrity. (Entity integrity is a component of SAA SQL and is implemented in both OS/2 DM and DB2.) One serious drawback of the current OS/2's DM implementation is its lack of support for forward recovery from media failure (a recovery from the last backup forward to the point of failure).

A separate DM component, Remote Data Services, represents an extension to the base Database Services. It enables users and programs to access remote OS/2 Database Managers (homogeneous DBMS connectivity) across various communications links—LAN (using NetBIOS), SNA (using SDLC protocol), or WAN (X.25 support). Remote Data Services communications take advantage of the SNA's Advanced Program-to-Program Communications (APPC) and support two types of connectivity:

- DRDA's homogeneous Remote Unit of Work between OS/2 Database Managers

- Remote Procedure Call (called Remote Program Link, or RPL), which allows an OS/2 application to call a program running on an IBM host under CICS

Continued development of these distributed facilities in conjunction with distributed DB2 will lead to the creation of a distributed OS/2 DM (DB2 client/server environment) on currently existing hardware platforms (PS/2 and IBM mainframes).

## 13.2.3 AIX and RDBMS

The open systems market is growing faster than the computer industry as a whole. AIX (Advanced Interactive eXecutive operating system—IBM's version of Unix) is IBM's solution for this new requirement. Despite the common perception that AIX is a "nonstandard" Unix, AIX conforms to all key standards, including those from POSIX, X/Open, ISO, and other standards groups. Indeed, AIX was certified to be XPG3-compliant (X/Open Portability Guide version 3) even before such a major Unix operating system as SunOS.

Even though to date IBM does not offer a native relational DBMS for AIX, it has stated repeatedly that its goal is to provide AIX distributed databases on all AIX platforms. IBM plans to develop an AIX RDBMS that will fully participate with SAA distributed DBMS implementations. The goal of SAA-AIX interoperability implies that DB2, SQL/DS, OS/400 Database Manager, and OS/2 DM will be able to distribute and access data among themselves and the yet-to-be-released AIX RDBMS. When that happens, SAA and AIX users will be able to share common relational data. What is more, since AIX is based on open systems standards, AIX RDBMS should be able to distribute and share relational data between itself, SAA DBMSs, and such Unix-based DBMSs as Oracle, Sybase, Ingres, and Informix, to name just a few.

Even though IBM, like every other DBMS vendor, states that multivendor DBMS connectivity within the scope of the open systems standards (such as ISO RDA and ANSI SQL) is one of its goals, IBM's distributed DBMS and client/server computing strategy is beginning to pay off as its mainframe DBMSs (DB2 and SQL/DS), midrange DBMS (OS/400 Data Manager), and workstation DBMSs (both OS/2's DM and AIX RDBMS) become more capable of supporting data distributed among them transparently, reliably, and efficiently.

## 13.3   OTHER CLIENT/SERVER DBMS SOLUTIONS

Of course, IBM is not the only player in the distributed client/server DBMS arena. There are several DBMS products designed to work in client/server environments based on various hardware and operating system platforms. Among them, several Unix-based and DOS/OS/2-based DBMS solutions appear to be ahead of OS/2 DM in multiuser environments. Some of these products (Unix-based Ingres, Sybase, Informix and Oracle) are discussed here.

### 13.3.1   Ingres RDBMS

Ingres DBMS offers advanced database technology for both OLTP and Decision Support System (DSS) Unix-based environments. The version 6.3 of the Ingres DBMS is one of the most technologically advanced relational database management systems on the market today. Ingres RDBMS consists of three components: a relational DBMS server, a Knowledge Management Extension, and an Object Management Extension. Ingres RDBMS server is a robust, high-performance multidatabase, multithreaded database management system, that includes cost-based optimization, hashed tables, asynchronous I/O, and stored procedures.

Ingres multithreaded architecture is well suited to either single-processor or multiprocessor, especially Symmetric Multiprocessor (SMP) computers. Ingres RDBMS features include:

- ANSI standard SQL support
- parallel database query implementation
- referential integrity
- multilevel locking
- support for very large databases and binary large objects
- integrated graphical application development environment (Windows 4GL)
- access control, security, and remote database administration
- online backup/recovery

The Knowledge Management Extension allows users to create and store triggers that enforce referential and domain integrity, implement server-enforced business rules, and control resource utilization. The Object Management Extension allows users to define their own data types, functions, and operators, which enhances the base functionality of SQL, simplifies application development, and increases programmer productivity.

Ingres supports distributed DBMS with such products as Ingres/Gateways, Ingres/Net, and Ingres/Star. Ingres/Gateways provide the capability to access such databases as DEC's RDB/VMS, IBM's DB2, SQL/DS, and IMS (the last is for read-only). Ingres/Net connects Ingres applications across such networking protocols as DECnet, Asynch, SNA, TCP/IP, and OSI. Ingres/Star provides distributed Ingres RDBMS capability by supporting distributed cost-based optimization, multisite update with automatic two-phase commit, and data location transparency. Currently, Ingres/Star is offered on DEC VMS platforms.

By combining Ingres RDBMS with Ingres/Net, Ingres/Star, and Ingres/Gateways, users can implement distributed client/server environments across different networks, platforms, and database management systems.

### 13.3.2 Sybase RDBMS

Sybase is another major client/server RDBMS player in the Unix arena. Sybase's RDBMS (SQL Server) is a multithreaded database management system known for its high performance in both uniprocessor and SMP systems. Sybase's latest release (4.8) (the Virtual Server

Architecture, or VSA) can take advantage of Symmetric Multiprocessors in such a way that a System/DBA administrator can decide on the number of processors to be used by the RDBMS.

Sybase RDBMS features include:

- cost-based optimization
- ANSI standard SQL support
- stored procedures
- server-enforced referential integrity, triggers, and business rules
- user-defined data types
- clustered indexes
- asynchronous I/O
- multilevel locking
- programmer-controlled two-phase commit
- support for binary large objects (TEXT and IMAGE BLOBs)
- access control, security, and remote database administration
- online backup/recovery

Sybase supports software disk mirroring and provides integrated graphical application development environment (APT). Beginning with its release of version 4.0, Sybase offers an advanced implementation of Remote Procedure Calls (RPC).

Sybase distributed databases are supported by RPCs, Net/Gateway, and Open Client/Server Interfaces (C/SI) that are based on ISO Remote Database Access protocol. Data location transparency and programmable two-phase commit for multisite updates are enhanced via the use of RPCs. Sybase's Open Client is a programmable interface which manages all communications between clients and the SQL Server. Sybase's Open Server provides a consistent method of receiving SQL requests or RPC from Sybase applications and passing them on to a non-Sybase application.

For heterogeneous (relational, nonrelational databases and files) data access, Sybase provides the Open Gateway solution which allows a Sybase application to issue an RPC to access any mainframe data available through CICS. Sybase's Net/Gateway supports standard TCP/IP and SNA APPC/LU6.2 protocols. The latter uses APPC CONFIRM level conversations to implement reliable host data access.

Sybase's Client/Server architecture is a proven solution for integrating heterogeneous data and applications. Sybase RDBMS is also available in an OS/2 version (SQL Server) offered by Microsoft.

### 13.3.3 Informix RDBMS

One of the most popular RDBMS for low-end Unix platforms, Informix, offers an impressive software development tool (Informix/ 4GL), excellent performance, and has relatively few hardware/software requirements.

Informix OnLine, the latest version of the Informix RDBMS, includes disk mirroring, on-line backup and recovery, asynchronous parallel I/O, and cost-based optimization. Informix OnLine supports Binary Large Objects (BLOB) for image, graphics, voice, and large text objects. In fact, Informix is so efficient in multimedia applications that it is often chosen as the underlying DBMS for commercial image systems. Informix distributed database support is provided by Informix Star, and includes distributed cost-based optimization, data location transparency, and distributed queries. However, Informix Star supports only single site updates. In other words, Informix does not support distributed two-phase commit. For heterogeneous DBMS connectivity, Informix uses third party software vendors to implement its mainframe Gateway strategy. The gateway from Sterling Software allows Informix RDBMS to access mainframe data in batch mode for read only operations.

### 13.3.4 Oracle RDBMS

Oracle is the largest RDBMS vendor outside of IBM. Oracle DBMS is available on practically every hardware platform and every operating system. Oracle offers not just a relational database management system, but the entire suite of integrated software tools, including an Integrated Computer Aided Software Engineering (I-CASE) toolset.

Oracle front-end tools include SQL*FORMS graphical tools for application development, SQL*ReportWriter, and SQL*Menu products.

Oracle RDBMS offers standard SQL implementation with several useful extensions and two programming interfaces: low-level Oracle Call Interface and embedded SQL with SQL precompilers. Even though Oracle RDBMS is not a multithreaded database server, it offers sophisticated concurrency control, row-level locking, contention-free queries, event-related triggers, and asynchronous I/O.

Oracle supports very large databases, on-line backup/recovery, active data dictionary and on-line, remote database administration.

Oracle distributed DBMS implementation supports distributed query (but not distributed updates), data location transparency, site autonomy, and network independence. Oracle supports DECnet, TCP/IP, SNA LU0, LU2 and LU6.2/APPC, Novell, Named Pipes, NetBIOS, and Banyan Vines, to name just a few. Oracle heterogeneous DBMS connectivity is supported by gateways—SQL*Connect to DB2, SQL/DS, and VAX RMS. The current version of the Oracle RDBMS (V 6.0) does not, however, support cost-based optimization, clustered indexes, stored procedures, disk mirroring, or BLOB data types. Oracle plans to implement these features in its version 7.0. Despite these deficiencies, Oracle is very popular, mainly because of its excellent portability, which includes even Macintosh support.

Of course, there are many other DBMS servers available today that offer comparable advanced features (examples include Gupta, which offers a relational DBMS for DOS and OS/2 environments, and Sybase's new serious competitor, InterBase, which provides an RDBMS for Unix-based environments). However, the discussion of every available DBMS server is beyond the scope of this book. The products described here were chosen to illustrate the state of the DBMS industry on representative examples of database management systems available today in a client/server environment.

# Transaction and Workflow Management in Client/Server Environments

*Transaction processing is the backbone of daily business activities throughout organizations and industries. Major governments and such industries as transportation, communications, distribution, financial services, manufacturing, and retailing rely on transaction processing systems to manage mission-critical information. Today, transaction processing technology is becoming increasingly important because of the computer industry direction to perform OnLine Transaction Processing (OLTP) on open, distributed systems and in the client / server architecture.*

*The client / server computing model, which can be viewed as a special case of cooperative processing, facilitates the development and implementation of networked, distributed environments. Indeed, linking multiple computers together through a communications network allows users to access and share all available distributed resources, while at the same time effectively distributing the computing workload. From a client / server architecture perspective, the workload distribution between clients and servers may allow clients to manage input, output, and presentation functions, as well as some application logic functions and even certain local data access functions.*

*Servers, on the other hand, perform database access functions and common shareable application functions. Most importantly, the server's role is to perform workload distribution and management, synchronization, and control of access to centralized resources based on client requests. As a result, the cost-effectiveness of the computing environment is maximized and the environment itself becomes flexible, scalable, and reliable.*

*Workload distribution, synchronization of client / server interactions, and management of resource access are the functions of transaction and workflow management described in the following chapters.*

# Distributed Transaction Processing

Traditionally, transaction processing has been performed on centralized systems, typically running proprietary operating systems. Naturally, such centralized (nondistributed) transaction processing has been supported, often quite successfully, by transaction monitors native to the underlying mainframe hardware and operating systems. The last several years have been characterized by the advent of distributed heterogeneous computing architectures and open systems, often based on the Unix operating system. As a result, transaction processing is evolving to satisfy two complementary goals:

- On the one hand, it provides support for the traditional, nondistributed transaction management in the new, open systems environment.

- On the other hand, it provides a focal point for a distributed, enterprise-wide transaction processing system.

Needless to say, a transaction processing system that satisfies both requirements will enable users of proprietary TP monitors to take advantage of distributed environments and open systems while protecting and leveraging users' investment in existing proprietary TP systems. Such a transaction processing system will allow customers to choose freely among various vendor products. It will support nondisruptive growth of systems and applications, and will allow sharing of computing resources among customers and service suppliers across a worldwide open enterprise.

Let's follow the evolution of transaction processing by taking a closer look at the concepts of Distributed Transaction Processing and DTP implementations using the example of one of the most successful TP monitors: IBM's Customer Information Control System (CICS).

## 14.1    DTP CONCEPTS

To illustrate the emerging TP management trends, the definition and properties of transactions described in the previous chapters can be expanded to include the concepts of distributed transaction processing (DTP).

### 14.1.1    Transactions

In Chap. 9, a transaction was described as a sequence of predefined actions performed on behalf of the application. A transaction takes a computing system and its resources from one consistent state to another, in order to accomplish the desired business functionality. Transactions possess the following properties:

- *Atomicity.* The entire sequence of actions (Logical Unit of Work) must be either completed or aborted. The transaction cannot be partially successful.

- *Consistency.* A transaction takes a computing system and its resources from one consistent state to another.

- *Isolation.* A transaction's effect is not visible to other transactions until the transaction is committed.

- *Serializability.* As long as a transaction in progress depends on certain information, this information is locked to prevent any other transaction from changing it.

- *Durability.* Changes made by the committed transaction are permanent and should tolerate system failures.

These transaction properties have been illustrated in the previous chapters in the example of database transactions.

### 14.1.2    TP monitors

By supporting these transaction properties, transaction processing, as the name implies, deals with the execution and control of transactions and provides users with on-line, near-instantaneous access to many types of information. Computer systems that support OnLine Transaction Processing (OLTP) are typically called Transaction Processing Monitors, or TP monitors. TP monitors perform the following major functions:

- They provide software tools (data access tools, screen painters, intersystem communications) that are used to develop custom business applications.

- They provide an execution environment that ensures the integrity, availability and security of data, fast response time, and high transaction throughput by managing synchronization and distribution of the transaction workload among available resources.

- They provide administrative support that permits users to perform custom installation, configuration, monitoring, and management of their computing systems.

In a nondistributed environment, TP monitors perform their functions by running on the same system where the application functions, presentation functions, and database management systems reside. Therefore, the resources that the TP monitor must manage are local and appropriate interprocess communications mechanisms that can be used to control and coordinate all participants in a transaction.

However, when the business logic functions and, therefore, the work they are designed to do, are distributed among several systems, the role of the TP monitor must be expanded to manage transactions affecting multiple systems in a distributed transaction processing environment (DTP). Even though each distributed node performs its share of the work in its portion of the still atomic "local" transaction (with all its local transaction properties intact), distributed transaction processing requires a new concept of distributed atomicity, consistency, isolation, and durability. These new distributed transaction properties are provided by new distributed Transaction Processing Managers (TPM).

### 14.1.3 Distributed transaction processing

Distributed transaction processing is the evolution of traditional, centralized transaction processing into the world of open distributed computing. The result of this evolution is the creation of Enterprise Transaction Processing, in which the entire enterprise is involved in the execution of business transactions under the control of Enterprise Transaction Management.

In distributed transaction processing, a business transaction that is executed across a network of distributed systems is actually comprised of multiple participants—"local" transactions. Every local transaction is executed on its own system, under the control of a distributed transaction manager. The communication between participants in Distributed Transaction Processing is synchronous. Each transaction can be designed in such a way that its processing depends directly on the results of the processing performed by another transaction. In a DTP environment, synchronization (consistency) points taken by one transaction can be coordinated with the corresponding synchronization points in another. So, all changes made to local and remote resources can be committed or rolled back synchronously.

To illustrate this important point, consider the infamous Funds Transfer Problem. A customer of the Central Bank wants to transfer funds from his/her checking account into the savings account. The checking account resides in the checking accounts database in New York City, while the savings account is handled by the data processing unit located in Des Moines, Iowa.

In the conventional way of thinking, the New York branch will submit a transfer (delete) request to the New York Home Office Data Processing department via a Home Office transaction program. At the same time the transfer (add) request is wired to Des Moines to be processed by the nightly batch program. Such a transfer will probably take place overnight. However, in today's fast moving business environment such slow, batch processing may not be appropriate. In a real-time OLTP environment two different transactions should take place practically simultaneously. What will happen if either one of these transactions fails? Will the customer get an unexpected credit to his savings account without reducing his/her checking, or will a certain amount be debited from the checking account without being credited on the savings side?

Without distributed transaction management to provide for the consistency and integrity of resources, the results of such a transaction could be unpredictable. Enterprise-wide Distributed Transaction Processing should be managed to ensure that the funds are either transferred successfully or not at all.

Conceptually, an Enterprise Distributed Transaction Processing (EDTP) environment should support the local Transaction Processing Manager (TPM) on each distributed node. At the same time, EDTP should provide for a global, logically centralized TP coordinator (manager) that can communicate with and control each of its participant TPMs.

This concept can be illustrated on the example of a three-tiered client/server OLTP computing environment (see Fig. 14.1). Here, the client workstations may perform local transactions under the control of a local TPM. Concurrently, they may participate in a workgroup trans-

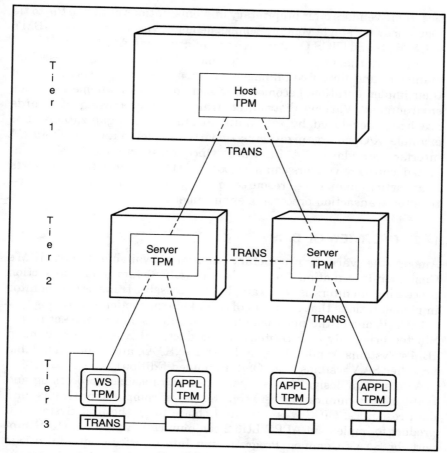

**Figure 14.1** DTP in a multitiered client/server environment

action coordinated by a Server TPM. Conversely, servers may participate in a distributed transaction spanning multiple servers and/or in a
global transaction initiated and coordinated by a host TPM.

All these distributed transactions must be coordinated, and all participating transaction monitors must be integrated into a "centralized"
distributed TP Manager.

The key to such integration is the existence of a common Transactional Application Programming Interface (TP-API), which is understood by all participants—transaction managers and resource
managers (e.g., database). Implementations of these APIs are based on
two major cooperative processing techniques: Advanced Program-to-
Program Communications (based on IBM's SNA LU6.2 protocols) and
Remote Procedure Calls (RPCs). Despite considerable technical difficul-

ties, some vendors offer proprietary implementations of such APIs to tie together even single-vendor, homogeneous environments (e.g., IBM's CICS/MVS and CICS OS/2 intercommunication via APPC/LU6.2).

However, the importance of common APIs between Transaction managers and Resource Managers (RM), as well as the complexity of their implementation, becomes even more obvious in an open systems environment. Various distributed transaction processing standards are being developed by international standards organizations. For example, X/Open organization has nearly completed its DTP TPM/RM interface standard—XA interface. Once these standards are completed, software vendors can incorporate DTP APIs into their products (transaction managers, resource managers) to make an open distributed transaction processing environment a reality.

## 14.2    OVERVIEW OF CICS

Among the various proprietary solutions available today, IBM's Customer Information Control System (CICS) family of transaction processing monitors is an example of successful transaction monitor implementations that supports distributed transaction processing.

CICS is one of the most popular TP monitors on the market today. Started originally as a System/370 product, CICS is a participant in IBM's Systems Applications Architecture (SAA), and is now available for other SAA systems (e.g., OS/2 Extended Edition).

As a system designed to support on-line transaction processing and real-time communication between the users, computer programs, and data resources, CICS was a natural choice to be the first System/370 product to implement APPC/LU6.2 communication protocol. CICS support for SAA's Common Programming Interface for Communications (CPI-C) provides CICS users with a high-level consistent interface (API) to the LU6.2 session services of the SAA Common Communication Support (CCS).

CICS API facilitates application developers in building distributed applications designed to work in a distributed transaction processing environment. This documented Application Programming Interface is provided by the CICS family of TP monitors (CICS) on all of their supported platforms. The common documented API and supporting CICS facilities allow programmers to write portable applications across all supported environments.

In a multiple-system environment, CICS can communicate with other systems that have suitable communication facilities. Such a cross-system communication partner can be another CICS system (like CICS/ESA, CICS OS/2, CICS/MVS, CICS OS/400, or CICS/AIX—IBM has stated its intent for cross-system support for the latter two CICS implementations), or an IMS/VS system (version 1.3 or later). Most importantly, however, CICS can communicate with any system or workstation that supports APPC/LU6.2 protocols. This last feature makes CICS an ideal choice for implementing a client/server computing environment across platforms that support APPC/LU6.2 application programming interfaces.

### 14.2.1 CICS intercommunication methods

To describe CICS intercommunication methods, let's consider the most popular CICS implementation under mainframe IBM operating systems: MVS and ESA. In general, there are two ways in which a local CICS system can communicate with other (remote) systems: Intersystem Communication (ISC) and Multiregion Operation (MRO).

*Multiregion Operation.* MRO is designed for CICS-to-CICS communications by enabling CICS systems that run in the same host but are located in different address spaces to communicate with each other. MRO does not support communications between CICS and non-CICS (such as IMS/VS) systems. SNA networking facilities and access methods (ACF/VTAM) are not required for MRO, and all data transfers between address spaces are handled by either a CICS-supplied Interregion Communication Program (IRC) or by MVS cross-memory services (XMS).

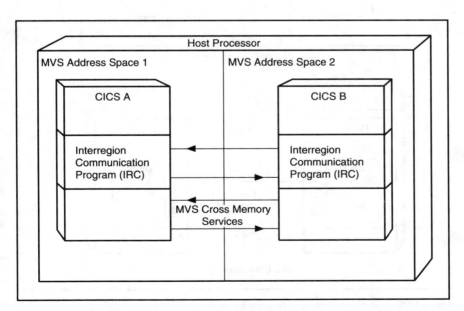

**Figure 14.2**  CICS multiregion operations

*Intersystem Communication.* Communication between systems residing in different locations implies the existence of a network linking these locations. Such communication also requires some sort of communication access method to provide the necessary communication protocols. The CICS implementation of Intersystem Communication is, in fact, an implementation of IBM's Systems Network Architecture. The SNA access method, ACF/VTAM, is used to provide the necessary communication protocols for ISC. The principal protocol used for ISC is APPC/LU6.2, even though SNA LU6.1 protocols are also available for certain connections.

*Note:* Intersystem Communication via ACF/VTAM can be used between systems in the same host processor. In this case, the application-to-application facilities of ACF/VTAM are used.

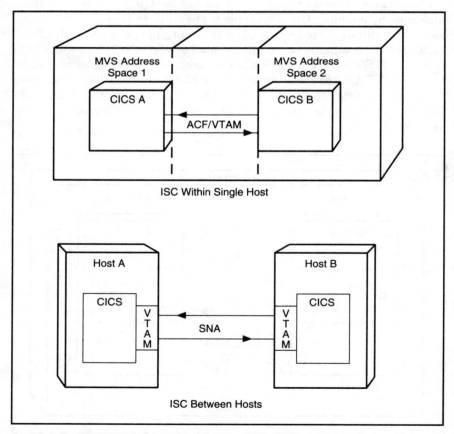

**Figure 14.3**   CICS intersystem communications

There are three basic forms of ISC: ISC within a single processor (intrahost ISC), ISC between physically adjacent processors, and ISC between physically remote processors. From the CICS point of view, intrahost and interhost ISC are indistinguishable. Compared with MRO, ISC offers a wide variety of configurations for both local and remote systems, including the APPC-based client/server computing model.

Therefore, the discussion that follows is concentrated on the CICS intersystem communication facilities.

### 14.2.2   CICS intercommunication facilities

CICS Intersystem Communication (ISC) provides four basic types of intercommunication facilities: CICS Function Shipping, Asynchronous Processing, CICS Transaction Routing, and CICS Distributed Transaction Processing (DTP). For completeness, a brief description of each is provided below, even though these facilities are not universally available for all forms of CICS intercommunication.

*CICS Function Shipping.* This facility is available only for CICS-to-CICS intercommunication via MRO or ISC LU6.1 and LU6.2 links. Function Shipping is designed to enable an application program running in one CICS system to access a resource owned by another CICS system.

The remote resource can be a file or DL/I data base, a transient data queue, or a temporary storage queue. Application programs that access remote resources can be designed and coded as if the resources were local to the system in which the application is to run. CICS handles the function shipping by passing a request from a local system to a special transaction (known as a mirror transaction) in the remote system. CICS supplies a number of mirror transactions, each of which corresponds to a particular function.

*Asynchronous Processing.* This facility enables a CICS transaction to distribute the required processing between systems in an Intersystem Communication environment by initiating a transaction in a remote system and passing data to it. The reply does not have to be returned to the task that initiated the remote transaction, and no direct correlation can be made between a request and a reply (other than the application-provided code). The processing is thus called asynchronous. It differs from synchronous Distributed Transaction Processing (in which a session is held by two transactions for the period of a conversation between them), and requests and replies can be directly correlated. Asynchronous Processing is available via MRO or ISC LU6.1 and LU6.2 links.

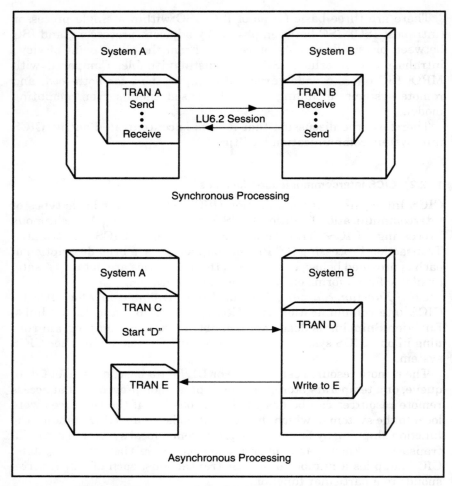

**Figure 14.4**  CICS synchronous and asynchronous processing

*CICS Transaction Routing.* This facility is available only for CICS-to-CICS intercommunication via MRO and ISC LU6.2 links. It enables a device (terminal) that is owned by one CICS system, to initiate a transaction that is owned by another CICS system. For ISC links, the two systems can be connected via LU6.2 protocols only. CICS supplies a special relay program which provides the communication mechanism between the local terminal and the remote transaction.

As with Function Shipping, the intricacies of the actual communication are handled by CICS itself, and applications can be designed in a way that makes it transparent that the terminal is connected to another CICS system.

*CICS Distributed Transaction Processing.* This is the CICS facility that actually implements SAA distribution. It enables a CICS transaction to communicate with a transaction running in another system for the purpose of distributing the required processing between two or more systems in an intercommunication environment. The other system can be another CICS connected via MRO, ISC LU6.1 and LU6.2 links, IMS/VS connected via LU6.1 links, or any other system supporting APPC/LU6.2 protocols.

Synchronous CICS DTP communication using APPC protocols means that a session is acquired and held by two transaction programs for the duration of a conversation between them. The transactions have exclusive use of the session, and the messages that pass between transactions as part of the conversation can be directly correlated. Each transaction can be designed in such a way that the processing of one depends directly on the results of the processing performed by the other.

## 14.3  OVERVIEW OF CICS APPC API

Let's use the funds transfer application to illustrate the basic concept of DTP in CICS-to-CICS intercommunication. Assume that checking funds transfer transaction TRANA in CICS system A (CICS-A) is being initiated by a terminal attached to system A (see Fig. 14.5). It is associated with the transaction program, which for the purpose of this illustration is also called TRANA. Its function is twofold: to debit a checking account database, and to initiate a savings account funds transfer transaction TRANB in the remote system B (CICS-B). TRANA and TRANB must coordinate their actions by either committing the changes to their respective protected resources (if both transactions succeeded in their tasks), or by rolling back the changes they could have effected on their respective protected resources (if either transaction fails). In this scenario, TRANA is the *Front-End* transaction that initiates the conversation, and CICS-A is the front-end system. Conversely, transaction TRANB is initiated by TRANA. TRANB is the *Back-End* transaction and CICS-B is the back-end system.

The communication between TRANA and TRANB is performed via the use of CICS intercommunication facilities. It is based on the CICS implementation of the APPC/LU6.2 protocol, which is the key to CICS Distributed Transaction Processing.

APPC API consists of a set of commands (verbs) that are issued by each participant of the conversation depending on the transaction logic and the state the transaction is in.

This is how CICS uses APPC to implement DTP. After being initiated, TRANA acquires exclusive use of the ISC session with CICS-B by

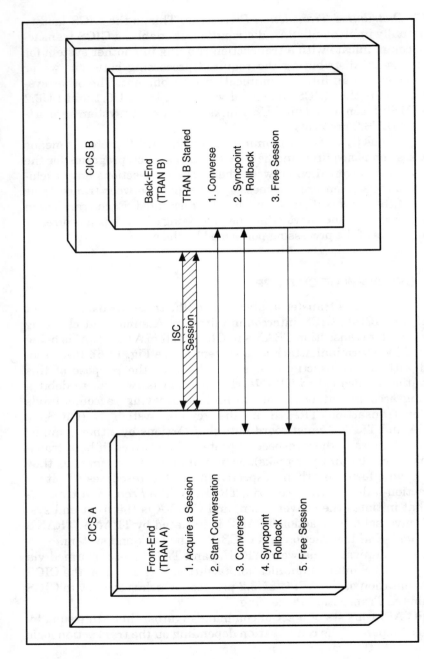

**Figure 14.5**  CICS distributed transaction processing

using a CICS ALLOCATE command. TRANB, in CICS-B, is initiated by another CICS command, CONNECT PROCESS, which is unique to CICS APPC API. TRANA performs all the necessary application-dependent actions (debiting the checking account), and sends the appropriate message to TRANB to credit the customer's savings account. TRANB complies and sends back a confirmation or rejection message. At that point, both transactions can either take a joint sync-point (successful transfer) or joint rollback (transfer failed).

In CICS, the session that TRANA acquires is called an *alternate facility* of the transaction TRANA. On the other hand, the facility that causes TRANA to be initiated (for example, a terminal) is called the *principal facility* of the transaction. A transaction can have only one principal facility, but several alternate facilities. This means that both TRANA and TRANB can hold conversations with other remote trans-actions as well as with each other.

Typically for APPC/LU6.2 conversations, the front-end transaction begins its conversation with the back-end transaction in the Send state, while the back-end transaction is initiated in the Receive state.

CICS implementation of APPC/LU6.2 defines its own CICS-specific Application Programming Interface (API) that provides the LU6.2 pro-tocol boundary for CICS Distributed Transaction Processing applica-tions. CICS provides high-level language support for APPC API. Application programs must use the CICS Command Level interface, and can be written in COBOL, COBOL II, PL/I, C, and Assembler language.

### 14.3.1  Mapped and basic conversations

CICS APPC API supports two types of LU6.2-based conversations: mapped conversations and basic (unmapped) conversations.

Mapped conversation programs can be written in any of the pro-gramming languages, mentioned above. In place of LU6.2 verbs, CICS API uses Command Level interface commands—EXEC CICS ALLO-CATE, EXEC CICS CONNECT PROCESS, EXEC CICS EXTRACT PROCESS, EXEC CICS CONVERSE, EXEC CICS ISSUE ABEND, EXEC CICS ISSUE CONFIRMATION, EXEC CICS ISSUE ERROR, EXEC CICS ISSUE PREPARE, EXEC CICS ISSUE SIGNAL, EXEC CICS FREE, EXEC CICS RECEIVE, EXEC CICS SEND, EXEC CICS SEND CONFIRM, EXEC CICS WAIT—to request LU6.2 services. The data that transactions exchange on a mapped conversation is just application data, and the LU6.2 mapping takes care of all necessary formatting, including record headers, length indicators, and logical record prefixes.

The distinguishing feature of CICS APPC API for mapped conversa-tion is its support for coordinated syncpointing between all conversation partners. LU6.2 syncpoint levels of 0, 1, and 2—NONE, CONFIRM, and SYNCPT—are specified when the remote transaction is started. CICS APPC API provides EXEC CICS SYNCPOINT and EXEC CICS SYNCPOINT ROLLBACK commands to request syncpoint and backout services.

In other words, CICS supports a two-phase commit protocol and acts as a transaction coordinator in the two-phase commit processing. For unmapped conversations, programs must be written in Assembler. To use the unmapped conversation API, applications must understand the formats of the LU6.2 message units, logical records, General Data Stream variables, and Function Management headers, perform the necessary conversions, and build appropriate data structures. Therefore, CICS APPC API provides special CICS GDS commands to handle basic conversation requests.

### 14.3.2 Front-end and back-end transactions

To start a distributed transaction, a front-end transaction must initiate a conversation with its partner (back-end transaction) over a session between logical units (LU-LU session). So, the first action the front-end transaction should perform is to acquire an LU-LU session to the required remote system by issuing an ALLOCATE command to CICS (and its LU6.2). The front-end transaction specifies the name of the remote system as a parameter of the ALLOCATE command.

After the session has been allocated, the front-end transaction should initiate a back-end transaction. For LU6.2 sessions, CICS APPC API provides a special command—CONNECT PROCESS—which the front-end transaction must issue before the first SEND or CONVERSE. On its conversations with the back-end transaction, the front-end transaction must specify what conversational resource (conversation-id) it is using. This conversation-id is supplied by LU6.2 when the session is allocated, and it must be used by the front-end transaction on every command it issues for that conversation. The exceptions to this rule are CICS SYNCPOINT and ROLLBACK commands that apply to every conversation in which this transaction is involved.

While in conversation, the front-end and back-end transactions exchange messages by issuing SEND, RECEIVE, or CONVERSE CICS commands. The state of the conversation at either end of the link is determined by the previous state and the most recently executed command. The front-end transaction always starts in the Send state; the back-end, in the Receive state. The conversation follows LU6.2 half-duplex flip-flop protocol. The state change can be initiated only by a transaction in the Send state issuing the CONVERSE or SEND commands, even though it can be requested by the transaction in the Receive state.

Specifically, a transaction in the Receive state can use the ISSUE SIGNAL command to request a change of direction (change of states). Irrespective of the current state, a transaction can issue ISSUE ERROR and ISSUE ABEND commands to inform its partner that an error has occurred.

### 14.3.3  Syncpoints

APPC/LU6.2 protocols define the way in which synchronization of distributed processes can be performed. LU6.2 architecture supports three synchronization levels: NONE, CONFIRM, and SYNCPT. CICS APPC supports all three synchronization levels. They can be specified on the CONNECT PROCESS command:

- Level 0 (NONE) indicates that no synchronization is possible.

- Level 1 (CONFIRM) indicates that LU6.2 SYNC_LEVEL (CONFIRM) is selected. As defined in the LU6.2 architecture, confirmation exchanges are supported. CICS APPC API supplies special commands—SEND CONFIRM, ISSUE CONFIRMATION, ISSUE ERROR, ISSUE ABEND—to implement this protocol.

- Level 2 (SYNCPT) corresponds to the LU6.2 SYNC_LEVEL (SYNCPT). This means that in addition to the confirmation exchanges, full CICS syncpointing (SYNCPOINT and SYNCPOINT ROLLBACK commands) is available for distributed transaction processing.

The maximum synchronization level available on the session must be agreed upon by both ends of the session, and is determined at the session BIND time. The synchronization level for a particular conversation over that session is specified in the CONNECT PROCESS command, even though it cannot exceed the maximum allowed for the session.

Synchronization level 2 conversations support and participate in the syncpointing activity also known as the two-phase commit protocol. The two-phase commit process consists of two distinctive portions: the "prepare" phase and the "commit" phase. Typically, during both phases of the commit process, the response of every application involved in the transaction is written to that application's permanent log. This insures that the data managed by the application is correctly updated even in the event of a system failure.

CICS commit actions are called syncpoints. CICS syncpoints are implemented by APPC/LU6.2 protocols and, according to the two-phase commit rules, include a designation of one of the distributed transaction participants as the coordinator. The coordinator is in charge of coordinating the phases of the two-phase commit. The CICS syncpoints are initiated and coordinated by any one of the transactions connected by the level 2 conversations when it issues the SYNCPOINT or SYNCPOINT ROLLBACK command. These commands always apply to *all level 2 conversations* held by a transaction. However, CICS APPC API supplies a special command (ISSUE PREPARE), that requires the conversation-id and allows individual conversations to be prepared for the syncpointing activity.

The CICS transaction that initiates the syncpoint is called the *syncpoint initiator*. It must be in the Send-state when the SYNCPOINT command is issued. All transactions that receive the syncpoint request are in a Receive state relative to the syncpoint initiator, and are called *syncpoint slaves*. For the syncpoint slave, the normal response to a syncpoint request is to issue the SYNCPOINT command.

However, in the distributed transaction processing environment, the slave may hold level 2 conversations with other transactions. Therefore, it must participate in the distributed syncpoint (distributed commit process). The slave becomes the syncpoint initiator for these transactions, and must ensure that it is in the Send state in relation to its slaves before SYNCPOINT commands can be issued.

In the terminology of the two-phase commit protocol, during the first, "prepare" phase, the initiator's SYNCPOINT command sends the Prepare-To-Commit (PTC) request to its first slave. PTC requests are then propagated down the syncpoint tree. The slaves exchange positive Request Commit (RC) responses when they are ready to commit.

Once all slaves but the "*last*" have answered with the RC, the initiator starts the second, "commit" phase, by sending the RC to its last slave. At that point, the Committed (CTD) responses are exchanged between the syncpoint tree nodes as the resources are being committed (see Fig. 14.6).

While the syncpoint activity is in progress, one of the slaves may detect an error. The syncpoint request is then rejected. The rejecting slave can use the SYNCPOINT ROLLBACK, ISSUE ERROR, or ISSUE ABEND commands to answer with a negative response.

In a CICS environment, the ISSUE ERROR command, issued in response to a syncpoint request, causes the syncpoint initiator to abort, thus initiating a rollback among participating transactions (CICS Dynamic Transaction Backout). The ISSUE ABEND command goes even further by causing the syncpoint initiator to abend the conversation. Therefore, the recommended negative response to a syncpoint request is the SYNCPOINT ROLLBACK command. This command can be issued regardless of whether the transaction is in a Send or Receive

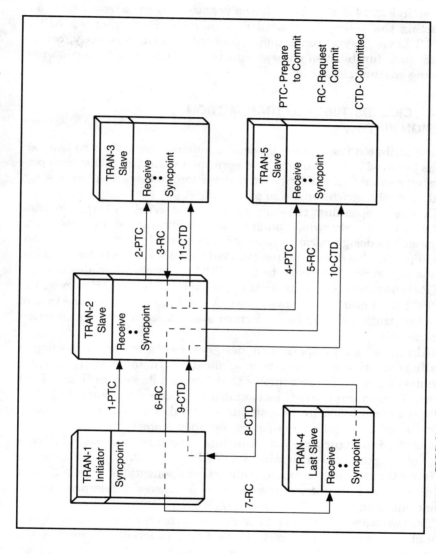

**Figure 14.6** CICS distributed syncpoint

PTC- Prepare to Commit

RC- Request Commit

CTD- Committed

339

state. When issued, it causes the current logical unit of work to roll back unconditionally. The rollback request (RB) is propagated to all level 2 conversational partners of the transaction. The syncpoint tree, shown in Fig. 14.7, illustrates how a negative response from TRAN-5 is affecting the entire distributed unit of work. By supporting APPC/LU6.2 Level 2 synchronization, CICS ensures the atomicity, consistency, and durability of transactions in a distributed transaction processing environment.

## 14.4 CICS DISTRIBUTED TRANSACTION DESIGN HINTS

In a distributed transaction processing environment, the two transactions involved in the conversation perform a variety of tasks: local processing related to the distributed transaction, conversation processing, and, possibly, synchronization processing.

Generally speaking, the conversation- and synchronization-related activities are somewhat outside the traditional data processing approach to design because these activities involve not only local processing, but also direct interactions with another, remote transaction. Certainly, strict adherence to the APPC protocols when designing a DTP transaction should make this task relatively easy. However, the APPC/LU6.2 architecture is so powerful and universal that the task of synchronization should be performed automatically by a Transaction Manager.

Otherwise, an inexperienced designer can attempt to develop a really sophisticated peer-to-peer application. In so doing, a designer can develop a system so complex that it would be very difficult, if not impossible, to implement, test, and use. Lacking the automatic distributed transaction processing support in distributed DBMS and/or distributed transaction managers, detailed knowledge of the APPC protocols, data structures, and functions is required to take full advantage of the peer-to-peer capabilities of APPC/LU6.2.

In most cases of distributed transaction applications, it is sufficient to design two conversing transactions as a "master" (main program, or front-end) and a "slave" (or back-end).

The two transactions should be designed together, so that conversational partners do not have to be designed to handle an unexpected request or response from each other. In general, the front-end transaction should be a master initiating a conversation, and should contain as much of the conversation logic as possible. The master should send requests to its slave. The slave should respond to the requests from its master by performing the appropriate actions and replying to its master before it receives the next request.

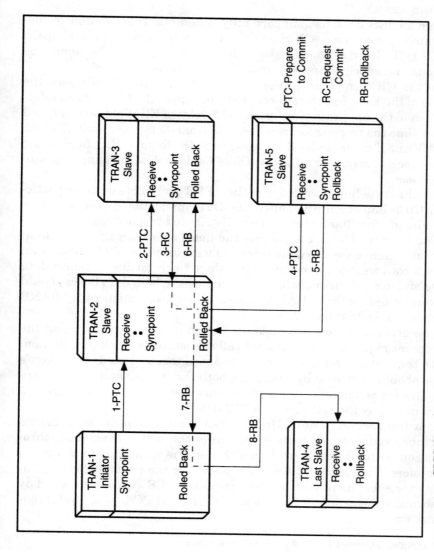

**Figure 14.7** CICS distributed rollback

PTC-Prepare to Commit

RC-Request Commit

RB-Rollback

341

If the application requires the distribution of logic between two transactions on a peer basis, then it is easier to design two symmetrical pairs of transactions, each pair having its own master that controls its own slave.

Since CICS does not support fully automatic coordination of distributed transactions, CICS APPC API has to be used to implement CICS DTP. Even a "master-slave" design requires that the communications and synchronization protocols are observed.

In the CICS implementation of APPC/LU6.2, APPC API uses the fields of the Exec Interface Block (EIB) to supply the LU6.2 state information to the application program. DTP-related EIB fields are updated every time the transaction receives data from its partner (RECEIVE or CONVERSE commands). It is good practice to save EIB fields after every receive request and to test these fields to determine appropriate responses.

To illustrate how knowledge of the APPC protocols and their particular CICS implementation affect the DTP application design, consider the already familiar funds transfer distributed transaction.

The master (TRANA) performs the debit operation against a local customer data base. In communication with its slave (TRANB) over an LU6.2 conversation, it requests the slave to credit its customer data base and to send the reply back. The changes to both data bases should be committed, so that TRANA allocates the conversation with TRANB at synchronization level 2.

The designer takes into account that on a level 2 conversation the syncpoint request can be automatically generated at task termination. Both the master and the slave are designed together, and the master's logic should be driven by the states both the master and its slave are in. The transactions states and various state change indicators are determined by the setting of the EIB fields.

If a transaction issues LU6.2 verbs irrespective of its own and its partner's conversation state, violation of the APPC Level 2 synchronization protocol can occur, in which case the transaction will abend. Therefore, the command sequence, shown in the example below, contains tests for the implicit commit request (CICS syncpoint) issued by a normal transaction termination on a CICS APPC/LU6.2 level 2 conversation.

**Example.**    Correct LU6.2 Mapped Conversation.

```
            TRANA                    |    TRANB

    ... Local Processing ...         |
              ..                     |
      EXEC CICS ALLOCATE             |
      EXEC CICS CONNECT PROCESS      |
```

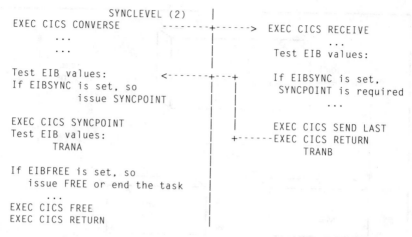

```
                     SYNCLEVEL (2)     |
   EXEC CICS CONVERSE      --------+-----> EXEC CICS RECEIVE
       ...                         |           ...
       ...                         |        Test EIB values:
                                   |
   Test EIB values:       <-------+---+     If EIBSYNC is set,
   If EIBSYNC is set, so          |   |      SYNCPOINT is required
        issue SYNCPOINT           |   |         ...
                                  |   |
   EXEC CICS SYNCPOINT            |   |     EXEC CICS SEND LAST
   Test EIB values:               |   +------EXEC CICS RETURN
        TRANA                     |              TRANB
                                  |
   If EIBFREE is set, so          |
      issue FREE or end the task  |
        ...                       |
   EXEC CICS FREE                 |
   EXEC CICS RETURN               |
```

Notice that TRANA tests EIB values after the CONVERSE command has been issued. It obtains the state indicators sent by TRANB immediately after control has been passed back to TRANA. Thus, the determination of the conversation state can be made based not only on the local command sequence, but also on the results of the command execution at the remote transaction.

In fact, a designer of CICS DTP applications should not try to guess at what command should be issued next, but instead should design both the master and the slave together and examine the conversation state indicators to determine the appropriate course of action.

## 14.5  CICS DISTRIBUTED TWO-PHASE COMMIT

Complex distributed transaction processing applications may require several transactions in different systems to be executed in order to perform the needed application function. One way to accomplish this is to use the structured approach of the master/slave tree (see Fig. 14.8). In this case, the initial request starts the front-end transaction (master of the entire tree), which in turn allocates a conversation with another remote transaction (its slave), which then initiates its slave, and so on.

In a CICS environment, this approach, while offering the least complicated design, involves multiple LU6.2 sessions. As a result, the synchronization points in that particular distributed transaction can involve all tree nodes. Unless the request for synchronization (either commit or backout) originates from the tree master, the synchronization is unlikely to succeed.

The tree master (transaction coordinator) must perform the following functions:

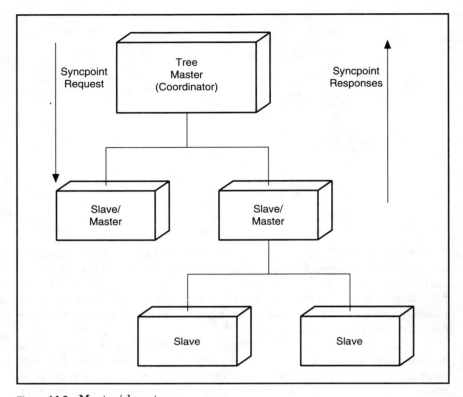

**Figure 14.8** Master/slave tree

- Identify all participants involved in the transaction.
- Send "Prepare-to-Commit" (PTC) requests to all participants.
- Insure that all participants successfully acknowledge the PTC request.
- Log the fact that all participants are prepared.
- Send the "Commit" request to all participants.
- Insure that all participants successfully acknowledge the Commit request.
- Log the fact that all participants have committed.

Logging of the commit phases is critical to transaction consistency and durability, i.e., implementation of a successful two-phase commit. Therefore, a transaction selected as the distributed transaction coordinator (a syncpoint initiator) must be able to log the commit phases or interact with the transaction logging services provided by the Transaction Manager. Notice that CICS logging is supported by CICS automatically.

To support proper synchronization of the two-phase commit protocol, the transaction coordinator (tree master) should initiate the commit process, and the synchronization signals should be propagated all the way down the tree. The syncpoint responses flow in the opposite direction, from the leaf nodes through the intermediate masters to the tree master. The transactions should be designed in such a way that if any of the transactions attempting to execute the SYNCPOINT command (explicit or implicit) abends, that abend should be propagated to every other transaction in the tree, and all transactions should back out their protected resources.

## 14.6   CICS TO NON-CICS COMMUNICATION

So far, distributed transaction processing has been described from the point of view of CICS-to-CICS communications. However, CICS can communicate with other systems and transactions running in other systems. To work with the CICS APPC API, these systems should support the LU6.2 principal and/or optional function sets. Examples of other such systems and transactions are: application transaction programs written for ACF/VTAM APPC (version 3.2 and higher), OS/400 using APPC and APPN, and OS/2 with the Communication manager.

Specifically, as a transaction manager, CICS/MVS (and CICS/ESA) supports distributed transactions not only for a homogeneous CICS-to-CICS environment, but also those that include such resource managers as IBM DB2 RDBMS. In fact, a distributed transaction processing environment supported by CICS family of TP monitors may include a front-end CICS transaction running on one system that is in synchronous DTP communications with another CICS transaction running on a remote system. The latter, in turn, may be connected to a DB2 subsystem that accesses relational data distributed between this and yet another distributed system. This scenario includes presentation, processing, and data distribution, albeit in a homogeneous (single vendor) environment. Such an environment can be expanded into the world of client/server architecture by including client workstations running OS/2 Extended Edition and CICS OS/2 that are attached to the host CICS (possibly via a LAN Server). In turn, the host CICS may be connected to any resource manager that is supported by the CICS APPC API.

IBM's family of CICS products continues to be extended by offering CICS implementations for the OS/400 and RS/6000 AIX operating systems. Reliance on common documented CICS APIs helps to make the transition of the CICS family of products into the Open Systems arena.

IBM's stated goal is to provide the broadest range of connectivity in the industry by supporting all important standards-compliant network and communication interfaces. Even today, open interfaces are provided to support transaction processing with integrity in conjunction with many different vendors of resource managers (e.g., DBMSs).

For example, if CICS/AIX is designed to support standard cross-TPM and TPM/RM interfaces, the users and developers will be able to build truly distributed enterprisewide transaction processing client/server applications that can span both SAA and AIX worlds.

The need for a global, cross-platform Enterprise Transaction Manager is becoming more apparent as users' demands for open systems, distributed computing, and client/server continue to grow. One possible solution for this problem is the "opening" of proprietary TP monitors like CICS. The other solution is the development of Enterprise Transaction Managers that are designed to operate in open systems environments. Some of these ETP Managers are discussed in the next chapter.

# Transaction Managers for Open Systems

Transaction management technology is evolving to reflect such current computing trends as client/server computing, platform downsizing, increased modularity, and especially, architected interfaces for open systems. The users' view of open systems is gradually focusing on two major open systems benefits: interoperability and portability. These benefits become even more desirable as major governments and industries (such as communications, financial services, transportation, manufacturing, retailing, and distribution) rely on OnLine Transaction Processing (OLTP) systems to manage critical strategic information in heterogeneous, multivendor, multiplatform and multioperating system environments. Centralized OLTP systems are moving to distributed computing via such architectures as client/server. At the same time, user demands for the open system's promise of interoperability and portability continue to grow. As a result, users and vendors alike have begun to realize that transaction management will become a unifying force that can glue the various components of distributed transaction processing into a single, global system image.

This need for a global, standards-based cross-platform transaction manager has resulted in the emergence of a variety of approaches to transaction management. One of these approaches was illustrated with an example of the most widely installed, however proprietary,

CICS TP monitor. Other approaches follow the direction of developing a transaction management system for what is perceived as the precursor for open systems—Unix-based environments. Among the transaction managers being developed for Unix-based operating systems are AT&T's Tuxedo, NCR's Top End, and Transarc's Transarc.

## 15.1  TUXEDO

AT&T's transaction manager product offering for Unix-based OLTP—Tuxedo—is designed to address today's trends of distributing centralized transaction management to such computing models as client/server architecture. Tuxedo software is available from Unix Software Laboratories, whose strategy is to create end-user demand for Tuxedo via its functionality and openness. As of release 4.0, Tuxedo is supported on several hardware platforms including Amdahl, AT&T, Pyramid, Sequent, and Unisys. Major Unix RDBMS vendors have announced compatible products, or stated their intention to support Tuxedo TPM/RM interfaces. Among them are Oracle, Informix, Ingres, and Sybase.

### 15.1.1  Tuxedo overview

The Tuxedo System (referred to as Tuxedo throughout this chapter) is designed to operate in a heterogeneous client/server environment that includes workstations, servers, and mainframe hosts. To date, Tuxedo is the only UNIX TPM available. It can deliver support for LAN-oriented client/server OLTP by providing such important services as transaction name serving, two-phase commit, and flexible queuing. Tuxedo supports publicly available standard interfaces that can enable hardware and software vendors to support OLTP applications using Tuxedo as a central hub—the coordinator of all OLTP activities.

To understand Tuxedo design goals, let's consider the Enterprise Transaction Processing model (see Fig. 15.1). This model consists of workstations running MS DOS, OS/2, or Unix operating systems on the first tier, Unix-based servers on the second tier, and mainframe class machines running proprietary operating systems and proprietary TP monitors on the third tier (e.g., IBM MVS and CICS). Such a model reflects real-life situations where organizations attempt to decentralize transaction processing and downsize operations while maintaining existing applications and databases. In this model, Tier-2 servers play the central role by providing TPM services to workstations and connections to mainframes.

As a transaction management system designed to operate in a heterogeneous distributed client/server environment, Tuxedo provides the following functions:

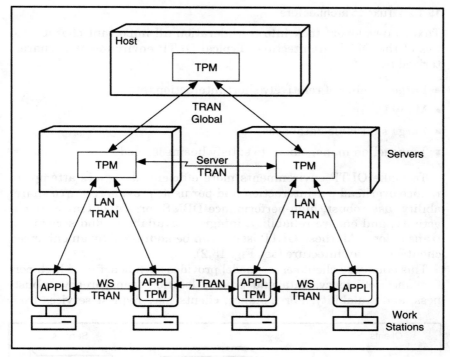

**Figure 15.1** Enterprise transaction processing

- Sending and receiving messages between clients and servers across a network
- Managing the flow of transactions
- Interacting with Resource Managers (e.g., DBMS) using standardized, generic interfaces
- Defining and supporting global transactions that span multiple distributed systems
- Interfacing with a data entry system that enables users to create and manage data entry forms available on user's workstations through any supported presentation manager

The last function can be supported by the Tuxedo-provided Data Entry System (DES), although any data entry system can be selected by users. In a complete Tuxedo System environment, service requests entered through a data entry system are managed by the Tuxedo TPM and are treated as transactions against the appropriate Resource Managers (i.e., database transactions against various DBMSs).

### 15.1.2 Tuxedo architecture

Tuxedo developers took into consideration all important characteristics of the OLTP architecture. Typical OLTP environment is characterized by:

- Large number of relatively short interactions
- Many Users
- Large shareable databases
- Transaction management to satisfy business needs

To make OLTP environments more efficient, designers attempt to reduce overhead per interaction and per user, provide resource shareability, use robust, high-performance DBMS, prioritize transactional activity, and ensure reliability, integrity, availability and security of transactions. All these OLTP issues can be addressed by an enhanced client/server architecture (see Fig. 15.2).

This enhanced client/server model provides such benefits as high performance, efficiency, data and process location transparency, robustness, and scalability. For instance, clients may request services from

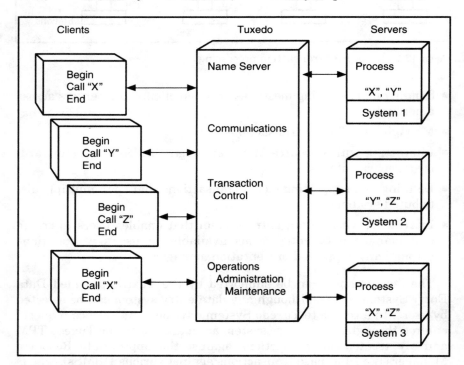

**Figure 15.2** Enhanced client/server model and Tuxedo

servers by calling a particular server process. Tuxedo intercepts these requests and routes them transparently to the appropriate server to the application. Service locations and descriptions are handled by the Name Server. For example, as shown in Fig. 15.2, the first and last clients request the same service. The Tuxedo Name server decides where the required service resides, and, in the case of multiple locations, even routes requests in such a way that the workload balance is ensured.

Tuxedo expands the enhanced client/server model by employing modular architecture and incorporating standards-based interfaces and protocols for communications and interactions with resource managers. The Tuxedo system consists of a Transaction Manager (known as System/T), a System Resource Manager (known as System/D), a High Performance File System, and a Data Entry System, or DES (little more than a demonstration tool). System/T provides such facilities as the Name Server, Communications Manager, Transaction Control, and Operations, Administrations, and Maintenance (OA&M) to control client/server interactions. System/D includes server applications and their interfaces for database access and access to remote applications.

The Tuxedo Transaction Manager and Resource Manager employ such standard interfaces as Application Transaction Manager Interface (ATMI) and X/Open XA interfaces for communication with resource managers.

ATMI provides client/server communications, including service location transparency, load balancing, priority processing, network independence, context-sensitive routing, and transparent data representation conversion.

The ATMI and XA interfaces provide for transaction control by using such constructs as "transaction begin", "transaction commit", "transaction abort", "transaction end", etc.

Tuxedo's openness in respect to resource managers is derived from its conformance to X/Open's DTP Reference Model (see Fig. 15.3), which specifies the Resource-Manager-server-to-Transaction-Manager interfaces (XA).

The Tuxedo implementation of the X/Open model is shown in Fig. 15.4. Notice that in order to support transaction processing across heterogeneous platforms in a distributed environment with consistency and integrity, the Tuxedo architecture requires all participating applications and resource managers to adhere to standard interfaces. The ATMI and XA interfaces are only two of the standards required for a truly open environment. Other interfaces and standards, such as SQL, RPC, and RDA (Remote Data Access) must be agreed upon to provide for interoperability across heterogeneous systems.

Another side of the openness issue—portability of the client and server code—requires the development of and agreement on such stan-

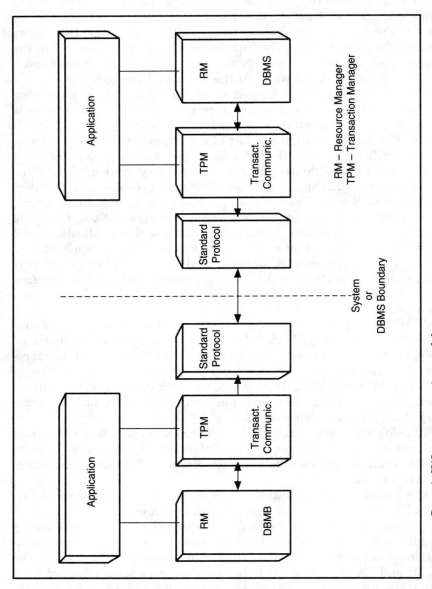

**Figure 15.3** Generic X/Open transaction model

RM – Resource Manager
TPM – Transaction Manager

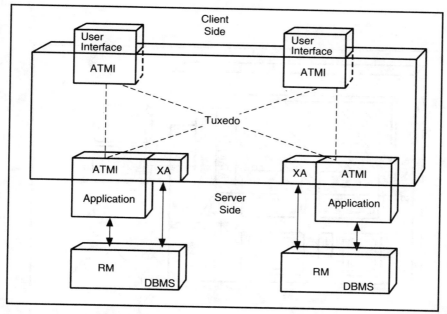

**Figure 15.4** Tuxedo and X/Open model

dards as Graphical User Interfaces (GUI), forms presentation (FIMS), and even operating systems.

### 15.1.3 Tuxedo distributed transaction management

The Tuxedo ATMI allows the transaction manager to define and support global transactions. A global transaction is one that allows work that may involve more than one resource manager and span more than one physical location to be treated as one logical unit of work. Global transactions may be composed of several "local" transactions, each accessing a local Resource Manager (a database, a file, etc.) under the control of the local Tuxedo TPM (see Fig. 15.5).

A given local transaction may be either successful or unsuccessful in completing its work. A global transaction is treated by the Tuxedo Transaction Manager as a specific sequence of events that is comprised of all local transactions. Both the global and local transactions are characterized by the previously described transaction's properties of atomicity, consistency, isolation, and durability.

Global transactions are defined to the Tuxedo TPM using ATMI primitives. The Tuxedo Transaction Manager provides a directory service—Name Server—which contains all service locations on the system.

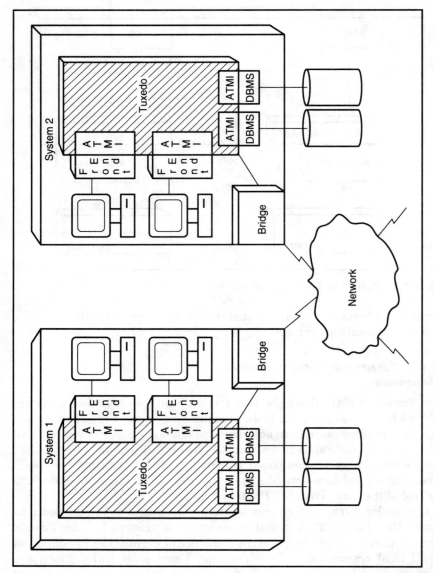

**Figure 15.5** Tuxedo distributed architecture

Name Server is used by the Tuxedo TPM to provide service location transparency in a global transaction. Once a global transaction is defined, the Tuxedo System TPM is responsible for managing its status and ensuring that its atomicity, consistency, isolation, and durability are preserved. In other words, in a distributed transaction processing environment, Tuxedo TPM coordinates global transactions by:

- Creating transaction identifiers
- Tracking the status of all participants
- Executing the Two-Phase Commit algorithm by acting as the coordinator for all participating Resource Managers
- Detecting and resolving global deadlocks
- Coordinating transaction recovery

Resource managers participating in a global transaction must also adhere to the interoperability standards. In fact, all major Unix DBMS vendors have adopted the strategy of building XA-compatible interfaces. This strategy allows their DBMSs to work with and benefit from such a standard-oriented TPM as Tuxedo. From the network interoperability point of view, Transaction Manager uses Unix System V Transport Layer Interface (TLI), which supports TCP/IP, NetBIOS, OSI protocols, BSD socket interfaces, and APPC/LU6.2, thus isolating the Tuxedo System from the underlying network technologies.

### 15.1.4 Tuxedo and CICS

All relational DBMS architectures address a somewhat uniform set of requirements and use various dialects of a common language (SQL). The underlying architecture and even design goals of various transaction managers are quite different. This difference is best illustrated by a comparison between the most widely installed, although proprietary, TP monitor—IBM's CICS—and the leader among TP monitors for Unix-based systems—Tuxedo.

CICS (described in the previous chapter) evolved as a self-contained operating subsystem designed to augment batch-oriented mainframe processing with on-line transaction processing. Real business needs (applications such as airline ticket reservations) resulted in the development of CICS to implement the OLTP in a mainframe-based, centralized environment. As a complete transaction processing system, CICS provides all four major services required from an OLTP application program:

- *User I/O Services,* which consist of Presentation and Communications management

- *Intersystem and Interapplication Services,* which include Queue and Remote Procedure Calls management (e.g., CICS Remote Program Link, XCTL, LINK, Transient Data Queue), as well as CICS Intersystem Communication based on APPC/LU6.2

- *Data Management Services,* which are implemented via interfaces to various Resource Managers (i.e., VSAM, IMS and DB2)

- *Operating System Services,* which include Storage Management, Trace and Dump Management

By contrast, Tuxedo performs only a subset of the functions provided by CICS. Even though since its inception it has had an open, accessible design, Tuxedo provides virtually no user I/O services and no terminal communications functions. Instead, Tuxedo concentrates on program-to-program communications, and addresses a few data management and operating environment issues. The assumption under which Tuxedo was designed is that all missing services should be provided by the operating system (Unix), Resource Managers (e.g., DBMS), or the application itself. Even where the functions performed by Tuxedo are similar to those of CICS, the services delivered by Tuxedo differ in the manner in which they are performed. For example, Tuxedo conforms to the Unix Transport Level Interface (TLI). Thus, Tuxedo can be independent of the networking mechanism used for data communications, and can, therefore, be migrated easily between different LAN protocols. CICS, as was already shown, may use proprietary MRO protocols to communicate between CICS regions within the same processor. CICS Intersystem Communications (ISC), on the other hand, is a valuable alternative to the MRO and is based on de facto interprogram communication standard—APPC/LU6.2.

While still very different, Tuxedo and CICS are evolving in similar directions. Both are likely to migrate communications functions into lower layers of system software. CICS already started the migration of LU6.2 functionality into the communications access method—ACF/VTAM. Even more important, both products are evolving their client/server communications capabilities. Specifically, Tuxedo allows clients to talk to servers on different, heterogeneous processors. It also supports generalized location-transparent communications and name services. CICS, while having similar facilities implemented in a mainframe environment (e.g., Function Shipping and CICS DTP), now offers a location-transparent client/server communication mechanism—Remote Program Link. RPL allows applications running on CICS/OS/2 to execute an RPC-like request to the host CICS. In addition, IBM plans to migrate CICS into a Unix-based (AIX) environment. When that happens, CICS AIX may prove to be a serious competitor to Tuxedo and similar systems.

### 15.1.5 Tuxedo/Host

To penetrate the commercial OLTP market, Tuxedo developers are expanding their efforts to migrate Tuxedo into the domain of CICS—the mainframe environment. The latest release of Tuxedo (5.0)—Tuxedo Enterprise Transaction Processing (Tuxedo/ETP)—consists of Tuxedo/WS and Tuxedo/Host. Tuxedo/WS provides APIs which allow MS-DOS, Windows 3.0, OS/2, and PC Unix workstations to be Tuxedo clients. Tuxedo/Host, on the other hand, is designed to provide a seamless migration path from non-Unix platforms to open, distributed client/server architectures by extending the concepts of interoperability to non-Unix hosts. Generic Tuxedo/Host consists of request/response interactions with host processes, and will continue to evolve to support DTP and conversations that can span multitiered heterogeneous environments.

Generic Tuxedo/Host provides a framework for building gateway servers. One such application of the Tuxedo/Host is the Tuxedo/Host for CICS. Tuxedo/Host for CICS includes a gateway server that can be linked with an APPC/LU6.2 communication library, a CICS-resident gateway program, a CICS Application Programming Interface (API), and CICS administrative utilities (see Fig. 15.6).

Tuxedo/Host for CICS includes the following capabilities:

- Use of APPC/LU6.2 protocols for peer-to-peer communications between Unix-resident and CICS-resident processes
- Support for data conversion for the ATMI-supported data types (to be performed by the Tuxedo System)
- Invocation of CICS programs by a Tuxedo/Host CICS-resident gateway program—services which retrieve and return messages via CICS-specific Tuxedo-supplied function interface
- Providing CICS service software in a style acceptable and familiar to CICS and host operating systems

Even in implementing Tuxedo/Host for CICS, the design goals of openness have not been compromised. In release 5, gateway communications between Tuxedo and CICS are performed by calls to X/Open's CPIC (Common Programming Interface for Communications) routines. This interface is the result of standardization of the APPC protocol.

Even though CICS is a complete OnLine Transaction Processing environment manager delivering high throughput and efficiency, Tuxedo, despite its limited functionality, offers the advantages of open systems and flexibility of its unbundled architecture.

By promoting interoperability rather then displacement, Tuxedo/Host allows data and functionality, currently existing in "legacy" mainframe applications, to be integrated with Unix products. Thus, Tuxedo/

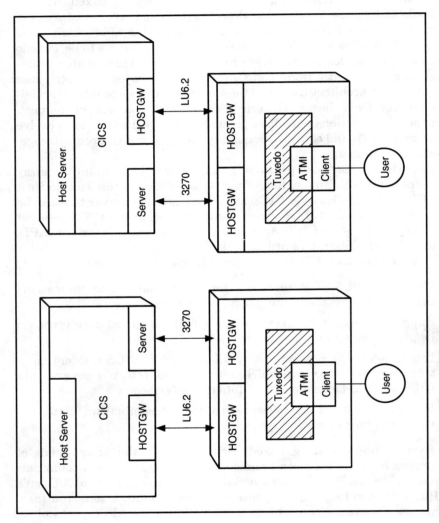

**Figure 15.6** Tuxedo/Host architecture

Host helps leverage investments already made in applications, software, hardware, and networks.

## 15.2 TOP END

TOP END is the Distributed Transaction Processing (DTP) system designed by the NCR Corporation especially for the open system OLTP environment. TOP END, scheduled for commercial availability in the third quarter of 1991, appears to be a direct competitor for the Tuxedo System, especially considering the merger between AT&T and NCR. In fact, industry experts believe that TOP END will eventually replace Tuxedo as a more robust OLTP manager for open systems. TOP END is built from NCR's years of experience in OLTP and point-of-sale applications. TOP END's developers believe that their product is superior to the Tuxedo System, even though Tuxedo is getting its release 5 ready while TOP END is offering its first release—release 1.0. Let's review TOP END's features.

### 15.2.1 TOP END overview

TOP END is a robust, full-featured DTP system that meets comprehensive requirements of OLTP users—high performance, workload distribution, global transaction management, database interoperability, and powerful and flexible system administration.

TOP END offers a complete execution environment with levels of administration, security, performance, and message-handling capabilities that surpass existing TP managers for Unix OLTP environments. In addition, TOP END is designed to provide users with price/performance benefits by supporting large numbers of users per system with greater flexibility. The design principals used by NCR in the TOP END development include:

- support for transaction management services in a way that requires minimal special application programming
- support for the X/Open Distributed Transaction Processing model
- support for TOP END portability by incorporating standard languages and interfaces, and isolating platform-unique dependencies
- integration of major Unix-based DBMS products by developing strategic relationships with DBMS vendors
- availability of TOP END on open systems platforms by developing strategic relationships with hardware vendors
- support for both the source and the binary distribution of TOP END
- building robust OLTP products to become a performance leader for open systems OLTP

Key TOP END deliverables for release 1.0 include:

- support for the Distributed Transaction Processing, including geographically distributed transactions, implementation of X/Open DTP standards, and provision of distributed recovery and software fault tolerance
- support for enhanced client/server interactions by providing for intranode and internode communications, dynamic workload balancing, and security authentication (using Kerberos Authentication)
- support for leading Unix-based Relational DBMSs
- implementation of such application services as support for C, C++, and COBOL languages, distributed debugging facilities, and context sensitive help management
- user friendly system administration, including interactive system definitions with definition integrity, and system control
- support for Unix-based and DOS-based workstations
- national language support

Similar to Tuxedo, TOP END achieves these goals by providing X/Open DTP environment (shown in Fig. 15.3) for its components—applications, resource managers, and communication managers.

### 15.2.2  TOP END components

The TOP END architecture is based on the client/server computing model. Therefore, TOP END simplifies transaction processing by dividing it into two separate processing entities: service requester processes and service provide processes. To achieve greater system performance and failure isolation, TOP END enhances client/server architecture with modular system design.

The TOP END modules (components) are used to facilitate the implementation of distributed transaction processing. TOP END splits transaction processing into major component areas that can either be distributed across the network for greater flexibility and efficiency, or replicated for concurrency and location autonomy. To support this distribution, TOP END provides a sophisticated system administration component which includes security authorization and password authentication across the network. In addition, similar to the Tuxedo System, TOP END ensures a global transaction integrity by supporting the X/Open-compliant two-phase commit protocol that is totally transparent to the applications.

Major TOP END components are designed for a distributed message-passing environment. These components, shown as an extension of the X/Open DTP Reference Model in Fig. 15.7, include a Transaction Manager (TPM), Application Server instances (AS), a Resource Manager (RM), a Communication Resource Manager (CRM), and the Network Interface (NI).

The Transaction Manager regulates the TOP END execution within a processing node and performs transaction routing, scheduling, commit/rollback coordination, security, and timer functions. Application Server instances execute application programs. The Communication Resource Manager provides a means for application programs to communicate in cooperative processing. The Network Interface allows the TOP END TPM to communicate with other TOP END transaction managers on the network. TOP END allows these components to be distributed across the network in order to implement and easily support applications in a distributed environment. To support its modular design in a distributed transaction processing environment, TOP END keeps track of the component distribution throughout the network. TOP END uses this information for dynamic workload balancing. TOP END routes scheduled transactions to the least busy components, attempting to send transaction to its originating node whenever possible. To isolate a system from potential failures in environments where multiple address spaces are supported, TOP END attempts to use different address spaces for the applications and TPM components.

What is more, depending on the application priority and the selection of faster response time versus failure isolation, TOP END offers an alternative execution path for the transaction processing. Users can choose to speed up transaction execution by forcing TOP END to sacrifice application isolation in favor of reusing already existing application server instances.

### 15.2.3  Administration and security

TOP END provides sophisticated administration functionality which allows authorized users to administer changes to the network from any location. Administration functions include TOP END's start-up and shutdown as well as TOP END's status inquiry. Moreover, a TOP END administrator can control how many client terminals are in the network and how the initial login screen should look for local and remote users. For workload distribution and balancing, the TOP END administration functions include transaction routing as well as an alternative routing in case of busy or failed nodes. There are even administration functions that authorize users to perform various TOP END administration functions. This high level of administration functionality is enhanced by TOP END's ability to authorize and authenticate user passwords across the network. The TOP END security

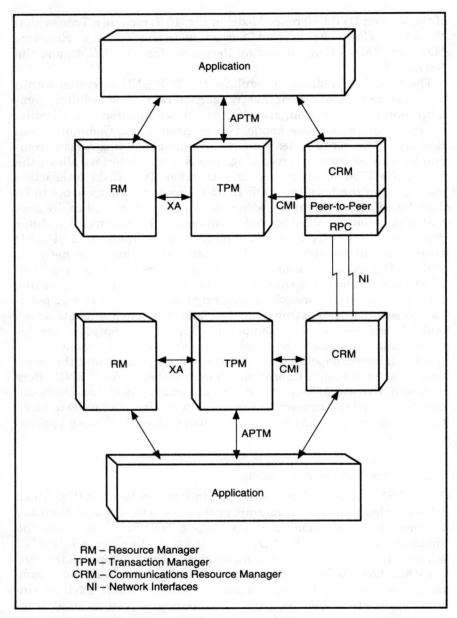

**Figure 15.7** TOP END components

system is based on the Kerberos security system discussed in the description of the Open Software Foundation's Distributed Computing Environment, or DCE (see Chap. 1 for details).

The Kerberos system places users in a multilevel security schema where each user or group of users are assigned an allowed set of functions. Users can classify messages as either "safe" or "private." Safe messages do not get encrypted, although they contain a check sum value to ensure the integrity of message content. Private messages are encrypted. The Kerberos system allows users to exchange encrypted information with the Kerberos authentication server. In effect, user messages carry Kerberos tickets that can prove a user is who he/she claims to be. The security system provides the access control list mechanism that awards data access to authorized users.

TOP END security administration includes extensive security audit capabilities. Therefore, TOP END administrators can audit all authentication requests, authorization requests, and transactions from a given location or user. TOP END security administration functions support dynamic security modifications for a given location, or globally, by propagating the security changes to all TOP END locations across the network.

### 15.2.4   TOP END and Tuxedo

TOP END and the Tuxedo System appear to be very similar in their architecture and functionality. However, despite their similarity in design and supported environments, Tuxedo and TOP END are different products. Tuxedo, being the first available transaction manager for Unix operating systems, has a significant timing advantage over other Unix transaction managers. TOP END, on the other hand, developed after the Tuxedo System became available, has the advantage of correcting Tuxedo's weak points while still in the design phase.

TOP END features differ from those of the Tuxedo System mainly in the area of administration, security, communications, timer services, and load leveling.

In the area of administration and security, TOP END supports an interactive resource definition and stores definitions in the RDBMS repository. In contrast, Tuxedo uses Unix editor for these definitions and the Unix file system for storage.

As described previously, TOP END supports the Kerberos security system, while Tuxedo currently does not offer this support.

TOP END's communication support includes *direct* support for the Unix TLI, ISO's OSI, APPC, and IPC, while Tuxedo uses the Unix TLI for network interfaces in order to take advantage of the TLI independence of the underlying network protocols.

TOP END's application support includes C, C++, and COBOL languages as well as the provision of timer services. Tuxedo timer services may be available in its next release.

Workload balancing in Tuxedo is predefined, while in TOP END it is dynamic network-sensitive.

Since the merger between AT&T and NCR has been completed, users may see one of these competing products gradually phased out in favor of the other. Industry analysts believe the winner will be TOP END. Until this happens, and regardless of the differences in the design and implementation, both Tuxedo and TOP END represent good examples of transaction management directions in the arena of Unix OLTP.

## 15.3 TRANSARC

Transarc is the name of Transarc Corporation's Transaction Manager. Announced in January of 1991, it was planned for release in the third quarter of 1991. Transarc's founders are professors from Carnegie Mellon (CMU) and Stanford Universities. Their OLTP product—Transarc—is based on research projects (Camelot from CMU, Argus from MIT, and Quicksilver from the IBM Almaden Research Center). Transarc incorporates technologies from the X/Open Consortium and OSF's Distributed Computing Environment (DCE). The affiliation with OSF's DCE resulted in Transarc's endorsement by such major hardware and software vendors as IBM, Hewlett-Packard, Stratus, Sybase, Informix, and Jyacc. In fact, IBM intends to use Transarc TPM as a component of its CICS/AIX product. Transarc has stated as its main goal its dedication to providing users with an extremely high-quality, long-lived, highly reliable, and easy-to-use transaction processing environment based on the best available open systems, client/server, and distributed computing technologies.

### 15.3.1 Transarc strategy overview

The Transarc strategy is based on the belief that open distributed transaction processing technology is the key technology for distributed systems. Therefore, Transarc has decided to develop a flexible DTP environment that is powerful, flexible, and portable to all platforms that comprise distributed transaction processing environment—PC DOS, OS/2, Unix, and any other open or proprietary operating system running on microcomputers, minicomputers, and mainframes. To achieve these ambitious goals, the Transarc strategy is to use and extend the services of the OSF's Distributed Computing Environment (DCE).

Transarc is justifying the DCE decision by the fact that DCE's resource location transparency, communication, and security components are receiving broad industry support, and should be available on a wide variety of hardware and software platforms. The DCE gives Transarc a powerful set of distributed processing communication and management tools. These include Apollo Network Computing System's (NCS) Remote Procedure Calls (RPC), the Andrew File System (AFS), X.500 Directory Services, and Kerberos Authentication. In turn, Transarc intends to augment DCE's transaction processing with the additional facilities that can simplify application programming while providing high throughput and reliable access to large amounts of data.

Another important feature of the Transarc strategy is the decision to build advanced technology directly into its internal architecture. The two main architectural advantages Transarc may have over its competition are its multithreaded architecture and nested transactions. The multithreaded architecture, described earlier in the book, provides better efficiency, performance, interprocess communications, and task management than is possible with the traditional multiprocessing. This architecture is a desirable feature from both the Transaction Management and DBMS perspective. In fact, NCR's TOP END is ready to incorporate a multithreaded architecture as soon as X/Open standards for threads become available.

Nested transactions have originated in the object-oriented technology, and are rarely used in the traditional OLTP due to their complexity in managing coordination of recovery and synchronization of commits and rollbacks. In addition, neither X/Open nor OSI are currently considering standardization of nested transactions.

However, as the technology evolves, the difficulties of the nested transaction management will be overcome. As a result, even Transarc's main competitor—Tuxedo—is considering emulating Transarc's nested transaction facility in its next release.

### 15.3.2    Transarc architecture and components

Transarc's technology is built on the basis of client/server architecture and principles of extreme modularity. As a result, Transarc components can be used to build distributed transaction managers, resource managers, or integral parts of other systems. Conformance to such open system standards as X/Open interfaces ensures that Transarc's modules will interoperate with other open-system standards-compliant systems. This standards compliance will support interoperability among large numbers of heterogeneous systems across networks.

Transarc components are designed to work together with the OSF's DCE. Transarc provides DCE with its AFS Distributed File System. The components (see Fig. 15.8) are designed to perform some specific

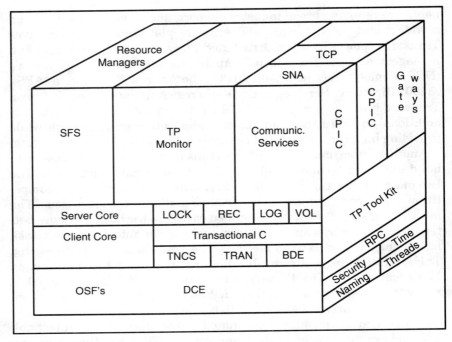

**Figure 15.8**   Transarc components

client and/or server functions, and to interact with each other to support full-featured TP managers, Resource Managers, or other distributed systems.

These Transarc components can be grouped into client and server components. They consist of the Transarc TP Toolkit (Client Core and Server Core), Transarc TP Monitor, Structured File Service, Transarc CPIC Services (including Peer-to-Peer Communications, or PPC) and the PPC Gateway/SNA. CPIC stands for the Common Programming Interface for Communications.

Transarc's Client Core components perform the beginning and end of a transaction, exceptional conditions handling, and Transactional RPCs. Client Core components include:

- *TNCS Services.* These transactional communications include Transactional RPCs (based on Apollo's NCS) and a run-time library for the asynchronous communications needs of TRAN.

- *TRAN Services.* These distributed transaction services provide an optimized two-phase commit, isolated recovery, communication and operating system interfaces, nested transactions, and heuristic outcome support. In addition, TRAN supports a general TP interface which includes RPCs and peer-to-peer communications, TRAN-to-TRAN communications, and X/Open's XA interfaces.

- *Base Development Environment* (BDE). This allows for operating system portability, supports POSIX-style threading and process synchronization, signal handling, time and alarm services, and dynamic storage allocation.

- *Transactional C.* These "C" language libraries support transactional applications, threads of control, locks, recoverable variables, and prepare/commit/abort operations.

Transarc's Server Core components enable the construction of recoverable servers, provide for full transaction integrity, and support archiving and backup. Server Core components include the following:

- *LOG Services* provide for a stable reliable data storage with archiving support (possibly to tape), common-log storage, and administrative support.

- *REC Services* provide for the undo/redo logic and administrative support, buffer management, and physical/logical logging of changes for committed data.

- *LOCK Services* provide for transactional shared, exclusive, and intentions locks.

- *VOL Services* provide support for the large file disk management, data storage on multiple volumes with the reduced disk fragmentation, support for high concurrency of access, fast sequential retrieval, and disk mirroring.

### 15.3.3 Transarc TPM features

One of the key Transarc features is the extension of remote procedure calls into Transactional RPCs. With transactional RPCs, applications can use the DCE's RPC facility to invoke transactions on a network as if they (transactions) were local. The Transactional RPC invocation is contained within a distributed transaction. All necessary transaction processing, including state information, is delivered over an existing client/server RPC connection totally transparent to users and applications. Another important feature of the Transactional RPC is its support of the DCE authentication and security all the way down to the RPC level.

Transactional RPCs are supported by the Transarc distributed transaction services, which manage distributed (global) transactions and use an advanced synchronization protocol—"presume-abort" protocol.

Other basic features of the Transarc TPM are as follows:

- It uses an object-oriented paradigm to encapsulate both the code and data in the server process. Therefore, multiple servers or multiple instances of the same server can operate on each distributed node.

- It supports the two-phase commit protocol over multiple processors and network nodes. Local optimized two-phase commit protocol is used for nondistributed transactions executing on a single node.

- It supports Nested Transactions. These can invoke other transactions and assemble results. Nested transactions help isolate failures within a transaction. Failing transactions are retried automatically and transparently to users. Thus, system reliability is improved. Nested Transactions help utilize multiple servers on a network, therefore improving transaction throughput and data availability. Nested transactions are supported by nested commits, logging, and recovery, which Transarc TPM accomplishes with logical locks and complex atomicity functions.

- Its support for a distributed and/or mirrored logging increases system reliability and availability in a distributed environment.

- Its node management utilities permit authorized users to install servers on remote nodes. Servers can be started, stopped and restarted dynamically, without interruptions to user access.

- It supports user-defined and abstract data types directly within Client Core and Server Core programs, without participation of an advanced DBMS.

- Its built-in record-oriented file system supports the X/Open ISAM API.

- It supports the X/Open XA interfaces between Transarc TPM and XA-compliant resource managers (e.g., DBMSs).

- Support for the Heuristic Outcome allows Transarc's TPM to work with other transaction protocols. In a heterogeneous distributed environment, heuristic outcome support allows individual sites to recover from failures even if they cannot communicate with the rest of the nodes.

- APPC/LU6.2 support over SNA and TCP/IP networks will be extended to incorporate X/Open's Peer-to-Peer API and the ISO TP protocol.

- Coordinator migration allows transactions to originate on workstations or PCs without sacrificing transaction reliability. Transaction coordinator's responsibilities can be automatically migrated from a local PC to a more reliable server system.

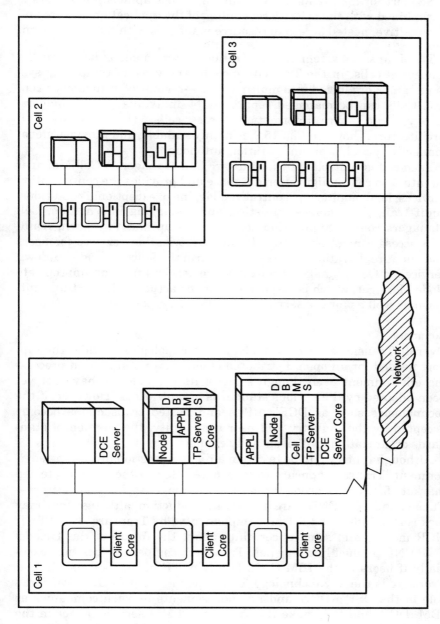

**Figure 15.9** Transarc TPM cell architecture

- Support for a dynamic load balancing across application servers is combined with the priority scheduling of the application servers and repetitive, nested access to resource managers within a transaction.

The Transarc system administration environment is based on the concept of cells. In the Transarc model, a network of computing systems can be organized into multiple cells—regions of autonomous control. Cells can be managed separately by individual Cell Managers, and yet can share information across cells. The Transarc Cell Architecture, shown in Fig. 15.9, is highly scalable, and provides global connectivity and local configuration autonomy.

Each cell is controlled by a Transarc Cell Manager. A Cell Manager maintains a cell configuration database and provides the configuration services, load monitoring, centralized logging of exceptional conditions, audit trail, performance statistics, and debugging information. Cell Managers control application servers start-up and shutdown, maintain access control lists, provide the authorization services for users and client registration services. To perform the start-up and shutdown services, a Cell Manager requests these services from an appropriate Node Manager, which is responsible for the actual node start-up/shutdown as well as for the server process failure reporting.

**Summary**
Overall, Transarc's use of new advanced technologies provides the support needed for an open distributed client/server transaction processing environment even though some of its technologies have not yet been adopted by the various standards organizations. However, if the technologies such as DCE's RPCs and nested transactions become accepted by the industry and user community, the position of standards organizations will eventually change.

Although it has yet to be tested in a real transaction processing environment, Transarc appears to be a pacesetter in the hotly contested market for Unix-based transaction managers. Its competitors—Tuxedo and TOP END—are already in production, although they may lack certain advanced features implemented by Transarc. The AT&T/NCR merger and some uncertainty about the future of the Tuxedo/TOP END product line may help Transarc's competitive position, especially if users of the IBM CICS family of TP monitors consider that Transarc is the key technology for the planned CICS/AIX. Transarc's role in the OSF's DCE, and its endorsements by such companies as IBM, DEC, and HP, make the Transarc TPM a serious player in the open system OLTP arena.

# Workflow and Information Distribution Management in a Client/Server Computing Environment

A client/server architecture is a special case of cooperative distributing processing. It offers many significant user benefits. At the same time, it is a complicated technology which presents many serious design, administration, and operation issues to developers and users alike. Some of these issues—networking and communications, hardware/software platform specialization, distributed data management, transaction management, portability and interoperability in open system environments—have been discussed previously.

To complete the picture, this chapter deals with two important but little discussed issues of a client/server computing environment: workflow management and information distribution management.

## 16.1  WORKFLOW MANAGEMENT

One of the results of using the client/server computing model is the emergence of the groupware—groups of users that are linked electronically via a network in a client/server computing environment. These users work together, possibly sharing common data and applications.

Ideally, such a groupware computing model requires that all its components—clients, servers, network, application, and management tools—are integrated to work together in a cohesive, user-transparent fashion. As a result, these working groups become integrated into office systems where users are allowed to control the flow of work activities throughout the entire environment by dealing with it as a whole.

### 16.1.1   Workflow Management overview

The goals of a Workflow Automation Management environment include overseeing processes, controlling events and their outcome, and increasing the effectiveness of individuals and workgroups by providing the necessary tools, information, and communication services for the purpose of reduced manual intervention or coordination. In other words, Workflow Management automates everyday, routine tasks associated with the normal business office activities. For example, Workflow Management is a critical component of an image office system. Image systems allow the replacement of interoffice envelopes and manila folders with electronically stored documents. As a result, more information is readily available to users. On the other hand, more information leads to the need to provide automated management of work with image documents—search, archiving, and delivery.

In general, Workflow Management includes a series of consecutive or simultaneous tasks that follow the process model of a particular business activity. Workflow Manager automates each step of this activity, keeps track of the status of activities performed, and fills gaps in the otherwise cohesive processing flow by either supplying necessary information or requesting an answer from an end user. The idea behind the Workflow Manager is to trust the computing system with the routine tasks while freeing end users to perform more important duties—thinking and making decisions.

Let's look at client/server interactions in a work group environment from the perspective of performing a particular task for one or several clients. In such a model, clients interact with servers and users by sending Work Items to the proper parties. From the client perspective, the request and reply Work Items are always presented to the end users and may involve:

- a confirmation or rejection reply to an original request (e.g., a YES or NO response by a manager to a client question)

- an informational message, which may recommend to the end user that a particular activity should be started (e.g., reminder, calendar, alarm signal, etc.)

- a request for information, documents, or services

- a request for the authorized user to make a decision based on the information attached to this request (e.g., supported documents to approve/reject a mortgage application)
- selection and initiation of an appropriate end user tool (e.g., spreadsheet, statistical analysis tool, etc.)
- exporting of a document from a server to a user (client) workstation
- printing of a document based on user's request, a prearranged list of documents, or a prepared schedule

To perform these functions, a Workflow Manager should support the concepts of naming services, time deadlines, reminders, and prearranged schedules. Therefore, naming and time services play an important role in the implementation of a Workflow Manager. Also, to simplify the development and use of such a Workflow Manager, object-oriented concepts should be used. Object orientation can facilitate the design of the Workflow Manager knowledge system. Specifically, a Workflow Manager should "know" what work has to be done, where, and when. Indeed, all this information will have been defined to the Workflow Manager up front. In other words, like a conductor in an orchestra, a Workflow Manager orchestrates the work in the workgroup by following the directives that are defined to the Workflow Manager. These directives may include:

- WHAT items (data needed, its location, its owner, steps involved to process it)
- WHEN items (schedules, deadlines, delays, reminders, sequences of steps)
- WHO items (list of users involved and their roles)

Finally, it is highly desirable that such a Workflow Manager is designed and can operate in the open system environment, so that the goals of portability and interoperability are not sacrificed by the automation of the workgroup environment.

An example of such a Workflow Manager is AT&T's Rhapsody Workflow Automation System.

### 16.1.2  AT&T Rhapsody

The underlying concept behind the AT&T Workflow Manager—Rhapsody—is to coordinate, or "orchestrate" business activities of groups of people working together.

*Architecture.* The Rhapsody product is based on an open systems approach to client/server architecture. Therefore, Rhapsody architecture contains client and server components (see Fig. 16.1).

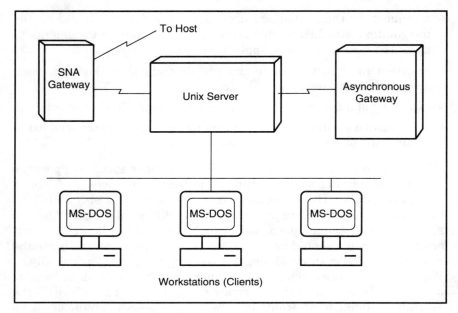

To Host

SNA Gateway

Unix Server

Asynchronous Gateway

MS-DOS        MS-DOS        MS-DOS

Workstations (Clients)

**Figure 16.1** Rhapsody architecture

On the client side, Rhapsody supports personal computers running DOS operating system with Microsoft Windows. Both the local and remote clients are supported.

Rhapsody's server platform is a Unix-based (currently i386-based machine running Unix System V version 3.2) system. Rhapsody clients and servers are interconnected over a network utilizing existing AT&T products—PMX/Starmail for LAN-based electronic mail with Microsoft Windows clients, AT&T distributed directory services (DDS), and Stargroup LAN Manager/X. In addition, Rhapsody offers two unique features:

- The extension to the office automation system from Hewlett-Packard (HP NewWave) allows direct access to fax machines from a Rhapsody client via a fax icon.

- It offers Workflow Automation Software, which is described below.

*Components.* Rhapsody consists of many different components, but the central role among them is given to the Workflow Automation Software. Rhapsody's components are placed on either the server or the client side of Rhapsody's client/server architecture. These components can be placed into several major groups—a Workflow Automation System, an End User Desktop, and a Developer/Administrator Desktop. The Rhapsody component groups are shown in Fig. 16.2.

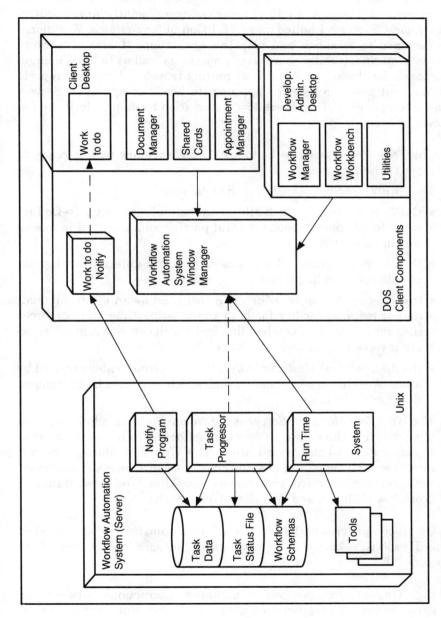

**Figure 16.2**  Rhapsody components

375

Server-based Workflow Automation System provides the workflow management through its Workhorse software, jointly developed by Workhorse Systems Limited and AT&T Computer Systems. Workhorse is designed to establish and help the workgroups (teams of workers given a specific, usually short-term project), as well as to handle large, corporate-level work tasks such as routing travel and expense reports throughout the company for appropriate levels of approval. Server-based components of the Workflow Automation System include the following items.

- The *Task Progressor* checks to see if any workflow task is ready to move to the next step.
- The *Run Time System* includes the following.
  - the *Task Manager,* which allows an "action item" (e.g., To-Do List item) to be shared among several participants involved in execution of this action
  - the *Notify Program,* which is used to notify different workgroup members of pending tasks
  - the *Meeting Manager,* which is a tool used as an electronic mail and scheduling facility for both the meeting time and resources (i.e., conference rooms schedule), and which can also remind workers involved about their meetings
  - the *Appointment Manager,* which is an electronic calendar used by other Workhorse components, and which may also be present on the client's desktop
- The *Workflow Manager-Server* is a development and administration tool providing the means to develop and define to Rhapsody a set of workflows across the organization. The Workflow Manager-Server interacts with the client desktop resident Developer/Administrator workflow management components (Desktop Workflow Manager, Workflow Utilities, and Workflow Workbench).

Client components of the Workflow Automation System are based on the Hewlett-Packard's NewWave office automation system. They include:

- the *Window Manager,* which manages interactions between the client-based applications/end-users and the Run Time System (server component)
- *Desktop Components,* consisting of the *Developer/Administrator Desktop* and *End User Desktop* components

The Developer/Administrator Desktop components include:

- the client portion of the Workflow Manager—starting, stopping, and editing workflow tasks
- the Workflow Workbench—a development environment for the Workflow Automation System
- Workflow Utilities—adding/deleting users, etc.

End User Desktop components include:

- A "Work To Do" component which provides access to work items, appointment and work item reminders, and appointment requests.
- A "Work To Do Notify" component which notifies an end user of a new work item.
- A Document Manager which provides access to documents stored by the Server-based Workflow Automation System. The documents may include library documents, notes, archives, etc.
- Shared Cards which represent an electronic analog of index cards. Cards may be of different types (Customer card, Company card, etc.), and may have document forms attached to them. (For example, a new driver's card may have a driver's license application form attached to it.)
- A Desktop Appointment Manager component which is a client portion of the Appointment Manager. This facility can be initiated by the Workflow Automation System when the Meeting Manager finds it efficacious to place appointments on a user's local (client desktop) calendar.

The Desktop components of the Workflow Automation System support several interesting features that extend the capabilities of the Desktop foundation—HP's NewWave. Specifically, in addition to simple documents, Rhapsody's Document Manager supports complex documents known as variable documents. These documents are similar to form letters. However, they can be more sophisticated. For example, variable documents may have workflow scripts attached to them. Such scripts may direct the Workflow Manager to retrieve workflow data, start a workflow, ask one or more questions, make a decision based on workflow data and the answer received from the end user, or merge a given document with other documents accessed by the Document Manager.

Another important Rhapsody feature is the desktop integration of the presentation, communications, and application tools. Rhapsody's desktop integration includes all NewWave-ready applications at the object level. Furthermore, Rhapsody desktop environment offers:

- the extension of the standard NewWave object-oriented encapsulation, which, for example, allows direct access to fax machines from a Rhapsody client via a fax icon
- Desktop Controller, which helps bridge NewWave and Microsoft Windows environments
- Application Programming Interfaces to facilitate import and export of objects to and from the desktop, edit/view/print a document, and run various desktop tools

In addition to desktop interfaces and AT&T-developed products like Desktop FAX and Windows StarMAIL, Rhapsody supports several popular front-end user tools in the Microsoft Windows environment. Among them are Lotus 1-2-3, Excel, WordPerfect, Microsoft Word for Windows, Micrografx Graph Plus, and DynaComm terminal emulator.

Among tools and facilities integrated into Rhapsody, one tool is noticeably absent. So far, an image system is not integrated into Rhapsody. However, the database that is chosen as the foundation for the Workhorse is the Informix, known for its ability to process IMAGE data types and often used in image systems. Therefore, it is possible that future releases of Rhapsody will be integrated with image processing.

### 16.1.3  Workflow management advantages

Workflow management coordinates the steps of the flow of work items, manages office automation and business routines, automates the production of complex documents and orchestrates people's activities within the office environment.

By coordinating various elements of the business enterprise and workgroup efforts, Workflow Automation System in general, and Rhapsody in particular, offers the following advantages:

- Relieves office workers and workgroup members from day-to-day monitoring and tracking of routine business activities, thus increasing personal and workgroup productivity
- Reduces hardware requirements by off-loading expensive mainframe CPU- and I/O-bound applications into smaller, less expensive workgroup servers and client desktop microcomputers
- Integrates heterogeneous hardware and software systems into a seamless client/server computing environment, thus distributing various office automation functions close to the people working with them
- Integrates local and remote productivity tools into a cohesive, automated desktop office environment without users being aware of the location of the tools and data (documents)

- Supports client/server interactions by distributing work items and business functions between workgroup client systems, as well as between different workgroups and even between different environments

Rhapsody is the perfect example of the well-designed business solution built on client/server architecture. Using client/server architectural principles, Workflow Automation Systems like Rhapsody can deliver the desired workflow management functionality directly to the end user desktop.

## 16.2  INFORMATION DISTRIBUTION AND MANAGEMENT IN CLIENT/SERVER DISTRIBUTED ENVIRONMENT

The client/server computing model represents a special case of the cooperative processing. As such, client/server computing must solve multiple issues relevant to a distributed cooperative processing environment. Among them are the basic issues of distribution of the presentation, application, database logic, and data among several systems across the network. Making all these distributed components of the client/server architecture work together in a cooperative fashion is what the design of the client/server computing environment is all about.

So far, the focus of this book has been directed at issues of the distribution of application components and data between clients and servers, and on the cooperative processing interactions performed by clients and servers. However, one critical, but often forgotten, issue of the client/server architecture and distributed computing deserves special attention. This is the issue of the information distribution management in a distributed client/server environment.

### 16.2.1  Overview of the information distribution

A distributed client/server architecture may be composed of heterogeneous systems connected via a network. Each of these systems may be acting as either a client, a server, or both. When an existing business enterprise undergoes a transition from a centralized hierarchical architecture to a distributed client/server architecture, a three-tier computing model is often used as the blueprint of such a rearchitecture project.

This three-tiered approach is evolutionary, and has its roots in the familiar hierarchical master-slave computing architecture. The evolution of this architecture is based on additional capabilities offered by distributed cooperative processing of the client/server computing model.

Three-tiered architecture is the result of distributing the computing resources vertically. When the resources are to be delivered to end users on their workstations, these end user workstations are acting as clients with the ultimate server being the most powerful system and the source of the corporate data—the mainframe. This is the two-tiered architecture. However, such an architecture does not take advantage of all the benefits offered by the client/server computing model and the power available in the new microcomputer technology. For instance, if independent clients are to be organized into workgroups, their inter-client communications are to be routed through the central hub—a possibly remote mainframe computer. Obviously, this is not the best approach.

Besides, the centralized computer has to deal with vast numbers (potentially thousands) of clients directly. The client base growth may result in the need to continuously increase mainframe capacity. The same is true for communication and networking aspects of the issue.

The answer to this problem is the organization of end users (clients) into workgroups via Local Area Networks (LAN), and the introduction of the middle tier which contains powerful LAN servers. These servers have dual properties. They act as clients for the top tier and send appropriate requests to the mainframe. At the same time, they function as servers for the workstations and PCs that reside in the third tier (see Fig. 16.3).

Figure 16.3 shows an example of such a three-tiered architecture. It can be an organization that extends its central single-host data center capabilities by building LANs in each of its headquarters departments and connecting corresponding LAN servers to the host. This architecture can be expanded by adding mainframes to the top tier, local area networks servers to the second tier, and client workstations to the third tier. For example, an organization that desires to extend its East Coast operations by building a second data center on the West Coast can put LANs into each regional sales office. Office LAN servers can be physically located in remote locations, and can be connected to either host via a wide area network (WAN).

The complexity of this three-tiered client/server architecture is caused not only by the issues of applications and data distribution, but also by the problems of network management, system performance, workload balancing, and SOFTWARE DISTRIBUTION and MAN-AGEMENT.

Indeed, consider the three-tiered environment shown in Fig. 16.3. Let's assume that the corporate headquarters are responsible for the overall management of the environment, as well as for development, purchase, installation, and maintenance of all the software running on every node of the network. This means that every client workstation,

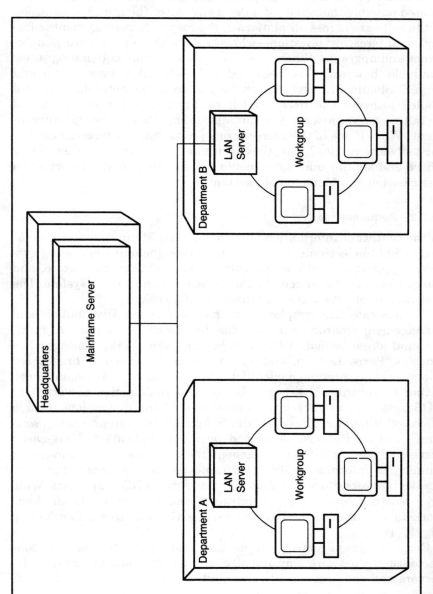

**Figure 16.3**  Three-tiered architecture

for example, runs a set of programs provided by a corporate division located possibly thousands of miles away. After the initial installation of the software across all platforms, the corporate management is facing an interesting question—what to do with the software maintenance and upgrades. When a new version of an application program is available, how will it be delivered and installed at every client and server? Should the new version be put on a magnetic diskette and mailed to every end user? And if so, are the end users capable of installing new software without disrupting their existing environment? What if one of the users (or one group) has not received the latest software version? Can they continue to use their workstations? These and similar questions should be answered by the Information Distribution and Management system.

### 16.2.2  Requirements

In the context of Information Distribution and Management, *information* refers to electronic data in all its forms, including operating systems, application and user executable files, text, graphic, voice, and image objects, not managed by the database management system. The distribution of data is the responsibility of a DBMS.

To illustrate the complexity of the Information Distribution and Management environment, consider the following situation. A multinational organization with branches in New York, Chicago, Los Angeles, Paris, London, and Tokyo has implemented a three-tiered client/server computing model that is built on several IBM mainframes acting as centralized servers, Unix-based middle tier servers, and DOS-based end user (client) workstations. Client applications include Microsoft Windows, dBase III DBMS, MultiMate word processing software, and an in-house developed business application. Unix-based servers support both the development and operational environment by running an Informix DBMS. Mainframes are the residence of the corporate data repository distributed among several DB2 databases. Wide area network connects all mainframes and servers, while all client workstations are attached to their servers via local area networks (see Fig. 16.4).

Corporate management has decided that since all users are connected on the network, any and all changes to the software used by the servers and end users will be distributed electronically, over the network.

Let's assume that the business application program has been upgraded, and the new version is available at the corporate headquarters. The new version of the program requires an additional 2 Mbytes of the hard disk space and a special driver which must be specified in

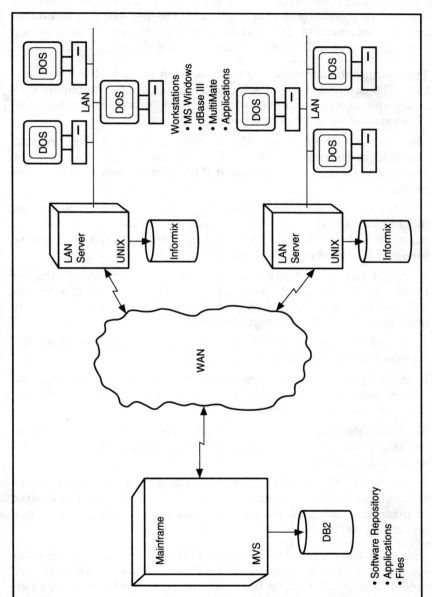

**Figure 16.4** Three-tiered distributed environment

383

the CONFIG.SYS file. This new program must be installed under MS Windows. To distribute a simple program change like this to all end users, the information distribution and management system should support several complex requirements. Among them:

- The system should know the configuration of each client workstation. The configuration data includes the amount of available disk space and memory, number of disk drives, drive name where MS Windows software is installed, etc.

- The system should know the current version of the program installed, so that the distribution/installation software can save the previous version and can restore it if the new version does not work properly.

- The system should have the ability to schedule the distribution/ installation job at a time when users do not use the system. For example, if the CONFIG.SYS file has been changed, the PC has to be rebooted for the changes to take effect.

- It should have the ability to provide technical support utilities for those clients that need them. For example, a utility can be distributed to make a backup copy of the existing configuration and to print installation and/or upgrade notes.

- It should be able to provide remote management support for the recipient nodes as well as for the network.

- It should provide the required level of security while distributing information, so that unauthorized access and tempering with the distributed software is prevented.

- The system should be "smart" enough to rely on the underlying networking protocols for the transport, notification, and optimum network routing selection.

- It should be able to take advantage of and be integrated with the Distributed DBMS software, as well as with the Distributed Transaction Management in a distributed client/server cooperative processing environment.

And most important, the Software Distribution and Management system should provide users with a single view of the distributed environment. The Single System Image should be supported even in a heterogeneous distributed environment, where disparate networking protocols interconnect different hardware platforms running different operating systems and different database management systems. In other words, the ideal Software Distribution and Management system should be designed to operate in an open systems environment.

### 16.2.3  Management components

Clearly, the requirements listed above are rather difficult to satisfy. It is not surprising, therefore, that at the time of this writing there were no products available in the marketplace that could satisfy even this incomplete list of the functional requirements. One logical conclusion, though, follows the principles of the distributed client/server architecture. A complex system like the Information Distribution and Management system should be designed in a modular fashion, where different components should be dedicated to performing specialized tasks while cooperating with other components to successfully distribute and manage information. These components and their functions can be divided into the following major groups:

- The *Centralized Change Management* is a system designed to manage the ongoing control, monitoring, installation, and updates of relevant information while maintaining the integrity of the entire environment.

- A *High-Performance Communication Networking* component is designed to provide a highly secure, error-free message transport mechanism, capable of transporting atomic and compound (integrated binary executable, text, graphics, voice, and image) objects. Remote control of the network nodes with the ability to run diagnostics and (re)configuration software is also highly desired.

- *Support Services* consist of software designed to support end users receiving software distribution. Support services should include various help and self-training facilities, "read-me" files, tutoring, and on-line technical support (including the communication software).

These major component groups of the Software Distribution and Management system should include the following facilities:

- *Network Interfaces and Route Management* may include single logon, dynamic route selection, peripheral devices support (e.g., access to the attached and centralized printers), LAN-to-WAN and LAN-to-LAN bridges.

- *Information Collection Management* may include node profile database that contains all relevant information regarding a particular node's configuration, access, directories, and available resources, a configuration management software, queue management, and similar facilities.

- *Configuration Management* should automatically maintain an accurate, up-to-date hardware and software inventory, notify Distribution Management regarding any problem preventing a successful distribution, and keep track of any changes to the system configuration.

- *Version Control Management* should include control of software contracts and licenses, and should notify management of any license agreement violations.

- *Remote Support and Job Scheduling* should include functions like scheduling collection and/or distribution jobs, assigning job priorities, backup of the previous software version/recovery to the previous versions. Job scheduling should allow remote users to schedule their own jobs.

- *Security Management* should support access control to individual programs and software packages, prevent software piracy, protect against computer viruses by scheduling a regular virus detection program, provide monitoring of changes and important events, and maintain accurate audit trail support.

These Software Distribution and Management components and their functional requirements represent an incomplete list of features that today are likely to appear in a Request For Information/Request For Proposal document, typically submitted by users of a distributed client/ server environment to the software vendors. Indeed, these requirements are so complicated that any one vendor would have an extremely difficult task to satisfy them all, even within the limitations of a particular architecture. For example, if the target environment is limited to IBM's SAA platforms, IBM's Software Distribution and Management solution consists of the NetView/Delivery Manager (NetView/DM) and SAA Delivery Manager (SAA/DM). This combined solution includes administrative functionality (License/Asset Management, User Access Control, Version/Release Control, Centralized Resource Management) and Network Control Functions (Automatic Software Installation, Distribution Tracking, Automatic Transmission). However, this solution does not satisfy all the requirements of the open heterogeneous Software Distribution and Management system. Specifically, the SAA/DM provides a rather rich administrative functionality, while its Network Control functions are currently limited to LU2 (3270-type) links. NetView/DM functionality is reversed—poor administrative functionality and robust, APPC/LU6.2-based network control functions. Furthermore, both products are limited to the OS/2 operating systems.

There are several other products on the market today that provide a reasonable subset of the desired functionality, but on a limited platform. One example of such a solution is the "Network Navigator" from Annatek Systems, Inc. (Boulder, Colorado).

However, the problem of software distribution and management is serious enough, and real enough, for such technology organizations like Open Software Foundation to begin the search for the right solution. Such a solution could be the OSF Distributed Management Environment, or DME.

### 16.2.4   OSF's Distributed Management Environment

The Distributed Management Environment (DME) is OSF's technology for a standardized uniform framework for efficient object-oriented cost-effective management of open systems. The DME is based on technology offerings submitted by such vendors as IBM, Hewlett-Packard, Groupe Bull, and Tivoli Systems. These companies are providing Application Programming Interfaces and Object-Oriented technology that OSF's DME will use to allow vendors to build standardized applications capable of running on, and being managed by, centrally controlled hardware and software across heterogeneous networks.

True to its goals of openness, OSF is designing the DME to be usable with both Unix and proprietary systems. The OSF Distributed Management Environment has two main components. The first is a set of application services providing some of the most common system management functions.

The second DME component is a framework which provides the building blocks needed to develop software and applications to manage heterogeneous systems. The DME architecture is shown in Fig. 16.5.

The DME architecture contains distributed application services provided as a set of modules and Application Programming Interfaces. DME application services are the fundamental set of services designed to facilitate interoperability. These services are extensible in many ways. For instance, they can add value to the applications and can add new services. In addition to the application services, the DME includes management applications that use the underlying application services to perform their tasks. DME Management Applications include DME Software Management, DME License Management and DME Printing Services. The DME Software Management facilitates packaging, distribution, installation, and management of software. The DME Distributed License Management offers extensive means to track software licenses. The DME Printing Services combines high functionality and the flexibility needed in heterogeneous distributed environments.

All DME management operations can be performed via a single interface and style—an object-oriented communication. At the core of the DME framework is a mechanism designed to allow all network components, including heterogeneous hardware and software on every node, to be represented in standardized, easily manipulated data packages—objects. This mechanism is called a Management Request Broker, and is based on IBM's Data Engine, Tivoli's WizDOM, and HP's OpenView Network Management Server.

The Management Request Broker manages communications between objects using standard API formats. Standard APIs allow heterogeneous systems and multivendor applications to talk to each other and reuse application code in a modular fashion. The Management

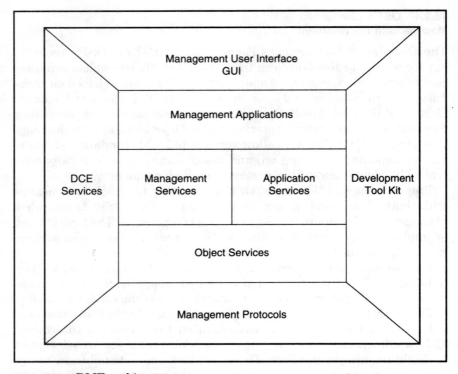

**Figure 16.5** DME architecture

Request Broker is similar in functionality to the object-oriented technology (Object Request Broker) proposed for standardization by X/Open and Object Management Group (OMG). Objects are maintained by Object Servers, which are divided into two classes—object servers for short-duration tasks (e.g., password change task), and object servers for long-running tasks (e.g., network monitoring).

Also included in the DME is the object-oriented software from Wang Laboratories. An Event Logger (part of the DME Event Management Services) monitors events and traffic on the network, and can be configured to filter certain events.

DME's Application Programming Interfaces are based on the Consolidated Management API (CM-API) that was jointly developed by Groupe Bull, IBM, and HP. CM-API allows software developers to continue writing software using traditional methodology, rather than forcing them to learn object-oriented programming and design.

DME APIs are part of the DME Development Toolkit, which provides developers with a rich programming environment designed to facilitate the development of DME applications. DME APIs support the development of DME applications written in either standard C language or object-oriented C++ language. These applications can use communication protocols based on the Simple Network Management Protocols, or SNMP (TCP/IP's network management protocol), the Common Management Information Protocol, or CMIP (the equivalent of the Open System Interconnection protocol), and Distributed Computing Environment's Remote Procedure Calls (RPC). Access to multiple management protocols helps promote DME portability and interoperability. The DME is designed to solve many software distribution and management requirements. DME's layered architecture is built to operate in tandem with the OSF's Distributed Computing Environment (DCE), and includes the following DME Application and Management Services components (as well as those which have been already mentioned above):

- Host-based Configuration Manager, which is based on WizDOM

- License Control Manager, designed to enforce licensing of applications on a network (based on HP/Apollo Net LS)

- Software Installation Manager, which provides on-line installation and application update services on the network (based on HP's Software Distribution Utilities)

- Network Management software for personal computers (based on Gradient Technology's networking products)

- Print Manager, which is based on the Palladium Print Server from MIT

The DME satisfies many software distribution and management requirements in the open, standardized fashion. However, to become an undisputed leader in the software distribution field, the DME (and similar products) should also satisfy key requirements of scalability and support for both hierarchical (centralized) and peer-to-peer management.

The Distributed Management Environment appears to be a step in the right direction. Of course, it is not alone in the very competitive Software Distribution and Management field. For example, distributed computing architecture from the Unix International—Atlas— is expected to be compatible in functionality to OSF's DCE and DME.

The issues related to Software Distribution and Management have been discussed to illustrate one more difficulty in building a truly open, distributed client/server environment. Fortunately, these difficulties can be overcome.

When architectures like the DME and Atlas are fully implemented, the resulting Software Distribution and Management products will provide a solid foundation for the development of truly open systems management applications for a distributed client/server environment.

## 16.3 CLIENT/SERVER COMPUTING— ARCHITECTURE FOR TOMORROW

Up to this point, the discussion on the client/server architecture has been aimed mostly at the evolution of the computing environment, clarification of the client/server paradigm, and analysis of the various client/server architecture components—presentation, business logic, and data management.

The client/server computing model has been shown to include the specialized client and server platforms. And the critical role of data communications between clients and servers has been demonstrated on examples of various Local and Wide Area Networks and networking protocols. The analysis of the client/server architecture has extended a widely accepted view of client/server computing as the architecture for the distributed database environment. This extended view includes such important issues as workflow management, networks and data communications, distributed presentation, and distributed transaction processing.

Most importantly, the client/server architecture has been discussed from the point of view of standards and open systems. And hopefully, the result of all these discussions has demonstrated the client/server paradigm as a special case of the distributed cooperative processing. Client/server computing can bring to the users some extremely important and tangible benefits, especially if the client/server architecture is built upon and takes advantage of the open systems.

### 16.3.1 Benefits and advantages of client/server computing

Client/server computing continues its advance, mainly because its current and prospective users—extensive networked enterprises and organizations looking to decentralize, downsize, and distribute their data processing operations—continue to demand enhancements in functionality and technology.

Among these demands is the need to migrate to open distributed systems. As a rule, most users are facing the problems of portability and interoperability in heterogeneous networked environments. Indeed, portability and interoperability, and not a particular operating system, are what users are looking for in the open systems arena. Such openness can be achieved by:

- building the entire computing environment and its various components in compliance with the international and industry accepted standards

- distributing various application components between clients and servers and interconnecting them via efficient, standards-based networks

- integrating all distributed system, heterogeneous hardware and software platforms, and various presentation and database management systems into a seamless, cohesive, reliable, and secure single system image

- providing tools and mechanisms to effectively manage and control this new, open, distributed client/server environment

- ensuring that the openness of the environment does not compromise the security and integrity of applications and data

The client/server architecture is not the "end" of all architectures, and it has some serious drawbacks. Complexity is one of them. However, users find that there are real benefits in adopting the client/server architecture.

Specifically, client/server architecture can effect the following:

- It allows corporations to better leverage emerging desktop computing technology. Today's workstations deliver considerable computing power, previously available only from mainframes, at a fraction of mainframe cost.

- It allows the processing to reside close to the source of data being processed, therefore reducing network traffic and response time. As a result, the effective network throughput is increased and the network bandwidth requirements and associated costs can be reduced.

- It facilitates the use of standards-based graphical user interfaces (GUI) available on powerful workstations. These new intuitive easily-navigated and consistent interfaces can be delivered to customers in a variety of visual presentation techniques. As a result, investment in training and education can be better leveraged, and new products exceeding customer expectations can be developed faster. End user resistance in accepting new products can be minimized.

- It allows for and encourages the acceptance of open systems. Indeed, by its own nature, the client/server computing model calls for the specialization of client and server platform. The need to interconnect heterogeneous systems, to port applications between client and server systems, and to be able to participate in cooperative processing allows end users to free themselves from proprietary architectures. Thus, users are able to enjoy economical, marketing, and competitive advantage of the open systems market.

The client/server computing model holds many promises to both developers and end users. Some of these promises are achievable today, while others will hopefully be solved tomorrow.

And, while client/server architecture will not turn nontechnical users into professional software developers, it can, if properly implemented, reduce software maintenance costs, increase software portability, boost performance of existing networks, and even eliminate application backlog by increasing developers' productivity and shortening the development lifecycle.

### 16.3.2    What is next

The client/server architecture does not end the evolution of the computing environment. The next evolutionary step may be towards an intelligent, networked peer-to-peer computing model where all participant systems are equal, and can request and provide services to and from each other.

Very few products today claim to support such an advanced peer-to-peer computing. This architecture appears to be the ultimate in distribution of application processing. The processing is performed wherever there is available computing resources, including shared devices, CPU, and memory. A single system in peer-to-peer processing can act as a client for other servers and a server for itself and other clients. In an intelligent peer-to-peer processing, one server cannot only distribute a workload among available servers, but can also optimize such a distribution based on network characteristics, available routes, and system resources. As a result, multiple systems can cooperate in order to perform a particular task, and the number of such systems can depend on the nature and requirements of the task.

If the client/server architecture demonstrates the wealth of complex, not always easily solvable issues, the spectrum of outstanding technical issues relevant to the implementation of a peer-to-peer computing architecture is far greater.

However, the client/server computing model, as an evolutionary step towards the goal of peer-to-peer computing, is a promising and powerful architecture. It provides business solutions that allow the development of open distributed systems *today*.

# SNA PU Types

The Systems Network Architecture assigns types to various physical units (PUs). All physical units are implemented as a combination of software and hardware within each node.

Typically, PUs are assigned the same numeric type as the SNA node in which they reside. The Physical Unit can represent to the network a processor, a controller, a workstation, or a printer. The following physical unit types are currently defined in the SNA:

- *PU Type 1* represents products such as IBM 3271, IBM 6670, IBM 3767.

- *PU Type 2.0* describes a Peripheral node that contains PU type 2.0. PU 2.0 supports the following logical unit (LU) types—LU2, LU3, LU6.2, and LU1 (the latter is for non-SNA interconnection)—and provides end users with access to the network and end-user services. PU 2.0 represents such products as IBM 3174, IBM 3274, IBM 3276, IBM/PC, IBM 3770, and AS/400.

- *PU Type 2.1* describes a Peripheral node that contains its own control point, which provides PU services. PU 2.1 supports LU1, LU2, LU3, LU6.2 and direct link connections to other Type 2.1 nodes; it provides end-user access to the network and end-user services. PU 2.1 represents such products as IBM System/36, IBM System/38, IBM/PC, TPF, AS/400, ACF/VTAM V3.3, and ACF/NCP V5.3.

- *PU Type 4* describes a Communication Controller Subarea node that contains PU Type 4. PU 4 routes and controls the flow of data through the network. PU 4 represents such products as IBM NCP, IBM 3720, IBM 3705, IBM 3725, and IBM 3745.

- *PU Type 5* describes a Host Subarea node that contains a System Services Control Point (SSCP). PU 5 supports all LU types. Its primary functions are to control network resources, to support application and transaction programs and end-user services, and to provide network operators access to the network. PU 5 represents products such as IBM's ACF/VTAM, IBM 4300, IBM 308X, IBM 9370, IBM 3090, and IBM 3900.

# SNA LU Types

| LU TYPE | Description | Examples |
|---------|-------------|----------|
| 0 | LUTYPE 0 uses non-SNA protocols; these protocols are implemented by the LU itself. | TCAM, IMS, CICS, JES2/NJE use 3270-BSC terminals |
| 1 | LUTYPE 1 is used for application program that communicates with single or multiple-device WS in an interactive, batch data transfer or distributed data processing environment using IBM's SNA data stream. | Application program uses IBM IMS/VS and communicates with an IBM 8100 Information System. |
| 2 | LUTYPE 2 is for an application program that communicates with a single workstation using the SNA 3270 data stream. | Application program uses IBM IMS/VS and communicates with IBM 3179 Display station. |
| 3 | LUTYPE 3 is for an application program that communicates with a single printer using IBM 3270 data stream. | Application program uses IBM CICS/VS to send data to IBM 3287 printer through 3274 Controller. |

| 4 | LUTYPE 4 is used for: (1) application program that communicates with single or multiple-device WS in an interactive, batch data transfer or distributed data processing environment; the data stream confirms to the IBM's SNA character string (SCS); or (2) logical units in peripheral nodes that communicate with each other. | (1) Application program uses IBM CICS/VS and communicates with an IBM 6670 Information Distributer; (2) two 6670 that communicate with each other. |
|---|---|---|
| 6.1 | LUTYPE 6.1 is for an application sub-system that communicates with another subsystem in a distributed data processing environment. | Application program uses IBM CICS/VS and communicates with IBM IMS/VS. |
| 6.2 | LUTYPE 6.2 supports sessions between two applications in a distributed environ-ment, using SNA General Data Stream (GDS), or user-defined data stream (see note below). | Advanced Program-to-Program Communication— CICS/VS communicates with another CICS/VS. |
| 7 | LUTYPE 7 supports sessions between host application and a midrange system, such as IBM System/3X, or a single display station. | Application, running at 3090 communicates with System/36. |

NOTE: LU6.2 is also known as Advanced Program-to-Program Communication, or APPC. It is the most recent and the most advanced LU type, and it provides functions over and above those of the previous logical units. LU6.2 sessions provide communication between different node types—between two type 5 nodes, a type 5 node and a type 2.1 node, and between two type 2.1 nodes.

# LU6.2 Verbs

Mapped and Basic Conversation Verbs.

```
+--------------------------------------------------------------+
I Verb:   [MC_] ALLOCATE                                       I
+--------------------------------------------------------------+
I Common Parameters:                                           I
+--------------------------------------------------------------+
I Mandatory Input parameters:                                  I
I    - LU_NAME (OWN)       or                                  I
I              (OTHER (remote-LU-name))                        I
I                                                              I
I    - MODE_NAME (mode-name)                                   I
I                                                              I
I    - TPN (remote-TP-name)                                    I
+--------------------------------------------------------------+
I Optional Input parameters:                                   I
I    [                  ( WHEN_SESSION_ALLOCATED )         ] I
I    [ RETURN_CONTROL ( DELAYED_ALLOCATION_PERMITTED )]    I
I    [                  ( IMMEDIATE )                      ] I
I                                                              I
I    [            ( NONE )    ]                                I
I    [ SYNC_LEVEL ( CONFIRM ) ]                                I
I    [            ( SYNCPT )  ]                                I
I                                                              I
I    [            ( NONE )                              ]  I
I    [ SECURITY  ( SAME )                               ]  I
I    [            ( PGM ( USER_ID (user-id)             ]  I
I                        PASSWORD (password)            ]  I
I                        PROFILE (variable) ) ]            I
I                                                              I
I    [ PIP (NO) ]                                              I
I    [       (YES (pip-1 pip-2 pip-3 pip-4...) ]           I
+--------------------------------------------------------------+
I  For Basic conversation only:                                I
I                                                              I
I     [ TYPE (BASIC_CONVERSATION) or ]                         I
I     [      (MAPPED_CONVERSATION)   ]                         I
+--------------------------------------------------------------+
I  Returned parameters:                                        I
I                                                              I
I     - RESOURCE (resource-id)                                 I
I     - RETURN_CODE (rc)                                       I
+--------------------------------------------------------------+
I  ABEND Conditions:                                           I
I   - PARAMETER_ERROR (Invalid LU or mode name)                I
I   - ALLOCATION_ERROR                                         I
I   - UNSUCCESSFUL (if RETURN_IMMEDIATE is specified)          I
I                                                              I
+--------------------------------------------------------------+
I  States from which the verb can be issued:                   I
I     RESET                                                    I
+--------------------------------------------------------------+
I  State after successful execution: SEND state                I
I                                                              I
 --------------------------------------------------------------
```

```
+------------------------------------------------------------+
I Verb:  [MC_] CONFIRM                                       I
+------------------------------------------------------------+
I Common Parameters:                                         I
+------------------------------------------------------------+
I Mandatory Input parameters:                                I
I                                                            I
I    RESOURCE (resource-id)                                  I
I                                                            I
+------------------------------------------------------------+
I  Returned parameters:                                      I
I                                                            I
I     - RETURN_CODE (rc)                                     I
I     - REQUEST_TO_SEND_RECEIVED (yes/no)                    I
+------------------------------------------------------------+
I  ABEND Conditions:                                         I
I   - PARAMETER CHECK (If SYNC_LEVEL (NONE) is used or       I
I     if resource-id is not assigned)                        I
I   - STATE CHECK (if conversation is not in SEND or         I
I                      DEFER states)                         I
+------------------------------------------------------------+
I  States from which the verb can be issued:                 I
I     SEND, DEFER                                            I
+------------------------------------------------------------+
I  State after successful execution:                         I
I     RECEIVE State, if CONFIRM is issued in Defer State I
I                    after PREPARE_TO_RECEIVE                I
I     RESET State,   if CONFIRM is issued in Defer State I
I                    after DEALLOCATE                        I
I     SEND State,    if CONFIRM is issued in Send State I
 ------------------------------------------------------------
```

```
+----------------------------------------------------------------+
I Verb:  [MC_] CONFIRMED                                         I
+----------------------------------------------------------------+
I Common Parameters:                                             I
+----------------------------------------------------------------+
I Mandatory Input parameters:                                    I
I                                                                I
I    RESOURCE (resource-id)                                      I
I                                                                I
+----------------------------------------------------------------+
I  Returned parameters:                                          I
I                                                                I
I      None                                                      I
+----------------------------------------------------------------+
I  ABEND Conditions:                                             I
I    - PARAMETER CHECK (If resource-id is not assigned)          I
I    - STATE CHECK (if a conversation is not in CONFIRM          I
I                                                      state)     I
+----------------------------------------------------------------+
I States from which the verb can be issued:                      I
I     CONFIRM                                                    I
I                                                                I
+----------------------------------------------------------------+
I State after successful execution:                              I
I RECEIVE State, if CONFIRM is received on preceeding            I
I               RECEIVE_AND_WAIT or RECEIVE_IMMEDIATE            I
I SEND State, if CONFIRM_SEND is received on preceeding          I
I               RECEIVE_AND_WAIT or RECEIVE_IMMEDIATE            I
I DEALLOCATE State, if CONFIRM DEALLOCATE is received on         I
I       preceeding RECEIVE_AND_WAIT or RECEIVE_IMMEDIATE         I
+----------------------------------------------------------------+
```

```
+------------------------------------------------------------+
I Verb:  [MC_] DEALLOCATE                                    I
+------------------------------------------------------------+
I Common Parameters:                                         I
+------------------------------------------------------------+
I Mandatory Input parameters:                                I
I   RESOURCE (resource-id)                                   I
+------------------------------------------------------------+
I  Optional input for basic conversation:                    I
I             ( SYNC_LEVEL ) ]                               I
I             ( FLUSH      ) ]                               I
I             ( CONFIRM    ) ]                               I
I    [ TYPE   ( ABEND_PROG ) ]                               I
I             ( ABEND_SVC  ) ]                               I
I             ( ABEND_TIMER) ]                               I
I             ( LOCAL      ) ]                               I
I                                                            I
I    [ LOG_DATA (NO)                            ]            I
I              (YES (log-error-variable) ]                   I
+------------------------------------------------------------+
I  Optional input for mapped conversation:                   I
I             ( SYNC_LEVEL ) ]                               I
I             ( FLUSH      ) ]                               I
I    [ TYPE   ( CONFIRM    ) ]                               I
I             ( ABEND      ) ]                               I
I             ( LOCAL      ) ]                               I
+------------------------------------------------------------+
I  Returned parameters:                                      I
I    RETURN_CODE (rc)                                        I
+------------------------------------------------------------+
I  ABEND Conditions:                                         I
I   - PARAMETER CHECK (if resource-id is not assigned,       I
I       if TYPE(CONFIRM) is specified, but conversation      I
I          is allocated with SYNC_LEVEL(NONE),               I
I       if specified parameters are not supported)           I
I   - STATE CHECK, if:                                       I
I   1.FLUSH, CONFIRM or SYNC_LEVEL specified not from        I
I           SEND State                                       I
I   2.ABEND_PROG, ABEND_SVC or ABEND_TIMER specified notI
I          from SEND, DEFER, RECEIVE, CONFIRM or            I
I                                   SYNCPOINT states I
I   3.LOCAL is specified not from DEALLOCATE  state          I
+------------------------------------------------------------+
I States from which the verb can be issued:                  I
I  SEND, RECEIVE, CONFIRM, SYNCPOINT, DEALLOCATE -           I
I          depends on the TYPE specified                     I
+------------------------------------------------------------+
I State after successful execution:                          I
I DEFER State, if SYNC_LEVEL is specified and the            I
I               synchronization level is SYNCPT              I
I RESET State, if:                                           I
I     - FLUSH, CONFIRM, LOCAL or ABEND  is specified         I
I     - SYNC_LEVEL is specified, and sync level is NONE I
I                                    or CONFIRM.             I
+------------------------------------------------------------+
```

```
+-------------------------------------------------------------+
I Verb:   [MC_] FLUSH                                         I
+-------------------------------------------------------------+
I Common Parameters:                                          I
+-------------------------------------------------------------+
I Mandatory Input parameters:                                 I
I                                                             I
I    RESOURCE (resource-id)                                   I
I                                                             I
+-------------------------------------------------------------+
I  Returned parameters:                                       I
I                                                             I
I        None                                                 I
+-------------------------------------------------------------+
I  ABEND Conditions:                                          I
I    - PARAMETER CHECK (If resource-id is not assigned)       I
I    - STATE CHECK (if a conversation is not in SEND or       I
I                                       DEFER states)         I
+-------------------------------------------------------------+
I States from which the verb can be issued:"                 I
I     SEND, DEFER                                             I
I                                                             I
+-------------------------------------------------------------+
I State after successful execution:                           I
I RECEIVE State, if FLUSH is issued in DEFER state afterI
I               [MC_] PREPARE_TO_RECEIVE                      I
I RECEIVE State, if FLUSH is issued in DEFER state afterI
I               [MC_] DEALLOCATE                             I
I SEND State, if FLUSH is issued in SEND state               I
-------------------------------------------------------------
```

```
+-------------------------------------------------------------+
I Verb:   [MC_] GET_ATTRIBUTES                                I
+-------------------------------------------------------------+
I Common Parameters:                                          I
+-------------------------------------------------------------+
I Mandatory Input parameters:                                 I
I                                                             I
I  RESOURCE (resource-id)                                     I
+-------------------------------------------------------------+
I  Optional Returned Parameters:                              I
I  [ OWN_FULLY_QUALIFIED_LU_NAME (LU-name) ]                  I
I  [ PARTNER_LU_NAME (partner-LU-name) ]                      I
I  [ PARTNER_FULLY_QUALIFIED_LU_NAME (partner-LU-name)]       I
I  [ MODE_NAME (mode-name) ]                                  I
I  [ SYNC_LEVEL (sync-level) ]                                I
I  [ SECURITY_USER_ID (user-id) ]                             I
I  [ SECURITY_PROFILE (profile) ]                             I
I  [ LUW_IDENTIFIER (LUW-id) ]                                I
I  [ CONVERSATION_CORRELATOR (syncpt-conv-correlator) ]       I
+-------------------------------------------------------------+
I  ABEND Conditions:                                          I
I   - PARAMETER CHECK (If resource-id is not assigned,        I
I      or one of the specified returned parameters is         I
I                                    not supported)           I
I                                                             I
I   - STATE CHECK - NONE                                      I
+-------------------------------------------------------------+
I States from which the verb can be issued:                   I
I     SEND, DEFER, RECEIVE, CONFIRM, SYNCPOINT,               I
I                            BACKED OUT, DEALLOCATE           I
+-------------------------------------------------------------+
I State after successful execution: no state changes          I
+-------------------------------------------------------------+
```

```
+-----------------------------------------------------------+
I Verb:   [MC_] POST_ON_RECEIPT                             I
+-----------------------------------------------------------+
I Common Parameters:                                        I
+-----------------------------------------------------------+
I Mandatory Input parameters:                               I
I   RESOURCE (resource-id)                                  I
I   LENGTH (length)                                         I
+-----------------------------------------------------------+
I Optional input for basic conversation only:               I
I   [ FILL (LL)      ]                                      I
I           (BUFFER) ]                                      I
+-----------------------------------------------------------+
I  ABEND Conditions:                                        I
I   - PARAMETER CHECK (If resource-id is not assigned)      I
I   - STATE CHECK - conversation is not in RECEIVE stateI
+-----------------------------------------------------------+
I States from which the verb can be issued:                I
I    RECEIVE                                                I
I                                                           I
+-----------------------------------------------------------+
I State after successful execution: no state changes        I
-------------------------------------------------------------
```

```
+----------------------------------------------------------------
I Verb:   [MC_] PREPARE_TO_RECEIVE                         I
+---------------------------------------------------------------+
I Common Parameters:                                       I
+---------------------------------------------------------------+
I Mandatory Input parameters:                              I
I                                                          I
I    RESOURCE (resource-id)                                I
+---------------------------------------------------------------+
I  Optional input parameters:                              I
I            (SYNC_LEVEL) ]                                 I
I    [ TYPE  (FLUSH     ) ]                                 I
I            (CONFIRM   ) ]                                 I
I                                                          I
I    [ LOCKS (SHORT)     ]                                 I
I            (LONG )     ]                                 I
+---------------------------------------------------------------+
I  Returned parameters:                                    I
I                                                          I
I        RETURN_CODE (rc)                                  I
+---------------------------------------------------------------+
I  ABEND Conditions:                                       I
I    - PARAMETER CHECK (If resource-id is not assigned,    I
I        or parameter specified is not supported)          I
I    - STATE CHECK (if conversation is not in SEND state,  I
I      or it is, but TP started and did not finish         I
I                      sending logical record)             I
+---------------------------------------------------------------+
I States from which the verb can be issued:                I
I    SEND                                                  I
I                                                          I
+---------------------------------------------------------------+
I State after successful execution:                        I
I RECEIVE State, if CONFIRM or FLUSH is specified, or      I
I          SYNC_LEVEL is specified, but sync level is      I
I                      NONE or CONFIRM                     I
I DEFER State, if SYNC_LEVEL is specified, and sync        I
I              level is SYNCPT                             I
I                                                          I
----------------------------------------------------------------
```

```
+----------------------------------------------------------+
I Verb:   [MC_] RECEIVE_AND_WAIT                           I
+----------------------------------------------------------+
I Common Parameters:                                       I
+----------------------------------------------------------+
I Mandatory Input parameters:                              I
I    RESOURCE (resource-id)                                I
+----------------------------------------------------------+
I Optional input for basic conversation only:              I
I    [ FILL (LL)      ]                                    I
I            (BUFFER) ]                                    I
+----------------------------------------------------------+
I Input-output parameters:                                 I
I    LENGTH (length)                                       I
+----------------------------------------------------------+
I  Returned parameters:                                    I
I     RETURN_CODE (rc)                                     I
I     REQUEST_TO_SEND_RECEIVED (yes/no)                    I
I     DATA (data-area)                                     I
I     WHAT_RECEIVED (receive-indicator)                    I
+----------------------------------------------------------+
I  Optional for mapped conversation only:                  I
I     MAP_NAME (map-name)                                  I
+----------------------------------------------------------+
I  ABEND Conditions:                                       I
I   - PARAMETER CHECK (If resource-id is not assigned,     I
I        or if MAP_NAME is specified and not supported)    I
I   - STATE CHECK (if a conversation is not in SEND or     I
I        RECEIVE state, or from the SEND state the LR      I
I        transmission is not finished)                     I
+----------------------------------------------------------+
I States from which the verb can be issued:                I
I     SEND, RECEIVE                                        I
I                                                          I
+----------------------------------------------------------+
I State after successful execution:                        I
I RECEIVE, if verb is issued in SEND or RECEIVE states,    I
I         and receive-indicator = DATA_COMPLETE or         I
I                                 DATA_INCOMPLETE or        I
I                                 FMH_DATA_COMPLETE or      I
I                                 FMH_DATA_INCOMPLETE       I
I SEND State, if receive-indicator = SEND                  I
I CONFIRM state, if receive-indicator = CONFIRM or         I
I                                 = CONFIRM_SEND or         I
I                                 = CONFIRM_DEALLOCATE      I
I SYNCPOINT state, if receive-indicator =                  I
I                         TAKE_SYNCPT              or       I
I                         TAKE_SYNCPT_SEND         or       I
I                         TAKE_SYNCPT_DEALLOCATE            I
-------------------------------------------------------------
```

```
+-------------------------------------------------------------+
I Verb:   [MC_] RECEIVE_IMMEDIATE                             I
+-------------------------------------------------------------+
I Common Parameters:                                          I
+-------------------------------------------------------------+
I Mandatory Input parameters:                                 I
I    RESOURCE (resource-id)                                   I
+-------------------------------------------------------------+
I Optional input for basic conversation only:                 I
I    [ FILL (LL)      ]                                       I
I           (BUFFER) ]                                        I
+-------------------------------------------------------------+
I Input-output parameters:                                    I
I    LENGTH (length)                                          I
+-------------------------------------------------------------+
I   Returned parameters:                                      I
I      RETURN_CODE (rc)                                       I
I      REQUEST_TO_SEND_RECEIVED (yes/no)                      I
I      DATA (data-area)                                       I
I      WHAT_RECEIVED (receive-indicator)                      I
+-------------------------------------------------------------+
I   Optional for mapped conversation only:                    I
I      MAP_NAME (map-name)                                    I
+-------------------------------------------------------------+
I   ABEND Conditions:                                         I
I    - PARAMETER CHECK (If resource-id is not assigned,       I
I        or if MAP_NAME is specified and not supported)       I
I    - STATE CHECK (if a conversation is not in RECEIVE       I
I                                                state)       I
I                                                             I
+-------------------------------------------------------------+
I States from which the verb can be issued:                   I
I      RECEIVE                                                I
I                                                             I
+-------------------------------------------------------------+
I State after successful execution:                           I
I RECEIVE, if verb is issued in RECEIVE state, and            I
I              receive-indicator = DATA_COMPLETE or           I
I                                  DATA_INCOMPLETE or         I
I                                  FMH_DATA_COMPLETE or       I
I                                  FMH_DATA_INCOMPLETE        I
I SEND State, if receive-indicator = SEND                     I
I CONFIRM state, if receive-indicator = CONFIRM or            I
I                                   = CONFIRM_SEND or         I
I                                   = CONFIRM_DEALLOCATE       I
I SYNCPOINT state, if receive-indicator =                     I
I                       TAKE_SYNCPT            or             I
I                       TAKE_SYNCPT_SEND       or             I
I                       TAKE_SYNCPT_DEALLOCATE                I
-------------------------------------------------------------
```

```
+------------------------------------------------------------+
I Verb:   [MC_] REQUEST_TO_SEND                              I
+------------------------------------------------------------+
I Common Parameters:                                         I
+------------------------------------------------------------+
I Mandatory Input parameters:                                I
I                                                            I
I    RESOURCE (resource-id)                                  I
I                                                            I
+------------------------------------------------------------+
I  Returned parameters:                                      I
I                                                            I
I       None                                                 I
+------------------------------------------------------------+
I  ABEND Conditions:                                         I
I   - PARAMETER CHECK (If resource-id is not assigned)       I
I   - STATE CHECK (if a conversation is not in CONFIRM,      I
I                  RECEIVE or SYNCPOINT states)              I
+------------------------------------------------------------+
I States from which the verb can be issued:                 I
I      RECEIVE, CONFIRM, SYNCPOINT                           I
I                                                            I
+------------------------------------------------------------+
I State after successful execution: no state changes         I
+------------------------------------------------------------+
```

```
+----------------------------------------------------------+
I Verb:  [MC_] SEND_DATA                                  I
+----------------------------------------------------------+
I Common Parameters:                                      I
+----------------------------------------------------------+
I Mandatory Input parameters:                             I
I                                                         I
I  RESOURCE (resource-id)                                 I
I  DATA (record) - data-record for mapped conversation    I
I               - logical-record for basic conversationI
I  LENGTH (length)                                        I
+----------------------------------------------------------+
I  Optional Input for mapped conversation only:           I
I  [ MAP_NAME (NO)              ]                          I
I            (YES (map-name) ) ]                          I
I  [ FMH_DATA (NO)   ]                                    I
I            (YES) ]                                      I
+----------------------------------------------------------+
I  Returned parameters:                                   I
I     RETURN_CODE (rc)                                    I
I     REQUEST_TO_SEND_RECEIVED (yes/no)                   I
+----------------------------------------------------------+
I  ABEND Conditions for mapped conversation:              I
I  - PARAMETER CHECK (If resource-id is not assigned,     I
I    or if MAP_NAME is specified and not supported,       I
I    or if FMH_DATA is specified and not supported)       I
I                                                         I
I  - STATE CHECK (if conversation is not in SEND state I
I  ABEND Conditions for basic conversation:               I
I  - PARAMETER CHECK (If resource-id is not assigned,     I
I    or if DATA contains invalid logical record length)I
I  - STATE CHECK (if conversation is not in SEND state I
I                                                         I
+----------------------------------------------------------+
I States from which the verb can be issued:               I
I    SEND                                                 I
I                                                         I
+----------------------------------------------------------+
I State after successful execution:   SEND                I
----------------------------------------------------------
```

```
+--------------------------------------------------------------+
I Verb:  [MC_] SEND_ERROR                                     I
+--------------------------------------------------------------+
I Common Parameters:                                          I
+--------------------------------------------------------------+
I Mandatory Input parameters:                                 I
I                                                             I
I  RESOURCE (resource-id)                                     I
+--------------------------------------------------------------+
I  Optional Input for basic conversation only:               I
I  [ TYPE (PROG) ]                                            I
I         (SVC)  ]                                            I
I  [ LOG_DATA (NO)                            ]               I
I             (YES (error-log-variable)) ]                   I
+--------------------------------------------------------------+
I  Returned parameters:                                       I
I    RETURN_CODE (rc)                                         I
I    REQUEST_TO_SEND_RECEIVED (yes/no)                        I
+--------------------------------------------------------------+
I  ABEND Conditions for mapped conversation:                 I
I   - PARAMETER CHECK (If resource-id is not assigned)        I
I                                                             I
I   - STATE CHECK (if conversation is not in SEND,            I
I                 RECEIVE, CONFIRM or SYNCPOINT states)       I
I  ABEND Conditions for basic conversation:                  I
I   - PARAMETER CHECK (If resource-id is not assigned,        I
I     or if LOG_DATA is specified and not supported)          I
I   - STATE CHECK (if conversation is not in SEND,            I
I                 RECEIVE, CONFIRM or SYNCPOINT states)       I
I                                                             I
+--------------------------------------------------------------+
I States from which the verb can be issued:                  I
I     SEND, RECEIVE, CONFIRM, SYNCPOINT                       I
I                                                             I
+--------------------------------------------------------------+
I State after successful execution:  SEND State               I
--------------------------------------------------------------
```

```
+-------------------------------------------------------------+
I Verb:  [MC_] TEST                                           I
+-------------------------------------------------------------+
I Common Parameters:                                          I
+-------------------------------------------------------------I
I Mandatory Input parameters:                                 I
I                                                             I
I    RESOURCE (resource-id)                                   I
+-------------------------------------------------------------+
I Optional Input parameters:                                  I
I                                                             I
I    [ TEST ( POSTED ) ]                                      I
I             ( REQUEST_TO_SEND_RECEIVED ) ]                  I
+-------------------------------------------------------------+
I Returned parameters:                                        I
I                                                             I
I        RETURN_CODE (rc)                                     I
+-------------------------------------------------------------+
I  ABEND Conditions:                                          I
I   - PARAMETER CHECK (If the verb is not supported)          I
I   - STATE CHECK (if TEST (POSTED) is specified, and         I
I        conversation is not in RECEIVE state;     or         I
I        TEST (REQUEST_TO_SEND_RECEIVED) is specified,        I
I        and conversation is not in SEND, DEFER or            I
I                                 RECEIVE states              I
+-------------------------------------------------------------+
I States from which the verb can be issued:                  I
I SEND, RECEIVE, DEFER                                        I
I                                                             I
+-------------------------------------------------------------+
I State after successful execution: no state changes          I
I                                                             I
-------------------------------------------------------------
```

Type-Independent Verbs.

```
+-----------------------------------------------------------+
I Verb:  BACKOUT                                            I
+-----------------------------------------------------------+
I Common Parameters:  NONE                                  I
+-----------------------------------------------------------+
I  ABEND Conditions:                                        I
I   - PARAMETER CHECK (If the verb is not supported)        I
I   - STATE CHECK (if at least one protected resource isI
I       not in SEND, RECEIVE, DEFER, CONFIRM, SYNCPOINT orI
I              BACKED OUT states                            I
+-----------------------------------------------------------+
I States from which the verb can be issued:                I
I SEND, RECEIVE, CONFIRM, SYNCPOINT, DEFER, BACKED OUT   I
I                                                           I
+-----------------------------------------------------------+
I State after successful execution: state is the same asI
I       it was after last sync point                       I
-------------------------------------------------------------
```

```
+-----------------------------------------------------------+
I Verb:  GET_TYPE                                           I
+-----------------------------------------------------------I
I Mandatory Input parameters:                               I
I                                                           I
I   RESOURCE (resource-id)                                  I
I                                                           I
+-----------------------------------------------------------+
I  Returned parameters:                                     I
I                                                           I
I      TYPE (conversation-type)                             I
+-----------------------------------------------------------+
I  ABEND Conditions:                                        I
I   - PARAMETER CHECK (If resource-id is not assigned)   I
+-----------------------------------------------------------+
I States from which the verb can be issued:                I
I SEND, RECEIVE, CONFIRM, SYNCPOINT, DEFER, BACKED OUT, I
I                                          DEALLOCATE     I
+-----------------------------------------------------------+
I State after successful execution: no state changes     I
-------------------------------------------------------------
```

```
+----------------------------------------------------------------+
I Verb:  SYNCPT                                                 I
+----------------------------------------------------------------+
I   Returned parameters:                                        I
I       RETURN_CODE (rc)                                        I
I       REQUEST_TO_SEND_RECEIVED (yes/no)                       I
+----------------------------------------------------------------+
I   ABEND Conditions:                                           I
I   - PARAMETER CHECK (If resource-id is not assigned)          I
I   - STATE CHECK:                                              I
I     1. Protected resource is not in SEND, DEFER or            I
I        SYNCPOINT state;                                       I
I     2. Protected resource is SEND state, but TP               I
I        started and did not finish sending LR (basic           I
I                            converstion only)                  I
+----------------------------------------------------------------+
I States from which the verb can be issued:                    I
I    SEND, DEFER, SYNCPOINT                                     I
I                                                               I
+----------------------------------------------------------------+
I State after successful execution:                            I
I 1. RESET, if SYNCPT is issued in DEFER state after           I
I            DEALLOCATE was issued;                             I
I 2. RECEIVE, if SYNCPT is issued in DEFER state after         I
I            PREPARE_TO_RECEIVE, or if SYNCPT is issued in      I
I            SYNCPOINT state after TAKE_SYNCPT was received     I
I            from RECEIVE_AND_WAIT or RECEIVE_IMMEDIATE;        I
I 3. SEND, if SYNCPT is issued in SYNCPOINT state after        I
I            TAKE_SYNCPT_SEND was received;                     I
I 4. DEALLOCATE, if SYNCPT is issued in SYNCPOINT state        I
I            after receiving TAKE_SYNCPT_DEALLOCATE.            I
I                                                               I
------------------------------------------------------------------


+----------------------------------------------------------------+
I Verb:  WAIT                                                   I
+----------------------------------------------------------------+
I Mandatory Input parameters:                                  I
I                                                               I
I    RESOURCE_LIST ( resource-id-1, resource-id-2,....)        I
I                                                               I
+----------------------------------------------------------------+
I   Returned parameters:                                        I
I       RETURN_CODE (rc)                                        I
I       RESOURCE_POSTED (posted-resource-id)                    I
+----------------------------------------------------------------+
I   ABEND Conditions:                                           I
I   - PARAMETER CHECK (If one of resource-id from              I
I                  RESOURCE_LIST is not assigned)               I
+----------------------------------------------------------------+
I States from which the verb can be issued:                    I
I    RECEIVE                                                    I
I                                                               I
+----------------------------------------------------------------+
I State after successful execution: no state changes           I
------------------------------------------------------------------
```

Control-Operator verbs.

Change-Number-Of-Session Verbs.

```
+-----------------------------------------------------------+
I Verb:   CHANGE_SESSION_LIMIT                               I
+-----------------------------------------------------------+
I Mandatory Input parameters:                               I
I                                                           I
I    LU_NAME (lu-name)                                      I
I    MODE_NAME (mode-name)                                  I
I    LU_MODE_SESSION_LIMIT (limit)                          I
I    MIN_CONWINNERS_SOURCE (number-source-cont-winner)      I
I    MIN_CONWINNERS_TARGET (number-target-cont-winner)      I
+-----------------------------------------------------------+
I Optional Input parameters:                                I
I                                                           I
I    [ RESPONSIBLE (SOURCE) ]                               I
I                 (TARGET) ]                                I
+-----------------------------------------------------------+
I  Returned parameters:                                     I
I     RETURN_CODE (rc)                                      I
+-----------------------------------------------------------+
I  ABEND Conditions:                                        I
I     PARAMETER CHECK:                                      I
I     - the verb is not supported                           I
I     - TP does not have CNOS privilege                     I
I     - LU_MODE_SESSION_LIMIT specifies 0                   I
I     - one of the specified parameters is not supportedI
I                                                           I
+-----------------------------------------------------------+


+-----------------------------------------------------------+
I Verb:  INITIALIZE_SESSION_LIMIT                           I
+-----------------------------------------------------------+
I Mandatory Input parameters:                               I
I                                                           I
I    LU_NAME (lu-name)                                      I
I    MODE_NAME (mode-name) or                               I
I            ('SNASVCMG')                                   I
I    LU_MODE_SESSION_LIMIT (limit)                          I
I    MIN_CONWINNERS_SOURCE (number-source-cont-winner)      I
I    MIN_CONWINNERS_TARGET (number-target-cont-winner)      I
+-----------------------------------------------------------+
I  Returned parameters:                                     I
I     RETURN_CODE (rc)                                      I
+-----------------------------------------------------------+
I  ABEND Conditions:                                        I
I     PARAMETER CHECK:                                      I
I     - the verb is not supported                           I
I     - TP does not have CNOS privilege                     I
I     - LU_MODE_SESSION_LIMIT is greater than 1 for a       I
I                              single session               I
I     - LU_MODE_SESSION_LIMIT is equal to 0                 I
I     - one of the specified parameters is not supportedI
I                                                           I
+-----------------------------------------------------------+
```

```
+------------------------------------------------------------+
I Verb:  RESET_SESSION_LIMIT                                I
+------------------------------------------------------------+
I Mandatory Input parameters:                               I
I   LU_NAME (lu-name)                                       I
+------------------------------------------------------------+
I Optional Input parameters:                                I
I                                                           I
I [              (ALL)                 ]                     I
I [ MODE_NAME (ONE (mode-name) ) ]                          I
I [              (ONE ('SNASVCMG')) ]                       I
I                                                           I
I [ DRAIN_SOURCE (NO)   ]                                   I
I [              (YES) ]                                     I
I                                                           I
I [ DRAIN_TARGET (NO)   ]                                   I
I [              (YES) ]                                     I
I                                                           I
I [ RESPONSIBLE (SOURCE) ]                                  I
I               (TARGET) ]                                  I
I                                                           I
I [ FORCE (NO)   ]                                          I
I [       (YES) ]                                           I
+------------------------------------------------------------+
I  Returned parameters:                                     I
I     RETURN_CODE (rc)                                      I
+------------------------------------------------------------+
I  ABEND Conditions:                                        I
I     PARAMETER CHECK:                                      I
I     - the verb is not supported                           I
I     - TP does not have CNOS privilege                     I
I     - one of the specified parameters is not supportedI
I                                                           I
+------------------------------------------------------------+


+------------------------------------------------------------+
I Verb:  PROCESS_SESSION_LIMIT                              I
+------------------------------------------------------------+
I Mandatory Input parameters:                               I
I   RESOURCE (resource-id)                                  I
+------------------------------------------------------------+
I  Returned parameters:                                     I
I     LU_NAME (LU-NAME)                                     I
I     MODE_NAME ( variable1 variable2 )                     I
I     RETURN_CODE (rc)                                      I
+------------------------------------------------------------+
I  ABEND Conditions:                                        I
I     PARAMETER CHECK:                                      I
I     - the TP that issued the verb is not SNA service  I
I       TP identified as CNOS (HEX '06F1')                  I
I                                                           I
+------------------------------------------------------------+
```

Session Control Verbs.

```
+-----------------------------------------------------------------+
I Verb:  ACTIVATE_SESSION                                         I
+-----------------------------------------------------------------+
I Mandatory Input parameters:                                     I
I                                                                 I
I   LU_NAME (lu-name)                                             I
I                                                                 I
I   MODE_NAME (mode-name)                                         I
I             ('SNASVCMG')                                        I
I                                                                 I
+-----------------------------------------------------------------+
I  Returned parameters:                                           I
I     RETURN_CODE (rc)                                            I
+-----------------------------------------------------------------+
I  ABEND Conditions:                                              I
I     PARAMETER CHECK:                                            I
I     - the verb is not supported                                 I
I     - TP does not have session-control privilege                I
I                                                                 I
+-----------------------------------------------------------------+


+-----------------------------------------------------------------+
I Verb:  DEACTIVATE_SESSION                                       I
+-----------------------------------------------------------------+
I Mandatory Input parameters:                                     I
I                                                                 I
I   SESSION_ID (session-id)                                       I
+-----------------------------------------------------------------+
I Optional Input parameters:                                      I
I                                                                 I
I  [ TYPE (CLEANUP) ]                                             I
I  [      (NORMAL)  ]                                             I
I                                                                 I
+-----------------------------------------------------------------+
I  Returned parameters:                                           I
I     RETURN_CODE (rc)                                            I
+-----------------------------------------------------------------+
I  ABEND Conditions:                                              I
I     PARAMETER CHECK:                                            I
I     - the verb is not supported                                 I
I     - TP does not have session-control privilege                I
I                                                                 I
+-----------------------------------------------------------------+
```

LU6.2 Definition Verbs.

```
+----------------------------------------------------------+
I Verb:  DEFINE_LOCAL_LU                                   I
+----------------------------------------------------------+
I Mandatory Input parameters:                              I
I                                                          I
I    FULLY_QUALIFIED_LU_NAME (lu-name)                     I
+----------------------------------------------------------+
I Optional Input parameters:                               I
I                                                          I
I  [ LU_SESSION_LIMIT (NONE)                        ]      I
I  [                      (VALUE (session-limit) ) ]       I
I                                                          I
I  [              (ADD (USER_ID (u-id) PASSWORD (pw)       I
I  [ SECURITY                       PROFILE (prof))) ]     I
I  [              (DELETE (USER_ID (u-id) PROFILE (prof))) ]I
I                                                          I
I  [ MAP_NAME (ADD (map-name)      ]                       I
I  [              (DELETE (map-name)) ]                     I
I                                                          I
+----------------------------------------------------------+
I  Returned parameters:                                    I
I      RETURN_CODE (rc)                                    I
+----------------------------------------------------------+
I  ABEND Conditions:                                       I
I     PARAMETER CHECK:                                     I
I     - the verb is not supported                          I
I     - TP does not have LU define privilege               I
I                                                          I
+----------------------------------------------------------+
```

```
+------------------------------------------------------------+
I Verb:  DEFINE_REMOTE_LU                                    I
+------------------------------------------------------------+
I Mandatory Input parameters:                                I
I                                                            I
I    FULLY_QUALIFIED_LU_NAME (lu-name)                       I
+------------------------------------------------------------+
I Optional Input parameters:                                 I
I                                                            I
I [ LOCALLY_KNOWN_LU_NAME (NONE)            ]                I
I [                       (NAME (name) ) ]                   I
I                                                            I
I [ UNINTERPRETED_LU_NAME (NONE)            ]                I
I [                       (NAME (name) ) ]                   I
I                                                            I
I [ INITIATE_TYPE (INITIATE_ONLY)       ]                    I
I [               (INITIATE_OR_QUEUE) ]                      I
I                                                            I
I [ PARALLEL_SESSION_SUPPORT (YES) or (NO)]                  I
I                                                            I
I [ CNOS_SUPPORT (YES) or (NO) ]                             I
I                                                            I
I [ LU_LU_PASSWORD (NONE)          ]                         I
I [                (VALUE (pw) ) ]                           I
I                                                            I
I [                      (NONE)              ]               I
I [ SECURITY_ACCEPTANCE (CONVERSATION)      ]               I
I [                      (ALREADY_VERIFIED) ]               I
+------------------------------------------------------------+
I  Returned parameters:                                      I
I      RETURN_CODE (rc)                                      I
+------------------------------------------------------------+
I  ABEND Conditions:                                         I
I      PARAMETER CHECK:                                      I
I      - the verb is not supported                           I
I      - TP does not have LU define privilege                I
I                                                            I
+------------------------------------------------------------+
```

```
+----------------------------------------------------------+
I Verb:  DEFINE_MODE                                        I
+----------------------------------------------------------+
I Mandatory Input parameters:                               I
I                                                           I
I    FULLY_QUALIFIED_LU_NAME (lu-name)                      I
I                                                           I
I    MODE_NAME (mode-name)                                  I
+----------------------------------------------------------+
I Optional Input parameters:                                I
I                                                           I
I  [ SEND_PACING_WINDOW (size)                   ]          I
I                                                           I
I  [ RECEIVE_PACING_WINDOW (size)                ]          I
I                                                           I
I  [ SEND_MAX_RU_SIZE_LOWER_BOUND (variable) ]              I
I                                                           I
I  [ SEND_MAX_RU_SIZE_UPPER_BOUND (variable) ]              I
I                                                           I
I  [ RECEIVE_MAX_RU_SIZE_LOWER_BOUND (variable) ]           I
I                                                           I
I  [ RECEIVE_MAX_RU_SIZE_UPPER_BOUND (variable) ]           I
I                                                           I
I  [ SYNC_LEVEL_SUPPORT (CONFIRM)              ]            I
I  [                    (CONFIRM_SYNCPT) ]                  I
I                                                           I
I  [                              (OPERATOR)     ]          I
I  [                              (PLU)          ]          I
I  [ SINGLE_SESSION_REINITIATION (SLU)          ]          I
I  [                              (PLU_OR_SLU)   ]          I
I                                                           I
I  [ SESSION_LEVEL_CRYPTOGRAPHY (NO)           ]            I
I  [                            (YES)          ]            I
I                                                           I
I  [ CONWINNER_AUTO_ACTIVATE_LIMIT (limit)    ]             I
+----------------------------------------------------------+
I  Returned parameters:                                     I
I      RETURN_CODE (rc)                                     I
+----------------------------------------------------------+
I  ABEND Conditions:                                        I
I      PARAMETER CHECK:                                     I
I      - the verb is not supported                          I
I      - TP does not have LU define privilege               I
I                                                           I
+----------------------------------------------------------+
```

```
+----------------------------------------------------------+
I Verb:  DEFINE_TP                                         I
+----------------------------------------------------------+
I Mandatory Input parameters:                              I
I                                                          I
I   TP_NAME (tp-name)                                      I
+----------------------------------------------------------+
I Optional Input parameters:                               I
I                                                          I
I  [           (ENABLE)       ]                            I
I  [ STATUS (TEMP_DISABLE)  ]                              I
I  [           (PERM_DISABLE)  ]                           I
I                                                          I
I  [ CONVERSATION_TYPE (MAPPED or BASIC)  ]                I
I                                                          I
I  [ SYNC_LEVEL (NONE or CONFIRM or SYNCPT)   ]            I
I                                                          I
I  [                         (NONE)              ]         I
I  [                         (CONVERSATION)      ]         I
I  [ SECURITY_REQUIRED (ACCESS (PROFILE) )       ]         I
I  [                           (USER_ID) )       ]         I
I  [                           (USER_ID_PROFILE) ) ]       I
I                                                          I
I  [                  (ADD (USER_ID (u-id)       ]         I
I  [ SECURITY_ACCESS        PROFILE (variable) ) )  ]      I
I  [                  (DELETE (USER_ID (u-id)       ]      I
I  [                            PROFILE (variable) ) )]    I
I                                                          I
I  [ PIP (NO)         ]                                    I
I  [     (YES (pip) ) ]                                    I
I                                                          I
I  [ DATA_MAPPING (NO or YES) ]                            I
I                                                          I
I  [ FMH_DATA (NO or YES)  ]                               I
I                                                          I
I  [ PRIVILEGE (NONE)                              ] I     I
I  [           (CNOS or SESSION_CONTROL or DEFINE or ] I   I
I  [            DISPLAY or ALLOCATE_SERVICE_TP)       ] I  I
+----------------------------------------------------------+
I   Returned parameters:                                   I
I        RETURN_CODE (rc)                                  I
+----------------------------------------------------------+
I   ABEND Conditions:                                      I
I      PARAMETER CHECK:                                    I
I      - the verb is not supported                         I
I      - TP does not have LU define privilege              I
I                                                          I
+----------------------------------------------------------+
```

```
+-------------------------------------------------------------+
I Verb:  DISPLAY_LOCAL_LU                                     I
+-------------------------------------------------------------+
I Mandatory Input parameters:                                 I
I   FULLY_QUALIFIED_LU_NAME (lu-name)                         I
+-------------------------------------------------------------+
I  Returned parameters:                                       I
I      RETURN_CODE (rc)                                       I
+-------------------------------------------------------------+
I Optional Return parameters:                                 I
I                                                             I
I  [ LU_SESSION_LIMIT (limit) ]                               I
I                                                             I
I  [ LU_SESSION_COUNT (count) ]                               I
I                                                             I
I  [ SECURITY (verification-list) ]                           I
I                                                             I
I  [ MAP_NAMES (map-list)  ]                                  I
I                                                             I
I  [ REMOTE_LU_NAMES (remote-LU-list)  ]                      I
I                                                             I
I  [ TP_NAMES (tp-name-list)              ]                   I
I                                                             I
+-------------------------------------------------------------+
I  ABEND Conditions - PARAMETER CHECK:                        I
I      - the verb is not supported                            I
I      - TP does not have LU display privilege                I
+-------------------------------------------------------------+


+-------------------------------------------------------------+
I Verb:  DISPLAY_REMOTE_LU                                    I
+-------------------------------------------------------------+
I Mandatory Input parameters:                                 I
I   FULLY_QUALIFIED_LU_NAME (lu-name)                         I
+-------------------------------------------------------------+
I  Returned parameters:                                       I
I      RETURN_CODE (rc)                                       I
+-------------------------------------------------------------+
I Optional Return parameters:                                 I
I                                                             I
I  [ LOCALLY_KNOWN_LU_NAME (lu-name) ]                        I
I                                                             I
I  [ UNINTERPRETED_LU_NAME (lu-name) ]                        I
I                                                             I
I  [ INITIATE_TYPE (type) ]                                   I
I                                                             I
I  [ PARALLEL_SESSION_SUPPORT (variable) ]                    I
I                                                             I
I  [ CNOS_SUPPORT (variable) ]                                I
I                                                             I
I  [ SECURITY_ACCEPTANCE_LOCAL_LU (sec-level)  ]              I
I                                                             I
I  [ SECURITY_ACCEPTANCE_REMOTE_LU (sec-level) ]              I
I                                                             I
I  [ MODE_NAMES (list) ]                                      I
+-------------------------------------------------------------+
I  ABEND Conditions - PARAMETER CHECK:                        I
I      - the verb is not supported                            I
I      - TP does not have LU display privilege                I
+-------------------------------------------------------------+
```

```
+----------------------------------------------------------------+
I Verb:  DISPLAY_MODE                                            I
+----------------------------------------------------------------+
I Mandatory Input parameters:                                    I
I   FULLY_QUALIFIED_LU_NAME (lu-name)                            I
I   MODE_NAME (mode-name)                                        I
+----------------------------------------------------------------+
I  Returned parameters:                                          I
I      RETURN_CODE (rc)                                          I
+----------------------------------------------------------------+
I Optional Return parameters:                                    I
I                                                                I
I  [ SEND_PACING_WINDOW (size)                    ]              I
I  [ RECEIVE_PACING_WINDOW (size)                 ]              I
I                                                                I
I  [ SEND_MAX_RU_SIZE_LOWER_BOUND (variable) ]                  I
I  [ SEND_MAX_RU_SIZE_UPPER_BOUND (variable) ]                  I
I                                                                I
I  [ RECEIVE_MAX_RU_SIZE_LOWER_BOUND (variable) ]              I
I  [ RECEIVE_MAX_RU_SIZE_UPPER_BOUND (variable) ]              I
I                                                                I
I  [ SYNC_LEVEL SUPPORT (level)                 ]              I
I                                                                I
I  [ SINGLE_SESSION_REINITIATION (variable)    ]              I
I                                                                I
I  [ SESSION_LEVEL_CRYPTOGRAPHY (variable)   ]                 I
I                                                                I
I  [ CONWINNER_AUTO_ACTIVATE_LIMIT (limit)   ]                 I
I                                                                I
I  [ LU_MODE_SESSION_LIMIT (limit) ]                            I
I                                                                I
I  [ MIN_CONWINNERS (count)               ]                    I
I  [ MIN_CONLOSERS (count)               ]                    I
I                                                                I
I  [ TERMINATION_COUNT (count)          ]                     I
I                                                                I
I  [ DRAIN_LOCAL_LU (yes/no)            ]                     I
I  [ DRAIN_REMOTE_LU (yes/no)           ]                     I
I                                                                I
I  [ LU_MODE_SESSION_COUNT (count) ]                           I
I                                                                I
I  [ CONWINNERS_SESSION_COUNT (count) ]                        I
I  [ CONLOSERS_SESSION_COUNT (count)  ]                        I
I                                                                I
I  [ SESSION_IDS (list)                  ]                    I
+----------------------------------------------------------------+
I  ABEND Conditions:                                             I
I      PARAMETER CHECK:                                          I
I      - the verb is not supported                               I
I      - TP does not have LU display privileges                  I
I                                                                I
+----------------------------------------------------------------+
```

```
+------------------------------------------------------------+
I Verb:  DISPLAY_TP                                          I
+------------------------------------------------------------+
I Mandatory Input parameters:                                I
I                                                            I
I    TP_NAME (tp-name)                                       I
+------------------------------------------------------------+
I Optional Return parameters:                                I
I                                                            I
I  [ RETURN_CODE (rc)      ]                                 I
I                                                            I
I  [ STATUS (status)      ]                                  I
I                                                            I
I  [ CONVERSATION_TYPE (type)  ]                             I
I                                                            I
I  [ SYNC_LEVEL (level) ]                                    I
I                                                            I
I  [ SECURITY_REQUIRED (variable) ]                          I
I                                                            I
I  [ SECURITY_ACCESS  (variable)  ]                          I
I                                                            I
I  [ PIP (pip)         ]                                     I
I                                                            I
I  [ DATA_MAPPING (yes/no)    ]                              I
I                                                            I
I  [ FMH_DATA (yes/no)       ]                               I
I                                                            I
I  [ PRIVILEGE (variable)   ]                                I
I                                                            I
+------------------------------------------------------------+
I  ABEND Conditions:                                         I
I     PARAMETER CHECK:                                       I
I     - the verb is not supported                            I
I     - TP does not have LU display privilege                I
I                                                            I
+------------------------------------------------------------+


+------------------------------------------------------------+
I Verb:  DELETE                                              I
+------------------------------------------------------------+
I Optional  Input parameters:                                I
I                                                            I
I  [ LOCAL_LU_NAME (lu-name)  ]                              I
I                                                            I
I  [ REMOTE_LU_NAME (lu-name) ]                              I
I                                                            I
I  [ MODE_NAME (mode-name)    ]                              I
I                                                            I
I  [ TP_NAME (tp-name)        ]                              I
+------------------------------------------------------------+
I  Return parameters:                                        I
I  RETURN_CODE (rc)                                          I
+------------------------------------------------------------+
I  ABEND Conditions:                                         I
I     PARAMETER CHECK:                                       I
I     - the verb is not supported                            I
I     - TP does not have LU define  privilege                I
+------------------------------------------------------------+
```

# C. J. Date's Twelve
# Distributed DBMS Rules

The following rules have been compiled from the Summer 1987 article on distributed database systems published by Chris J. Date in *InfoDB* magazine.

### Rule 1—local autonomy

*Definition:* The sites in a distributed system should be autonomous, or independent of each other.

*Comments:* A DBMS at each site in a distributed system should provide its own security, locking, logging, integrity, and recovery. Local operations use and affect only local resources and do not depend on other sites.

### Rule 2—no reliance on central site

*Definition:* A distributed database system should not rely on a central site, because a single central site may become a single point of failure affecting the entire system. Also, a central site may become a bottleneck affecting the distributed system's performance and throughput.

*Comments:* Each site of a distributed database system provides its own security, locking, logging, integrity, and recovery, and handles its own data dictionary. No central site must be involved in every distributed transaction.

### Rule 3—continuous operation

*Definition:* A distributed database system should never require downtime.

*Comments:* A distributed database system should provide on-line backup and recovery, full and incremental archiving facility; the backup and recovery should be fast enough to be performed on-line without noticeable detrimental affect on the entire system performance.

### Rule 4—location transparency and location independence

*Definition:* Users and/or applications should not know, or even be aware of, where the data is physically stored. Instead, users and/or applications should behave as if all data was stored locally.

*Comments:* Location transparency can be supported by extended synonyms and extensive use of the data dictionary. Location independence allows applications to be ported easily from one site in a distributed database system to another without modifications.

### Rule 5—fragmentation independence

*Definition:* Relational tables in a distributed database system can be divided into fragments and stored at different sites transparent to the users and applications.

*Comments:* Similar to the location transparency rule, users and applications should not be aware of the fact that some data may be stored in a fragment of a table at a site different from the site where the table itself is stored.

### Rule 6—replication independence

*Definition:* Data can be transparently replicated on multiple computer systems across a network.

*Comments:* Similar to the data location and fragmentation independence rules, replication independence is designed to free users from the concerns of where data is stored. In the case of replication, users and applications should not be aware that replicas of the data are maintained and synchronized automatically by the distributed database management system.

### Rule 7—distributed query processing

*Definition:* The performance of a given query should be independent of a site at which the query is submitted.

*Comments:* Since a relational database management system provides nonnavigational access to data (via SQL), such a system should support an Optimizer that can not only select the best access path within a given node, but can also optimize a distributed query performance in regard to the data location, CPU and I/O utilization, and network traffic throughput.

### Rule 8—distributed transaction management

*Definition:* A distributed system should be able to support atomic transactions.

*Comments:* Transaction properties of atomicity, consistency, durability, isolation, and serialization should be supported not only for local transactions, but also for distributed transactions that can span multiple systems. An example of a distributed transaction management issue is transaction coordination in the distributed two-phase commit processing.

### Rule 9—hardware independence

*Definition:* A distributed database system should be able to operate and access data spread across a wide variety of hardware platforms.

*Comments:* Any truly distributed DBMS system should not rely on a particular hardware feature, nor should it be limited to a certain hardware architecture or vendor.

### Rule 10—operating system independence

*Definition:* A distributed database system should be able to run on different operating systems.
*Comments:* Similar to Rule 10, a truly distributed database system should support distribution of functions and data across different operating systems, including any combination of such operating systems as DOS, OS/2, Unix, MVS/VM, VSE, VAX, etc.

### Rule 11—network independence

*Definition:* A distributed database system should be designed to run regardless of the communication protocols and network topology used to interconnect various system nodes.

*Comments:* Similar to Rules 10 and 11, a truly distributed database system should support distribution of functions and data across different operating systems irrespective of the particular communication method used to interconnect all participating systems, including local and wide area networks. In fact, networks and communication protocols can be mixed to satisfy certain business, economics, geographical, and other requirements.

### Rule 12—DBMS independence

*Definition:* An ideal distributed database management system must be able to support interoperability between DBMS systems running on different nodes, even if these DBMS systems are unlike (heterogeneous).

*Comments:* All participants in a distributed database management system should use common standard interfaces (APIs) in order to interoperate with each other and to participate in a distributed database processing.

# Glossary

**Access Method**  A method used to move data between the main storage and peripheral devices (e.g., I/O devices such as tapes, disks, etc.). Access can be sequential (records are accessed one after another in the order in which they appear in the file), random (individual records can be referred to in any order), and dynamic (both sequential and random access is allowed).

**ACB**  In VTAM, this refers to application control block or access method control block.

**Advanced Communication Function**  A group of SNA-compliant IBM program products such as ACF/VTAM, ACF/TCAM, ACF/SSP, and ACF/NCP.

**Alert**  An error message sent to central network control point (e.g., SSCP) at a host system.

**ALLOCATE**  An LU6.2 application program interface verb used to assign a session to a conversation.

**Advanced Peer-to-Peer Networking (APPN)**  Data communication support that routes data in a network between two or more APPC systems that are not directly attached.

**Advanced Program-to-Program Communications (APPC)**  Peer level data communication support, based on SNA's Logical Unit Type 6.2 protocols.

**Advanced Interactive eXecutive (AIX)**  IBM's version of the Unix operating system.

**Architecture-Neutral Distribution Format (ANDF)**  A way to develop and distribute software independently from the hardware architecture platform on which the software is intended to run.

**American National Standards Institute (ANSI)**  An organization sponsored by the Computer and Business Equipment Manufacturers Association for establishing voluntary industry standards.

**American National Standard Code for Information Interchange (ASCII)**  The code, developed by ANSI for information exchange between data processing systems, data communication systems, and associated equipment. An ASCII character set consists of 7-bit characters plus one bit for parity check.

**API**  See Application Programming Interface.

**Application Enabling Interface (AEI)**    An API that supports the SAA programming requirements and is portable across all systems supporting that API.

**Application Program**    (1) A program written for or by a user that performs the user's work. (2) A program used to connect and communicate with stations in a network.

**Application Programming Interface (API)**    The formally defined programming language interface between a program (system control program, licensed program) and its user. In VTAM, API is the interface through which a program interacts with the access method.

**APPC**    See **Advanced Program-to-Program Communications.**

**APPN**    See **Advanced Peer-to-Peer Networking.**

**Application Requester (AR)**    In DRDA, the source of a request sent to a remote Relational Database Management System.

**AS/400**    Application System/400—a family of IBM's midrange computers.

**Application Server (AS)**    In DRDA, the target of a request from an AR.

**Asynchronous Processing**    A series of operations that are done separately from the job or transaction in which they were requested.

**Asynchronous Transmission**    In data communication, a method of transmission in which sending and receiving of data is controlled by control characters rather than by a timing sequence.

**Attach Manager**    In OS/2, the component of APPC that manages incoming ALLOCATE requests.

**Back-end program**    In CICS, a program that is initiated by the front-end program in order to support an LU6.2 conversation.

**Batch**    In contrast with interactive, a group of jobs to be run sequentially on a computer, with little or no operator intervention.

**Base set**    The set of functions, including verbs, parameters, return codes, and indicators, that is supported by all products in a particular architecture (e.g., LU6.2 architecture).

**Basic Conversation**    The conversation that supports the functions of the basic conversation protocol boundary defined by LU6.2. Contrast with the **Mapped conversations.**

**Bidder**    In SNA, the LU-LU half-session defined at session activation as having to request and receive permission from the other LU-LU half-session to begin a bracket. Contrast with **first speaker.**

**Binary Large Object (BLOB)**    Very large (may be several megabytes in size) binary representation of an image data type.

**Binary Synchronous Communications (BSC)**    A data communications line protocol that uses a standard set of transmission control characters and control character sequences to send binary-coded data over a communication line. Contrast with **synchronous data link control.**

**BIND**   A request to activate a session between two logical units.

**Boundary function**   In SNA, (1) capability of a subarea node to provide protocol support for adjacent peripheral nodes, such as transforming network addresses to local addresses, performing session sequence numbering, providing session-level pacing support. (2) A component that provides these capabilities.

**Bridge**   A means (device) of connecting two similar environments at relatively low protocol levels (such as two LANs at the logical link level).

**Buffer**   A portion of storage for temporarily holding input or output data.

**Carrier Sense Multiple Access with Collision Detection or Collision Avoidance (CSMA/CD, CSMA/CA)**   Popular LAN networking protocols.

**CCITT**   The International Telephone and Telegraph Consultative Committee.

**Change-direction protocol**   A data flow control function in which the sending logical unit stops sending requests, signals the receiver using the change-direction indicator, and prepares to receive requests.

**Channel**   A path along which signals can be sent (e.g., System/370 data channels).

**Channel-attached**   Attachment of a device directly to the computer channel.

**Character Data Representation Architecture (CDRA)**   In DRDA, the architecture that defines codes to represent characters and conversion to/from these codes.

**CICS (Customer Control Information System)**   A teleprocessing and transaction management system which runs as a VTAM application.

**Class of service (COS)**   In SNA, a designation of the path control network characteristics (security, priority, bandwidth) that apply to a particular session.

**Client**   A system entity (combination of hardware and software components) which requests particular services to be done on its behalf from another entity—server.

**Cluster controller**   A channel-attached or link-attached device that can control the input/output operations of more than one device connected to it (e.g., IBM 3174).

**Commit**   A process that causes the changes to the protected resources to become permanent. See also **Syncpoint.**

**Communication controller**   Communication hardware that operates under the control of the network control program (NCP) and manages communication lines, cluster controllers, workstations, and routing of data through the network.

**Communications Manager**   In OS/2, a component of OS/2 Extended Edition that lets a workstation connect to a host computer and use host services as well as resources of other personal computers to which the workstation is attached.

**Complex Instruction Set Computing (CISC)**   As the opposite of RISC (**Reduced Instruction Set Computing**), a computer system architecture that utilizes a relatively large set of complex instructions where each instruction requires more than one CPU cycle to execute.

**Congestion** An overload condition caused by traffic in excess of the network's capabilities.

**Contention** In the LU6.2 architecture, a situation in which two LU6.2s both attempt to allocate a session at the same time.

**Contention-winner** In contention, the LU6.2 which has been assigned by the control operator to win the contention, and grant or reject the bid from the contention loser.

**Contention-loser** In contention, the LU6.2 which has been assigned by the control operator to request permission (bid) from the contention winner to allocate a conversation on a session.

**Contention polarity** In APPC, a designation that an LU6.2 is the contention-winner or the contention-loser.

**Control operator** For LU6.2, a service transaction program that describes and controls the availability of certain resources.

**Control point (CP)** A **system services control point** (SSCP) which provides hierarchical control of a group of nodes in the network; a control point local to a specific node that provides control of that node.

**Conversation** The logical connection between a pair of transaction programs for serially sharing a session between two type-6.2 logical units. Conversations are delimited by brackets to gain exclusive use of a session.

**Cryptography** The transformation of data to conceal its meaning.

**Database Management System (DBMS)** A software system that controls and manages the data in order to eliminate data redundancy and to ensure data integrity, consistency, and availability, among other features.

**Database Server (DS)** The target of a request received from an **Application Server** (AS) in DRDA.

**Data channel** A device that connects a processor and main storage with I/O control units.

**Data Definition Language (DDL)** A part of the **Structured Query Language** (SQL) that consists of the commands responsible for the creation/deletion of the database objects.

**Data flow control (DFC) layer** The SNA layer within a half-session that controls whether the half-session can send, receive, or concurrently send and receive RUs, groups related RUs into RU chains, delimits transactions through the use of brackets, controls the interlocking of requests and responses, generates sequence numbers, and associates requests with responses.

**Data link control (DLC) layer** The SNA layer that consists of the link stations that schedule data transfer over a link between two nodes and perform error control for the link.

**Data Manipulation Language (DML)**   A part of the **Structured Query Language** (SQL) that consists of the operators responsible for the data manipulation (e.g., SELECT, DELETE, UPDATE, INSERT).

**Data stream**   A continuous stream of defined format data elements being transmitted, or intended to be transmitted.

**Database Manager**   A component of OS/2 Extended Edition consisting of Database Services and Query Manager.

**Decipher**   To return enciphered data to its original form.

**Definite response**   A protocol that directs the receiver of the request to unconditionally return a positive or negative response to that request.

**Digital Network Architecture (DNA)**   A network architecture developed by the Digital Equipment Corporation.

**Directory services**   Services for resolving user identifications of network components to network routing information.

**Distributed Computing Environment (DCE)**   The standards-based environment developed by the Open Software Foundation (OSF) that provides interoperability and portability across heterogeneous distributed systems.

**Distributed Data Management (DDM)**   An architecture that allows application programs or users on one system to access data stored on remote systems.

**Distributed Management Environment (DME)**   A standards-based computing environment developed by the OSF that provides distributed management solution for the DCE.

**Distributed Relational Database Architecture (DRDA)**   A connection architecture developed by IBM to provide access to relational databases distributed across various (IBM) platforms.

**Distributed Request**   An extension of the **Distributed Unit of Work** (DUW) method of accessing distributed relational data where a single SQL statement may reference data residing in different systems; Distributed request support includes unions and joins across distributed DBMSs.

**Distributed Transaction Processing (DTP)**   A type of transaction processing that is characterized by synchronous communication between partners, accomplished via LU6.2 protocols.

**Distributed Unit of Work (DUW)**   A method of accessing distributed relational data where each SQL statement may reference only one system location, but the unit of work may consist of several SQL statements that can read and write data from several distributed DBMSs.

**Document Interchange Architecture (DIA)**   Protocols within the transaction services layer, used by distributed office application processes for data interchange.

**Domain**   A **system services control point** (SSCP) and **physical units** (PU), **logical units** (LU), **links, link stations,** and all associated resources that the control point can control.

**Duplex**    Simultaneous two-way independent data transmission in both directions.

**Dynamic Link Routine (DLR)**    In OS/2, a program or routine that can be loaded by an application as part of a program.

**EBCDIC**    Extended binary-coded decimal interchange code.

**Emulator High-Level Language Application Programming Interface (EHLLAPI)**    An OS/2 **Communications Manager** API that provides a way for users to access the 3270 host presentation space.

**Encipher**    To scramble or convert data prior to transmission in order to hide the meaning of data from unauthorized user.

**End user**    The ultimate source and destination of data in an SNA network.

**End-user verification**    For LU6.2, checking the identification of end users by means of passwords and user identifiers on attach function management headers (FMH).

**Ethernet**    LAN architecture that uses CSMA/CD for the media access control.

**Event control block (ECB)**    A control block used to represent the status of an event.

**Event Callback Model**    A presentation logic technique used in some graphical user interface (GUI) routines to handle events

**Event Loop Model**    A presentation logic technique used in some graphical user interface (GUI) routines to handle events

**Exception response**    The SNA protocol, that directs the receiver to return a response only if the request is unacceptable or cannot be processed.

**Exit routine**    Special-purpose, user-written routine.

**Extended recovery facility (XRF)**    A function that creates a backup for an LU-LU session.

**Fiber Distributed Data Interchange (FDDI)**    High-performance networking standard based on the token-passing technique used in the optical fiber cable.

**Finite-state machine**    An architectural entity that can be placed in a limited number of defined states as the result of applying allowed input sequences.

**First speaker**    The LU-LU half-session defined at session activation time as being able to begin a bracket without requesting a permission from the other LU-LU half-session.

**Flow control**    The process of managing the rate at which data traffic passes through a network.

**Flushing**    For LU6.2, the process of sending through the network all remaining data generated by a transaction program and held in the buffer.

**Formatted Data Object Content Architecture (FD:OCA)**    An architectured collection of constructs used to interchange formatted data.

**Front-end program**    In CICS, a program that is responsible for starting an LU6.2 conversation with the back-end program.

**Full duplex**  See **Duplex.**

**Function Management Header (FMH)**  In SNA, one or more headers, optionally presented in the leading RUs of an RU chain, that allow one half-session in the LU-LU session to carry a conversation establishment request, carry session and conversation error-related information, carry LU-LU password verification data, select, change, or transmit a destination as a session partner.

**Function shipping**  A CICS facility that allows certain CICS functions, requested in one CICS system, to access resources on another, remote CICS system.

**Gateway**  In SNA, the combination of a gateway node and one or more gateway control points that provide the name translation, network address translation, and CP rerouting functions between connected networks.

**Gateway function**  The capability of a subarea node to interconnect subarea path control elements that reside in different networks.

**Gateway node**  A subarea node with gateway function.

**General data stream (GDS)**  Data and commands that are defined by length and identification bytes.

**Graphical User Interface (GUI)**  An interface used by display workstations to interface with end users that provides a consistent API and a standard "look and feel." Microsoft's Windows, OSF's Motif, Sun's Open Look, and OS/2 Presentation Manager are some of the most popular GUIs.

**Half-duplex**  In data communications, alternate, one-way-at-a-time, independent transmissions.

**Half-session**  In SNA, a component that provides data flow control and transmission control at one end of a session. In LU6.2, a component, that provides half-session functions to the logical unit.

**Host node**  A subarea node that contains a telecommunications access method.

**Host processor**  In SNA, a processor where telecommunications access method resides.

**Interclient Communications Conventions Manual (ICCM)**  A set of specifications published by the X Consortium that allow client applications to communicate and work together.

**Interface Definition Language (IDL)**  A language used to interconnect clients and servers via **Remote Procedure Calls** (RPC) in the OSF's DCE.

**Internet Protocol (IP)**  A part of the TCP/IP protocol suite that performs data packet segmentation and routing.

**Intersystem communications (ISC)**  In CICS, a way of providing communications between two CICS systems, residing in different processors, by using ACF/VTAM access method. Contrast with CICS Multiregion Operations (MRO).

**Layer**  An architectural grouping of related functions, that are logically separated from the functions of the other layers.

**Link**   The combination of the link connection and link stations that join adjacent nodes in the network.

**Link connection**   The physical equipment that provides two-way communication between link stations.

**Link station**   The combination of hardware and software that allows a node to attach to, and provide control for, a link.

**Local Area Network (LAN)**   The physical connection that allows information exchanges among devices (typically, personal computers) located on the same premises.

**Logical unit (LU)**   A port through which an end user accesses an SNA network in order to communicate with another end user.

**Logical Unit of Work (LUW)**   A work that is performed between the start of a transaction and COMMIT or ROLLBACK of the same transaction.

**LU6.2**   Logical unit type 6.2—a special type of logical unit that supports **Advanced Program-to-Program Communications** (APPC) between programs in distributed processing environment. APPC/LU6.2 is characterized by peer-to-peer communication support, comprehensive end-to-end error processing, optimized data transmission flow, and generic application programming interface.

**LU-LU session**   A session between two logical units.

**LU Network Services**   An LU6.2 component that is responsible for the interactions between the LU6.2 and the network.

**LU Presentation Services**   An LU6.2 component that is responsible for processing of LU6.2 verbs.

**LU Resources Manager**   An LU6.2 component that manages LU6.2 and local resources.

**LU Services Manager**   An LU6.2 component that consists of the **LU Resources Manager** and **LU Network Services.**

**Management services**   In SNA, one of the types of network services in the network control point and **physical units** (PU) that provide functions for problem management, performance, accounting, configuration, and change management.

**Mapped conversation**   In APPC, a type of conversation in which the data can be sent and received in a user-defined format, while the data transformation is performed by APPC/LU6.2.

**Message unit**   A generic term for the unit of data processed by any SNA layer.

**Metropolitan Area Network (MAN)**   A network using a city infrastructure to connect nodes within the geographical limits of a city.

**Modem**   A device that modulates and demodulates signals transmitted over data communication facilities in order to convert digital signals into and from an analog form.

**Motif**  A popular window manager selected by the **Open Software Foundation** for the presentation management in its version of the open system environment.

**Negative response**  A response indicating that a request did not arrive successfully or was not processed successfully by the receiver.

**Network address**  An address that identifies a link, a link station, or a network addressable unit.

**Network File System (NFS)**  Popular method of accessing remote files in a Unix system environment (developed by Sun Microsystems).

**Network Operating System (NOS)**  A generic term for the operating system level software used to manage and control networks.

**NetView**  A System/370-based IBM licensed program used to monitor, manage, and diagnose an SNA network.

**Network addressable unit (NAU)**  A **logical unit** (LU), a **physical unit** (PU), or a **system services control point** (SSCP), which is the origin or the destination of the data transmitted by a path control network.

**Network Control Program (NCP)**  An IBM licensed program that runs on a communications controller and supports single-domain, multiple-domain, and interconnected network capabilities of the controller.

**Node**  In SNA, an endpoint of a link, or a junction common to two or more links.

**Object**  A named unit that consists of a set of characteristics that are encapsulated within the object and describe the object and data. Certain characteristics of an object are inherited from its "parents" and can be inherited by its "children." Operations valid for the object are stored together with the object as its methods. In computer architecture, an object can be anything that exists in and occupies space in storage (e.g., programs, files, libraries) and on which operations can be performed.

**Open Look**  A popular window manager that is used primarily by the members of the Unix International (UI).

**Open Network Computing (ONC)**  Unix International's architecture for an open distributed computing environment.

**Open Software Foundation (OSF)**  A not-for-profit technology organization that intends to develop an open computing environment by selecting technology solution from its members.

**OS/2**  Operating System/2—a multiprogramming, multitasking operating system developed for PS/2 family of personal computers.

**OSI**  Open Systems Interconnection—a layered architecture that is designed to allow for interconnection between heterogeneous systems.

**Pacing**  A technique by which a receiver controls the rate of transmission by the sender.

**Packet** A data transmission information unit consisting of a group of data and control characters.

**Packet switching** The process of routing and transferring data by means of addressed packets.

**Parallel sessions** Two or more concurrently active sessions between two logical units using different pairs of network addresses.

**Path** In SNA, a series of path control components that are traversed by the information exchanges between two NAUs.

**Path control layer** An SNA layer that manages the sharing of link resources and routes information units through the SNA network.

**Path control network** The part of SNA network that includes data link control, path control, and physical control layers.

**Peripheral node** An SNA node that uses local addresses for routing and therefore is not affected by changes in network addresses.

**Physical control layer** The SNA layer that provides a physical interface for any transmission medium to which it is attached.

**Physical unit (PU)** The SNA component—a type of NAU—that manages and monitors a node's resources.

**Positive response** A response indicating that a request has been successfully processed.

**Presentation Manager (OS/2 PM)** An OS/2 component that provides graphics API.

**Presentation services (PS)** The LU6.2 component that processes LU6.2-defined verbs.

**Presentation services layer** In SNA, a layer that provides transaction programs with services such as conversation-level communication (e.g., process verbs, perform mapping, etc.)

**Primary logical unit (PLU)** The logical unit that sends the BIND request for a particular LU-LU session.

**Professional Office System (PROFS)** A facility that allows users to receive, create, send, store, and search for information within an office environment.

**Protocol boundary** A synonym for the architecturally defined LU6.2 application program interface.

**Queued attach** In OS/2 APPC, an incoming ALLOCATE request that is queued by the **Attach Manager** until the transaction program issues an appropriate APPC verb.

**RAS programs** *R*eliability, *A*vailability, and *S*erviceability programs that facilitate problem determination.

**Recommendation X.21** A Consultative Committee on International Telephone and Telegraph (CCITT) recommendation for a general purpose interface between data terminal equipment and data circuit equipment for synchronous operations on public data networks.

**Recommendation X.25** A Consultative Committee on International Telephone and Telegraph (CCITT) recommendation for an interface between data terminal equipment and packet-switched networks.

**Reduced Instruction Set Computing (RISC)** As the opposite of CISC (**Complex Instruction Set Computing**), a computer system architecture that utilizes a relatively small set of computer instructions where each instruction is "simple" enough to require one CPU cycle to execute.

**Remote Data Access (RDA)** A proposed ANSI standard to access remote relational databases.

**Remote Program Link (RPL)** A mechanism used in OS/2 CICS to link to and execute a program residing on a host (mainframe) CICS.

**Relational Database (RDB)** A database built to conform to the relational data model (includes the catalog and all the data described therein).

**Remote Procedure Call (RPC)** A connectionless method of communication between two programming systems where a requester (client) issues an RPC to execute a procedure on a remote system (server).

**Remote Request** The form of SQL distributed processing where the application runs on a system different from the one housing the RDB (contains a single SQL statement referencing data located at a single site).

**Remote Unit of Work (RUW)** The extension of the Remote Request form of SQL distributed processing where multiple SQL statements may reference data located at a single remote site.

**Report Program Generator (RPG)** An SAA programming language designed for report-oriented business applications.

**Rhapsody** A workflow management software developed by AT&T.

**Rollback** The process of restoring protected resources to the state at the last commit point.

**Secondary logical unit (SLU)** In SNA, the logical unit that contains the secondary half-session for a particular LU-LU session (i.e., the LU that receives the session activation request).

**Server** A system entity (combination of hardware and software components) which performs particular services on behalf of another entity—client.

**Server-Requester Programming Interface (SRPI)** An API used by requester and server programs to communicate with PC or hosts.

**Session** In SNA, a logical connection between two **network addressable units** (NAU) that allows them to communicate.

**Session-level pacing** In SNA, a flow control technique that permits the receiver to control the data transfer rate.

**Session-level security** For LU6.2, partner LU verification and session cryptography.

**Session limit**   In SNA, the maximum number of concurrently active LU-LU sessions a particular LU can support.

**Session partner**   In SNA, one of the two NAUs participating in an active session.

**Structured Query Language (SQL)**   A standard for the nonnavigational data access and definition language used in relational databases.

**Subarea**   In SNA, a portion of an SNA network that consists of a subarea node, attached peripheral nodes and associated resources.

**Subarea node**   In SNA, a type 4 or type 5 node that uses network addresses for routing and whose routing tables are affected by changes in the network configuration.

**Symmetric Multiprocessing (SMP)**   A computer architecture where several tightly-coupled CPUs share a common memory and common workload.

**Syncpoint**   (1) A point in time when all protected resources accessed by an application are consistent. (2) An LU6.2 verb that causes all changes to protected resources to become permanent, and, therefore, consistent. See also **Commit.**

**Synchronization level**   In APPC, the specification indicating that the conversation allows no synchronization (SYNCLEVEL=NONE), supports confirmation exchanges (SYNCLEVEL=CONFIRM) or full synchronization (SYNCLEVEL=SYNCPT).

**Synchronous Data Link Control (SDLC)**   A communication protocol for managing synchronous code-transparent, serial-by-bit information transfer over a link connection.

**Synchronous transmission**   In data communication, a method of transmission where the sending and receiving of characters is controlled by timing signals.

**Systems Application Architecture (SAA)**   A set of software interfaces, protocols and conventions that provide a framework for designing and developing consistent, portable applications across various computer environments.

**Systems Network Architecture (SNA)**   The description of the logical structure, formats, protocols, and operational sequences for transmitting information and controlling configuration and operation of networks.

**Systems Network Architecture Distributed Services (SNADS)**   An IBM architecture that defines a set of rules to receive, route, and send electronic mail across networks.

**System Services Control Point (SSCP)**   In SNA, a central location point within an SNA network for managing the configuration, coordinating network operator and problem determination requests, and providing directory support and other session services for end users.

**Target**   In APPC, a program or system to which the communication or processing request is sent.

**Task Manager**   In OS/2, the function that controls starting and stopping of programs.

**Terminal**   In data communication, a device capable of sending and receiving information.

**Time Sharing Option (TSO)**   A feature of an operating system (i.e., MVS) that provides conversational time-sharing of system resources from remote stations.

**Top End**   A transaction monitor developed by the NCR Corporation to provide transaction management in the open systems (Unix-based) distributed environment.

**Transaction**   In communications, a unit of processing and information exchange between a local and a remote program that accomplishes a particular action or result.

**Transaction program (TP)**   In APPC, a program that uses APPC API to communicate with a partner transaction program on a remote system.

**Transaction Routing**   In CICS, a facility that allows CICS transactions, initiated on a local CICS system, to be executed on a remote CICS system.

**Transaction Monitor/Transaction Manager (TPM)**   A software system that provides control and management functions to support transaction execution, synchronization, integrity, consistency, atomicity, and durability.

**Transarc**   A transaction monitor developed by Transarc Corporation and adopted by the OSF to provide transaction management in the open systems distributed environment.

**Transmission control (TC) layer**   In SNA, the layer within a half-session that synchronizes and paces session-level data traffic, checks session sequence numbers of requests, and enciphers/deciphers user data.

**Transmission Control Protocol/Internet Protocol (TCP/IP)**   Communication protocols used mostly in a Unix environment—popular because of its openness and easy interoperability features.

**Tuxedo**   A transaction monitor developed by AT&T to provide transaction management in the Unix system distributed environment.

**Two-phase Commit (2PC)**   A protocol that ensures the integrity and consistency of all protected resources affected by a distributed transaction.

**Unit of work**   In APPC, the amount of processing that is executed from the time the transaction is started to the time the transaction is ended.

**Verb**   In APPC, an LU6.2 command, defined in the APPC API.

**Virtual Machine/System Product (VM/SP)**   An IBM licensed program which is an operating system that manages the resources of a real processor to provide virtual machines to end users.

**Virtual Telecommunications Access Method (VTAM)**   An IBM licensed program that controls communication and data flow in an SNA network.

**VTAM application program**   A program that (1) has identified itself to VTAM by opening an ACB and (2) can issue VTAM macro instructions.

**Wide Area Network (WAN)**   A network connecting nodes located across large geographical areas.

**Windows**  Popular presentation management software developed by Microsoft to support an easy-to-use multiprogramming environment in the PC DOS platform.

**Workstation**  A terminal or personal computer at which a user can run applications.

**XA Interfaces**  X/Open's proposed standards for the portable application programming interfaces between transaction managers and resource managers (DBMS).

**X/Open**  A nonprofit organization founded to develop standards for interoperability between unlike systems. Its specifications for system interoperability and portability are listed in the *X/Open Portability Guide Issue 3* (XPG3).

**X Window System**  A distributed presentation management system developed by MIT for Unix-based environments.

**X.21**  See **Recommendation X.21**.

**X.25**  See **Recommendation X.25**.

# List of Abbreviations

| | |
|---|---|
| **ACB** | Application control block or access method control block |
| **AIX** | Advanced Interactive eXecutive |
| **ANDF** | Architecture-Neutral Distribution Format |
| **ANSI** | American National Institute of Standards |
| **API** | Application Programming Interface |
| **AEI** | Application Enabling Interface |
| **APPC** | Advanced Program-to-Program Communications |
| **APPN** | Advanced Peer-to-Peer Networking |
| **APPCCMD** | VTAM macro instruction (implements LU6.2 verbs in ACF/VTAM application programs) |
| **AR** | Application Requester (in DRDA) |
| **AS** | Application Server (in DRDA) |
| **AS/400** | Application System/400 |
| **BIU** | Basic Information Unit |
| **BLOB** | Binary Large Object |
| **BSC** | Binary Synchronous Communications |
| **CDRA** | Character Data Representation Architecture |
| **CCITT** | The International Telephone and Telegraph Consultative Committee |
| **CICS** | Customer Information Control System—a teleprocessing and transaction management system which runs as a VTAM application |
| **CISC** | Complex Instruction Set Computing |
| **CNM** | Communication network management |
| **CNOS** | Change number of sessions |
| **CP** | Control point |
| **COS** | Class of service |
| **CSDA/CA** | Carrier Sense Multiple Access/Collision Avoidance |
| **CSDA/CD** | Carrier Sense Multiple Access/Collision Detection |
| **DB2** | Database 2 (IBM) |
| **DBMS** | Database Management System |
| **DCE** | Distributed Computing Environment |

| | |
|---|---|
| **DDF** | Distributed Data Facility |
| **DDM** | Distributed Data Management |
| **DFC** | Data flow control layer |
| **DFS** | Distributed File System |
| **DIA** | Document Interchange Architecture |
| **DLC** | Data link control layer |
| **DLR** | Dynamic Link Routine |
| **DME** | Distributed Management Environment |
| **DML** | Data Manipulation Language |
| **DNA** | Digital Network Architecture |
| **DTP** | Distributed Transaction Processing |
| **DRDA** | Distributed Relational Database Architecture |
| **DS** | Database Server |
| **DUW** | Distributed Unit of Work |
| **EBCDIC** | Extended Binary-Coded Decimal Interchange Code |
| **ECB** | Event Control Block |
| **EHLLAPI** | Emulator High-Level Language Application Programming Interface |
| **FDDI** | Fiber Distributed Data Interface |
| **FD:OCA** | Formatted Data Object Content Architecture |
| **FSM** | Finite-State Machine |
| **FMH** | Function management header |
| **FTP** | File Transfer Protocol |
| **GDS** | General Data Stream |
| **GUI** | Graphical User Interface |
| **ICCM** | Interclient Communications Conventions Manual |
| **ICF** | Intercommunication Function |
| **ISC** | Intersystem Communications |
| **ISDN** | Integrated Services Digital Network |
| **ISV** | Independent Software Vendor |
| **LS** | Link Station |
| **LAN** | Local Area Network |
| **LR** | Logical Record |
| **LU** | Logical Unit |
| **LUW** | Logical Unit of Work |
| **LU6.2** | Logical Unit type 6.2 |
| **LU-LU session** | A session between two logical units |
| **LNS** | LU6.2 Network Services component |
| **MAN** | Metropolitan Area Network |
| **MAP/TOP** | Manufacturing Automation Protocol/Technical and Office Protocol |
| **MC** | Mapped Conversation |
| **MCA** | Micro-Channel Adapter |

| | |
|---|---|
| **MLFLOPS** | Millions of Floating Point Instructions per Second |
| **MIPS** | Millions of Instructions per Second |
| **MRO** | Multiregion Operations |
| **MSA** | SNA Management Services Architecture |
| **NAU** | Network Addressable Unit |
| **NCP** | Network Control Program |
| **NFS** | Network File System |
| **NOS** | Network Operating System |
| **OLTP** | On-Line Transaction Processing |
| **ONC** | Open Network Computing |
| **OS/2** | Operating System/2 |
| **OSF** | Open Software Foundation |
| **OSI** | Open Systems Interconnection |
| **PC** | Path Control network |
| **PIU** | Path Information Unit |
| **PLU** | Primary Logical Unit |
| **PM** | OS/2 Presentation Manager |
| **POSIX** | Portable Operating System Interface |
| **PS** | LU6.2 Presentation Services |
| **PROFS** | Professional Office System |
| **PU** | Physical Unit |
| **PWS** | Programmable Workstation |
| **RAS programs** | Reliability, Availability, and Serviceability programs |
| **RDA** | Remote Data Access |
| **RDBMS** | Relational Database Management System |
| **RH** | Request/response Header |
| **RISC** | Reduced Instruction Set Computing |
| **RM** | LU6.2 Resources Manager |
| **RPC** | Remote Procedure Call |
| **RPL** | Remote Program Link |
| **RU** | Request/response Unit |
| **RUW** | Remote Unit of Work |
| **SAA** | Systems Application Architecture |
| **SCSI** | Small Computer System Interface |
| **SDLC** | Synchronous Data Link Control |
| **SLU** | Secondary logical unit |
| **SMP** | Symmetric Multiprocessing |
| **SRPI** | Server-Requester Programming Interface |
| **SNA** | Systems Network Architecture |
| **SNADS** | Systems Network Architecture Distributed Services |
| **SQL** | Structured Query Language |
| **SSCP** | System Services Control Point |

| | |
|---|---|
| **SVID** | Unix System V Interface Definitions |
| **SVR4** | Unix System V Release 4 |
| **TC** | Transmission Control layer |
| **TCOS** | Technical Committee on Open Systems |
| **TCP/IP** | Transmission Control Protocol/Internet Protocol |
| **TH** | Transmission Header |
| **TP** | Transaction Program |
| **TPM** | Transaction Processing Manager |
| **TPS** | Transactions Per Second |
| **TSO** | Time Sharing Option |
| **UI** | Unix International |
| **UOW** | Unit of work |
| **VAN** | Value Added Network |
| **VM/SP** | Virtual machine/System Product |
| **VR** | Virtual Route |
| **VTAM** | Virtual Telecommunications Access Method |
| **WAN** | Wide Area Network |
| **XPG3** | X/Open Portability Guide issue 3 |
| **XRF** | Extended Recovery Facility |
| **X.21** | A Consultative Committee on International Telephone and Telegraph (CCITT) recommendations for a general-purpose interface between data terminal equipment and data circuit equipment for synchronous operations on a public data networks. |
| **X.25** | A Consultative Committee on International Telephone and Telegraph (CCITT) recommendations for an interface between data terminal equipment and packet-switched networks |

# Further Reading

## IBM BOOKS AND MANUALS

### SAA Publications

*SAA: An Overview* (SC26-4341)
*Writing Applications: A Design Guide* (SC26-4362)
*SAA: Application Generator Reference* (SC26-4355)
*SAA: C Reference* (SC26-4353)
*SAA: COBOL Reference* (SC26-4354)
*SAA: Communications Reference* (SC26-4399)
*SAA: Database Reference* (SC26-4348)
*SAA: CPI Database Level 2 Reference* (SC26-4798)
*SAA: Dialog Reference* (SC26-4356)
*SAA: Presentation Reference* (SC26-4359)
*SAA: Procedures Language Reference* (SC26-4358)
*SAA: Query Reference* (SC26-4349)
*SAA: Framework for an Enterprise Information System* (G580-4005)
*SAA: Distributed Files for SAA* (G321-5330)
*SAA: Distributed Database for SAA* (G321-5331)

### LU6.2 Publications

*SNA Format and Protocol Reference Manual: Architecture Logic for LU Type 6.2* (SC30-3269)
*SNA Transaction Programmer's Reference Manual for LU Type 6.2* (SC30-3084)

### SNA Publications

*SNA Concepts and Products* (GC30-3072)
*SNA Technical Overview* (GC30-3073)
*SNA Format and Protocol Reference Manual: Architectural Logic* (SC30-3112)
*SNA Reference Summary* (GA27-3136)
*SNA—Sessions Between Logical Units* (GC20-1868)
*IBM SDLC General Information* (GA27-3093)
*SNA Network Product Formats* (LY43-0081)
*SNA Format and Protocol Reference Manual: Distribution Services* (SC30-3098)

### VTAM Publications

*VTAM Installation and Resource Definition* (SC31-0111)
*VTAM Operation* (SC23-0113)
*VTAM Programming* (SC23-0115)

*VTAM Programming for LU6.2* (SC30-3400)
*VTAM Reference Summary* (LY30-5600)
*VTAM Messages and Codes* (SC23-0114)
*VTAM Directory of Programming Interfaces for Customers* (GC31-6403)

## DRDA-Related Publications

*DRDA: DDM General Information* (GC21-9527)
*DDM Reference Guide* (GC21-9526)
*Concepts of Distributed Data* (SC26-4417)
*Introduction to Distributed Relational Data* (GC24-3200)
*DRDA Distributed Data Management Level 3 Architecture* (GC21-9526)
*DRDA Reference* (SC26-4651)
*DRDA Implementation Programmer's Guide* (SC21-9529)
*An Architecture for a Business and Information System* (*Information Warehouse*) (G321-5311)

## OS/2 Communications Publications

*OS/2 Information and Planning Guide* (G360-2650)
*OS/2 Extended Edition System Administrator's Guide for Communications* (90X7808)
*OS/2 Extended Edition User's Guide*
*OS/2 Extended Edition APPC Programming Reference* (90X7910)
*OS/2 Extended Edition Programming Services and Advanced Problem Determination for Communications* (90X7906)

## CICS/VS Intersystem Communications Publications

*CICS/VS General Information* (GC33-0155)
*CICS/VS Release Guide* (GC-0132)
*CICS/VS Facilities and Planning Guide* (SC33-0202)
*CICS/VS Intercommunication Facilities Guide* (SC33-0230)
*CICS/VS Resource Definition* (*Online*) (SC33-0186)
*CICS/VS Resource Definition* (*Macro*) (SC33-0237)
*CICS/VS Application Programmer's Reference Manual* (*Command Level*) (SC33-0241)

# STANDARDS DOCUMENTS

*ISO: Database Language SQL,* ISO-9075-1987
*ISO: Database Language SQL With Integrity Enhancement,* ISO-9075-1989(E)
*ANSI: Database Language SQL,* X.3.135-1986
*ANSI: Database Language SQL With Integrity Enhancement,* X.3.135-1989
*ANSI Database Language: Language Embedding,* X.3.168-1989

# Index